Matters for
JUDGMENT

Matters for
JUDGMENT
An autobiography
Sir John Kerr

Foreword by
Lord Hailsham of St. Marylebone
P.C., C.H., F.R.S., D.C.L., LL.D.

Epilogue by
Senator Eugene Forsey
O.C., PH.D., LL.D., D.LITT., F.R.S.C.

St. Martin's Press
New York

Library of Congress Cataloging in Publication Data

Kerr, John Robert, Sir, 1914–
    Matters for judgment.

    Bibliography: p.
    Includes index.
    1. Kerr, John Robert, Sir, 1914–
2. Australia—Politics and government—
1945–   3. Australia—Constitutional history.
4. Australia—Governors—Biography.
5. Judges—Australia—Biography.   I. Title.
DU117.2.K47A35   1979   994.06′092′4   [B]
ISBN 0-312-52305-X   79-17249

To Anne, my wife

Contents

'. . . Governments are instituted among men, deriving their just powers from the consent of the governed.'

The American Declaration of Independence,
4 July 1776

Foreword

The journey to Australia is not an easy one. I had broken the journey at Singapore to get a good night's rest. But all the same, two nights in a plane in the same week are not good for an elderly man, and I was sixty-seven years of age. It was about 6.30 in the morning, local time, when I emerged in a somewhat bemused and dishevelled condition on to the concourse at Sydney airport. It was May 1974.

Coming to meet me I saw a large man, with a mane of white hair. It was Sir John Kerr, Chief Justice of New South Wales, and, as I happened to know from my Foreign Office briefing, Governor-General designate of the Commonwealth of Australia. I was immensely flattered that anyone in so exalted a position should get up so early to greet me, by now a private citizen since the Labour victory of February 1974. I was there to represent the English profession at the sesquicentenary of the Sydney Law Courts. But I had not expected to be greeted by the Chief Justice in person.

During the few days that followed I got to know Sir John Kerr fairly well, and have since regarded him as my friend. I was, or became, aware that he was of working class origin and that, at an earlier period of his life, he had been a Labor lawyer with leanings rather to the right of centre of the Labor Party. I became greatly impressed with his intellectual integrity, and his obvious understanding and grasp of the nuts and bolts problems of judicial administration, a subject somewhat neglected in our schools of politics and law and, perhaps in consequence by the English Bench and Bar. We discussed most problems from religion to

xi

politics. But it never crossed my mind, nor, I think, his that he was going to be at the centre of one of the great crises of Australian constitutional history.

The Governor-General's post is in the gift of the Crown, but, in modern constitutional practice, the appointment is made on the recommendation of the Prime Minister, at that time the head of a Labor Government, Mr Gough Whitlam. I doubt not that it never crossed his mind, any more than Sir John's, that this apparently safe appointment of a competent Chief Justice with a past background of Labor politics was destined to bring his own flamboyant political career to an end. If, though I assume he did not, he thought about the matter at all, I expect he imagined that, since the appointment was at pleasure, and not for an assured term of years, he could always recommend dismissal in terms which Her Majesty, as Queen of Australia, would be constitutionally bound to accept. In fact, however, he had given Sir John reason to believe that, if he accepted the post, he could expect re-appointment for a second term.

The next time I came to Sydney Airport, this time with my wife on our way to our private Gethsemane, was only four years later, in May 1978. By that time the crisis was over. Mr Fraser was in office. Two whole General Elections had taken place, the first of both Houses, the second of the House of Representatives and half the Senate. Mr Whitlam was no longer Leader of the Labor Party. Sir John Kerr, after the most brutal persecution from the left, had virtually gone, at least for a period, into exile, and all this had happened as the result of the dramatic happenings in November 1975.

Labor authors have certainly been fairly active in canvassing opinion about these events. This is Sir John Kerr's account. I hope it is widely read, but I trust it will not be read in a spirit of acrimony or in a quest to see who went wrong where. In particular I must protest against the vindictiveness against Sir John personally. What Gough Whitlam said about 'maintaining rage' more than anything else cost him two elections and the leadership of Australian Labor. Constitutional problems, especially when they are not foreseen, are difficult of solution, seldom recur in the same form twice running, and are usually argued about by constitutional experts for decades after the event. But the poor men and women who have to take the crucial decisions have to take them in days rather than weeks, sometimes in hours rather than days, and perhaps minutes rather than hours. There is plenty of room, when an honest man acts in good faith, for argument afterwards. But there is none for want of charity. Sir John Kerr was an honest man placed in an intolerable position which was not of his creation. I personally believe with Dr Forsey, who writes an epilogue to this book, that he had in fact no option. Be that as it may, he acted honestly, and he should have been spared insult and persecution. He is certainly entitled, as he has done here, to have his say, and recount the facts as he saw them.

Has the record any lessons for us in the United Kingdom or for other Commonwealth countries? Yes, I think it has, but before we study them we must, I think, be on our guard against too easily translating Australian experience into British terms. The Governor-General may be the representative of the Sovereign. But he is not the Sovereign. He can be dismissed at pleasure, and in modern practice this means at the pleasure of the Commonwealth Prime Minister for the time being. This means that he is in danger of becoming a puppet on a string, and should he deem it his duty to use the reserve powers of the Monarchy against a would-be Mussolini, or a Prime Minister who wishes to govern unconstitutionally, he must make his preparations in secret or not at all. He must exercise the powers of the Crown before the Prime Minister advises the Queen to take them away from him. This is obviously unsatisfactory and Sir John Kerr more than once speaks of the undignified 'race to the Palace' which it could produce. Should the Governor-General be appointed for a term of years or be subject to an Australian Council of State? That is for Australians to decide. It does not arise here, since the Queen's powers for better or for worse are exercised by the Queen herself. Secondly, Australia has a written constitution of the Federal type with complicated provisions for amendment, for elections of one, or both Houses, or for half of one. Despite superficial resemblances, the Australian game is played with different rules, and differently shaped pieces on the board.

The origin of the problem with which he was faced was as I

have said, not of Sir John Kerr's making. This should have been taken into account in his favour. He was not the author of crisis. It was thrust upon him. Apart from antagonisms common to most industrial countries, the key to Australian politics lies in the tension between the states, so widely separated round the circumference of a continent with blank spaces in the middle, and the Commonwealth or Federal Government at Canberra. The Commonwealth would never have come into existence at all had an attempt been made to follow Canadian precedent and put into the hands of the centre all that had not been allotted to the States. The Constitution dates from 1900, before the House of Lords made its mad attempt in 1909 to reject the Lloyd George budget and so permanently maimed the British Constitution. The Australian Constitution is modelled on what was thought to be the British position at the end of Victoria's reign, but with an elected Senate representing the separate identities of the States, as in America. Though it is smaller, of a different tenure, and representative of units rather than numbers it can as much claim to be elected as the House of Representatives. Under the Constitution, though it cannot amend financial measures, it can reject them altogether. There is reason for this. Executive Government can be used discriminatively against particular states, representing numerically smaller but separate communities. There is no doubt that, in 1975, there was a legal power in the Senate to withhold supply. It was a question debated between Australian constitutional authorities as to whether it was politically proper for the power to be used and, if so, for what purposes. There was a respectable body of opinion which has always asserted that it could be used quite properly. It was used in 1975, and, there being deadlock between the two Houses, Sir John Kerr as Governor-General, Gough Whitlam as Prime Minister and Malcolm Fraser as Leader of the Opposition were all placed in the position of deciding what was to happen next. Since Mr Fraser and the Senate would not resile and Mr Whitlam refused to resign or advise a dissolution, in the last resort Sir John Kerr had to decide what to do in order that the Queen's Government could be carried on. He decided in favour of dismissing Mr Whitlam and commissioning Mr Fraser on condition he advised a dissolution of both Houses. In the election which followed, the electorate, within its sovereign rights, endorsed the decision.

So far there is nothing which could happen here. The House of Lords has no power now over supply and, if it had, the Government could pack it with new peers as Mr Asquith threatened to do at one stage. No reformed House of Lords or elective Senate created to take the place of the House of Lords is likely to be given the right to reject a budget and so stop Government in its tracks. But this is virtually what the Senate did in Australia in 1975, by constantly deferring consideration of the Budget, and that not especially because it objected to the particular financial proposals but because it wished to force a general election. This, it may be argued, is precisely what a second chamber should not do. But that again is something about which British people cannot generalise from their own experience. Ours is a unitary state and not comparable to a federal system with inherent emphasis on state rights. To this extent, too, it could not happen here.

What then is the bearing upon Britain of the Australian experience of 1975?

The first is a political lesson for any Government operating the British system as it existed prior to 1909 and, up to a point, even today. If one of the two Houses of Parliament challenges the Government of the day to the point at which Government becomes impossible, the right course, both constitutionally and politically, is for the Government to resign or advise a dissolution, and thus challenge its opponents to fight it out at a General Election. It is both morally and constitutionally wrong and politically unwise to bring the Crown into the situation by refusing so to act. Mr Asquith showed the way in 1909 and established his authority by so doing. Even had he lost the ensuing election the foundation would have been laid for a return to power, probably rapid, but at least eventual, when an adequate constitutional revenge would no doubt have been exacted. Apart from his selection of Sir John Kerr instead of the Senate and Mr Fraser for his 'rage', Mr Whitlam's eclipse was due, in my opinion, to his failure to take up the Senate's challenge as did Mr Asquith in 1909, and to attempt instead to govern without supply.

The second lesson to be learned regards the position of the Crown.

Dicey's original view that the Crown is in some way an arbiter of public opinion so as to put it in a position to force a dissolution after making a judgment concerning the popularity or unpopularity of a Government has long been rightly, and, I think, universally, discredited. This would be a prescription for bringing the Crown directly into party politics. Under a Cabinet system of Government, either Parliaments must be of fixed duration, or, if a premature dissolution is provided for, it must either be undertaken on the advice of a Minister who is prepared to take responsibility, or under some legal rules prescribed in writing and ultimately justiciable. The Crown is the trustee of the constitution and not the arbiter of public opinion.

To say, however, that the Crown is a trustee is to say that it is not a cipher, and may not be turned into a rubber stamp. There are reserve powers, although it is impossible in advance to say what they are, or when it will be necessary to use them. One hopes that they will never be used. No doubt, when Sir John Kerr took the oath of office, it never crossed his mind that he would ever have to use them. But he was faced with a situation in which two of the working parts of the Australian Constitution, namely the executive, supported by their majority in the House of Representatives, and the Opposition, supported by their majority in the Senate, had brought the machinery of the State to a grinding halt. If he had not acted in some way the constitution would have broken down, since payments, even of the most ordinary kind, by Government would have dried up. Whatever he did, he was bound to incur criticism. If he failed to act he would have incurred criticism. If he acted he would incur criticism, as he did. What on earth is it suggested that he should have done? Let supply run out? At one time Mr Whitlam suggested that he might present for the Royal Assent Bills which had not passed both Houses. Such Assent would not merely have been unconstitutional but illegal and, I believe, its illegality could have been established in the Courts. In any event, Mr Whitlam did not pursue this suggestion. Mr Whitlam himself had devised a harebrained scheme of governing without supply through an arrangement with the banks. Given the determination neither to give in to the Senate nor to ask for a dissolution himself this was no doubt well-intentioned. But was it legal? Could it have worked? Above all, was it constitutional? Governing without Parliamentary sanction is precisely the error which cost Charles I his head. Mr Whitlam got off cheaply with a double electoral defeat and the loss of the leadership of his Party. If he had acted earlier he could have advised Sir John to call a half Senate election. But he only decided to do this when it was too late. He has now gone on record as favouring a Republican form of Government for Australia, and what was an internal Australian issue has become a Commonwealth affair. Commonwealth statesmen would do well to reflect that a republican form of Government, in which the executive assumes independence of the trusteeship of the Crown, leads straight along the path to Tea Pot Dome, Watergate or Mulder and the Sanjay motor factory, and possibly to Idi Amin or worse, and voters in Commonwealth countries might care to consider that a Government which thinks it can go on governing without continued Parliamentary sanction and without an appeal to the people, is well on the way to becoming an elective dictatorship. It has only to find means to prolong its own life to become a dictatorship without being elective.

But there are lessons here too for the Crown. Though it be the business of British statesmen to avoid a situation which may bring reserve powers into action, the Crown cannot avoid its obligations if they fail to observe this rule. If Mr Heath had failed to resign in March 1974, the Queen would have been bound to dismiss him as soon as he had failed to carry the Queen's Speech and if instead of resigning he had asked for a second dissolution, she would have been wise to refuse it. If Mr Callaghan had failed to carry the Queen's Speech in 1978 and then refused to resign or ask for a dissolution, the Queen would have been forced to dismiss him and ask Mrs Thatcher to form a Government which would then have asked for a dissolution which the Queen would have had to grant. If someone blew up Parliament and killed all the occupants of the Front Benches, the Queen would be bound to act on her own initiative, one does not know how. It is clear that sovereignty lies with the people. But the Queen is a trustee for her people. Trustees are not ciphers, and cannot safely act as rubber stamps. Victor Emmanuel dismissed Mussolini too late to save his throne. Sir John Kerr dismissed Mr Whitlam just in time to avert an Australian catastrophe. Had he not been supported by the electorate, he would have had to resign. If the Crown makes a mistake, and is not endorsed by the electorate, there are only two possibilities, admission of error and reconciliation, or abdication in favour of a successor. That is the fate of trustees, and the sanction which must sober their use of power. Where Mr Whitlam erred was not in precipitating the crisis (though I myself think this an error) but in not accepting the verdict of the sovereign people, and in pursuing Sir John Kerr instead of Mr Fraser and his Party on party political lines after the verdict had gone against him. Had he not done this he might have lived to fight another day with success. Instead he has chosen to retire into the waterless desert of republican opinions, when no fault can be attributed to the Crown itself, and, so far as I am concerned, none to the Crown representative whom he had himself caused to be appointed.

Can anything be done in Britain which has not already been done to avoid constitutional crisis here? I doubt it. Of their very nature, constitutional crises are unpredictable and are due to the adherents of strong political views straining their legal rights under a constitution to breaking point. Political leaders are under an obligation to prevent this happening. But happen it certainly will from time to time as political history unfolds. The Crown, using its powers as a last resort, and not in order to influence policy, is a fail-safe mechanism. The Crown is a trustee for the Constitution on behalf of the Sovereign people. It would be no proof against armed force. But it is proof against much else. In the meantime, one sobering reflexion is in order. No constitution will work indefinitely unless there is an underlying determination on the part of the politicians concerned to make it work. If that underlying determination exists almost any constitution may be made to work, whatever inherent defects it may possess. But the people is sovereign and a general rule for politicians who suffer electoral defeat is to pick themselves up and dust their trousers, and live to fight another day. There is no future in whining about injustice, still less in assaulting the referee.

Hailsham of St Marylebone

xviii

Preface

This book gives an account of certain happenings in Australia between 1974 and 1978, of decisions of mine taken then as Governor-General and of the reasons for them. Although partly autobiographical in character it is not an intimate personal narrative but tells so much of my story as bears upon my Governor-Generalship, and something of the man who occupied the vice-regal office at a time of great constitutional and political significance in Australian history.

My book is, in part, a defence which I am entitled to make now, in bare justice to myself, against an extreme and bitter attack upon me and my actions. More importantly, the book should be published now because in the public interest the facts of my role in the happenings of 1975 should be known—in the interests of truth and of maintaining freedom of discussion and the development of knowledge on matters of great public importance. In relation to these matters there is a gap due to the silence I have maintained until now. That gap is being filled by gossip, rumour, error, bogus history, falsehood and invention. The longer the delay the greater the difficulty in displacing and correcting all of this. Two elections have been held since November 1975 and the time has come to allow the public interest in knowledge of constitutional matters of vital significance to prevail. Apart from all other considerations, constitutional amendments are under discussion and the public is entitled in our democracy to be fully informed about the happenings of 1975 so that the people can properly play their role under the Constitution by determining whether any amendment is needed because of those happenings.

There has been continuous discussion about the rights and wrongs of what took place in 1975, which has been conducted under the handicap of ignorance about what I have to say. Australia is a federal democracy in which the people have been given a direct responsibility for the evolution of the constitutional machinery, and their right to full information on constitutional matters is unquestionable. I therefore select the present as the best time to provide the people with important information to which they have not yet had access.

I see the book primarily as an exposition of constitutional principles as I came, over a lifetime, to understand them — the constitutional principles on which certain little known powers of the Governor-General rest. These have been generally referred to as the reserve powers of the Crown, although in Australia they derive from the Australian Constitution.

Although the book discusses, inevitably, some historical, constitutional and legal questions it is not a technical treatise in constitutional law, government or history. There have been and will be books of an analytical kind in those disciplines, dealing with what has been called the greatest constitutional crisis in Australian history. When that crisis came, in October–November 1975, I was the person that life had by then made me, equipped by education, experience and character in a particular way. I brought to my role in that crisis such legal and constitutional knowledge as I had developed over many years. I had been a practising lawyer and a serving judge. I present my knowledge of the relevant constitutional principles as part of my life story and my account of the application of those principles as living action in stirring and momentous times.

Many Australian personalities cross the pages of this book and I hope that Australians of widely different interests and activities will find much in them that reveals my own deep commitment to Australia. I have met very many Australians in all parts of the country, especially during my Governor-Generalship, and I am proud to be one myself.

We have come through the great crisis of 1975, and the last quarter of the twentieth century now unfolds. It will be a quarter-century, I believe, of achievement for an Australia with stable constitutional and political institutions—a period of acceptance and understanding of our federal constitutional heritage which rests securely upon the base of a democratic constitutional Monarchy.

The period of my Governor-Generalship embraced some troubled times. We have passed through them, and as Australians have a duty to reflect on and understand them, expending the effort necessary to do so.

My personal passage through those troubled times was made endurable by the support of enormous numbers of Australians, of my staff, under my Official Secretary David Smith, of my family and friends and above all my wife Anne whose dignity and courage, loyalty and never wavering understanding and love sustained me always. To her I have dedicated this book.

My thanks go to Senator Eugene Forsey, one of the great living authorities on the reserve powers of the Crown, for the epilogue he has written to this book. I tell later how my acquaintance with Senator Forsey developed over the period since the eleventh of November 1975. I greatly appreciate his taking the time, in the midst of his busy active life of constitutional leadership in the Canadian Senate, to read my work and write his epilogue.

Finally, I cannot sufficiently thank Lord Hailsham for the foreword he has contributed to the British edition of this work. It is a masterly summary of the situation and its implications, and I express my sincere gratitude to him for what he has said.

It is impossible to make particular mention of the many others to whom I owe so much. They will all know I am grateful.

John Kerr

The Consent of the Governed

In Australia in the latter part of 1975 a very serious political crisis occurred which rapidly developed into a constitutional crisis. A political drama, with unprecedented constitutional elements, was enacted on our national stage. The two powerful political leaders, who with their respective parties and supporters became locked in a vital struggle, were the Prime Minister Edward Gough Whitlam, leader of the Australian Parliamentary Labor Party, and John Malcolm Fraser, leader of the Opposition coalition of the Liberal and National Country Parties—each motivated by his political position and objectives and acting politically. As Governor-General of Australia I occupied at that time the neutral position of representative of the Crown in Australia and repository under the Australian Constitution of reserve powers which it has vested in the Governor-General alone.

The crisis and its aftermath created acute tensions, stresses and strains in the Australian community. The three principal participants faced decisions of great moment for the community and for themselves. More than three years have now passed since the confrontation: in two successive elections held since for the national Parliament—in December 1975, immediately after the crisis, in a national mood still of agitation and suspense; and in December 1977, with an electorate unusually calm and undemonstrative as it went to the polls—record landslide results confirmed and reconfirmed that the Australian people by its political judgment upheld the separate and different decisions made at that time by two of the protagonists in the drama and rejected those of the third. In 1975 Malcolm Fraser's coalition parties were returned, in a House of only 127 seats, with the phenomenal majority of 55 seats over the Labor Opposition under Gough Whitlam. In December 1977 Malcolm Fraser and the coalition were returned with an again phenomenal majority of 48 in a House of 124 seats. At both elections the Liberal Party, of which Mr Fraser is the leader, was given an outright majority. The 1977 result represents an even more significant expression of view, since the lapse of time had allowed passions to cool and given an opportunity for a calm perspective upon the events of 1975.

The decisions that as Governor-General I was called upon to make in the course of the 1975 crisis were crucial action decisions against the background of a tough national political struggle. They were abnormally difficult decisions and their timing and nature were critical for Australia.

In summary: the Senate, where the Government did not have a majority, in October 1975 denied supply to the Government. In Australia the Senate has this right; but it was the first time supply had actually been denied federally, the threat of denial having on an earlier occasion sufficed to achieve the result desired. Supply had however on a number of occasions been denied in recent times at State level.

The Prime Minister, instead of yielding as he had done eighteen months previously when denial of supply had been threatened, embarked on a course of attempting to govern without supply, whereas it is the responsibility of the Government to obtain supply in order to provide for the ordinary annual services of government and to meet its other commitments. If it cannot, it must let the people decide at an election what is to happen.

Over some four weeks of deadlock each leader became more firmly committed to his position. It became increasingly clear that neither would retreat. There was as I saw it an implacable quality in the unfolding of events. Each leader must have been fully aware that he was leading his party to a political brink and that upon his ultimate judgment his party's future, his personal career and his share of historic responsibility for the outcome substantially rested.

Mr Whitlam, as the threat became real that the money needed
for the conduct of government would run out, stated his intention
of governing with the aid of financial arrangements which I
believe would have been makeshift, precarious and probably
illegal even if obtainable, and further destructive of public
stability and confidence.

As October advanced and the deadlock tightened there was
mounting public anxiety, argument and outcry. It was clear that
I was being forced towards a position where I must be prepared
to make a personal decision of dramatic consequence to the
leaders and their parties, to the country and to myself. Failing a
compromise, or retreat by one side or the other, it was only by my
having recourse to the reserve powers of the Crown that the
situation could be resolved and the whole issue placed in the
hands of the electorate for decision.

On 11 November 1975, time having in practical terms run out,
I acted to end the deadlock. In exercise of the Governor-
General's reserve powers under the Constitution I withdrew the
commission of the Prime Minister of Australia, Mr Whitlam, and
of his ministerial colleagues; appointed the leader of the
Opposition, Mr Fraser, as caretaker Prime Minister, and swore
in a caretaker Government. I obtained immediate passage
through the Senate of the blocked supply Bills, and dissolved the
House of Representatives and the Senate. In a statement issued
that day I said:

> The result is that there will be an early general election for both
> Houses and the people can do what, in a democracy such as ours, is
> their responsibility and theirs alone. It is for the people now to decide
> the issue which the two leaders have failed to settle.

An election for the two Houses of the national Parliament
followed a month later.

Action such as I took, generally referred to as dismissal and
forced dissolution, had been taken only once before in Australian
history: when the Governor of the State of New South Wales, Sir
Philip Game, dismissed the New South Wales Premier, Mr Jack
Lang, in 1932 and forced a dissolution of the New South Wales
Legislative Assembly.

3

In a scene which attracted world headlines, when on the steps of Parliament House, Canberra, in the afternoon of 11 November my Official Secretary, David Smith, ended his reading of the Proclamation dissolving the two Houses with the words 'God save the Queen', Mr Whitlam addressed the crowd and said 'You may well say "God save the Queen"; nothing will save the Governor-General'; and in words that have since become notorious exhorted his followers: 'Maintain your rage'. Further incitement followed, in immoderate language which was much quoted later.

The scene on the steps might have been explained away as a temporary loss of control. But the failure by the Labor Party to regain balance — on the contrary, the building up from the initial outburst to a campaign of hate against the Governor-General which seemed at times to be virtually the only plank in the Labor platform — was, I feel sure, deeply harmful to Mr Whitlam and the Labor Party as a whole, and bitterly divisive in the community.

There followed in Australia a period of passionate public argument. Before the dismissal, political and constitutional controversy had centred upon the Senate's actions, some claiming that they were entirely constitutional, some claiming that they were illegal and some that they were in breach of binding conventions to the effect that, if the powers of the Senate existed, they could never properly be resorted to. Following the shock of the dismissal new controversy raged: did I or did I not have, had I or had I not improperly and in breach of convention exercised, the powers that I had asserted?

In the community at large, already under severe strain from the prolonged deadlock and the threat of financial insecurity on a nation-wide scale, one could not exclude the possibility of widespread incomprehension and confusion as an immediate reaction to the dismissal. In fact, when a month later the nation went to the polls the degree of confusion and incomprehension turned out to be far less than might have been expected. A striking fact emerging almost at once from the great number of supportive letters that flooded in to Government House after the dismissal, from people having clearly a wide range of education

4

and background, was the grasp exhibited of the essential realities of what had taken place.

However, at the level of understanding of the law and constitutional principles involved, in particular of the rightness or wrongness of the Senate's action in blocking supply and of my action in dismissing the Prime Minister, a considerable stutter was to be heard for a time in the machinery of the nation's intellectual life. A situation had arisen so unprecedented as to necessitate recourse to the reserve powers of the Governor-General, powers the mere existence of which is expected to be sufficient to prevent such a situation from arising and so make recourse to them unnecessary, but which exist and are real nonetheless. Being so rarely invoked, the reserve powers are unfamiliar to the public at large (although interestingly enough, as will be seen, there had been in the weeks leading up to the dismissal quite an amount of media and other comment to the effect 'the Governor-General can act; will the Governor-General act?'). But they appeared to be unfamiliar too to many lawyers — the reserve powers constitute a rather recondite area of the law which does not give rise to many issues. Academic lawyers, even those specialising in constitutional law, did not all seem to be in a position to assess, let alone to elucidate for the public in an objective way, the law concerned.

It happened, because of chance circumstances and friendships in my youth, that I had acquired an intellectual interest in the law relating to vice-regal prerogatives and powers when I was a law student in the thirties and had retained it, within the wide sweep of my legal interests, since then. Of course, when contemplating vice-regal office and subsequently assuming it I had applied my mind to the subject in a more direct way. The law and constitutional principles which governed the course of events will be examined in later chapters. At this point I will say merely that in the result neither the action of the Senate nor my action was challenged or tested in the courts, and that it was my view, on the basis of my training and experience, that they would not be challenged in the courts because a challenge could not succeed.

In the election of December 1975 Mr Whitlam made alleged

5

unconstitutionality of the Senate's refusal to grant supply and my dismissal of him the main issues on which he fought his campaign. For my part I am glad that the constitutional questions were strongly raised and canvassed as election issues: Mr Whitlam's landslide defeat must be accepted as meaning that the people gave judgment on the constitutional issues, from the political point of view, against him. Mr Fraser, while strongly defending the constitutionality of what had been done, refused to be diverted during the campaign from economic issues. The political judgment of the people was not directly relevant to the constitutionality of my decision which rested upon constitutional principle as I shall later show.

It is significant that in the 1977 election campaign no attempt was made by the Labor Party to make it a re-run of 1975: the constitutional battles of 1975 were not fought again. Nevertheless my opinion is that the 1975 crisis and Mr Whitlam's subsequent actions were vividly remembered, and taken together amounted to a 'sleeping' issue on which the people's verdict was dismissive of Mr Whitlam. The latter has now been succeeded as leader of the Australian Parliamentary Labor Party by William Hayden.

Nonetheless the national constitutional debate continues on many levels.

I have made no attempt since 11 November 1975 to answer the endless arguments about what could or should have been done. The subject is so important and the debate so continuous and my silence leaves such a gap that I decided I would write this book when I left the Governor-Generalship. I believe that it is essential for the sake of national debate and the orderly unfolding of our national life that insofar as it is possible to disclose it at this time the history of these events should be known, and that the law and constitutional principles relating to them should be understood.

The Australian public is entitled to know, from fact and not from fiction, something of the man who occupied the seat of Governor-General at a decisive moment of its history.

My desire is not to enter the controversy in any continuing way but to make this contribution and, as far as I can see at the present time, leave it at that. Perhaps it will trigger off new arguments, but at least, for those who so wish, they can be arguments based on a true account and not on invention or conjecture. I hope the arguments that prevail .will be those founded on truth and reason and aimed at pursuing sense and perhaps a more resistant and resilient consensus for the future.

I have called this chapter 'The Consent of the Governed', a phrase from the *American Declaration of Independence*, because it serves to emphasise the part that had necessarily to be played by the people in the events I report. While the Australian and the United States Constitutions are in significant respects different, the latter provided an important example for the Australian founding fathers to consider when they wrote our federal Constitution, which combines, with the notion of federation, two traditional British constitutional tenets — constitutional Monarchy as a democratic instrument, and responsible government, under which Ministers of the Crown must be members of the Parliament. When the Australian Constitution was written, the seminal principles of the United States democratic philosophy, so lucidly and felicitously stated at the time of their founding, were equally appropriate in the monarchical democratic system embraced by Australia. The people were made a key element in the constitutional apparatus of Australian government, not as legal sovereign or original constituent authority as in the United States, but by virtue of the fact that upon their consent — the consent of the governed — depended not only electoral decisions but also changes in the Constitution and the passage into law of a proposed law blocked by the Senate.

In the spirit of those provisions of the Constitution the reserve powers of the Crown, exercisable by the Governor-General, to dismiss a Government and force a dissolution of Parliament can nowadays be used, in exceptional and critical circumstances, only to obtain the decision of the people as to a solution of that crisis. The book deals with critical contemporary events which illustrate in action the valuable union between the democratic philosophy and the residual reserve powers of the Crown.

7

2

Appointment as Governor-General

On 19 November 1975, soon after my decision of the eleventh, Sir Robert Menzies wrote to me. I quote an extract from his letter:

> I fear that some people when they nominate some distinguished man to be Governor-General of Australia imagine that he is their humble, obedient servant and that he must do as they say. This is, of course, pathetic nonsense. It is not only an insult to the holder of the office, but it converts the Governor-Generalship into a mere automatic post in which the Governor-General must, under all circumstances, do what his advisers tell him to do. If this is what a Governor-General is for, we might just as well not have one; we might as well have an automatic machine — a kind of robot. And if that is what we are to have, then plainly we do not need a Governor-General at all, but merely a recording machine.

I place this quotation from Sir Robert's letter early in this book because it raises in Sir Robert's highly personal style what is to be a focal question. Is the Governor-General, under the Constitution, a robot, a rubber stamp, a cipher? Is he — to borrow a refreshing new image from the press — 'a cigar-store Indian standing wooden-faced and blind in a corner'?[1]

Did Mr Whitlam have such a concept of the office in mind when he nominated me for it? Did he aspire to reduce the office to such a level?

It is not in doubt that the principles of responsible government require the Governor-General normally to act upon the advice of the Ministry and in practical terms in the vast majority of cases he will undoubtedly do so. The point at issue between those who support and those who deny the rubber stamp theory is whether the true doctrine is that the Governor-General must in all circumstances so act. The rubber stamp theory negates the existence of the reserve powers, of all vice-regal personal discretion. Its opponents regard the reserve powers as having a real existence: they will rarely be exercised and in the daily routine of government their existence will be irrelevant, but at moments of great crisis they can become crucial. The existence of the reserve powers is a question of profound constitutional significance.

Professor (later Sir Kenneth) Bailey in his introduction to the first edition of H. V. Evatt's book *The King and his Dominion Governors* said, in 1936:

> The fate of the constitution itself will depend on the adequacy of the provision it makes for what may be called emergency or crisis or reserve powers.[2]

At no time, before or after appointment, would it have been possible for me to concede that the reserve powers did not exist.[3] If Mr Whitlam wished to have a Governor-General who accepted that the reserve powers did not exist, then it is puzzling, to say the least, that he wished to nominate me.

There was ample material available about my political and other activities and views, including my writings and other public utterances, to enable Mr Whitlam to assess my likely attitude to the office were I to assume it. In any event, presumably he could have asked me, if he had wanted to know.

The decision to accept appointment to the office of Governor-General of Australia is not a decision to be made lightly, especially by one who at the time the matter is raised is fifty-eight years of age and is Chief Justice of New South Wales and Lieutenant-Governor of that State. There is certainly an obligation upon anyone holding such offices, if asked to serve as the Queen's personal representative in the office of Governor-General of Australia, to consider the matter with great care, realising that it is commonly believed there is a duty, though not an absolute one, to agree to serve the Queen and the country in high office if requested to do so, unless countervailing considerations of great weight over-ride this duty.

In August 1973 when the question of appointment to the

Governor-Generalship was raised with me by Mr Whitlam[4], the offices of Chief Justice of New South Wales and Lieutenant-Governor had been occupied by me only since June 1972 and my retirement would not in the ordinary course come until 24 September 1984. The appointments had been made by the Askin Government of New South Wales, a Liberal-Country Party coalition. I had earlier accepted the judicial way of life when, in June 1966, I was appointed to the federal Bench on the recommendation of the Hon. B. M. Snedden, Q.C. (now the Rt Hon. Sir Billy Snedden), Attorney-General in the federal Liberal-Country Party coalition Government at that time.

The judicial way of life is very different from the vigorous life of the Bar and from political life, both of which have their great attractions. Having once chosen the Bench I found that judicial life gave opportunities for constructive, creative and challenging work. This was especially so with the Chief Justiceship. The administration of justice in New South Wales, and the work of the judicial branch of government, in 1973 called for vigorous planning. A role of leadership in that field, combined with ordinary judicial work, makes a strong call. This happened with me. The fifteen months between appointment as Chief Justice and August 1973 were happy ones of co-operation with colleagues, with heads of other jurisdictions, with the State Government and Attorney-General, with the New South Wales Law Reform Commission and with other authorities.

The challenge of judicial administration is more appealing in days when reform in that field is clearly needed, when lists are long, delays excessive, jurisdictions as between judicial levels in the various courts in need of adjustment, when the impact and development of legal aid services and demand for law reform are socially significant, and when relations between the federal and State judicial systems are fluid. All of these matters were pressing in 1972, 1973 and 1974.

The Supreme Court of New South Wales made judges available for enquiries of various kinds at the request not only of the State but also at federal level at the request of the McMahon and Whitlam Governments. This activity placed burdens upon the Court. Some controversy surrounds the principle of having

Supreme Court judges engage in enquiries for Governments, and opinion among judges is divided.[5]

With a Supreme Court consisting generally of thirty-six judges, I had to decide too how far I would allow administrative work to eat into my time as against ordinary judicial work.[6] Each Chief Justice approaches this in his own way. Involvement with the reform of judicial administration made heavy inroads into my time from the moment of my appointment. However, the judicial side of the life was also of absorbing interest, indeed one aim of my reorganisation was to have the courts working as smoothly as possible to enable the Chief Justice to devote his time increasingly to the judicial role.[7] My writings of the period contain ideas and reflections deriving from my work as Chief Justice.[8]

It is relevant to appreciate all of this in assessing the attractions and the opportunities, the demands and the duties of a Chief Justice in New South Wales at the time when the Governor-Generalship was under consideration by me, and what I had to face in making the decision to give up my New South Wales appointments.

A further aspect of the problem was that having accepted such offices as the Chief Justiceship and Lieutenant-Governorship one has the duty to carry out the responsibilities for a period sufficiently long to make one's contribution. Those who have offered such appointments and had them accepted are entitled to this. This was a duty pressing upon me in August 1973 when Mr Whitlam approached me, and one which I recognised. It had to be balanced against another call of duty.

On the personal side, the office permitted continuous residence and presence, with minor exceptions, in Sydney, which was very pleasing to my wife (my first wife, Alison), to my family and to me. I love Sydney, Sydney life and Sydney associations. Anyone considering the position objectively in 1973 would have come to the conclusion, and it would have been true, that happiness and satisfaction had flowed from work and life in Sydney after June 1972 and that the final stage of my career, for a period of twelve years given life and health, would be in the office of Chief Justice of New South Wales, with occasional enjoyment of vice-regal life as Administrator of the State. Thereafter retirement in my home city at seventy on a Chief Justice's pension would, as my wife and I saw it, be pleasant indeed.

On the other hand much of my life had been lived at the national level. My practice at the Bar had taken me to various parts of Australia, my work in the professional organisations and in particular the Law Council of Australia had done much to increase my Australia-wide contacts, while responsibilities as a federal judge had widened their range. Interest in New Guinea and Asia had further enlarged my horizon. Dominant concerns of mine had for a long time been national and international. Taking on the Chief Justiceship had meant in a real sense having to abandon all of this and return to New South Wales and its problems. My feelings when I did so were mixed, although I had immediately started to enjoy the challenges of office and the pleasures of living and working in Sydney full time.

The nature and duties of the Governor-Generalship of Australia attract the occasional thoughts of most lawyers and especially those with some interest in constitutional law; but at no stage in my life had I contemplated occupying that office. I had at no time any aspiration to do so. I had been interested in the men who held the office during my adult life, and especially, for constitutional reasons, in the periods of office of Sir Isaac Isaacs, Sir William McKell, Sir William Slim, Lord Casey and Sir Paul Hasluck. Several of the Governors-General I knew personally; and I had admired the way in which these men had impressed their personalities on the country and symbolised its national identity and institutions, giving expression to national values and aspirations. In 1932 I had lived through the Game-Lang crisis when at the age of seventeen I was studying constitutional law at Sydney University Law School, and had read, when it was first published in 1936, Dr Evatt's *The King and his Dominion Governors*. So the broad concept of vice-regal office was of interest to me generally and constitutionally and indeed my own office as Chief Justice included an occasional vice-regal element; but none of this had ever led me even remotely to contemplate occupying the office of Governor-General of Australia.

It was in these circumstances that at a State dinner in Sydney during the Constitutional Convention held in August 1973 the

Prime Minister said to me and my wife as the three of us walked in to dinner, 'I want to say something which affects both of you. Paul Hasluck is going from the office of Governor-General next year and I have in mind to put your name before the Queen, John. Will you give it some thought? You do not, of course, have to react now'—or words to that effect. I expressed my surprise and my appreciation of the honour implied, while adding that clearly the question would require a great deal of serious consideration. We had by then reached the table and there was no further time or opportunity for talk that night.

It is an ironic circumstance that this occurred during the first sitting of the Constitutional Convention which still meets and at the time of writing has before it proposals deriving from the crisis of October–November 1975—namely Mr Whitlam's proposal that the Senate's powers over money Bills be effectively abolished, and the proposal of the Premier of Western Australia, Sir Charles Court, that if the Senate denies supply for thirty days there should be a double dissolution automatically, with provisions for temporary supply and for the wishes of the House of Representatives to prevail after the ensuing election.

To my wife and me the idea of taking the Governor-Generalship was, in a sense, a disconcerting one. If appointment were offered and accepted our conception of how life would go until retirement from judicial office would have to be jettisoned.

Mr and Mrs Whitlam were, over the years, associates but not personal friends of my wife and myself. Mrs Whitlam and my wife had been students at the same time in the department of Social Studies at Sydney University. When the former Prime Minister was called to the Bar, I came to know him as a professional colleague. We had, so far as I can remember, no cases together or against one another. When he entered politics in 1952 he quickly became absorbed in that way of life and we saw little of him at the Bar. When the new Wentworth Chambers were occupied in 1957 he acquired chambers on the same floor as mine and we met from time to time at social floor gatherings. At such gatherings, in the build-up to the 1972 election campaign there would sometimes be talk between us as to how he saw his prospects. My recollection is that my wife and I accepted one invitation to visit the Whitlams at home. Both before and after the 1954–5 split in the Labor Party we were of different opinion about fundamental party strategy on the communist issue. There was no intimacy, no real friendship, no political communion at any stage. Nevertheless I had followed his 1972 campaign with some admiration.

A more detailed conversation with the Prime Minister than the brief exchange at the dinner was necessary, and after some time I had that conversation with him in my chambers at the Supreme Court. I asked him if the proposal were a serious one and he said that, though informal, it was, and asked me to consider it as such.

He then raised three matters which he said I would doubtless like to take into account since he realised that it would be impossible for me to consider the proposal unless I understood what he had in mind about these. The three matters were, first salary, secondly pension and thirdly period of tenure. These were not questions that I raised with him but were considerations which he wished to put to me. It is necessary for this to be understood because there has been innuendo to the effect that I bargained for these things as conditions before I would accept the office. The contrary is the truth.[9]

It would be obvious to anyone that I could not resign from the Chief Justiceship without the security of a pension. I had not served long enough as a judge to qualify for a judicial pension if I resigned voluntarily. At the time there was no provision for a pension for the Governor-General. It was equally obvious to a lawyer that the salary, which could not because of provisions in the Constitution be changed during the period of office of a Governor-General, needed adjustment because of the in-flationary times — times which later became very much more inflationary. It was also obvious that I was being asked to give up an office I would hold until I was seventy and to take an office to be held at pleasure.

On all these matters Mr Whitlam had thought out his position and knew what he was prepared to do before he spoke to me at all. He did so in order to suggest to me that I should seriously consider his suggestion. He told me that legislation would be introduced to increase the salary to take account of predictable inflation in the coming years[10] — an inadequate change as it turned out since the coming inflation proved to have been far from predictable. The Governor-General's salary is the only salary which by virtue of the Constitution cannot be changed or adjusted to take account of inflation during the whole period of his incumbency.

Further, the Prime Minister said that legislation would be introduced to provide a pension. This would be applicable to Sir Paul Hasluck, to me if I accepted the office, and to future Governors-General. It would provide for a pension equivalent to the pension that would be payable to a retiring Chief Justice of Australia at the relevant time.

Thirdly, he said that security of tenure was, under the Constitution, a matter which could not be assured as the office was one held at pleasure, but that he realised he was asking me to give up a securely held office and so far as he personally was concerned he would undertake to recommend to the Queen the renewal or extension of the commission beyond the first normal term of five years for a second similar term if I were interested. He added that although he could not talk to the leader of the Opposition at that stage he had no doubt that Mr Snedden would see the point that in the circumstances an extension ought to be available if I wanted one after the first five years. He would later talk to him about this and I understand that after the appointment he did so. However he said politics being politics this was something which could not constitutionally be guaranteed and made into a binding obligation. Up to a point I would have to take the political risks. How true that was.

These points have only to be grasped for it to be clear what the position was. This was not an office I was seeking. I was being asked to take it and the considerations just outlined were put to me persuasively to induce me to think about it. The whole history of the next four or five months shows how I gradually overcame reluctance, after knowing what the Government was proposing to do and after careful thought about the office in the light of my reading followed by discussions which Mr Whitlam invited me to have.

Between this conversation and a conversation with the Prime Minister in October 1973 the main talks were between my wife Alison and myself. She, to begin with, was not unattracted by the idea of accepting the offer. But the more she thought about it the more opposed to it she became. She was happy with things as they stood. She enjoyed the life which came to her as wife of the Chief Justice and she enjoyed life in Sydney with her family around her. She also loved her voluntary professional life as a marriage counsellor at Life Line.[11]

But, more importantly, my wife did not trust politicians. She held the view that the offer was a political one being made for political reasons, that it would be unwise to give up constructive and creative work in my chosen profession only to find myself at the mercy of unpredictable political forces including, whatever he said, Mr Whitlam's politics. It will not be profitable to go into the detailed marital discussions of that time, especially as my wife's instincts were supported by my own personal interest in continuing with the reforms in the administration of justice in New South Wales upon which I was embarked, and because my political experience and judgment taught me that there was a great deal to be said for my wife's opinions about insecurity.[12]

Nevertheless I had a contrary pull upon me to which I was responsive almost from the beginning — the pull to return to work at the national level and to interest myself in national problems, which I knew would be possible because of what I understood to be the information and insights that come to the Governor-General. I was aware that broadly speaking the role did not involve power and its exercise; but it would offer the fascination of knowledge and, perhaps, the occasional opportunity to offer comment or advice. These points did not much interest my wife, by then fully settled in a Sydney context she enjoyed.

The issue remained a domestic one until October 1973.

In October the Prime Minister spoke to me and said that the Queen would be in Australia for the opening of the Opera House and that he would have to talk with her about the Governor-Generalship. He appreciated that I had not made up my mind about it and could not be expected yet to have done so — the office would in any case not be vacated until nine or ten months later.

But he would like to be in a position to put a name before the Queen while she was in Australia: if I would indicate only that I would seriously consider accepting, he would be able to say to her that he wished to ask me to undertake the task.

There are stages of informal talk between the Monarch and the Prime Minister on these matters and his concern was to let her know how he was thinking. I told him that I could certainly say I would seriously consider accepting, but that my wife was not enthusiastic about it. Nevertheless domestic discussion and my own thinking were proceeding. He said on that basis he would mention to the Queen that he had my name in mind. This conversation was of a tentative, informal and exploratory kind binding on neither of us.

Once this had happened it became essential for me to give thorough and detailed consideration to the nature of the office of Governor-General. Between October and December 1973 I reread and refreshed my knowledge of Evatt's *The King and his Dominion Governors* — from an Australian point of view an outstanding work on the subject of the Governor-Generalship. Although I was no longer involved in politics and, as everyone knew, had not been associated with the Australian Labor Party since 1955, I regarded Evatt's views on vice-regal office as being informed not by a party-political but by a liberal-minded approach. Rereading his work in late 1973 was an exercise of an attractive but abstract kind. As things later turned out the subject was to be of great significance for me, though at the end of 1973 I of course did not read the book in that light.

At no stage before my appointment did Mr Whitlam seek to ascertain my views as to the nature of the role and functions of the Governor-General.[13] Nor, very properly, did he ask me anything about my political views or my attitude to the political parties or their federal policies. He had no reason to believe that I had since 1955 been committed in any way to the Australian Labor Party nor indeed to any party; on the contrary, as a Sydney lawyer he had every reason to know that I had not. The Bench and Bar of Sydney form a very small community.

Mr Whitlam had come into the federal Parliament soon after the double dissolution election of 1951. He was in Parliament for many years under Dr Evatt's leadership and also at the time of publication of the second edition of Evatt's book, with its introductions by Professor Kenneth Bailey and Professor Zelman Cowen, in 1967 just after Evatt's death. I took it for granted, without particularly thinking about it, that as a lawyer and Labor parliamentarian he was well aware of his former leader's views about the reserve powers of the Crown, and familiar with the detailed study of these matters which had so deeply engaged the attention of his leader.

I had no reason to think, nor do I now believe, that Mr Whitlam in approaching me about appointment had any expectation of political partisanship or subservience from me in the office of Governor-General.

My reading in late 1973 confirmed my belief that the office was worthwhile and not that of a mere ceremonial figurehead. I was not at the time of reading contemplating the possible need to exercise the reserve powers. It was obvious, since the two Houses were in the control of different political parties, that deadlock could occur, and this I did think about, but rather in terms of section 57 of the Constitution (which deals with double dissolution) than anything else.

There was some public discussion towards the end of 1973 about the possibility of the Senate denying supply. It did not do so in November 1973 and the first Whitlam budget was passed. Yet the possibility of denial of supply existed, and this too was something to which I gave passing thought in an academic kind of way. Not even in a remote corner of my mind did I then contemplate that there could be a denial of supply under circumstances leading to a dismissal of a Government in possession of the confidence of the Lower House. To the extent that I thought about this matter of supply it was along the line that such a development would lead to an election. May 1974 was to bear out this view.

As Christmas neared Mr Whitlam spoke to me and indicated that he would soon have to ask me for a firm reaction. He enquired how my thinking was going. I said I was seriously interested. The Prime Minister expounded some views of his own in regard to the office: he said it was really nowadays that of a viceroy and the Governor-General was in many respects the Head of State; his view was that we should 'show the flag', through the office of the Governor-Generalship, by State visits to selected overseas countries.[14] He then asked whether it would be helpful if he arranged for me to have a talk about the Governor-Generalship with Sir Paul Hasluck. In due course I had that talk, followed by one shortly afterwards with Sir John Bunting, then head of the Prime Minister's department; and after that I made up my mind. The talks took place at the beginning of 1974.

Since Sir Paul has made his general views about the office of Governor-General known to the public in his Queale Memorial Lecture delivered at the University of Adelaide on 24 October 1972, I feel I can say that the comments he made to me when I visited him at Admiralty House were along the lines of his published views. His Queale Lecture was given to me by the Prime Minister's department as background reading early in 1974. I shall quote from it later.

My talk with Sir John Bunting also was arranged at the suggestion of the Prime Minister, who said, 'You know Jack Bunting. Would it help to talk to him about the way the office works from day to day, relations with the Ministers in the Executive Council and with Bunting and with me?' Sir John explained to me the way the system worked, how the Prime Minister kept the Governor-General in the picture, how he, Sir John, by regular talks supplemented this in detail, how the Governor-General saw all Cabinet documents and minutes and all important despatches and cables and was able to have an up-to-date picture of what was happening. All of this strengthened the pull upon me of national-level affairs. I said to him, 'Jack, you know the sort of chap I am. Do you really think I would like this job?' He said that it was a difficult question to answer but he thought I would.

Sir John arranged for some further reading material to be sent to me. As a result of all my thought I came to the conclusion that I should allow my name to go forward to the Queen. The decision was supported by my wife, who came to look with pleasure at the possibilities of the new life once it became clear that I felt my proper decision was to undertake it. The appointment was announced on 28 February 1974. Soon afterwards I resigned as Chief Justice as from 27 June 1974 and on 10 April 1974 my successor to that office was announced to be the Hon. Mr Justice (now Sir Laurence) Street.

It was not long after the announcement was made that my wife suddenly became seriously ill. Therapy gave her a real chance of some years of life and she was well enough to travel to London with me in May 1974 to be received by the Queen. Before we went to London she felt that in view of her illness Mr Whitlam should be given an opportunity to reconsider my appointment even though by then I had resigned the Chief Justiceship and my successor had been appointed. I spoke to the Prime Minister who asked that we should carry on if we felt able. Had the decision been otherwise I should have been without any office at all and without any pension. I should have been looking for some other work.

We returned to Australia and I was sworn in as Governor-General on 11 July 1974. During an early period of relative well-being my wife said that after actual experience of the life she felt that, if the doctors were right in giving her a real chance of moderate health, she would enjoy it. Soon afterwards however she had a serious relapse and died on 9 September 1974.

The earlier part of the year had been marked by activity on the political scene which is of relevance to the 1975 crisis. In May 1974, whilst I was still Governor-General designate Mr Whitlam and his colleagues had to face a threatened denial of supply by the Senate. This episode demands comparison with 1975. Mr Whitlam's attitude in 1974 was classically correct: he accepted an election as the proper solution. A double dissolution followed with an election for both Houses, leaving Labor with a majority in the House of Representatives but not in the Senate.

One can readily imagine the intense interest of such a supply crisis for a Governor-General soon to enter upon his office. It was clear enough that Bills which had provided the occasion for the double dissolution could eventually come to the point of being considered at a joint sitting of both Houses of Parliament. This had never happened before in Australian history but was to take place soon after I took office, as will be recounted later. When it did I had my first experience of having to act, upon advice, on what I believed to be an erroneous view of the law.[15]

Following in Hansard the events that led to the double dissolution of May 1974 I found nothing said on either side that could cause me any qualms about the correctness of parliamentary attitudes nor about continuing on the path upon which I had now entered. On 4 April 1974 the leader of the Opposition, Mr Snedden, said in the House of Representatives referring to two Appropriation Bills then before the House:

> We will oppose both these Bills. In opposing both these Bills we expect that they will be opposed in the Senate. If in the Senate all members of the Liberal Party, the Australian Country Party and the Democratic Labor Party oppose the Appropriation Bills they will fail to pass. If they fail to pass it will mean that the Government must go to an election. There must be a dissolution of the House of Representatives.[16]

Mr Whitlam, the Prime Minister, in the same debate on the same day said:

> Mr Deputy Speaker, it is not just time for the election of a government of Australia but for a parliament of Australia — an election of the whole Parliament of Australia. If the Senate rejects any money Bill — the first time that the Senate would have rejected a money Bill in the history of our nation — I shall certainly wait upon the Governor-General and I shall advise the Governor-General not merely to dissolve the House of Representatives but to dissolve the Senate as well.

He added:

> For all the bluster that the right honourable gentleman committed this afternoon, he knows perfectly well that the Appropriation Bills which we are debating will be passed by this chamber. If the Senate rejects them, not only is there a powerful argument of those matters which the Senate has already twice rejected and been twice passed by the House of Representatives but also there will be the additional powerful argument for the Prime Minister to give to the Governor-General that the Senate is deliberately withholding Supply — an unprecedented action.

In those circumstances, if the Senate refuses Supply I shall certainly wait upon the Governor-General. I shall advise that he issue writs not only for an election of the House of Representatives on 18 May but also for the election of a new Senate on 18 May . . . Until the Senate has rejected Supply, there is not one scintilla of ground for me to advise the Governor-General to dissolve the House of Representatives. But if the Senate gives me that ground then I shall certainly also have reinforced grounds — grounds which have never been available in the 73 years of this Federation — as well as those for rejection of Bills for advising the Governor-General that there should be an election for the whole of the Senate as well . . . On 18 May we can have a completely new Parliament.[17]

It will be noticed that the words used were *rejection* or *refusal* or *withholding* of supply. In 1975 we were concerned with deferral, which is a way of refusing or withholding supply.

On 8 April 1974 Mr Whitlam was asked a question by Mr Phillip Lynch, deputy leader of the Opposition. The exchange was as follows:

Mr Lynch: Is the Prime Minister aware of the statement made by his Attorney-General, Senator Murphy, to the Senate on 18 June 1970 as follows: 'The Australian Labor Party has acted consistently in accordance with the tradition that we will oppose in the Senate any tax, any money Bill or other financial measure whenever necessary to carry out our principles and policies.' Is the honourable gentleman also aware that Senator Murphy tabled at that time a list of 168 financial measures, including taxation and Appropriation Bills, which were opposed in whole or in part by the Labor Opposition between 1950 and 1970? If this was the clearly stated policy of the Australian Labor Party in Opposition, can the Prime Minister explain why he has suddenly reversed the Party's attitude in government, or is he simply running scared?

Mr Whitlam: I do remember that Senator Murphy tabled such a list in the Senate. I did not approve of his tabling it. I do not agree that that was the Labor Party's attitude. But I would have thought that honourable gentlemen would well know that I have consistently followed the attitude throughout my years in the Parliament — so has the Treasurer and so have all my senior colleagues — that it is inappropriate for the Senate to purport to cut off supply for the House of Representatives where governments are elected and to which governments are responsible. I have not always agreed with Senator Murphy in the past and I did not at that time. I would have thought that my attitude on this matter was well known. It has been expressed in committees of the Parliament — the Joint Committee on Constitutional Review — and on many occasions in the House itself. I do not have the same objection to the Senate or an upper house refusing Supply if it also faces the people at the same time. That is a point of view which I have stressed in the Constitutional Review Committee which sat in 1956, 1957, 1958 and 1959. It is a view to which I adhere. I believe that the honourable member for Moreton adheres to the same view and I support him in it. I believe it is quite wrong for any House of Parliament to refuse Supply to a government without facing the consequences itself. I am very happy for both Houses of this Parliament to face the consequences of any refusal of Supply.[18]

It will be seen that Mr Whitlam did not deny that the Senate could block supply. He freely recognised the power. His only point was that the Senate should not block supply without itself facing the people. He said he did not have the same objection to the Senate refusing supply if it faces the people at the same time as the House does.

In due course he recommended a double dissolution because it was clear that the Senate would deny supply. It should be kept in mind that refusal of supply occurs when it is not granted, which may be by rejection or deferral. Neither actually occurred in 1974.

In the Senate on 10 April during the debate on the Appropriation Bills Senator Willesee moved that the resumption of the debate be made an order of the day for a later hour of the day.

Senator Withers then moved an amendment to the effect that the debate on the Appropriation Bills be not resumed before the Government agreed to submit itself to the people at the time of the coming Senate election.

Later that day the Prime Minister told the House that he had asked for a double dissolution and that the Governor-General, Sir Paul Hasluck, had accepted his advice and granted an immediate simultaneous dissolution, provided supply was granted for the ordinary services of the Government during the period of time covered by the elections.

During this period, it will be understood, I carried no responsibility but watched what was happening from the sidelines. I knew the generally accepted opinion of the meaning of section 53 of the Constitution — a matter to be discussed in detail later — and fully subscribed to the view commonly held amongst jurists that the Senate could validly deny or fail to provide supply. From the events of May 1974 it was apparent to me that Mr Whitlam recognised this power and right of the Senate: he countered the Senate's move by forcing a double dissolution.

In 1975 I could not fail to interpret events in the light of Mr Whitlam's words and acts of 1974. I may point out, here at the beginning of this narrative, that on 11 November 1975, bearing in mind what Mr Whitlam said in 1974 I so disposed things that the Senate went to the people with the House, thus meeting a condition to which Mr Whitlam attributed importance (though it was not constitutionally necessary) and also giving him the opportunity, if he won the election in the House and had an absolute majority available for a joint sitting, of getting his twenty-one blocked Bills enacted.

So in July 1974, after the 1974 supply issue and election and before the 1974 joint sitting, I found myself installed in the office of Governor-General. The Government controlled the House but not the Senate.

My life up to 1974 made me the man Mr Whitlam recommended to the Queen. That life was a public one. I shall now tell the story of how it unfolded, beginning with my early life in Balmain from 1914.

3

Childhood and Youth — School, University and Early Post-graduate Life

I was born on 24 September 1914 and grew up in Balmain, then a working-class suburb of Sydney. A picture of the Balmain of those days may be useful because it is now becoming a very different suburb from what it then was. My family lived there until I was seventeen and it had quite an influence upon me. It is now, like other inner suburbs, after a period crowded with working-class family living, becoming popular with the intelligentsia, artists and other people who want to live close to the city. Old houses are being bought and renovated and real estate values have gone up.

In my childhood, Balmain was very much a workers' suburb. It is a peninsula which juts out into Sydney Harbour and around its shore there were, and to a lesser extent still are, waterfront workshops of various kinds—ship-building yards, ship repair yards and so on. There was also during my childhood a working coal mine and we used to watch the miners coming off-shift.

The people who lived there were mainly tradesmen and labourers and their families, together with shopkeepers and others who served them. There were a few professional people — doctors, dentists, bankers, solicitors, school teachers and public servants.

My father was a boilermaker and my mother had been a dressmaker. My father's family were all manual workers. His father and mother were immigrants who came from northern England. My paternal grandfather had been a butcher, but my only recollection of him is during the 1920s when he was a wharf labourer. They arrived here in the late 1880s, my father's elder brother having been born in England. My father was born here (in 1890) as were the other children. They settled in Balmain.

25

The family was by modern standards a large one—six boys and two girls.

In those days, there was little access to education. My father left school at the age of twelve, with special permission, because of the family circumstances. He later became an apprentice boilermaker and served his time in that trade at Mort's Dock, now long since vanished. Three of his brothers also became boilermakers, working on the waterfront; the fifth son became a butcher and the sixth a labourer. The two girls did manual work of some kind. They lived in a very small cottage in Short Street, Balmain, which I remember well.

My mother grew up in the country. She was born in Grenfell in New South Wales in 1889. Her father was born in Australia, as was her mother. My great-grandfather on that side was born in England and came out here to settle and married an Australian. He was an overseer on a station property. In my mother's family there had been a little more education on her father's side in earlier days but not in this country. My grandfather had very little schooling and became a miner in the country at places like Lucknow on the New South Wales goldfields, and was at one stage a coach driver. He married a Catholic girl who had been born in this country but whose parents came from Ireland.

The religious position therefore was that my grandparents on my father's side were Anglicans; my grandfather on my mother's side was an Anglican, but his wife was a Catholic and my mother was brought up as a Catholic. However, when my mother and father married, apparently her religion did not count much because she was married in an Anglican church and we, their children, became Anglicans. There was a lot of religious bigotry in Australia between Catholics and Protestants at that time and for long afterwards.

My father and mother met soon after she arrived from the country and they were married in 1913. They went to live in Rozelle which is an extension of Balmain within the peninsula. Soon after marriage my parents moved into a little newly built semi-detached cottage. It had, although across a timber yard, a beautiful view of the Harbour up towards the Parramatta River.

Balmain at the time had a highly developed suburban

patriotism largely because of its geographical and industrial character — the local rugby league and cricket teams were followed enthusiastically. My father took my brother and me regularly on Saturdays to the matches. Archie Jackson, who at first played in short pants, because he was so young when he joined the Balmain cricket club, was a local idol who whilst still young scored a century in his first test innings for Australia against England. There were tidal swimming baths on the shore of a waterfront park, where my father took us to swim and as children we played there and explored its rocky shores. There was mixed bathing only on nominated occasions. At other times the baths were a male preserve.

In the days before the depression, life was reasonably good. One anecdote of passing interest is that when my father was an apprentice at Mort's Dock Sir William McKell, later Governor-General of Australia, was also a boilermaker apprentice there. They knew one another in those days and Sir William and I still sometimes talk about my father. When they were in the last year of their apprenticeship the question arose of whether they were then sufficiently skilled to ask for adult pay — they were not legally entitled to it — and the 'boys', as the apprentices called themselves and were called by others, of that particular year met and decided that someone should approach the boss and put it to him that the work they were doing entitled them to a tradesman's pay. My father was selected to do this but he rather felt, so he always told me, that he did not quite have the necessary personality to put the case and it was put by William McKell, and put successfully. The boys, the apprentices in their final year, did achieve adult pay. My father always enjoyed a fantasy that if he, instead of Sir William, had put the case he might have been later able to launch himself on a career along the lines that opened up to Sir William, who became a politician in New South Wales, qualified for and was admitted to practice at the Bar, became a Minister and later Premier of the State and in due course Governor-General of Australia. At least he seemed to believe he might have been able to go a little distance along that path. In fact, though he was a fine man he was personally unambitious.

27

Since one reads in the papers these days about my being the son of a boilermaker and every now and again we are told that Sir William began as a boilermaker, there may be some interest in that early association. It was a reason for developing a Labor orientation, as I did, especially in university days. At home we followed Sir William's career with great interest, but as it will be seen, he and his career had much less influence on me than did that of Dr Herbert Vere Evatt. Nevertheless all the things that happened in Sir William's life were noted in the family. He was a member of the Lang Ministry at the time of the dismissal of Lang by Governor Sir Philip Game which, with its aftermath, was a striking event in my pre-war life.

My parents were not church-going people and brought us up without too much religious discipline; but we were expected to go to Sunday school. I was a religious believer, as an orthodox Low Church Anglican, until I was at university. Indeed, a great deal of my life was, until about the age of seventeen, centred around St Thomas' Anglican Church in Rozelle. I taught at Sunday school there for a while. But religion was never talked about at home. Certain regular weekly observances were insisted upon so far as the children were concerned, but nothing else. Neither of my parents ever went to church or said prayers as far as we knew, though their children whilst very young were taught to do so.

My mother strongly objected to a Catholic priest calling on her and telling her she was not properly married because she was married in an Anglican church. She at no stage showed any desire to return to active practice of Catholicism, though in her later life both before and after my father's death I raised the subject with her on the advice of some of my Catholic friends, in case she might have underlying worries and doubts about her religious position, especially in old age.

The family was quite unselfconsciously working-class. The house had two bedrooms, a living-dining room, a kitchen, laundry, bathroom with a sort of tin bath in it, fuel copper and a fuel stove. My father kept a neat little pocket handkerchief-size garden including a vegetable garden and lawn and, at one stage, a small chicken run. My parents were well enough off to buy a piano and I can remember people coming to parties and singing around the piano and dancing. There was no question of looking with envy or interest even, at the way other people lived. Nobody really had much idea how other people lived. Certainly there was no political animus directed against those better off, no class feeling, no Marxist attitudes.

As a small child I visited Cockatoo Island several times. My father worked great machines there. I think they were a punching and a shearing machine. The former punched out the holes through which the rivets were put in ship-building and another machine sheared off the plates to the correct pattern. It seemed to me an enormous, highly complicated, very busy and very noisy place. One visited it on high days and holidays, if a ship were to be launched, or on some such occasion.

At the church there was a tennis court and tennis was played on Saturday mornings by the young people until they graduated to be teenage players and could join the afternoon club. I met a family at that time which was different from my own. It seemed to me to be rather upper class — not that I knew what an upper-class family was. They were in fact shopkeepers and had a prosperous flower shop opposite the church and a comfortable, spacious waterfront home in nearby Drummoyne. They entertained in a way that seemed lavish to me, at the time. Young people came from the church — Saturday night dances were held on the verandah, Sunday evening suppers, picnics on the harbour and nearby islands, swimming, canoeing, rowing, sing-songs around the pianola and billiards. The company consisted generally of the young friends of their children. The children went to minor private schools. That way of life went on until the depression, which began in 1929 when I was in my third year at Fort Street Boys' High School and was about fifteen.

Another aspect of social life in Balmain was the special setting of Friday nights. Friday was the late shopping night, and everybody, after the washing-up was done, would get tidied and parade up and down the main street. We, and almost everybody else as far as I can remember, would set out at about half past six or seven o'clock — we all ate very early — and walk the two or three miles up the street and back to the Balmain shopping centre, stopping to meet people and talk or gossip and listen to a brass band which often played at the shopping centre. My brother and I were always given by our parents a penny each, with which we bought four Cook's caramels, which we would eat as slowly as possible in the hope that by various tricks and devices one of us would end up having one left when the others had run out. Then my father and his brothers and sisters and their husbands and wives and the children would all end up either at our grandparents' house or a bit further up the street where one of the brothers lived. They would play cards and we would all have supper. Generally it was a happy enough environment and there were lots of cousins who were put up to sing a song or recite a poem to the pride of their parents.

My mother's parents lived in Woollahra off Oxford Street and we frequently exchanged visits. In the summertime we went as a large family group for picnics on some Sundays, generally to Bronte Beach or Bondi. My grandfather went ahead early to get a summerhouse. Great supplies of food, baked meats, salads, jellies, fruit and cakes were carried with us in hampers by tramcar. Lunch and tea, swimming and games filled in the day till dusk. Holidays during my early childhood were spent at Woy Woy in rented cottages, with a hired rowing boat, fishing, picnicking and walking, often with other relatives holidaying nearby. After my father became a railway worker he was entitled to a family pass on the trains, and we usually went to Urunga on the north coast of New South Wales and spent a leisurely time rowing, swimming and fishing. Fellow workers and their families went there at the same time. Having the passes we did a lot of train travelling. My father once took my brother and me to Broken Hill. We arrived after a night in the train, stayed for lunch and returned: a journey of 2,378 kilometres and a long way to go for lunch, but a great adventure.

As to the rest of Sydney I was aware, of course, of 'town' from going there with my parents, mainly my mother, to buy clothes. This was always done on what was called the 'cash order' basis. They would obtain cash orders, say for five pounds, and these would be paid off to a collector who came around every week and who was paid sixpence or a shilling in the pound per week. We very rarely bought anything in the way of clothes for cash, although my mother always met her obligations weekly and the cash orders were always paid off at the proper time. She was a good and careful housekeeper. Although normally prudent she sometimes 'got into the red' and had to confess to my father that she really needed an extra few pounds.

The North Shore, the rest of the Eastern suburbs and the Western suburbs played no part in my childhood except for a visit I can remember to a small poultry farm or orchard in Turramurra on the North Shore of Sydney Harbour owned by a boilermaker who worked with my father. I later lived there for more than twenty years during my days as barrister and judge in a large house in reasonably spacious grounds, built at the turn of the century long before this early and first visit of mine to that suburb. I had not seen or heard anything of my father's friend for about fifty years. When I became Governor-General he wrote to congratulate me, reminding me that he had been a fellow-worker of my father and that we had visited him at Turramurra long ago. At the time the Harbour Bridge had not been built.

It was when I was ten or eleven that a most significant event occurred in my life which for many years afterwards influenced it.

In 1925 Dr Evatt, then a young barrister, stood for election as a Labor candidate for the Legislative Assembly of New South Wales in an electorate which from memory I think was a composite one. Evatt was a young man of about thirty-one. In 1925 he had not yet taken silk, but he was a prominent young junior barrister. He was a most unusual phenomenon to me not only because he was a strange being called a barrister but also because he was a doctor but not a medical doctor. He was, as I was told, a Doctor of Laws.

He did not know my parents and my parents did not know him, but in developing his campaign as a Labor candidate he was seeking canvassers and supporters and people to man polling booths, and in some way my parents joined his entourage. I can barely remember young men in straw boater hats coming to the house at that time to organise the campaign. I do not think my parents were members of the Labor Party but it was a Labor family and they voted Labor.

Evatt won that election in 1925 and soon afterwards he had a political fight with Jack Lang, the New South Wales leader, as a result of which he was expelled from the Labor Party. He fought the election again in 1927 as an Independent. It was a bitter campaign in Balmain and Evatt won again after suffering much abuse from Labor supporters.

Elections in those days were totally different from what they are now. They were very much street corner affairs and on Friday nights during active election campaigns, throngs of people would meet in the course of their perambulations at particular street corners where the candidates would talk. There was no radio or television. Interjections and questions were tough. There was a lot of noise and mob oratory.

My parents at that time (they supported him again in 1927) came, in a peripheral sort of way, to know Dr Evatt. He wrote a letter, as most candidates did, to all the people who supported and helped him, thanking them, and that letter my father kept.

I think I can fairly say that between the years 1925–6 I decided, without knowing what the problems were but influenced by the talk about Evatt, that I would like to be a barrister. Evatt had gone to Fort Street Boys High School. I concluded that I would have to go to Fort Street too.

When I say that I decided these things, this raises an interesting psychological comment on the relationship between myself and my parents. They had no experience upon which to base any aspirations that one could become a barrister; but they knew about high schools and they encouraged me.

I wanted to sit for the High School Entrance examination in 1925. My results had always been good in primary school—the Rozelle Junior Technical School—but according to the headmaster I was too young to sit for the High School Entrance examination. So I sat for and passed the Primary Final, which entitled me to go into the seventh class, corresponding roughly to first year at high school, but providing a different sort of course—woodwork and technical drawing were taught as the foundation for a move the following year to a Trades School, as well as some geometry and algebra, science and other subjects.

I remember quite distinctly making the decision half way

through seventh class to seek the permission of the headmaster to go back to sixth class and sit for the High School Entrance, and this he allowed me to do. I sat for the High School Entrance and got into Fort Street, where I wanted to go.

That seems to me, when I look back on it, an unusual thing to have happened because a boy of eleven did not normally do things like that. One just went on in the same track. To reverse direction and go back to sixth class I must have had a very strong desire to get to high school and to get into a line of education which would lead to the law. My parents did not, in this, pursue a policy of their own but supported me in my desire. Of my two parents my mother was the stronger and encouraged me throughout in everything, with my father willingly going along.

Looking back I see that my parents' acquiescence in my aspiration, at the age of eleven, to become a lawyer marked the beginning of a slow severance of roots which continued when they moved late in 1932 to Dulwich Hill. This was, I am sure (though it was never spelt out) an attempt by my mother to give her law student son and her other children an environment which she thought more suitable to the changing situation. By the time my sister reached secondary school some years later, I was twenty-four and at the Bar and it was taken for granted that she would go to high school. The years left their mark on my parents who gradually became more and more detached from their old environment and friends without ever really joining a different social group as their children were doing.

Gradually, and despite a rather closer relationship between my mother and sister (who is now a doctor and married to a doctor, while my brother became a major in the Army), it came about that my parents were not really living either in their former world or in that of their children. From my schooldays until their death they met a cross section of my school and university friends and their families and, later, lawyers including judges; there was never any attempt to keep them in a separate compartment of life, as sometimes happened in those days when children grew up and crossed class barriers in the conditions of social mobility that exist in Australia. All three of us children were concerned with this and in the fifties and sixties our parents had all the modern comforts including a motor car; but the old verve of their earlier days was missing. They paid a personal price in the cutting of their old roots.

In 1926 after spending a few months in sixth class and sitting for the examination I went back, for more abundant precaution as I would say nowadays, to seventh class, passed the end-of-year examination and at the beginning of 1927 was actually in eighth class for a couple of weeks and attending the Balmain Trades School when I was notified I had passed for Fort Street.

It was quite an experience to start at Fort Street, which was then a selective high school drawing pupils from a very wide area. I went there in the first year after its famous headmaster, A. J. Kilgour, had left. It was a school to which many sons of the middle class went, as well as some working-class boys. There was in my year a son of a professor, sons of bank managers, many sons of school teachers and of public servants; and these were all new types to me. I simply set out to do as well as possible amongst them.

I was never much interested in sports. I played tennis at school and at weekends but certainly not well enough to make any teams. But I was always interested in school life and particularly in debating and in drama. Fort Street was a school which had a regular play day and every class put on plays. Academic success came and in my final year I was vice-captain of the school. I think I got on well enough with the boys and on the whole with the masters. As I did not play sport I was not able to achieve popularity on the basis of sporting achievements, but I was not unpopular even though I did well academically. A reasonable friendship developed with boys who did play sport. A number of cricketers, footballers and athletes were my friends.

As a pupil I was a bit talkative and I rubbed a few of the masters up the wrong way by that sort of behaviour and by ill-conceived attempts at wit and so on. When the selection of the captain, vice-captain and prefects came around one of the masters whom I much admired and who was a fine history teacher gave me a hint to try and be sensible for a few weeks as I had a lot at stake. I have no doubt I tried and in the upshot I became vice-captain. This was a position created that year for the first time, ranking between captain and senior prefect.

Kilgour's mark was still very much on the school when I went there. One of the things that Fort Street offered in those days was a pathway, as I discovered soon after I got there, to the professions, in particular so far as I was concerned into the law. As well as Evatt, the lawyers Spender, Barwick and Ellis, men to be mentioned later, were Fortians, though not there in my day. They and others like them exemplified the great legal tradition of the school. So I had in fact gone to the right place.

Of the Old Fortians I have mentioned, Evatt spent ten years as a judge of the High Court, becoming a member when he was thirty-six, and then went into federal politics, became Attorney-General and Minister for External Affairs in the Curtin and Chifley war-time Governments and played a significant role in the founding of the United Nations, of which in 1948 he became President. Later he became deputy leader and then leader of the Labor Opposition after the death of Chifley. He ended his career as Chief Justice of New South Wales.

Spender, like Evatt and like Barwick after him, had a big practice as a silk; he entered Liberal Party politics, ended up as Minister for External Affairs, became Australian Ambassador to Washington and later a member and President of the World Court at The Hague. Barwick also, after brilliant achievements as a barrister, and after being President of the New South Wales Bar Association and of the Law Council of Australia, had a distinguished political career. He was Attorney-General and later Minister for External Affairs in the Menzies Government, finally becoming Chief Justice of Australia. Kevin Ellis entered Liberal politics in New South Wales and became Speaker of the New South Wales Legislative Assembly. All except Evatt (the Labor Party being against knighthoods) were knighted. Many other successful lawyers and judges came from Fort Street.

Amongst the pupils at school, there was one who was a friend — quite a good friend, but not a close one — Leonard Conlon. He was a brother of the later well-known Alfred Conlon who was during and after the war a close associate of mine and played quite a big part in my life from 1942–9; and who even today, long after his death, among certain groups is seen as a somewhat legendary figure whilst amongst others he is underestimated.

I visited the Conlons at their home quite a lot and came to know all three brothers. They were all at different times at Fort Street. Alfred, the eldest, left school in his fourth year.

Leonard became a doctor and Arthur a barrister. Alfred did his matriculation, probably by studying at night, working I think with the Shell Company in the day-time. He graduated as Bachelor of Arts. He studied for his Arts degree, also I think in evening classes, during the very early radical days of John Anderson. Anderson had a considerable influence on Alfred Conlon but he was no idolater of Anderson. I met Alfred in those days. Later on, when I was doing Law, he had become an articled clerk to his brother, who was then practising as a solicitor. Alfred was intending to become a lawyer, but later he gave that up and started to study Medicine at Sydney University. At the end of his fourth year, the war had broken out and he became, I think, Manpower Officer at Sydney University. He also became a student representative on the University Senate. Later he became an adviser to General Stantke, who was the Adjutant-General. He joined the Army and became a major, heading a Research Section on General Stantke's staff.

I did not have very much personal contact with Alfred Conlon until during the war. He would be at home on occasions when I would call in with Leonard, and there would sometimes be conversation; he was always a stimulating fellow.

Similarly the poet James McAuley, whom I knew only slightly at Fort Street where he was in a lower form than mine, became a close friend during the war and later shared in many activities of which I will write.

Another school mate was Kenneth Gee, the son of a solicitor, who warned me of the difficulty of getting started in law. We went through both school and university together. He first became a solicitor. Starting out at university as a conservative, he gradually swung further and further to the left. During the early days of the war he gave up practice of the law and trained as a dilutee boilermaker. He met and became, as he still is, a friend of Laurie Short who later fought communism in the Federated Ironworkers' Union.

As the years went by Gee gradually moved back to the right

36

and ended up strongly anti-Marxist. He returned in other words to the conservative fold, became a barrister, a Crown Prosecutor and is now a District Court judge.

In common with many pupils I shared a tendency to try and be a bit smart. I recall on one occasion we were supposed to prepare ourselves to discuss Charles Lamb and I failed to do this, banking on the fact that in a class of thirty or so it would be most unlikely that I would be picked out. I went into class and on the way in I said to someone, 'Do you know anything about this fellow?' And he said, 'No, I don't. All I know is that he was a bit mad, and his sister was a bit mad too'. The teacher's eye lit on me and he said, 'Well, Kerr, come out and tell us what you know about Charles Lamb'. I had about three seconds to decide what to do, so I decided to play it for laughs and said, 'Charles Lamb was a bit mad and his sister was a bit mad too'. I then stopped and that produced a laugh. He said, 'Yes?' I replied, 'Well, that's all I know'. There was no caning or physical punishment at Fort Street. We could be detained, but this master did not impose detention. His way of humiliating me was simply to say, 'Yes. All right Kerr, I think you'd better go outside and play'.

My interest in English and history and the humanities was always keener than in anything else, but I also studied chemistry as well. I matriculated with first class honours in English, history and chemistry but my interest was far greater in English and history, partly I suppose because everybody told me that these were the subjects that led to the law.

Each year Evatt gave a prize for an essay. It had to be written under examination conditions and we were not allowed to take in any material with us. There were three hours to write it—it was meant to be of some length. The subject was given in advance and we could prepare fully for it. This prize Evatt gave in memory of his two brothers who were killed in the First World War—Raymond and Frank. The subject he set in the year when I entered for the prize was 'Australia should be more enterprising in the Pacific'. I can remember doing a lot of work in the Public Library on that subject, which even then I recognised as being designed to raise for discussion the real prospect of an independent foreign policy for Australia. This prize was competed for by the pupils in the final year and I won it in 1931.

The crash of 1929 made a vast difference both to Balmain and to many boys at the school. Great numbers were out of work in Balmain. Many houses were empty; all sorts of people went bush, people bunked in together; two or three of my father's brothers were at various times out of work. He by this time had moved to work for the railways as a boilermaker at the Eveleigh workshops. That was Government employment and although wages were not good he at least had constant employment during 1929–31 and afterwards, subject to some rationing of work. He had to help the out-of-work members of his family.

Employment collapsed for school-leavers. An annexe was added to Fort Street to take three or four hundred pupils from various intermediate high schools into the fourth and fifth years, because they could not get work. By the time I was vice-captain, Fort Street was a very big school for those days: the numbers went up from about six hundred to close on a thousand.

On leaving school at the end of 1931 I had to decide what to do. By that time my aspiration to read Law was taking a beating. My father was working, certainly. I won a bursary at the Leaving Certificate but I had, before then, personally decided that from an economic point of view there was going to be no way for me to study Law. I still wanted to do it but I felt I had to earn at least some money.

The best way to earn some money and still get a university education, without joining the public service which I did not want to do if I could avoid it, was to win a Teachers' College scholarship. It was not worth much but it was worth rather more than a bursary—about one pound per week. So I applied for an Exhibition, as it was called in those days, entitling one to pay no fees—but I applied in Arts rather than Law, and also for a Teachers' College scholarship and a bursary. I had a letter from the Education Department asking me, if awarded both a bursary and a Teachers' College scholarship, which I would take. The bursary gave me eight shillings a week. Although we had talked about it before and I had decided I could not tackle Law merely with a bursary, my father said we could have a go at it and he

38

would try to keep me for a while if I could see a way to get to Law School. My mother was urging me to explore the possibility. I had to make the decision whether there was any way of starting Law on eight shillings a week. I then made the second decision in my life which involved Evatt, and which brought me into personal contact with him for the first time.

At the end of 1931 Evatt, as a High Court judge, was an important person. He lived at Mosman in Sydney. There was no one for me to turn to in order to discuss Law. A fellow pupil who became a life-long friend and who was at Fort Street, the son of a solicitor and himself intending to go to Law School, said to me, 'It's absurd you wanting to do Law in the middle of the depression without any legal connections'. So, I have never understood quite how I came to do it, I looked up in the telephone book Evatt's address and went to see him at Mosman. It did not occur to me he might not be there when I arrived. I went bearing the letter that he had once written to my parents.

A story has been told that my father introduced me to Evatt at this point. It is unfounded; he had not had anything to do with Evatt since 1927. But when I suggested going to see Evatt to ask his advice as an Old Fortian, my father thought it was a good idea and produced the letter Evatt had written him in 1927 saying it might help.

A maid dressed in uniform answered the door — a phenomenon which I had never struck before. I said that I would like to see Mr Justice Evatt and thrust the letter into her hand. She went inside and spoke to someone who came out. It was Dr Evatt's wife, Mary Alice, as I later discovered everyone called her, whom in due course I came to know. I told her I wanted Dr Evatt's advice. She said, 'Oh, he's not here, he's at the High Court'. But she added, 'If you ring tonight, I'm sure he'll see you'.

I rang Evatt that night and he invited me to see him at the High Court. I told him my problem and he said, 'Well, the best way to do Law is to do Arts first and then Law. But I can see you won't want to do that because of the times. I'm sure if you ask them to change your Exhibition over to Law from Arts, they will do it'. He added, 'You'll have your bursary and you'll be able to find articles soon and become an articled clerk which, in the course of time, will bring in a few shillings'. I knew little about articles but believed them very difficult to get in those hard times; however, Evatt was optimistic.

He then said, 'I would like to do something myself. I would like to give you, personally, a scholarship to enable you to do Law'. I said, 'That is not what I've come for'. He said, 'I have no doubt it's not what you came for but you've got to consider your parents if you're going to do this. You're fully entitled to what I am offering. If there had been a scholarship around, you would probably have won it'. He added, 'I will give you a scholarship of fifty pounds a year'. I was amazed at this offer, indeed overwhelmed, and thanked him with some emotion but said that I would like to think about it and that I would not want it to be interpreted by him that I had come seeking financial help. He asked me to think it over and discuss it with my parents and take their advice. His view was that they would advise me to accept and they did. So I made a compromise. I got in touch with him again and said I would accept his scholarship with gratitude for one year only until I could work things out, but he said it was, subject to performance, available for the full course. He agreed to limit it, for the time being, to one year. He sent me a cheque for thirteen pounds a quarter, which with my bursary I knew would keep me going. Early in our discussion he had asked about my academic record and had learned among other things that I was the most recent winner of the Evatt Prize.

I changed my Exhibition over to Law. Then I heard from my friend Arthur Conlon that articles would be available with a firm called D. Lynton Williams, Ellis and Company in about May. Both partners were Old Fortians. I was given articles in their firm but this did not immediately bring in any income — I was to have nothing a week for the first twelve months. After the first twelve months I was to get ten shillings a week with increases of ten shillings a week each year. I was not required to pay a premium for my articles though this was still not uncommon in those days.

Towards the latter part of 1932 there was a change in my circumstances as an indirect result of the dismissal by Governor Game of Jack Lang.

My father by this time, even under Labor, was getting only four weeks work out of five. When B. S. Stevens won the election in 1932 after Lang's dismissal, it became possible for him, as the conservative leader, to make certain rearrangements in the constitution of the Industrial Commission of New South Wales. As a result of this salaries were reduced by ten per cent.

I had what was for me at the time a painful experience. I felt I had to go to see Williams, the senior partner. He knew that my father was a boilermaker and that there was not much money about. I had been accepted by the firm partly because of the Fort Street connection. I said, 'Mr Williams, you know my family situation. It's becoming a crucial question for me whether I can continue. Is there any chance of you giving me that ten shillings a week now instead of next May?' He said, 'Well, things are bad for all of us but I understand your position. I'll have a talk with Ellis'. Ellis had just graduated in Law and was a partner. At Fort Street, he also had done the English-history course and he had won the University Medal with first class honours in Law the year before I went to that office.

It took them about six weeks to make up their minds. Finally they agreed to give me the ten shillings. So by late November, or thereabouts, I had Evatt's fifty-two pounds a year; I had eight shillings a week from my bursary and I had ten shillings a week salary. This was adding up by now to a barely viable proposition. All my income was going back to my parents except that needed for tram fares, simple lunches and small change. At one time when I was in first year Law, I regularly walked most of the way from home to the Law School to save the fare.

At the end of first year there was a fifty pounds scholarship, which I shared with another student. When I won that, I said to Evatt, 'I'm over the worst of my troubles. I am very grateful for your help but I would prefer to give up your scholarship'. Now that I could, I preferred to compete with other students within the Law School system. He accepted my thanks and my point of view and we wound up the arrangement. I had seen him several times during the year. He used to lunch at Rainaud's, a restaurant at the top of King Street, Sydney, where I used to go and have lunch with him and others and he would talk about the law and sometimes about politics, including the Lang dismissal. He was making his name as a High Court judge.

Judges in Australia all have associates and Evatt offered me, during our early days, an associateship with him when I graduated, which when the time came I did not for various practical reasons take. My main reason was that I felt there was more real experience to be gained by responsible work in a law office than in an associate's job. He understood this point of view.

The Sydney Law School was, and still is, downtown in the heart of the legal precinct in the centre of the city of Sydney, whereas the main campus of the university is in Camperdown a few miles away. Those who entered the Faculty of Arts before going to the Law School therefore had experience of real university life, generally as full-time day students, in some cases living in a residential college. They would have two or sometimes three years in Arts and would enter the Law School older in years, education and experience than those just out of school.

Although the Law degree alone qualified one for admission to the Bar and articles of clerkship were necessary only for those wishing to become solicitors, most law students sought and found articles, which enabled them to postpone until after graduation in Law the choice between the two branches of the profession.

Inability to study in the Faculty of Arts thus deprived the law student, fresh from school, not only of the liberal full-time education on the campus provided by the actual courses of study but also of many aspects of ordinary university life. The result, especially after office experience and responsibility grew at the end of the first year or two of articles, was that in many if not most cases the typical law student straight from school became a city type, working full-time in the city and rubbing shoulders more and more with barristers and solicitors and clients. His principal student associations were with fellow law students.

A student from a background such as mine, living a full-time, downtown city life and seeing almost nothing of the university proper, had a lot of catching up to do. During term there was not time for substantial outside reading. All studying of law had to be done at night or at the weekend. Other demands on leisure limited the few available opportunities to absorb a liberal

42

education that would go beyond the mainly vocational approach of the Law School of those days. Looking back on it all I feel that I was lucky in my friendships and the influence upon me of a few people who introduced me to books and conversation of a kind entirely new in my life. I had grown up in a home where there was no reading or discussion of books, no music, no appreciation of art. It was not until I reached university and came to know a number of people who had studied Arts and read Philosophy that I discovered much about the world of ideas and art in its various forms. I gradually read my way, in an amateurish fashion, through some of the material that was talked about. Professor John Anderson, Professor of Philosophy at Sydney University, had a powerful influence in those times in Arts and all my friends who had been in Arts had studied under him.

Those were big days in Sydney for radicals because the thirties were the days of the great purges in Russia. Trotsky was still alive. His ideas were debated in Sydney University circles close to Anderson who, after abandoning a communist position, had been a Trotskyist for a time and later a critic of Trotsky: all of this led me both to follow the Russian purges and trials in detail and to read and buy Trotsky's *History of the Russian Revolution*, *The Revolution Betrayed* and other works. My son, years later as a radical university student, was astonished to find first editions of these and other such books on my shelves — they shed a new light on the paternal image. After my initial intellectual attraction to Trotskyism I read beyond it and became a strong anti-Stalinist social democrat.

Later, whilst at the Bar, I was overcome by a very strong desire to experience Anderson as a teacher. He was so obviously a teacher of impressive psychic impact that I felt I should have at least some experience of this. I enrolled as a student, not proceeding to a degree, in Philosophy I in Arts. The subject was logic. I had heard so much about Anderson's teaching methods that I approached the experience with eagerness and I was not disappointed. I did not sit for the examination at the end of the year and did not attempt to master the subject as taught by him. My desire was simply to listen.

Through another friend, my first wife's brother, I was led into

43

a whole range of reading which was not political in the same sense. I read my way through Bertrand Russell's books on social, moral and educational theory and much of his more popular philosophical work, and came close to pacifism under his influence. James Burnham's works, in particular *The Managerial Revolution*, had a big effect on me in the late thirties. I also began ranging more widely among the then modern English writers — Shaw, Wells, Lawrence, Huxley, Maugham, Spender, Auden and others. We debated it all and talked about it over coffee. So I achieved some kind of liberal and political education without actually doing Arts, developing into a typical radical product of Sydney University in the thirties. I was in a sense preparing for Labor politics.

One of my fellow students at Law School was Clarrie Martin, who became New South Wales Attorney-General in the forties. Martin was a lot older than the rest of us. He was the Labor member for Young until the time when Lang was dismissed in 1932. This was another reason why the Game-Lang crisis was so real for me — one of my Law School friends, in my class, suffered directly from the dismissal, losing his parliamentary seat in the ensuing election. This happened while he was, with the rest of us, studying Constitutional Law, including the constitutional principles relevant to the dismissal, under Sir John Peden.

Sir John Peden, in addition to being Dean of the Law Faculty, was a conservative and President of the Legislative Council in New South Wales. Some of us believed whilst students in 1932 that he played some kind of role, as an important establishment figure, in the events leading to the dismissal. Whether this was so or not I never knew — nor whether Sir Philip Game consulted him or anyone else in New South Wales — though then, as always in such a situation, conspiratorial theories were rife and the Governor's right to 'outside advice' was discussed before and after the dismissal.

As I came to the end of my Law School days I began, as many students do, to have serious doubts about the law as a way of life. We had at the Law School in those days A. H. Charteris, the urbane and witty Professor of Jurisprudence and International Law. These were subjects which interested me and I did well in them. I found in Professor Charteris an adviser both sympathetic and realistic. I had written an essay for him upon which he had made the comment, 'A very lawyerlike opinion. Go on and prosper'. This led me to open my developing doubts with him as a person who seemed to think that it was open to me to succeed on the practical as well as the academic side of the law. Having regard to my other political and social attitudes, the materialistic side of the law cut across my youthful idealism, but Charteris urged me to persevere, saying my reactions were understandable after four years of study. He simply said again, 'Go on and prosper.'

Those days between 1932 and 1938, when I was called to the Bar at the age of twenty-three, were exciting, demanding and varied. There was plenty of intellectual stimulus, especially after graduation, when more time became free for reading. After graduation I attended some valuable evening courses, sponsored by the Workers' Educational Association, in politics, government, and social and political philosophy by Percy Partridge and John Passmore (both members of Anderson's department and later professors) and in modern English literature by a colourful lecturer called Joe Bourke.

I was also lucky in the degree of responsibility given to me at Baldick Asprey and Company, the last office in which I was articled and, after I finished my articles, in the level of the legal work I was asked to handle by the two partners, Mr Baldick and Mr Asprey, later Mr Justice Asprey, a member of the Supreme Court and the Court of Appeal. He held the latter office during my Chief Justiceship. He was always a good friend and adviser to me.

The combination of influences on my life until then made me a different kind of legal product of Fort Street from Barwick and Spender, who were then young men at the Bar doing very well handling big work. My own desire was not well worked out although I wanted to become a Labor lawyer. I was a supporter of the Labor Party; I wanted to identify myself with the Labor Party and the trade unions and for a number of years I did.

This was due largely to my association and friendship with Evatt. I had become a student of his judgments when I was at

Law School. He had identified himself with the Labor movement, while Barwick, Spender and Ellis had been attracted to the problems of business and general legal work. I came to know Barwick, Spender and Ellis because they were involved in my daily life and work, Ellis as one of my master solicitors and Spender and Barwick as barristers briefed by my firm. But the choice I ultimately made meant that I identified myself when I first went to the Bar with Clive Evatt, the judge's brother, and Dick Kirby, later Sir Richard Kirby, President of the Commonwealth Conciliation and Arbitration Commission, Jock McClemen, who later became a Supreme Court judge and, while I was Chief Justice of New South Wales, Chief Judge at Common Law, and other Labor barristers. I set out to develop a Labor practice. That was, I soon saw, a mistake — putting oneself in a position where one would be able to do, as time passed, little else.

Evatt strongly advised me to go to the Bar early and to join the Labor Bar which was then emerging. I was doubtful about earning a living at the Bar during the aftermath of the depression and I wanted to get married during 1938. He asked how much I was earning in my office. I told him three hundred pounds per year. His response was that I would earn more than that, twice as much, in my first year at the Bar as a Labor lawyer. I knew that such a result in those days would be unusual for a young barrister and still expressed some doubt. His reply was typically Evatt. He said, 'What do you want me to do? Make out a deed poll guaranteeing you six hundred pounds a year?' I took his advice and was called to the Bar in February 1938, going into a newly organised set of chambers occupied exclusively by Labor lawyers. Dr Evatt arranged this for me.

I was married in the following November when my total accumulated capital was what I had left out of eighty-nine pounds after spending half of it on an engagement ring. In fact I made more than six hundred pounds in my first year, 1938.

During the thirties my approach to religion was undergoing change. I remained an orthodox Anglican until I left school. At the university, after much serious thought, reading and discussion, I abandoned religious observance and a positive belief in the Christian idea of God. All of this fitted in with my developing pattern of social and political ideas.

From time to time as the years went by I swung between a vague belief in forces of good which could be seen at work, on the one hand, and on the other, agnosticism and atheism. It was the problem of the existence in the world of evil and suffering, rather than rational arguments, that constituted the greatest barrier for me against accepting the Christian conception of God. Anderson and others had set out to prove the non-existence of God by methods of rational and logical argument. But when I was young I could not reconcile the idea of an all-knowing, all-powerful, all-loving God with the existence of evil and suffering on the mighty scale that because of war and depression during my lifetime lay revealed before me. This is not the time nor are these the circumstances in which a theological discussion on this great human dilemma should be undertaken, nor have I the knowledge and ability to undertake it. There was however from the beginning of my period of doubt and disavowal of orthodox religion in the thirties a countervailing line of thought which has since then gradually become stronger and which I shall touch upon briefly. The simplistic materialist interpretation of the Fort Street motto *Faber est suae quisque fortunae* — Every man is the maker of his own fortune — never appealed to me, but the notion that one's fate is in one's own hand stressed the idea of free will and did leave room, if one were so inclined, to regard the 'fortune' sought as embracing satisfaction of idealistic and ethical values. In any case I retained at the university my belief in the Christian ethic and in the moral values I saw in social democracy.

In swimming against the orthodox legal stream by becoming a Labor lawyer as a young man, I made a definite decision. It can be argued of course that I was in the grip of my childhood and past, but I also felt the pull of strong contrary influences; I believed and still believe that I was exercising my will.

Very early in life it became apparent to me that accident, contingency, the unexpected, the unpredictable crash in upon one. We are repeatedly knocked down by circumstances and have to pick ourselves up. We often have to start again. Great forces seem to be at work and we are at their mercy in a very real sense. But I believe that one acts in such a context pushed by existing pressures and circumstances and affected but not totally controlled by the influences that have operated in the course of one's life to that point.

The great unpredictable forces seemed to me as a young man to be a fact of life that supported my tendency to reject religion, because they appeared to be malign and to produce in the main evil and suffering rather than good. This fortified my religious doubt and agnosticism. As the years went by, and direct experience of life enabled me to develop a more mature approach, I came to see that the great forces were by no means all malign, and the accidental, contingent and unpredictable things that happened, limiting or affecting mastery of one's own fate, were not always bad but often good. Much of what has happened to me in life has been what could be called good luck rather than bad. Even the most stressful circumstances, the most agonising and lonely moments, the most difficult decisions, have had their creative aspects in their effect upon my life. Certainly I have experienced evil and suffering and destructive forces at work over the years but at the same time and in relation to the same circumstances I have also generally experienced love and support. Even when lonely in one or other aspect of life I have never felt that I was alone.

As time passed I came more and more to the view that a merely intellectual approach to the existence in the world of evil and suffering was not in itself enough to warrant denial of the existence or power or significance of the forces of good. Although I have not been able to get back completely to my simple youthful Christian notion of a personal God I have been more and more able to reconcile my acceptance of 'fate' and its impact upon one's life, and of one's real duty to make choices and decisions, with the existence of good and one's ability to embrace it. Although not interested in detailed theological discussions I have in recent years become happy to participate in the liturgical and sacramental ceremonies of my youthful Anglicanism. The great forces of good, including love, which have moulded my life and helped me to be the maker of my own fortune express the meaning that the word 'God' may be coming to have in my mind.

In fact, throughout life I have never succumbed to the view that my own will was irrelevant or non-existent—merely a reflection of the operation, in the world, of mechanistic principles and the total capture of the personality by determinist forces. I believe that there has been from my earliest days a separate and distinct though evolving person, namely myself—a person acted upon by outside circumstances but acting in turn upon them.

Given that one has a real opportunity to exercise one's will, if not freely of the outside world, at least within the boundaries of the possible as drawn by circumstances, duties flow from this fact. Values and a system of ethics necessarily evolve as one accepts responsibility for one's decisions and their consequences. This has always been one aspect of 'making one's own fortune'. Individual responses will vary in their balancing of realism and idealism, selfishness and selflessness, opportunism and self-sacrifice. But to cling to the notion of free will through all the vicissitudes of life, which appear from one point of view to dominate and control what happens irrespective of choice, in fact enables and indeed requires one to develop one's own formula and accept responsibility for it.

In big matters as in small it is impossible to take final refuge in inevitability and I do not think I have ever done so. I believe that I have made, many times—whilst a youth, even a child, and later up to the present time—decisions that were truly mine. For these I have to take personal responsibility because I could have elected to do otherwise. Accepting, as I do, freedom of will, the duties flowing from it have faced me up to creative possibilities for achieving good and to the fact of good in the world. For me, making my own fortune has increasingly consisted in trying to identify with the forces of good and to resist the destructive powers of evil. Legal and judicial codes of ethics, and the duties inherent in offices I have held have supported this aspiration of mine.

My beliefs on religious matters have their foundation in retained Christian ethics and a special personal approach to individual responsibility for one's life. They have emerged gradually as my life unfolded and are related to my reaction to some deep and bitter experiences of later years, to reading, and to talks with spiritual advisers that I have undertaken in more recent times. If I include these reflections in this chapter it is because of a need to be frank about my developing beliefs in the thirties. It is no more than a personal confession and is not meant to be a real contribution to the difficult problems discussed.

From my reading in the thirties one book left a deep impression on me; one image from that book, because it expressed an approach to life that I felt and needed to have expressed at that time, remained a reference point in my attitude towards life and its choices. Philip, the central character in Somerset Maugham's *Of Human Bondage*, towards the end of the novel is reflecting with melancholy upon the death of a friend. He asks himself what is the use of living at all. 'It all seemed inane . . . The effort was so incommensurate with the result. Pain and disease and unhappiness weighed down the scale so heavily. What did it all mean?' Then as he broods he calls to mind a Persian rug, which another friend now dead had given him, telling him that it answered his question upon the meaning of life. Suddenly he feels he has understood. 'As a weaver elaborated his pattern for no end but the pleasure of his aesthetic sense, so might a man live his life, or if one was forced to believe that his actions were outside his choosing, so might a man look at his life, that it made a pattern . . . Out of the manifold events of his life . . . he might make a design, regular, elaborate, complicated, or beautiful . . . A man might get a personal satisfaction in selecting the various strands that worked out the pattern'.[1]

Of Human Bondage was widely read and widely discussed amongst young people in the thirties. The passage impressed me deeply. It is, I suppose, an artist's way of giving the individual who believes in free will a feeling that the exercise of free will can be creative and can be the inspiration that gives pattern, unity and moral worth to a life buffeted by fortune. It also encourages a belief in free will which he can call to his aid — a belief that in creating his life, the age-old values which tell him what is good and help him to handle the malign are real. This helps him to accept the inevitable and to cope with it, to deal creatively with what must be accepted. At least he can, informed by such a philosophy, try to throw his weight on the side of truth and good.

For myself, as I read it then, Maugham's image of the Persian rug became a dominant one in my life. Accepting accident, contingency and the unpredictable I chose, of the two alternatives offered, the one that said 'a man might *live* his life that it made a pattern' and not the one denying free will, which left a man the prospect not of *living* but only of *looking at* his life, not of creating but only of seeing it as a pattern.

From that time, deeply impressed with that image, I have always regarded the materials accidentally to hand, the unforeseeable events, together with what the weaver himself has in his mind and personality, his knowledge and experience, as being the strands from which he, by living, creates his own ever-changing Persian rug or design. He does this by living his life, exercising his choices, making his decisions. The weaver weaves himself as a person, ever growing, into the design which, by living, he makes his own personal work of art—his life.

4

Evatt and the Reserve Powers

Because of my personal contacts with Dr Evatt from the early thirties onward, my views on the reserve powers of the Crown under the Westminster system, and in particular under the Australian Constitution, will emerge from this narrative in an autobiographical way. This is because my friendship with Dr Evatt meant that the whole question of the reserve powers became a reality for me from my early student days. His outstanding work on the subject was actually being written and his thoughts on it being discussed with me and other friends during the period of my Law School studies. The study of the reserve powers by this eminent jurist and Labor leader is well known to lawyers, but is less likely to be familiar to the average Australian. I shall therefore examine it in some detail as being an invaluable introduction to the subject of Australia's constitutional structure and functioning for anyone seeking to understand the events of 1975.

Evatt's book *The King and his Dominion Governors* was of great autobiographical significance for me. The Game-Lang crisis, Evatt's Labor orientation, the friendly relations between us, his offer to me to collaborate with him in preparing for publication his doctoral thesis on the prerogative powers (an offer which I found flattering but which I preferred not to take up because of the delay it would cause in my getting actively started at the Bar), all made Evatt's thoughts on the reserve powers, and the reserve powers themselves, far more vivid to me than they might have been from merely abstract study of a book by an author unknown to me. Reading Evatt led me to read other authorities, but he occupied, then as now, a key position as an authority on the reserve powers of the Crown; and his scholarly views not only were of great importance to me as the views of a distinguished lawyer and judge, but were real and alive to me from my student days onwards, even after I ceased to support him in his political activities and leadership.

Evatt can no doubt be criticised for excessive tenacity in arguing his thesis that the reserve powers should be codified, and for some heaviness and lack of style in his writing, but I could not have had a better or more realistic introduction to the subject of the reserve powers than I received from him. Although as the years passed I ceased to agree with him on some matters he discusses, his acceptance of the existence of the reserve powers remained important for me, even though he found them vague and complained that they were undefined.

Herbert Vere Evatt was in his political philosophy a social democrat. I learned this from talks with him in the thirties and it was confirmed by his entry into politics and by everything he said and did thereafter. He felt it was possible to hold the views he held, in the thirties and later, about the existence of the reserve powers and to be at the same time a social democrat. I was to discover later that the great Canadian authority Eugene Forsey also was able to accept the reality of the reserve powers of the Crown whilst being an active socialist.

In the first chapter of *The King and his Dominion Governors* Evatt refers to a major question which he later discusses in depth. It is whether and under what conditions the King or the Governor possesses sufficient constitutional authority to act against the advice of his Ministers possessing the confidence of the popular House, by dismissing the Ministers and dissolving that House. The Game-Lang crisis had made this a focal issue in Australia in the early thirties and it was of absorbing interest to Evatt.

Evatt discussed, as other writers have done, the uncertainties associated with the discretionary powers and their exercise, the confusion, stress and argument that can arise in the community and the burdens imposed upon and difficulties faced by vice-regal appointees in times of acute constitutional crisis because of the existence of the reserve powers, having regard to their lack of definition and to the differences of opinion to which this gives rise even among specialist theorists. The dominant theme of the book is Evatt's advocacy of legal codification of the reserve powers of the Crown, and of power in the courts to administer the legal code.

The main introduction (there was a short preliminary introduction by Harold Laski) written by Sir Kenneth Bailey to the first edition of *The King and his Dominion Governors* and reproduced, together with a new introduction by Professor Zelman Cowen, in the second edition in 1967, begins as follows:

> An age of great controversies puts to the test all institutions, however soundly established. When vital questions come to issue, each side is fain to invoke the full exercise of constitutional powers, and seeks to resolve in its own favour all that is obscure or ambiguous in the existing situation. The fate of the constitution itself will depend on the adequacy of the provision it makes for what may be called emergency or crisis or reserve powers. One of the distinctive features of the British constitution, as has often been remarked, is the combination of the democratic principle that all political authority comes from the people, and hence that the will of the people must prevail, with the maintenance of a monarchy armed with legal powers to dismiss ministers drawn from among the people's elected representatives, and even to dissolve the elected legislature itself. In normal times the very existence of those powers can simply be ignored. In times of crisis however, it immediately becomes of vital importance to know what they are and how they will be exercised.[1]

Bailey's statements in regard to the Monarch in Britain apply under the Australian Constitution to the Governor-General in Australia.

In the Game-Lang crisis 'vital questions came to issue' and the great controversy 'put to the test' our institutions which were believed to be soundly based and which in fact survived the crisis basically unchanged. The same is true of October–November 1975, to judge from all the evidence. Our stable institutions survive basically unchanged.

Professor Bailey in his introduction emphatically said that the whole future of the British constitutional system would depend on the extent to which in the few years ahead it was demonstrated that the reserve powers of the Crown 'are not the antithesis but the corollary of the democratic principle that political authority is derived from the people'.[2]

He clearly emphasised his belief not only that emergency or crisis or reserve powers do exist but that the Constitution has need of them and that they should retain a flexible form:

> The thesis maintained by Mr Justice Evatt is that the reserve powers of the Crown should be subjected to the normal and natural process of analysis and definition and reduction to rules of positive law, just as the relations between the two Houses of the Imperial Parliament, or of the Commonwealth Parliament in Australia, have been defined and expressed in the form of law . . . The risks of the process are of course great. A constitution in an emergency period has need of emergency powers, not over-rigidly defined. But the risks of undefined elasticity are also great.[3]

Bailey's reference to the two Houses of the Australian Parliament is noteworthy. It relates to section 53 of the Constitution and indicates that relations between those two Houses had been codified as constitutional law. The Senate's power over supply accordingly became from the beginning of Federation a matter of codified law. Some people believe that a convention can grow and limit or qualify such a statutory constitutional provision but this, in the case of section 53, is very doubtful and in any case it has not happened.

Towards the end of his introduction Professor Bailey stated:

> Any exercise of reserve powers by the Crown must inevitably involve the King, or his Dominion representative, in the assumption of very heavy personal responsibility, to his advisers, to Parliament, and to the people. It will inevitably entail unpopularity in some quarters. That is a serious matter even in the case of the Sovereign. But it is an absolutely vital matter in the case of a Governor, who is a temporary officer, and who now, it appears, holds his office upon the advice of his own ministers. Under such circumstances the Governor can readily be stripped of all personal discretion, and left entirely without reserve powers. Such considerations as these—fully discussed in this book—lend additional weight and urgency to the contentions of Mr Justice Evatt.[4]

This reference to the 'heavy personal responsibility' of the vice-regal appointee is, of course, quite inconsistent with any notion that his role is that of a puppet.

Exercise of the reserve powers may, obviously, lead to 'unpopularity' in some quarters, as the events of 1932 and 1975 showed.[5] It may also involve the risk of being 'stripped of all personal discretion and left entirely without reserve powers' by 'recall', that is by termination of the commission — the only way in which such a result could be achieved. It is emphasised as a real possibility at the very beginning of Evatt's book. I did not myself remember, nor until recently have I seen it suggested, that there was any actual risk in 1932 of Governor Sir Philip Game being dismissed or recalled. He and the then Premier appeared, so far as public material indicated, both to proceed on the basis that Game was going to be able to do his duty as he saw it without risk of dismissal. In any event Lang does not appear to have attempted to have Game dismissed at the critical time. Yet both Evatt and Bailey recognised the possibility of dismissal arising should there, in certain circumstances, be a risk of the reserve powers being exercised. The case of Sir Gerald Strickland, examined by Evatt, shows how true this is.[6]

Long before I became Governor-General myself, I read the introduction by Professor Cowen — now Sir Zelman and my successor in the office — to the 1967 edition of *The King and his Dominion Governors*. In 1973 when considering the nature of the Governor-General's role and whether I would be prepared to undertake it I took what Sir Zelman had written into account. Apart from the addition of his new introduction to the second edition, the 1936 text and Bailey's introduction were reproduced in 1967 unchanged. Some might argue that Evatt's book was written forty years ago, but its modern relevance is clear, first, from the fact of its reprinting unaltered only eight years before the 1975 crisis, and secondly from the absence of any attempt to codify the conventions in Australia between 1936 and 1967 or since. Sir Zelman wrote as follows:

Evatt's purpose was 'to reexamine some of the constitutional rules and practices whereby, both in Britain and in the self-governing Dominions, doctrines of overwhelming importance are treated as

56

being too vague to be defined at all, or, if defined, defined in an unsatisfactory manner, and never regarded as enforceable by the Courts of the land. These rules and practices relate, in general to what may be called . . . the "Reserve Powers" of the Crown'.

These reserve powers (exercisable by the Queen or by her representative in a Commonwealth country) include the powers to dismiss a ministry, to grant or refuse a dissolution of a legislative chamber, to designate a Prime Minister, and to appoint or to refuse to appoint Peers in the House of Lords or in a comparable Upper House.[7]

He then summarised Evatt's dominant theme in a way which was in accordance with my own understanding, in the thirties, of what Evatt then said and meant:

Evatt's detailed examination of past practice and of the writings of learned authorities disclosed 'the immense amount of sheer uncertainty and confusion in which the whole subject is involved'. He argued that the appropriate course was to deal with the matter by restating practice in the form of rules of law.

'The best method by which constitutional practice, determining the relationship between the Crown, the first and other ministers, the Parliament and each House thereof, and the electorate may be defined is by the passing of legislation by the Parliament possessing jurisdiction within the appropriate constitutional unit.'

Both the late Professor Harold Laski and Sir Kenneth Bailey, who wrote separate introductions to the original edition, stressed the importance of more precise definition, and Bailey pointed to the heavy personal responsibilities which rested upon the Crown and its representatives in exercising these powers.[8]

Despite the reality of these heavy personal responsibilities no codification, as I have pointed out, has ever been carried out in Australia. The position of the vice-regal appointee remains the same today as when Evatt, Bailey and Cowen wrote, and the same as when I studied Evatt's views in the thirties and talked to him about them. Attempts have, however, been made elsewhere. After 1947 when India and Pakistan gained independence and the decolonisation movement began in earnest, the new countries that emerged from the old British Empire acquired written Constitutions, and in many of these attempts were made to put into written form the conventions of the Constitution as they operated under the Westminster system or as modified to meet local needs. In Australia we watched with close attention, in the fifties, sixties and early seventies, the evolving movement towards independence in British colonies and in our territory of Papua New Guinea. I was myself very much interested in the debate on constitutional issues taking place in those areas, including attempts made in some to reduce the conventions to written form. I shall later quote from my writing on these questions as they arose in Papua New Guinea during the pre-independence period.[9] This writing provided one of several occasions for refreshing and reinforcing my understanding of Evatt's opinions, my own earlier memories of personal discussions with him, and my grasp of the basic principles embodied in the reserve powers of the Crown.

In the thirties I was substantially persuaded that there should be legal codification of the reserve powers. Sir Zelman Cowen in his introduction refers to the views of Sir Kenneth Wheare in his study *The Statute of Westminster and Dominion Status*. Wheare's view was that to commit agreed conventions to writing in *non-legal* form has much to commend it, though Wheare's approach to the problem reflects, Sir Zelman commented, general agreement with Evatt's argument, if not with the precise form of the remedy. For a country like Australia my present view is that non-legal codification might recommend itself because of the difficulty in amending the Constitution, but the binding quality of such non-legal codification might be of doubtful political strength. It would also be extremely difficult to achieve an agreed non-legal codification.

Evatt, in arguing for codification, points out that 'the power of dismissal of Ministers possessing the confidence of the majority of the popular Assembly is not precisely ascertained'; and that 'the power of the Crown or its representative to insist upon a dissolution against the will of Parliament and Ministers alike . . . is also undefined'.[10]

He had previously observed:

The truth is that the most important 'conventions' or rules of all, those relating to dissolution of Parliament and dismissal of Ministers, are concerned with the personal discretion of the Sovereign, and whatever the 'convention' or rule on the point may be, mere legal requirements have nothing to do with the matter. The reason is plain. The common law, in the case of Britain, and the Statute law, in the case of most of the Dominions, vests the relevant legal power in the King or the Governor. If the conventional rule is broken by the decision to dissolve, the legal power is merely applied. No question of *its* breach can arise.[11]

He said further:

If the situation is allowed to continue without alteration, the Sovereign, Governor-General and the Governor will have to determine for themselves, on their own personal responsibility, not only what the true constitutional convention or practice is, but also whether certain facts exist, and whether they call for the application of the rule which is alleged to be derived from, and consistent with, all constitutional precedents. Even if, upon the given occasion, no extraordinary exercise of the Crown's prerogative results, the possibility of its exercise has always to be reckoned with, and this inevitably creates uncertainty and distrust.[12]

Evatt here clearly recognises that failing codification of the reserve powers as law, and they have not been codified in Australia, the Governor-General will have to determine for himself on his own personal responsibility not only what the conventions and practices are but whether certain facts exist and whether they call for the application of the unwritten rule. This was the position in which I found myself in October–November 1975. Far from saying that a Governor-General has no such right or duty, Evatt firmly asserted that there were circumstances in which he would have to make up his mind on his own personal responsibility what to do, and bear the weight of the consequences. The truth of this was perfectly apparent to me when the Governor Sir Philip Game and the Premier Mr Lang were going through that very experience, and the situation is in no way altered today.

Evatt also analysed a great constitutional crisis which arose in the United Kingdom between 1909 and 1911. On 30 November

1909 the House of Lords denied supply, 'there being no precedent for such action for over two hundred years'.[13] On 2 December 1909 the House of Commons resolved:

> that the action of the House of Lords in refusing to pass into law the financial provision made by this House for the service of the year is a breach of the Constitution and a usurpation of the rights of the Commons.[14]

By 'breach of the Constitution' the conventions of the Constitution were undoubtedly meant and 'usurpation of the rights of the Commons' referred to conventional rights.

Despite this, on 3 December, the House was dissolved and Mr Asquith took the issue of the Lords' denial of supply to the people. He certainly did not attempt to govern without parliamentary supply, and accepted the legal power of the Lords to deny it even though he complained that its denial was a usurpation of the rights of the Commons.

Asquith wrote a memorandum after the election dealing with another matter, the constitutional powers and functions of the Sovereign. In it he said that it was 'not the function of a Constitutional Sovereign to act as arbiter or mediator between rival parties and policies; still less to take advice from the leaders of both sides, with the view to forming a conclusion of his own'.[15] I later deal with the right to arbitrate or mediate in discussing the 1975 crisis.[16]

Evatt however says about this proposition that such a theory, namely that no such right exists, 'is and will be regarded by many as an attempt to reduce the power of the Monarch to a nullity in those very times of great crisis when his intervention alone might save the country from disaster'.[17] Evatt also says:

> It cannot be taken for granted, as is so usually done, that the King's personal view of what is a just and proper exercise of the royal prerogative does not count.[18]

Even if a right to arbitrate or mediate does not exist the power to act in other ways does, and the personal view of the Monarch, or of his representative, as to what is 'just and proper' is what counts when it comes to the exercise of the prerogative.

In discussing his main theme, namely that the conventions should be legally codified, Evatt made the point:

It is not impossible that the right of personal intervention by the Monarch should be preserved but its proper scope and ambit carefully defined and restricted so that all concerned may attend and govern themselves accordingly.[19]

Evatt accepted that the right of personal intervention did exist and under some circumstances should be preserved. He did not press for its abolition.

Towards the conclusion of the book he stated:

It has been made abundantly clear:
1. That there is no generally recognised or binding rule to govern each situation of crisis.
2. That no independent tribunal is vested with any authority to determine either what the general rule is, or how it should be applied to the particular case.
3. That even where a general rule is recognised, no sanction is attached to secure its performance or to prevent its breach.
4. That as the Crown and its representatives cannot avoid being embroiled from time to time in the controversies created by a political crisis, the tendency to weaken the Crown as an institution is almost inevitable.
5. That, in the case of the self-governing Dominions, it is the very uncertainty as to the possible exercise by the Governor for the time being of prerogative or statutory powers which is likely to lead to the recall of the Governor by The King, the latter being advised to act by the Dominion Ministers, who tender it solely because they are not prepared to accept the risk involved if a constitutional crisis suddenly arises.
6. It follows that the tendency will be for the position of Governor (if it remains at all) to be filled at all times by the nominees of the Ministry in power, such nominee retiring from office when the Ministry is displaced.
7. That, in the event of a Governor's dismissing Ministers who retain the confidence of Parliament and dissolving Parliament on the advice of new Ministers, it is possible that the failure of the latter at the ensuing elections will be visited by some sanction. It cannot be supposed that, so long as parliamentary Government remains, members of Parliament may openly and with impunity flout the

majority of an existing Parliament, who not only appear to represent the majority of the electors, but who are proved to do so.[20]

Evatt's paragraph 5 above refers to the risk of recall on the possibility arising of a sudden constitutional crisis. Evatt was well aware of this practical possibility as of the risks mentioned in paragraph 7. He brought these right out into the open as early as 1936. They were understood at that time and have been understood ever since by those interested and informed on these matters. What Evatt says about the tendency of the Crown to be weakened (paragraph 4) and for the Governor to be always the nominee of the Ministry in power (paragraph 6) does not yet appear to have been demonstrated. He refers as follows to a Governor faced with the decision as to whether to give or withhold assent to a Bill that would prolong the life of the Parliament:

> This question of the extension of Parliament's life is quite sufficient to illustrate the somewhat dangerous position which now exists, for a Governor-General certainly runs the risk of immediate dismissal if, in any circumstances, he runs counter to the will of the Ministers holding office. For no impartial holder of the position of the Sovereign's personal representative can face with equanimity (say) a proposal analogous to that which Sir Gerald Strickland desired to veto in 1916.[21]

(In New South Wales in 1916–17 Sir Gerald Strickland was faced by what Evatt called 'such extraordinary legislation'[22] as a legislature setting out to extend its own life. He threatened to dismiss his Ministers or refuse assent to the Bill and was recalled by the Imperial Government.)

Evatt continues:

> Such proposals may, under certain circumstances, be nothing less than attempts to cheat the electors of their right to control the Legislature. Certainly a high-minded Governor may occasionally take such a view. At present, however, he is placed in the dilemma of being summarily removed from office if he seeks to protect the people, or of yielding to what may be an impudent attempt to thwart their will by a coup d'état under the forms of law.[23]

The *coup d'état* to which he was referring was a parliamentary and governmental one consisting of a Government's getting Parliament to extend its own life.

Evatt's approach to this problem, as to most such problems, was to say that the best way out is to define, declare and provide for the enforcement of rules to govern the exercise of the reserve powers of the Crown's representative. The formidable dilemma noted by Evatt can still arise in all cases that could attract the reserve powers, especially the reserve power of dismissal and enforced dissolution. Evatt accepts the existence of this reserve power and points out that its threatened exercise may produce 'immediate dismissal' of the Governor-General. It was hard to miss this important point in 1936 or to forget it thereafter.[24]

In an appendix to *The King and his Dominion Governors*, 'The New Status of South Africa', Evatt is more specific on the reserve power of dismissal and forced dissolution. Discussing the Status of the Union Act 1934 of South Africa he makes, under the heading 'Reserve Powers Unaffected', the following statement:

> The first and second aspects of these subsections [sections 4(1) and (2)] might be thought at first glance to safeguard both Ministers and Parliament against the possible exercise by the Crown of its reserve powers of dismissal and dissolution. This, however, is not so. The provisions are quite consistent with the exercise by the Governor-General of such reserve powers, so long as he can discover other Ministers ready and willing to vouch for the necessary executive acts, to 'carry on', and so accept 'responsibility' for the Governor-General's actions.[25]

He goes on to say:

> The reserve powers of the Crown in relation to dismissal and dissolution may still be exercised by the Governor-General for the time being. It is expressly provided, however, that he should be bound by the 'constitutional conventions relating to the exercise of his functions'.[26]

He points out that the reference to constitutional conventions raises difficulty because it is impossible to say what the conventions are and where they may be found. 'Is recourse to be had to Hallam or May? To Hearn or Bagehot? To Bryce or

Anson? To Asquith or Dicey? To Todd or Keith? To Jennings or Laski?'[27]

A lesson I learned early was that the controversy arising in a great crisis such as the Game-Lang crisis and the 1975 supply crisis will certainly include serious dissension among the 'experts'. In his main text Evatt had noted:

> It is abundantly clear from the opinions of text writers that there will seldom be lacking 'authoritative' support for those who suggest that the Crown should, upon some given occasion or crisis, exercise a reserve power in relation to dissolution or dismissal. No doubt the employment of the weapon may be accompanied by grave dangers, particularly as other text writers may, very likely, take a view which is hostile to the exercise of the reserve power in question. But the existence of those dangers will not, in themselves, prevent those interested in promoting or obtaining a desired exercise of the prerogative from advocating such an exercise. Amongst the text writers on the subject of constitutional conventions those interested will usually be able to find support for (or against) almost any proposition.[28]

One reason for his arguing in favour of codification lay in the difficulties a Governor-General or Governor could encounter in seeking to find his way through the jungle of expert opinion in the absence of such codification. I am not seeking to set out in this book the diverging opinions of the experts on relevant constitutional principles. My aim in this book, having been myself in the position of having to make up my mind whether or not to act under the reserve powers, and in what way and when, is to indicate the development of my own thinking and reasons for action.

Evatt in his appendix goes on to tackle Professor A. B. Keith for having avoided the difficulty when he wrote as follows:

> . . . the fact that any Government can provide itself with a Governor-General of its own party complexion renders these formal powers meaningless. It is noteworthy that a proposal to allow the King to act independently in the matter of the selection of the Governor-General was deliberately negatived. Yet, if the Governor-General is a nominee of the local Government and holds office at its pleasure, he departs vitally from the British parallel and the

constitution ceases to provide any control over the majority party in the Lower House for the time being.[29]

Evatt reacts with the following strong comment:

But is it permissible to agree that the occasion will never arise when, in the crisis of a political controversy, a Governor-General may think it proper to exercise his ultimate authority and even dismiss a Ministry which has the support of a majority of the Assembly, appoint the Opposition Leader as Prime Minister, and grant a dissolution of Parliament to the new Prime Minister? Surely it is wrong to assume that the Governor-General for the time being will always be a mere tool in the hands of the dominant party . . . That the possibility of similar action by a Governor-General against the advice of his Ministers for the time being is not merely academic, was shown in May 1932, when the Governor of New South Wales dismissed from office a Ministry in full possession of the confidence of the popular Assembly . . . Many constitutional students have attempted to justify that particular exercise of the reserve powers.[30]

Evatt quotes J. G. Latham, later Sir John Latham, for many years Chief Justice of Australia, on the subject of vice-regal discretion[31]:

Even in the case of the Governor-General of the Commonwealth, it has been stated that in the exercise of his 'discretion' under section 58 in dealing with Bills passed by both Houses of the Parliament, he need not always act upon the advice of his Ministers. Mr Latham, for instance, says:

'Exceptional cases may arise in which the Governor-General would be justified in disregarding their advice. The principles applicable for determining the existence of such exceptional cases can only be those which in fact have been applied in Australia (though not without controversy) by the Governor-General and by State Governors in dealing with the advice of a Ministry *that Parliament should be dissolved*. Such advice has on several occasions been rejected, but only when the Governor-General or Governor, as the case may be, has been able to secure another set of Ministers who do not repeat the advice given by their predecessors.'[32]

The appendix also quotes Lord Haldane's pertinent remarks on the powers of the Governor-General under the Australian

Constitution, made in December 1922 in the course of argument in an application by the State Governments of Australia for special leave to appeal from the decision of the High Court of Australia in the Engineers' case:

> Under sec. 61 it is declared 'The Executive power of the Commonwealth is vested in the Queen and is exercisable by the Governor-General as the Queen's representative and extends to the execution and maintenance of this constitution and of the laws of the Commonwealth'. No doubt that does not take away the powers of the Governors of the States as representing the Sovereign within their limits, but does it not put the Sovereign in the position of having parted, so far as the affairs of the Commonwealth are concerned, with every shadow of active intervention in their affairs and handing them over, unlike the case of Canada, to the Governor-General?[33]

This is the principle adopted by the Queen in relation to the 1975 crisis, as will be seen from the letter of her Private Secretary to Mr Scholes dated 17 November 1975.[34]

The two points that always remained in my mind from Evatt's study of the South African example, though I did not remember the details of it, were first, his acceptance of the vice-regal power of dismissal and secondly, his opinion that the Constitution itself gave all the reserve powers to the Governor-General.

The appendix also includes the following statement by Evatt:

> Perhaps the greatest advantage to be derived from defining the extent of the discretion as to the exercise of the reserve powers is that the absence of definition may prevent an over-careful Governor-General from acting when he should, just as it may enable an imprudent or over-zealous Governor-General to act where no reasonable ground for intervention exists. In each case an error may be fatal to the best interests of the people which are committed in the last resort to the care of the Governor-General or Governor.[35]

The weighty burden resting on the vice-regal shoulders not having been mitigated by codification remains unchanged. That it exists and must be borne in times of great crisis can hardly be doubted.

Professor Geoffrey Sawer, in his recent book *Federation Under Strain*, makes some comments on Evatt's opinions. In discussing the exercise of the power of dismissal in relation to electoral opinion he writes:

> Nevertheless, one must regard the wider statements about Queens or Governors keeping ministries in line with electoral opinion as among the 'more preposterous' reasons for the exercise of discretionary powers which Dr Evatt rightly said have been abandoned. The exercise of such a function by either a hereditary Monarch or a party-appointed Governor-General would, as Evatt says, be a denial of responsible government. But there can be equally little doubt that an emergency personal discretion does survive. Evatt's book (1936) is poorly organised and tendentiously written, but nevertheless it convincingly demonstrates the survival of the reserve power; one main theme of the book is thus summarised by the author: 'What may fairly be called the extreme Whig view of the Monarchy' (viz. that the Monarch must always act in accordance with the advice of his existing ministers) 'whatever validity it is thought to have in point of theory, is not true in point of fact'.[36]

Sawer then quotes from Evatt what Sawer calls 'a remarkable passage' defending the continued existence of a reserve power. It appears to have Sawer's approval and I shall repeat it as quoted by Sawer:

> Yet situations may arise in which the exercise of reserve power will be the only possible method of giving to the electorate an opportunity of preventing some permanent and far-reaching constitutional change.

Sawer passes on to refer to Eugene Forsey whose views I discuss in Chapter 14:

> Forsey similarly (1943) had no doubt that reserve powers exist, both in the United Kingdom and the other Westminster systems, and he gives an even wider scope for their operation — 'to protect the Constitution or to ensure that major changes in the economic structure of society shall take place only by the deliberate will of the people'. Indeed it is absurd to contend that the reserve power does not exist, when it plainly continues to exist as a matter of law, and has been exercised in the many cases discussed by Evatt and Forsey, many of them in this century, and in the 1952 Victorian case — and now the Kerr-Whitlam case of 1975.[37]

Evatt failed to achieve his main object, namely codification, in Australia and had no greater success in the United Kingdom and the other older Commonwealth countries. The absence of such a code, far from decreasing the power and responsibility of a Governor-General in a time of great constitutional crisis, increases his burdens and duties. The reason is obvious. Applying a known and precisely stated rule is easier than having to decide what the rule actually is, in the midst of difference of opinion on that subject. This was, according to Evatt, a burden, a responsibility and a power which should not have to rest upon the shoulders of a Governor-General. However, despite his vigorous argument he did not succeed in producing any relief for vice-regal appointees. When I came to be caught in the midst of a great crisis demanding the exercise of the reserve powers I had to find my way without the assistance of a precise code.

5

The Game-Lang Crisis

The events that led to the Game-Lang crisis began when Jack Lang was elected Labor Premier of New South Wales with a big majority in October 1930. I was then sixteen and in fourth year at high school. Problems presently arose over payment of interest on British loans, and a substantial difference of opinion on the subject developed between New South Wales and the Australian Commonwealth. Legislation of the New South Wales Government was rejected in the Upper House and the Government in the first half of 1931 asked for additional appointments to the Upper House, which was at that time an appointed House, but this was at first rejected by the Governor. Further conflict occurred and on 20 November 1931 the Governor appointed to the Council twenty-five Labor nominees (although this was not, according to Evatt's account of it, sufficient to secure the passage of all Government legislation).

The Scullin Federal Labor Government was replaced by the Lyons conservative Government in an election in December 1931 and the new Parliament carried legislation, later held to be valid by the High Court on 6 April 1932, with a view to compelling persons to pay to the Commonwealth their debts owing to New South Wales, in order to meet that State's liability. Mr Lang resisted the Commonwealth scheme and the Commonwealth then acted to force payment by the banks to the Commonwealth of certain moneys standing to the credit of New South Wales. This action was held to be valid by the High Court on 22 April 1932. Lang instructed his officers not to pay money into the banks from which it might be seized. He then, in order to acquire money to service his government, passed a Mortgage Taxation Bill on 13 May 1932.

The Governor of New South Wales at that time was Air Vice-Marshal Sir Philip Game. Professor John Ward describes him thus:

> A man of principle, honesty and courage for whom Lang had no private dislike . . . In World War I he joined the Royal Air Force and won many awards for exceptional gallantry. He commanded the RAF in India from 1922 to 1923 and was a member of the Air Council from 1923 to 1928. He was not chosen to govern NSW in order to thwart Lang, as Lang liked to think, but because . . . he was available for further service on retirement in 1929 at the young age of 53. After his term in NSW Game was Metropolitan Commissioner of Police in London. A pleasant, kindly, modest man . . . Game had an exacting sense of duty, a high level of administrative efficiency, great courage, undoubted humanity, and good judgment. He was not, however, a lawyer and the problems he had to face in NSW were among the most difficult in our constitutional history.[1]

On 12 May the Governor drew the attention of the Premier to the fact that his circular instruction of 12 April to public servants appeared to be in direct collision with a federal Proclamation, which directed officers of the State receiving revenue of a certain character to deal with the moneys in the manner directed by the Federal Treasurer. Evatt himself says that there was a direct collision between this Proclamation and the instruction issued by Lang requiring State officers receiving such revenue to deal with it as directed by the circular.[2]

But he points out that the validity of the application of this Proclamation was never tested in court; there were courts in which this could have been done, and if a decision adverse to Lang had been given, injunctions against Lang and all others concerned could have been granted. Sir Philip Game's letter of 12 May requested Mr Lang 'either to furnish me with proof that the instructions in the circular are within the law, or alternatively, to withdraw the circular at once'.[3] The Premier did not comply and refused to withdraw the circular. On 13 May the Governor by letter to Mr Lang made the point that Mr Lang did not dispute the illegality of the circular. On the same day the

Governor wrote to Mr Lang saying that, as he saw it, the Ministers were committing a breach of the law. He said: 'While you did not admit this, you did not deny it'.[4]

The Governor then told the Premier he should resign so that he could get Ministers who would obey the law. Lang refused and the Governor, on 13 May 1932, dismissed him. He had not by then assented to the Mortgage Taxation Bill and ultimately did not have to do so. The leader of the Opposition, Mr Stevens, formed a Government at the request of the Governor, advised dissolution, accepted responsibility for the Governor's actions, and won the ensuing election.

Game had relied on the illegality of the actions of his Ministers to justify his dismissal of them in 1932. Evatt believed that such illegalities were 'intended to be settled by recourse, not to action of the Executive power as represented by the Governor-General or the Governor, but by reference to the judicial power which alone is entitled to say whether the Commonwealth or the State has trespassed beyond the limits of its lawful authority'.[5] These views of Evatt about Game's acting in relation to a justiciable issue instead of leaving the matter to the courts were of considerable interest to me in the thirties and thereafter. He commented that cases may arise 'where, the illegality of ministerial action being either admitted or beyond dispute, no remedy whatever is available except the exercise of a prerogative by a Governor'.[6] How clearly this recognises the existence of that prerogative!

In the New South Wales case however Evatt believed that legal proceedings in the courts could have settled the matter. While recognising that Game did indeed have the powers he exercised, Evatt wrote as follows:

Although no person can confidently assert that Sir Philip Game was guilty of a breach of constitutional duty, that is mainly because the reserve powers have not yet been defined so as to exclude prerogative action when those interested in asserting illegality on the part of Ministers have it in their power to obtain redress from the ordinary Courts of law.

He concluded his chapter on this great issue by saying that

if the matter is carefully and dispassionately considered, it will become reasonably plain that the power of dismissal can hardly be regarded as properly exercised if a Governor justifies it merely by reliance upon the Ministers having broken the law, and it appears that there is available a competent legal tribunal which can determine the question of legality, and which has jurisdiction to issue appropriate orders and injunctions, and see that they are enforced.[7]

Sir Philip Game, on the other hand, obviously thought that to instruct that the valid Proclamation be defied was an illegal act 'beyond dispute'.

It is noteworthy that Evatt says, not that the power of dismissal is not legally available in such a case, but that it may be 'improper' to use it—that it should not, in his opinion, be exercised where the courts can determine the issue. He is thus making a specific point and even then does not apply the test to 'illegality beyond dispute'.

It is, *a fortiori*, quite impossible to show from Evatt that it is never permissible to resort to the reserve power of dismissal in cases that do *not* raise justiciable issues and hence cannot be solved in the courts, but which nevertheless can attract an exercise of the reserve power.

Evatt, whilst making his point that this matter of illegality should have been decided by the courts, said that Game 'might reasonably have insisted upon Mr Lang's calling the judicial power into action'.[8] He did not examine Game's right of dismissal had he insisted on Lang's going to the courts and had Lang refused, as he no doubt would have done. What would have been the position if this had happened, and if no one else, for example the Commonwealth, had managed within reasonable time to get the issue to the courts? If the crisis is serious enough and the illegality clear enough and if the prospect of getting to the court and getting an answer involves obstruction or delay, the very urgency of the matter may itself demand vice-regal action, always of course at the peril of later dismissal of the Governor.

Professor Ward has commented on the issue of justiciability. In 'The Dismissal'[9] he refers to a draft document prepared in the Dominions Office on 10 May 1932, but not sent to the

Governor because events moved too fast. This document discussed the illegality point, saying that the Governor *could* constitutionally allow his Ministers to commit the allegedly illegal acts until a court decided on their illegality. If the court condemned the acts as illegal and the Government persisted in committing them then the Governor would have to ascertain whether he could obtain other advisers capable of commanding a majority in the legislature, perhaps by dissolution of the House and appeal to the electorate.

This document would have told the Governor, had he received it, what he *could* do including apparently, in the last resort, deciding upon a forced dissolution.

Ward points out that Game did not have to take upon himself the difficult task of deciding the legality of the Commonwealth Proclamation and Lang's circular. The Commonwealth could have sought an injunction in the High Court to restrain the public servants of New South Wales from acting on the Lang Ministry's instructions. This did not happen and it is a little difficult to see how Game could have asked the Commonwealth to go to the High Court, though perhaps he could have said he would not act himself until the Commonwealth or some other party had taken the matter to the High Court. This would have tied his hands, at least for a time, and the degree of delay could not be foreseen: he may well have judged that he needed to keep his freedom of prompt action.

Sawer says that Game's action could be supported because Lang failed to answer a request for an assurance as to the legality of what he was doing, and could be taken as admitting illegality. I add that it could be supported also on the ground that, when asked to stop acting illegally, Lang refused to withdraw the circular. The illegal publication of the circular, and the refusal to withdraw it, engage Forsey's principle that a forced dissolution can properly be resorted to preventively, to give the people a chance to stop something which in basic principle should not be happening.[10]

Sawer remarks that Mr R. G. Menzies, K.C., 'when commenting on Game's action, did not go so far as to require judicial testing, but he did require that the "illegality" which he thought would alone justify dismissal should be "clear"'. Mr Menzies had written to Sir Philip in 1932:

Finally, we all felt that when you did exercise the power of dismissal for a clear illegality your action was not only timely but was all the more emphatic a vindication of the constitutional position of the King's representative because of your earlier patience and restraint.[11]

Professor Sawer continues:

High Court decisions had established the general legality of the course of coercing the Lang State Government which the Lyons Federal Government had undertaken, and this was a matter on which the Governor could satisfy himself. It was clear that the Lang tactic of trying to keep State funds in a form not readily subject to Commonwealth attachment could involve a series of particular steps, and it might be unreasonable to expect a Governor to wait until all such measures had been tried out and tested judicially. Perhaps Sir Philip Game acted too precipitately, but he could not have delayed much longer.[12]

As to the comment that 'perhaps Sir Philip Game acted too precipitately': once it is conceded that he had the power to do what he did and that he 'could not have delayed much longer'; once it became clear that the decision he made was going to have to be made; once it became simply a matter of timing, the judgment on timing must, I believe, be left to the person carrying the responsibility. It is a very small point of criticism that Sir Philip Game, who 'could not have delayed much longer', could 'perhaps' have delayed for a day or a few more days. The pressures upon him were extreme, what he did he inevitably had to do, and the timing was a matter for his judgment.

Professor Ward, in his 'The Dismissal' already referred to, has a section under the heading 'Did Lang court his own dismissal?' He rather implies that he did, in the general political situation which then existed, and probably because he had federal ambitions. Ward says:

Dismissal from office on a constitutional ground relieved him from having to clear up a mess while leaving his reputation as a strong, driving left-wing (but anti-communist) leader intact. Again by

74

allowing his political opponents to take power he was condemning them to cope with the depression while possibly he prepared the way for a new and longer term of office for himself, whether in Sydney or Canberra.[13]

If Lang felt that he was locked into a position from which he could not politically retreat he may have preferred dismissal to surrender.

Lang accepted his dismissal quietly. He and the Governor privately exchanged presents — a pipe and books. Professor Ward says Lang was not taken by surprise when he was dismissed because 'the possibility of dismissal had been canvassed in the newspapers and between him and Game for more than a year before the fateful decision was taken'.[14]

It is something of a mystery why Lang did not try to get rid of Game before he was himself dismissed. At the time it seemed to me that for some reason, unknown, Game was not at risk. My later reading, in 1977, of the book *Dismissal of a Premier* by Bethia Foott showed me that the question of possible dismissal of Mr Lang and allegations that Lang was considering cabling Downing Street to have the Governor recalled were in the air in 1931 and 1932, but until the end nothing came of either possibility.[15]

The dismissal of Sir Gerald Strickland in 1916, referred to earlier and discussed by H. V. Evatt and Eugene Forsey[16], had shown how risky for a Governor recourse to his reserve power of dismissal could be. Evatt contrasts the Game and Strickland cases:

The two cases of Sir Philip Game's action in 1932 and Sir Gerald Strickland's action in 1916 provide a somewhat extraordinary contrast. In the former case Ministers possessing the confidence of the Assembly were dismissed, and the Assembly itself dissolved because of a supposedly illegal act on the part of Ministers, although redress in respect of such illegality was obtainable in the Courts of law. In the latter case the Imperial authorities intervened on the side of Ministers, although everything indicated that at the time, they would have been decisively defeated upon an immediate appeal to the people. The object of Sir Gerald Strickland was to safeguard the electors against a Coalition Government which had never received any popular endorsement, and the first act of which was to suspend for a period of one year the electors' right to elect their representatives.[17]

The record offers no evidence that in making the decision to dismiss Lang Sir Philip Game took into account any guess as to the likely electoral result. My opinion in the thirties, as it is today, was that if there is in the view of the vice-regal representative a proper ground for dismissal and for reference of an issue to the people, getting the people's decision is all that matters, not predicting what it will be.

In parenthesis I may say that this view is contrary to the view held by A. V. Dicey, upon whose writings I was at that time being brought up at the Law School, and who argued that the King could dismiss according to his view of probable electoral results. Evatt reasoned that Dicey was forced to this view by his desire to reconcile two precedents, on the one hand George III's dismissal of Fox and North in which case the King apparently estimated accurately what the electorate would do, and on the other William IV's forcing the resignation of Melbourne, when the King misjudged the electoral outcome. Evatt said Dicey was led to conclude that a successful electoral outcome is not required to justify the exercise by the King of the prerogative of dismissal and dissolution; that 'so long as there is a "fair presumption", "valid and reasonable ground for supposing" that the Commons is out of step with its constituents, the King is justified in his action'.[18]

Evatt strongly criticised this approach and in my youth I agreed with him as I still do today. But all of this applies to an assertion of power to dismiss on the ground of an opinion that the House is out of step with the electorate. That is not in my view a valid ground for dismissal and dissolution; but where a valid ground exists, Diccy's point and Evatt's criticism of it are irrelevant. My view was and is that valid grounds can exist and when they are relied on the exercise of the reserve powers is unconnected with any judgment as to the result of an election following their exercise.

76

Evatt, then, in his discussion of the 1932 crisis stressed that the success of the Stevens Government at the election should not be regarded as concluding the constitutional issue, since it could hardly be accepted that 'the Sovereign or his representative may at any time dismiss a Ministry possessing the confidence of Parliament and force a dissolution and, so long as the popular verdict goes against the dismissed Ministers, the action of the King or Governor must necessarily be treated as right'. He recognised that it would be otherwise if Dicey's constitutional theory, previously referred to, were accepted; but he rejected that theory, as do I.[19]

If the decision of the electorate favours the dismissed Ministry it will, of course, prevail. A Governor or Governor-General in relying upon what he considers a proper ground of dismissal always faces that possibility. In that event the vice-regal representative will doubtless, as Evatt made clear, be in great peril. But just as a result in favour of the new Ministers does not prove of itself that a Governor acted properly in dismissing and forcing dissolution, so an electoral decision in favour of the dismissed Ministers does not necessarily mean that a Governor acted either illegally or improperly in dismissing and forcing dissolution. His duty is to do what he believes to be right upon proper legal and constitutional principles and run whatever personal risks are involved irrespective of his assessment of likely electoral results. Evatt expressed it as follows:

> The true test of the constitutional exercise of such a reserve power should direct itself to the circumstances existing when the power is exercised, disregarding the mere calculation as to the outcome of the subsequent electoral verdict.
> But in any case it would seem clear that if the reserve power of the Crown is exercised upon a specifically stated ground, the propriety of the exercise should be discussed solely in reference to such ground.[20]

Sir Philip Game did not in fact have to face the consequences that might have flowed from success of Lang in the election, because Lang was defeated and the Minister who had accepted responsibility for the Governor's actions in dismissing Lang and dissolving Parliament was returned to power. Evatt describes the confused reaction to that dismissal, which in his view resulted from the lack of binding and settled rules for the exercise of the reserve powers:

> I have not referred in any way to merely political attacks upon, and defences of, Sir Philip Game's action. Their number is legion. With extravagant praise from the one side was mingled violent blame from the other. For months prior to the dismissal of his Ministers the Governor was attacked by newspapers which were politically opposed to the Premier, because the latter was not dismissed. For months after his action, the Governor was attacked by the Labor Party for what he did. By the first group he was called a political poltroon because he allowed the Lang Ministry to retain office; by the latter he was called a political assassin because he decided to act. Such a controversy was calculated to injure the dignity and reputation of the office of King's representative. It is certain that the feared and actual exercise of exceptional pre-rogatives and reserve powers will often be followed by such consequences, unless the conditions and occasions of their exercise are perfectly well known to all concerned.[21]

This was the atmosphere of the early thirties and I shall never forget it.

It must be appreciated that once a situation of great social tension and danger to institutions had reached the brink at which the exercise of the prerogative had to be seriously faced, the Governor had to make all the relevant assessments. It is an area in which notoriously opinions may differ as to action and timing, especially when the matter is examined in retrospect. Mrs Foott, who as the young daughter of the Governor's Private Secretary was living in Government House during the crisis, in *The Dismissal of a Premier* vividly evokes the stresses that Sir Philip was enduring. She relates that he had a long period of sleepless nights. I readily confess to a similar experience in 1975.

Indeed I find myself looking at the Governor's decision in full and sympathetic awareness of the nature of the burden he was carrying. What is quite clear is that he was entitled to act as he did and there was little room left for delay. He cannot in my view be criticised for his decision.

Assuming that a Governor will act at his peril even though he has good grounds for acting, if the electorate subsequently supports the dismissed Ministers the question arises: is it inadmissible to rely upon his opinion as to the electoral outcome as the ground for action, but permissible to consider it as a factor when he has other grounds for discretionary action and is deciding what to do? My opinion has always been that it is not appropriate for a Governor to take possible electoral results into account. He should make up his mind where his duty lies, act and take the consequences. If a dismissal and a dissolution are in his view called for upon proper ground he should act. It is the right of the people then to decide who shall govern. Nothing since the thirties has caused me to change that opinion.

One thing, as I have said, that I came very early to understand was that the vice-regal office was in time of crisis a very chancy one indeed. The risk of the Governor-General himself being removed in the midst of a great constitutional crisis by Ministers who were themselves at risk of dismissal, so that he might be replaced by a successor of more subservient disposition, was and has in modern times always been great. There has always existed the real possibility of a 'race to the Palace' if there were an imminent prospect of the reserve powers being exercised.

The reserve powers, though ill-defined, are real. My early reading of Evatt led me as a young man to the conclusion, amply substantiated by the writers mentioned, that the vice-regal position is not merely ceremonial, and not a sinecure in times of crisis; that the holder of it has powers and duties that are his only, and may have to carry very heavy burdens in answering the call of duty as he hears it.

Mr Whitlam referred to the Game-Lang crisis early in the 1975 confrontation. A question was asked of, and answered by, the Prime Minister in the House. It had to do with Mr Menzies' letter to Sir Philip in 1932. The exchange is illuminating when following the events of October–November 1975.

On 15 October 1975 Mr Whitlam was asked a question by a Labor member:

> I direct my question to the Prime Minister. In view of the call by the Opposition for him to resign because it believes that this Government has lost the support of the people, I ask: Can the Prime

Minister recall the views of a former Prime Minister, Sir Robert Menzies, the father of the Liberal Party, on such a proposal? Is there any precedent for assuming such a lack of confidence without any such motion being moved in this House?[22]

Mr Whitlam replied:

> As honourable members will not be surprised to know, in the last few weeks I have been carrying out some research into the general question of dismissals of governments or rejections of Supply and the like.[23]

It was interesting to note that for a few weeks before 15 October 1975 Mr Whitlam, doubtless with all the resources available to him as Prime Minister, was doing this research. His answer continued:

> One of the great pieces of research which came to light was a letter which Mr Menzies wrote when he was Attorney-General and Deputy Premier of Victoria to the Governor of New South Wales, Sir Philip Game. It was among the Governor's papers, and his widow has made it available.

The full text of the letter was published in 1968 in Bethia Foott's book *The Dismissal of a Premier*, Lady Game having made it available to Mrs Foott, a close personal friend. It was public property at the time when Mr Whitlam was speaking.

Mr Whitlam then said, having been asked the date of the letter:

> It is 1932. It is relevant because there have been suggestions that in this day and age, the Viceroy of Australia, the Governor-General of Australia, should withdraw the commission of the Prime Minister who has the confidence of the House of Representatives. It is suggested that the Governor-General of Australia, the Viceroy, should take this action because, for the first time in history, the Senate, which cannot initiate and cannot amend money Bills might make so bold as to reject a money Bill. The last time in Australia that a vice-regal representative—it was a State Governor, a Crown Agent, in other words a British official—cancelled the commission of a head of government was in 1932.

This passage is of significance because it shows that Mr

Whitlam in the period before 15 October 1975 was giving thought to the question of the 'Viceroy's' powers of dismissal, in a context of denial of supply. Mr Whitlam continued:

> But what Mr Menzies, as he then was, wrote to Sir Philip Game is very relevant to present circumstances.

What Mr Menzies wrote was indeed relevant. But Mr Whitlam quoted it in part only, whereas the passage needs to be quoted in full. Mr Whitlam went on:

> He wrote: '. . . the newspaper demand that you should dismiss a Premier on the ground that there was some reason for believing that he no longer enjoyed the confidence of the electors always seemed to me to be based upon an absolute misconception of the constitutional position of a modern Governor. Under the Australian system of universal suffrage and triennial Parliaments, with a legally recognised and responsible Cabinet, it must, in my opinion, follow that so long as a Premier commands a majority in the Lower House, and so long as he is guilty of no illegal conduct which would evoke the exercise of the royal Prerogative, he must be regarded as the competent and continuing adviser of the representative of the Crown'.

Mr Whitlam was, by quoting this passage in the context he outlined, accepting the existence of the royal prerogative of dismissal if a Premier is guilty of illegal conduct. Mr Menzies makes this point absolutely clear in the final part of his letter, not quoted by Mr Whitlam but about to be quoted by me. Meanwhile it is most significant that Mr Whitlam without dissent quotes Mr Menzies' assertion in 1932 of the existence of the prerogative of dismissal.

Mr Whitlam quoted further:

> 'For a newspaper to urge a dissolution because in its opinion the Government has lost the confidence of the electorate is a mere impertinence. The constitutional authority of a Premier rests almost entirely upon his success at a general election, and upon his continued authority in the popularly elected House, and not upon irresponsible speculations as to whether he would have lost his majority if the Constitution had provided for annual and not triennial elections. Moreover these are days (and now I speak as a

politician) in which any Government may, in the stern discharge of its duty, be compelled to take steps which render it unpopular with the electorate. This, however, so far from being a good cause for its recall, may constitute its greatest claim to reputation, and one of the factors which strengthens the hand of a Government fresh from victory at the polls is that it may look forward to a period of office in which its policy may be dictated by convictions and not by the mere necessity of vote catching. It would, in my respectful opinion (and in this I am expressing the majority view among reputable lawyers in this State), have been nothing short of a calamity if during the very great constitutional crisis, New South Wales had possessed a Governor who had subordinated the constitutional authority of a Governor to the purely opportunist demands of those who found the constitutional restrictions irksome. This represents my considered view, in spite of the fact that I am a vigorous opponent of Mr Lang and his policy, and at all material times considered that policy to be actually disastrous to Australia'.

This is classically correct doctrine if the only ground of suggested dismissal or resignation is alleged unpopularity with the electorate. It is the answer to and refutation of the doctrine of Dicey.

Mr Whitlam concludes his answer:

I do commend the words of Sir Robert Menzies, the founder of the Liberal Party, the first leader of it, to the present incumbent.

But Mr Whitlam omitted to finish the quotation. What he omitted to quote was the concluding paragraph in which the purpose of Mr Menzies' letter is made clear:

Finally, we all felt that when you did exercise the power of dismissal for a clear illegality your action was not only timely but was all the more emphatic a vindication of the constitutional position of the King's representative because of your earlier patience and restraint.

Moreover, Mr Whitlam in what he did quote must be taken to have stated with approval Mr Menzies' doctrine of the legitimacy of dismissal in certain circumstances. His failure to quote the whole letter does not relieve him of the consequences of what he quoted.

6

Evatt and Outside Advice

In 1940 Evatt wrote an important article 'The Discretionary authority of Dominion Governors' in the January issue of the *Canadian Bar Review*.[1]

There had been a lot of speculation in 1932 about who, if anyone, had advised Sir Philip Game and whether it was right for him to have outside advice about exercising the reserve powers — advice, that is, coming from other sources than his constitutional advisers, the Ministers. I was especially interested in this because it seemed to me that he would have been in an extraordinary position, assuming that the right to dismiss existed, if he could turn to no one for advice. On the other hand suspicions would undoubtedly arise about whose advice he might seek. I did not then know whether he sought any. Professor Ward records that he consulted the Dominions Office by secret telegram on 23 April 1932: an answer was drafted on 10 May and the Attorney-General, Sir Thomas Inskip, concurred in the draft, but 'events outpaced it and it did not leave London'.[2]

The question whether ministerial advice as to a double dissolution was binding had been touched upon by Evatt in *The King and his Dominion Governors* in connection with the double dissolution of 1914, but it was in his 1940 article that he dealt with this and the right to outside advice in a more thorough fashion. In his 1936 book he discussed the 1914 double dissolution only in a limited way because he apparently did not then have the background documents that later became available to him.

In his *Canadian Bar Review* article Evatt examined the 1914 double dissolution in the light of the contents of the background documents, to which he had meantime gained access. These

83

included the learned and authoritative opinion of the then Chief Justice and founding father Sir Samuel Griffith.

The 1914 precedent happened a long time ago but Evatt's final view about it all was written when he was still a High Court judge, many years later than 1914, much nearer to the present time. Historically speaking 1940 is only yesterday. These great issues, especially issues involving the existence and exercise of personal vice-regal discretion, arise rarely, and historical precedent is of great value.

I shall refer to the 1914 case as an example of the exercise of a personal discretion — in that case a discretion under section 57 of the Constitution — by the Governor-General. That section deals with the resolution of deadlocks between the two Houses. No different considerations from those discussed in relation to the 1914 case could apply in discussing any exercise of the reserve powers committed to the Governor-General by the Constitution.

The Prime Minister, Sir Joseph Cook, in his memorandum to the Governor-General, had said that the latter had to act, in exercising his powers under section 57, on ministerial advice.[3]

Evatt when he discussed this in his book was obviously uneasy about this proposition of the Prime Minister. Cook had said that so far as the Imperial Parliament was concerned, though theoretically the King possessed a discretion as to granting or refusing a dissolution of the House of Commons, 'that discretion is always exercised in accordance with the advice of his responsible ministers'.[4]

Evatt commented that he had elsewhere demonstrated the error, 'perhaps the danger' in this assumption. Cook had taken his stand firmly on his proposition that 'it would be contrary to established constitutional usage for the Governor-General to reject the advice of his Ministers in the circumstances mentioned — that is in action under section 57'. Evatt said that Cook's reasoning did not appear entirely satisfactory. In his 1936 book he regarded this precedent, because the Governor-General in fact granted a double dissolution, as establishing that 'so long as the conditions mentioned in section 57 are complied with the Governor-General will grant a dissolution to Ministers who possess the confidence of the House of Representatives'. Evatt

84

was silent on whether the Governor-General or his ministerial advisers had the effective say as to whether the conditions of section 57 had been complied with.

The conclusion on the 1914 case in *The King and his Dominion Governors* was that the Governor-General had placed complete reliance upon the special parliamentary situation existing at the time of the double dissolution. Evatt had previously mentioned a Tasmanian precedent of 1914 in which there had been a despatch on the power of dissolution from Secretary of State Harcourt. In concluding his examination in 1936 of the 1914 double dissolution Evatt wrote:

> And the Harcourt despatch of 1914, whilst asserting the general principle that no exception can be admitted to the doctrine of ministerial responsibility for every official act or decision of the Governor, did not concern itself with an investigation of the circumstances and conditions which could justify a Governor in venturing upon an original exercise of discretion and subsequently obtaining Ministers to assume 'responsibility' for his decision.[5]

Evatt clearly regarded this as permissible in some circumstances.

Evatt was not in 1936 satisfied that 1914 had really elucidated one of the fundamental problems of section 57, namely whether the Governor-General was absolutely bound to act on ministerial advice. He was keeping this open.

He was able to speak authoritatively on this matter in his 1940 article 'The Discretionary Authority of Dominion Governors'. The significance of this is that we have jumped from 1914, through 1936 to 1940. The times in which this article was written are modern times. I remember in a general way having held views at that time along the lines adopted by Evatt.

What was being considered and dealt with in 1914 and discussed by Evatt in 1936 and 1940 was not a vice-regal dismissal designed to produce a forced dissolution, but other types of dissolution and the alleged automatic constitutional right of Prime Ministers to obtain them from a Governor at will. The denial of this right which crystallises from Sir Samuel Griffith's advice to the Governor-General and from Evatt's writings underlines at the same time the fallacy of any rubber stamp or figurehead theory of the Governor-Generalship, such as Cook had really argued for.

Evatt's article repudiates the idea that the Governor-General is a figurehead, and asserts the proposition that the Governor-General on matters in which he is exercising his own discretion is entitled to take outside advice.

Evatt said that the 1914 papers destroyed the argument that the decisions of Sir Ronald Munro Ferguson (later Lord Novar) as Governor-General were based upon the constitutional theory that in all cases whatsoever the Governor-General is bound to act upon the advice of his Ministers.

He mentioned Sir Samuel Griffith's opinion of the double dissolution provision in the Constitution (section 57) saying that he was then Chief Justice of the High Court, and was also an acknowledged authority on constitutional practice. He quoted Sir Samuel as saying that the double dissolution power under section 57

> should . . . be exercised only in cases in which the Governor-General is *personally satisfied, after independent consideration of the case*, either that the proposed law as to which the Houses have differed in opinion is one of such public importance that it should be referred to the electors of the Commonwealth for immediate decision by means of a complete renewal of both Houses, or that there exists such a state of practical deadlock in legislation as can only be ended in that way. As to the existence of either condition *he must form his own judgment*. (The italics are Evatt's.)[6]

Sir Samuel was of the view that the Governor-General does not have to act on ministerial advice 'but is in the position of an independent arbiter'. Evatt said that

> the Chief Justice added that, among other circumstances, the Governor-General should have regard to the state of parties, whether the resignation of Ministers would follow his refusal to act upon Ministerial advice, and whether, in such an event, another administration could be formed in the existing Parliament which would be able to carry on without a dissolution of the House of Representatives.[7]

Evatt also pointed out that Sir Samuel Griffith's memorandum on the Governor-General's duty in the double dissolution had concluded thus: 'The considerations applicable to a dissolution of the House of Representatives alone are in many respects of a different character, *but the element of the duty of independent exercise of discretion on the part of the Governor-General is common to both*'.[8] (The italics are Evatt's.) He comments on the importance of the conclusion

> that Lord Novar undoubtedly accepted the rulings of Sir Samuel Griffith and Sir Harrison Moore to the effect that, in relation to all applications for a single dissolution, the Governor-General of the Commonwealth not only possesses a right, but is under a duty to come to an independent judgment having regard, first to the parliamentary situation, and then to all the surrounding circumstances. Perhaps it should be added that sec. 28 of the Commonwealth constitution affirms the power of the Governor-General to dissolve the House of Representatives; the word used is 'may' — as is also the case in sec. 57 which deals with the simultaneous dissolution of Senate and House of Representatives.[9]

Evatt stated further:

> It is well settled that this general principle [that the Governor-General acts on the advice of responsible Ministers] does not mean that the King's representative must in all circumstances take positive action in accordance with the advice of Ministers for the time being. It means only that the King's representative must act constitutionally, not personally; in other words, he can only refuse to act upon the advice of existing Ministers if he is able to find another set of Ministers who, by accepting office after the refusal, will necessarily accept the full political responsibility for such refusal.[10]

It is not necessary to discuss here whether a vice-regal refusal of an advised dissolution can never occur unless new Ministers who accept responsibility for the refusal can be found. Such a refusal could conceivably be accepted by the Prime Minister who had advised the dissolution. This was presumably Mr Menzies' view in 1951 when he stressed to Sir William McKell that he must make up his own mind as to the double dissolution advised.[11]

Evatt added:

As the position stands at present, the dominion cases are quite inconsistent with the theory that the Governor-General has been stripped of all discretionary power.[12]

He made the further point:

One exception alone is sufficient to destroy the theory that in every case, whatever the parliamentary situation may be, the Governor-General must dissolve if asked to do so by the Prime Minister for the time being. There are many such exceptions.

And finally:

The fact that Lord Novar called in aid two 'outside', though very distinguished authorities on constitutional practice illustrates the difficulties confronting a King's representative who is not himself expert in a very difficult topic. Because of the lack of certainty in these matters, Dominion Governors have frequently felt themselves at liberty to adopt a similar course.[13]

Evatt was still a High Court judge, and a very eminent one, when he wrote all of this. He stepped down soon afterwards to enter politics on the Labor side. In 1940, in a development of his 1936 argument, he totally discredited the idea that the Governor-General of Australia is a figurehead. He expressed approval of the Governor-General's having taken the advice of Sir Samuel Griffith and Sir Harrison Moore. He laid it down that each Governor-General must exercise his own discretion. He stated as a fact that because of uncertainties in these constitutional discretions Dominion Governors have frequently felt themselves at liberty to consult outside constitutional authorities.

That article was written not only in my lifetime but after I became a practising barrister. Evatt followed Sir Samuel Griffith in rejecting the rubber stamp theory, and vigorously upheld the propriety of taking outside advice where in the vice-regal view the circumstances were such as to warrant it.

7

War Years and Choices

I was practising as a young barrister when I realised, soon after admission to the Bar, that about a third of my practice was coming from people I had known at the Law School and particularly from the last firm with which I had worked. About two-thirds of it was coming from Labor solicitors whom I had got to know. I reached the conclusion that the first third would not grow; the second two-thirds would grow and I would end up almost entirely with a negligence practice, cases arising from accidents to workers and so on. At this stage I had not done any industrial arbitration. My floor on top of the A.P.A. Building did not in those days handle much industrial arbitration.

I believed that I was on the wrong track — not politically, but professionally. Having the type of academic record I had at the Law School, where I had won prizes for Public International Law, Constitutional Law, and Political Science as well as winning or sharing the General Proficiency Scholarship at the end of each year, the point to which I had narrowed my activity was more and more evident to me. It was contrary to the advice of practically all my friends that I was giving up all that beckoned me in the great sweep of the law. I rationalised this as something I was doing for the Labor Party, but came increasingly to see that I had limited excessively the legal challenge I could have been meeting. I wanted to broaden my legal life and to escape from the confining effects of my previous decision.

I was helped to this view because early on, within a year or so of beginning practice, I had two very good equity briefs as junior to an equity silk Mr. R. Bonney, who later became Judge in Divorce. These came from a Law School friend. Very shortly after these cases Bonney sent for me and said, 'Kerr, I want to have a talk with you. You can cut it off if you want to as it's not really my business. But,' he said, 'I will tell you something that I haven't told anyone else. I'm about to accept an appointment to the Supreme Court as Judge in Divorce, and I would like to urge you to leave those chambers over there. I think I could arrange for you to take over my chambers'.

This was a kindly professional gesture. It meant that Bonney was willing to try to induce me to see that I should put myself into a more neutral position professionally so that I should have a chance of doing a wider range of work, which would not happen to me where I was. He said, 'Of course, I can understand the kind of reasons you have in your mind for what you're doing, but it will send you down one road from which, you know, probably there will be no turning'. I gave that advice a lot of thought. I knew that it was the right advice, just as the advice of others earlier had been, but my mind was in a state of conflict and I did not accept Bonney's offer.

Not many months after that, Leslie Herron (who many years afterwards became Sir Leslie Herron, preceding me in the office of Chief Justice) was appointed to the Bench. Another set of chambers thus became vacant in what had been Bonney's building, with the same clerk as Bonney had had; and I, being of the view that I had done the wrong thing in not going into Bonney's chambers, arranged to move in to the chambers vacated by Herron. I wanted to go my own way politically as a Labor man, but to be free as a barrister to develop an all-round practice.

I continued to do Labor work after moving to my new chambers. The Labor label stuck for a long time and nothing I did at that stage constituted an abandonment of the Labor Party politically. Indeed Dr Evatt, after he stepped across from the High Court to politics, took rooms in Denman Chambers to which I had moved, and I did some devilling for him on opinions which he was writing.

One of the things that attracted me about the chambers to which I had moved was that we were a diverse group. There was another Labor barrister, Eric Miller; I was to have a friend there in Asprey, who also went to the Bar. Eric Miller had a wider range of work than most Labor barristers of those days although his practice was significantly Labor.

Much of the same sort of briefs came to me for a time after I transferred to Denman Chambers as had come to me before. But gradually some other work came, and particularly work with Miller. Solicitors who briefed him in non-Labor work would often brief me as his junior. By then however the Japanese war was on and in April 1942 I was called up. It was all over for the time being.

During the first few months after the Japanese war started, age groups began to be called up. I was twenty-six; the inevitability of call-up presented itself to me; and despite a pacifist strain in my earlier thinking I found myself looking forward to my call-up notice. I was happy to let the authorities decide my future. So I was called up. I returned all my briefs and I went in to the Army. I was a nondescript sort of private soldier and was posted to a base supply depot in the Army Service Corps at Parkes, New South Wales, where I spent the first couple of months of army service. By that time the Japanese were already in New Guinea.

This was one of the few occasions when I allowed a big decision to be made for me by the sweep of events and was quite happy to acquiesce in the process.

My income was totally cut off from April 1942, except for the pay of a private. My wife got a job to help keep things going. In Parkes during that time I had the feeling, rare for me, of drifting with events. A friend John Ryan, who had been articled a couple of years after me at Baldick Asprey and Company, was called up at about the same time and went to Parkes too. Ryan had been at Fort Street, although I did not know him at school, where he was a couple of years behind me. He was not an Arts graduate, but was one of the group who before the war regularly formed our coffee circle in which politics, literature, philosophy and related subjects were discussed.

I had not heard what Alfred Conlon was doing in the Army. I do not think I even knew that he was in the Army, although by that time he had formed his little research section on General V. P. H. Stantke's staff at Land Headquarters. A friend of mine

Frank Hutley had become known to Conlon and been recruited into his section.

One morning I had a letter from Hutley saying that he had been marched into Conlon's section; that Conlon was putting together a group of able people, and that Hutley had been brought in and made a sergeant as a lawyer who could help with the sort of problems Conlon anticipated meeting as head of a research section under the Adjutant-General.

Hutley said that he had recommended that Conlon should include me in the group. He asked if I would be willing to join it, describing it as a research unit designed to help Stantke. Conlon had persuaded Stantke that it could be useful to have a group of capable people about him—the whole nation was being mobilised and there was going to be a very big Army with a number of rather new problems. They could advise the Adjutant-General on matters for which an orthodox military solution might not readily be available.

I received from the letter the impression that it was a rather unusual amateur outfit which the Adjutant-General could call upon as he needed it. The idea sounded attractive: I was, as I said, drifting. But it seemed to me that I could not accept Hutley's suggestion when Ryan and I had in effect said, 'Well, let's go on together and see what happens'.

I decided not to accept the offer to go to Land Headquarters, and I wrote and told Hutley this. I talked to Ryan about it, of course, and he said, 'If it interests you, who knows what's going to happen to any of us, you might as well take it and go down'. But I decided against it.

Despite my letter, a movement order came that I was to be marched out of my unit into Conlon's section.

Conlon had decided, perhaps because he knew about my career up to that point through his brothers, that I should not be given the choice. He had the power and he exercised it. I certainly had not had much in the way of military experience; it was only a short time since I had joined the Army. But I knew enough to realise when I reached the section that it was composed almost entirely of non-soldierly people. It was a curious experience.

At that time, in addition to Hutley, the group Conlon had persuaded to go with him into his research unit, which was about to work out an organisation, structure and job for itself under General Stantke, included among others two officers who were geographers — Major John Andrews, then a senior lecturer at Sydney University and later professor of geography at Melbourne University; and Captain Arthur Lowndes, who among other activities was later to be Chairman of the Australian Institute of Political Science. Another captain was James Plimsoll, now Sir James and a leading Australian diplomat. There was Lieutenant Edgar Ford, also a geographer who specialised in cartography; Lieutenant Duncan Macallum, later senior lecturer in history at Sydney University; Sergeant Eric Willis, who was to become, successively, Liberal Premier and leader of the Opposition in New South Wales; and another sergeant, Sam Cohen, a witty, amusing, radical-minded young lawyer who had been a student leader at Melbourne University and who years later became a Labor senator in the federal Parliament. All in all, they were an unusual bunch of soldiers to find together in the one place.

When I first arrived they were doing some work on what was called regional administration, which had to do with producing a detailed plan for dividing Australia up into sections such as might be self-sustaining in the event of invasion, if cut off, for as long as civilian control could continue. Andrews worked on the geographical division of Australia into suitable units; while the lawyers, including Hutley, worked on regulations for introduction under the National Security Act, to provide for the appointment of regional administrators with powers of government in case such a plan needed to be put into operation. The basic design was worked out by Conlon and others.

Government of civilians in such circumstances can be by armed forces or by civilians in association with them, the degree of flexibility varying according to the nature and seriousness of the disruption of normal government. Fortunately the plans came to nothing but in due course led to consideration of the analogous problem of governing civilians in New Guinea. Conlon and his group later, under the Commander-in-Chief, developed a deep interest in military government generally, with particular reference to New Guinea and Borneo. Eventually thought was given to the possible need to participate in military government in Japan.

Early in 1942, General Sir Thomas Blamey had come back from the Middle East and the Government decided to abolish the Military Board and to appoint him as Commander-in-Chief of the Australian Army. Very soon Blamey moved General Stantke from the position of Adjutant-General to General Officer Commanding the Queensland Lines of Communication Area, and appointed General C. E. M. Lloyd as Adjutant-General.

General Lloyd was the last soldier to think he needed a unit such as he found under Conlon. He brought Conlon over to describe to him what he was doing. Although Conlon had an extraordinary ability to persuade people to his point of view, he was not able to persuade Lloyd, and it seemed as though the unit would be disbanded. I remember Conlon coming back and quoting Lloyd as saying it would not be a bad idea for him to find himself a two-storey house somewhere out in the suburbs and move the whole outfit out there to do its thinking, as far away from Victoria Barracks as possible.

Some members of the section left. One or two—Samuel Cohen, and another lawyer, Warrant Officer E. J. Hook, also from Fort Street and a University Medallist in Law—left the Army at that stage because civilian departments were looking for capable people.

Hook many years later became Secretary of the Attorney-General's Department for some years, succeeding Sir Kenneth Bailey. Upon Sir Kenneth's retirement in 1964 the positions of Solicitor-General and Secretary of the Attorney-General's Department, both of which he had held for years, were to be given to two separate persons: Hook became Secretary of the Department and the office of Solicitor-General was offered to me. The fact that residence in Canberra was then thought to be necessary prevented me from accepting it. Had I been able to accept the office, two former members of our old section would have held the two top non-political legal positions in the Commonwealth at that time.

Gradually the section was being cut down. In the meantime, I had been promoted to sergeant. I was a kind of general handyman about the place, dealing with various problems.

Conlon, who was developing great skills in influencing people, came to know Blamey through Brigadier Eugene Gorman, a pre-war King's Counsel in Victoria — a man of influence and power, and a friend of Blamey's. He was then on Blamey's staff as an adviser. Gorman was a good friend of another King's Counsel at the Victorian Bar, Jack Barry, who later became a Supreme Court judge in Victoria. Conlon knew Barry and so came to know Gorman, and started to put a theory to Gorman about the use that the Commander-in-Chief could make of his collection of people. Through Gorman, Conlon had an opportunity of bringing his persuasive powers to bear on General Blamey, who saw point in the idea of having a group such as ours to think about what I have called the non-orthodox problems of the Army — problems of military government, the handling of some of his relations with Ministers. He needed advice about New Guinea matters, because although things had settled down in New Guinea to the point that the Japanese were in occupation of part of the country and the Australian Army in occupation of the rest, civilian administration had collapsed and it had been necessary for military government, with all the attendant problems, to be established.

A unit called ANGAU — the Australian New Guinea Administration Unit — headed by General B. M. Morris, was running the civil side of New Guinea. The unit included a number of district officers and others who had been in the Papuan and New Guinea administrations before the war. With other Army officers they had the task of administering the part of New Guinea that was not in enemy hands. This was an exercise in military government.

The Minister in control of New Guinea general policy was E. J. ('Eddie') Ward. He was regarded as radical in his views, while Blamey had a reputation of the opposite kind and was known to be tough-minded. This offered Conlon a challenge in the exercise of his capacity to influence people. He managed to persuade Ward that he and his staff could give valuable advice about the civilian situation in New Guinea as it developed. Administration was a matter for the Army, of course, on a day-to-day basis, nevertheless everything that happened in New Guinea would affect its future. It would be a good thing for Ward not only to keep his eye on the situation as it evolved, but to do so in co-operation with a part of the Army with which he could work. The Commander-in-Chief agreed with this point of view. Conlon became a friend of Ward's.

He also became a close adviser to Blamey. He acted in a liaison role between the Commander-in-Chief, who was ultimately responsible for military government in New Guinea, and the civilian Cabinet Minister who, though not responsible for day-to-day affairs in New Guinea, had a voice as to what should happen to the native people and how the stage was being set by Army activities for the resumption later of civilian administration. Conlon in those days was becoming a skilled political realist, able to deal with actualities of power and position. One of the great services he rendered the Commander-in-Chief was that he handled his relations with the Minister on New Guinea policy.

This meant also that Conlon was developing a position of some power. He was supported by the Commander-in-Chief. At the same time his influence with Ward enabled him to induce the two men to agree to various proposals. Together, Blamey and Ward made a strong combination. At this time Conlon was a major and I was a lieutenant.

In the latter part of 1941 and early 1942 the question had arisen as to how Australia's morale would stand up if there were an invasion. Conlon had persuaded the Prime Minister John Curtin, by direct contact, that there ought to be a committee to look at the question of civilian morale and to advise the Government as to what steps might need to be taken. Curtin at that time set up a National Morale Committee and appointed Conlon to chair it. When I first arrived at the research section Conlon was in a position to have meetings of this Prime Minister's committee and to travel backwards and forwards to Canberra for purposes connected with it. Accordingly he had apparent sources of power deriving in part from the Prime Minister, who was also Minister for Defence.

In the days when Alfred Conlon was still talked about a lot, during and after the war, people strove to explain the enigma of his influence in the war-time years. A person who is persuasive in the way Conlon was can gradually get into a position where he is fairly well protected and where any ideas he comes up with have a chance of being listened to and perhaps adopted.

He was still a youngish man; I suppose he was in his middle thirties. He had the theory that all doors are open. All one has to do is walk in. That, in a sense, is true, but that alone is not enough. Once inside a door it helps to be creative, impressive, persuasive. Conlon was able to talk to people about their own subject, whether it was one of the academic disciplines or some military or political problem. He had something to say in particular about military government — that the Army had to be watched in New Guinea in case it did irreparable harm to the civilian population while engaged in fighting the Japanese. It might leave behind a discontented and troublesome population for Australia to handle after the war was over. This was a proposition so important that it was convincing to Blamey, Ward and indeed others. As time passed Conlon's attention moved from regional administration and morale matters, which became academic, towards military and post-military government in New Guinea.

When Blamey took over Conlon's section he established it as a directorate of the Australian Army, called first the Directorate of Research and later the Directorate of Research and Civil Affairs, civil affairs being the phrase used in the British Army to cover military government. There was a Directorate of Civil Affairs in Britain at the War Office.

Within our Directorate there had gradually been brought together a larger number of people. We moved into new, bigger premises in Victoria Barracks, Melbourne.

The staff were both full-time and part-time. Full-time personnel included James McAuley and the anthropologists Camilla Wedgwood and Ian Hogbin.

Professor R. D. Wright of Melbourne University, at that time Professor of Physiology, was brought in as a colonel to work with the Directorate from time to time on medical matters relating to military government and other medical questions of interest to the Directorate. Professor Keith Isles, Professor of Economics at Adelaide University, joined the team part-time. He was later to become Vice-Chancellor of the University of Tasmania. Professor Julius Stone, Professor of Jurisprudence at Sydney University and a close friend of Conlon, joined us part-time as a general adviser. He and Isles held the rank of lieutenant-colonel.

Military government in New Guinea had become a big thing for the Directorate, and Conlon set out to establish a school to train officers who would be drawn from the ranks of the Army to take part in it. The old hands of the pre-war New Guinea District Services needed to be supplemented by some younger men as patrol officers and Assistant District Officers, and they would need training. Conlon established friendly relations with a number of leading New Guinea administrative figures then in uniform — people like Jim Taylor, who in the thirties had been one of the first Europeans to discover and contact the big primitive population of the New Guinea Highlands. All of them helped to shape Conlon's thinking about New Guinea and the future school.

In due course, that school was established at Duntroon. Its first Chief Instructor was Colonel J. K. Murray. He was already in the Army and had been the Principal at Gatton Agricultural College in Queensland before the war. He and Conlon mobilised the necessary academic staff and Army personnel.

Andrews was sent to Duntroon as principal assistant to Murray; James McAuley, Camilla Wedgwood and Hogbin also joined its staff. Ida Leeson, the former Mitchell Librarian, was involved in building the library, but stayed in the Directorate in Melbourne. Gradually, selected officers were brought in to study anthropology, geography, government and other subjects which would be needed if they were to participate with any degree of sophistication in responsible military government in New Guinea.

On the staff or assisting were anthropologists, geographers, colonial administration specialists, lawyers, economists, and they approached the task as an academic but practical exercise. In so far as it was a military problem, there was Army help. The students were officers, most of whom had had military experience of one kind or another, and the intention was that they would be the administrators in war-time New Guinea and later in Borneo. The planning was done in the Directorate before the school was established. Those who were to staff the school were given opportunities to go up to New Guinea for background experience.

My role in the meantime had become confirmed as that of practical problem handler as opposed to a researcher or teacher. There were many things to be done. Often when the Commander-in-Chief had a problem with an unusual ingredient he would turn to Conlon, and frequently I would end up working on some practical issue or problem.

A big thing that started to break in 1943 concerned the position of the Commander-in-Chief himself. Senior civilian officials of the Department of the Army and others held the view that the Military Board should be re-established. General Blamey, when he accepted the position of Commander-in-Chief, asked that he should have direct access to the Minister for Defence when and if he needed it. It would, of course, be resorted to rarely. But it meant that Blamey could, if he needed to, go over the head of the Minister for the Army to the Minister for Defence, who was the Prime Minister.

An attack ultimately began to be mounted on the position of Commander-in-Chief. A movement began which sought to achieve a return to orthodox methods of controlling the Army. Blamey had no intention of allowing his position to be undermined; he had Curtin's support, and as far as I could see he intended to stay until the war was over. And he did.

In that situation, Blamey became more and more influenced by Conlon, on all sorts of matters, because Conlon was helping him resist the movement to revert to the Military Board.

The Directorate was not an orthodox part of the Army. It had been recruited on the basis of intellectual attainment. It was not any kind of intelligence unit, nor was it concerned in a direct way with foreign policy. The Directorate never was a 'cloak and dagger' outfit, as was later asserted — a fiction that raises its head even to this day. It never did intelligence work, nor did I. I suppose I met an officer or two who were on the intelligence side at the LHQ Officers' Mess, but if so, I met them only socially. An absurd story was put about that I became some kind of intelligence operator in the war years and maintained some intelligence affiliations thereafter. Alleged later connections with the CIA have been the subject of rumour and gossip. This is and always has been false, in relation to the CIA and to all US and other intelligence activity. I have had no direct or indirect connections at any time, during or after the war, with any intelligence organisations including our own. Only the more gullible subscribers to the conspiracy theory of history could believe or want to believe such nonsense.

I gradually came to be Conlon's right-hand man. I turned out to have some skill as a crisis manager. My view at that time was that Conlon was a kind of psychological magician, able by his skills to persuade people to do things he wanted them to do. His persuading was done almost exclusively by talking. He had an influence on me which I found difficult to resist. By then too the subject of military government had begun to engage my serious attention. Conlon had a real need of me because although he could persuade, it often fell to me to give administrative substance to his ideas. I was useful in putting flesh on the bones of ideas of his which had merit and were accepted. Many of his ideas were good and some extremely creative. I was also able to persuade him to discard some ideas which seemed to me harebrained, and sometimes I persuaded him to adopt ideas of mine. I had influence on what Conlon would put to Blamey, on the one hand, and in getting done the things that Blamey authorised. But Conlon's personal influence on me was and remained strong for quite a time, even after the war ended. It took a genuine effort to shake it off.

During 1943 I was promoted to major, skipping the rank of captain. That gave me quite an important status in Conlon's outfit. He by this time had become a lieutenant-colonel. Though not yet in name, I was in effect his deputy director, specialising in military government.

Conlon's motivation was complex. He loved the power that came from being able to induce people, especially those who had power in their own right, to carry out his suggestions. He enjoyed very greatly being able to influence people. He had a minor kind of Leonardo complex: he believed he knew and understood a wide range of intellectual matters; he had an uncanny capacity for discussing what might be called the methodological and philosophical fringe of many subjects. He was a master of this and did it with wit, and some distinguished men came under his influence.

I went with Lieutenant-Colonel William Stanner, later Professor of Anthropology at the Australian National University, who was for a time with the Directorate, to London in 1944. We went as advisers to General Blamey, who accompanied Mr Curtin to the Prime Ministers' Conference held in London that year. There we came in contact with what were to be further problems in the military government field. Blamey presided at a conference, which Stanner and I attended, of people from the Colonial Office, the War Office and the Foreign Office on the subject of Borneo and Hong Kong, both of which were occupied by the Japanese and would have to be won back. It became part of my duties to maintain relations with two British units, the British Borneo Civil Affairs Unit and the Hong Kong Civil Affairs Unit, which had been formed with a view to planning the resumption of government in those areas when the time came.

The British were not going to be able to participate with troops in the retaking of British Borneo. It was expected that that would be done under MacArthur's general command, predominantly by Australians. The British knew that we should have to find, though not necessarily to finance, the men and the resources — the rice, the relief supplies, the necessities for military government of civilians as our troops established themselves in Borneo. It was to the British advantage to ensure that some of their people would be involved in civil affairs policy and activities, though the unit responsible would be Australian in the operational phase and would be operating under the Australian Army, which would run, in the field, the civilian side of Borneo. Australia fully accepted this and was co-operating. Planning was going on in 1944.

The British sent out an officer, Colonel Leonard Taylor, who spent a lot of time with our Directorate, to which he was seconded. He came from the British War Office, Civil Affairs Directorate. His job was to persuade us in advance how to organise the necessary military government unit for Borneo, with particular reference to the British role.

As far as I know Australia never aspired to post-war power in British Borneo, and the Directorate never engaged in the Borneo planning with any such aspiration in mind.

Getting ready for Borneo we had sent some officers to the School of Military Government at Charlottesville in Virginia, USA. Among those who went there were Stanner, Plimsoll, Reynolds (now a judge of the Court of Appeal in New South Wales) and several others, including Hutley, who was later with the military government in Japan, and Ryan, whom Conlon had brought from Army Education in to the Directorate. He, like Hutley, later went to Japan as a military government liaison officer. Several officers who did the Charlottesville course had a part later in military government in Borneo.

I went back to London in about April 1945. By that time a Borneo Civil Affairs group had been organised in Australia, with a British commander and a few senior British advisers in economic and other matters, in uniform — mostly either from the former colonial service or pre-war businessmen from Borneo. A separate Civil Affairs unit was established in the Australian Army under Australian control. The Directorate was in a position of power in relation to the British group because they could do nothing unless the Commander-in-Chief agreed to it.

Once it had become obvious that one of the dominant interests of the Directorate of Research was going to be military government in Borneo it was able, at Land Headquarters, with Blamey's support, co-operation and approval to take to itself some of the policy side of military government. Conlon, as Director, was able in these circumstances to exercise some power in his own right, not just to advise someone else to exercise power. People who merely advise others how to exercise power are protected by not having actual responsibility for decisions made and they are also protected by the fact that those who have power and who are listening to their advice can reject it. So they are safeguarded against the results of some of the things they may suggest.

Conlon was one of those adversely affected by acquiring personal power. On the only two occasions in my association with him where he found himself in a position of wielding some direct personal power — making day-to-day decisions — he ran into trouble, and one of those was with the British in connection with the running of the British Borneo Civil Affairs Unit.

In London in 1945 I had the task of smoothing things out and explaining to the British what we were endeavouring to do about military government in Borneo, because they were getting letters back from senior officers in the British group — private letters — which painted a picture of a person rather unpredictable and likely to over-rule them for the sake of over-ruling them, or to give them orders that did not seem to them to be reasonable. They found Conlon's action heavy-handed and his personality very difficult to understand and to handle. They felt that he was somewhat devious. I learned in London that his reputation with British officers in Australia was as a person very difficult to deal with indeed.

Colonel Taylor had returned to the War Office, travelling with me when I went to London in April 1945. A mounting movement was developing to make a complaint to the Australian Government or the Commander-in-Chief about the way Conlon was said to be running things. During my 1945 visit there was a meeting with War Office, Foreign Office and Colonial Office people. Colonel Taylor was there; we were about eight or nine round the table and they told me pretty frankly what they had been hearing. There was a lot of justification, as far as I could see, for some of their complaints. Some I had already been able to smooth over a little by my influence with Conlon; I was by this time thirty and a lieutenant-colonel. I said to them in effect that I would do my best, when I got home, to lessen their grounds for complaint, but it had to be accepted that Conlon's status with the Commander-in-Chief was such that they could not alter things by official complaints. As far as I could see they accepted this point of view.

I do not believe Conlon had any machiavellian post-war

intentions. Even if he had, they would have been irrelevant. The real problems were problems of his personality. Mysterious as his mental processes were, I am sure he expected Borneo to revert to the British and was not silly enough to aspire to continued Australian power there. Nothing he said to me indicated any such approach. The British in London had no feeling, so far as I could judge, that Australia wanted future power in Borneo.

May brought the end of the European war, and August the end of the Japanese war. Both VE and VJ Day occurred whilst I was in London. I did what I could from London to help Conlon but did not get back to do anything in Australia. I had to stay on in London after VE Day for reasons connected with Japan These the atomic bomb on Hiroshima presently made obsolete. The war was over.

My journey to London in 1945 had taken me via America where, as on my previous trip to London in 1944, I stopped over in Washington for talks with the Australian military mission and American military government officers. Plimsoll was at Charlottesville, and my train was to stop for half an hour at Grand Central in New York when I went through to Montreal from Washington to catch a plane to London. I let Plimsoll know I would be passing through the station. He had some leave which he was taking in New York and he came to the station to say 'hello'.

We were, at that time, of the view that we should get ready for military government in Japan, because we knew nothing about the bomb and believed that the following year Japan would be invaded. One of the things I had to do in London after VE Day was to explore British attitudes as to their participation and our in the invasion of Japan and in military government there. A British Commonwealth Force to consist of Indians, Australians New Zealanders and British was being thought about and the plan was that it would be an element in any army that invaded Japan. But, of course, the atomic bomb changed all that.

On the station that night at Grand Central I said to Plimsoll 'What about giving up the idea of getting ready to go to Borneo When I get to London I'll suggest that you should be promoted to major and be posted to the Australian Military Mission in

Washington to handle the American end of military government — to keep us informed of what's going on here in America in the military government field, get ready to play a role with the Americans who will be dominant in the military government side of the Japanese operation and occupation. How would that suit you?' He said the idea appealed to him.

When I reached London I sent back a signal and suggested this. It was done: Plimsoll was promoted to major and posted to the USA. When the war ended he was on the spot in America as an Australian already very well informed about what the Americans were doing and going to do in relation to military government in Japan. This enabled him to be very useful indeed to Australia, especially when the Far Eastern Commission was set up, and he remained in uniform until 1948.

The British Commonwealth sent an occupation force to Japan under General J. Northcott, but the Americans never gave Australians or British the power of military government in the area occupied by British and Australian troops. They sent their own military government people in to handle civil affairs. Some Australian military government officers, including Hutley and Ryan, acted as liaison officers with them.

Plimsoll's considerable and successful experience in the USA and on Japanese questions showed his clear vocation for diplomacy, and he moved from the Army into the Department of External Affairs. I feel I can fairly regard myself as having, on that visit to London, played a small part at the outset of Sir James Plimsoll's long and distinguished diplomatic career. I have in my turn, over nearly forty years, benefited greatly from his wisdom and friendship.

Lieutenant-Colonel (Professor) Isles was in London with me in 1945. He spent some time in Germany making a study of military government there, reporting back to Conlon. I urged that we should have, in London as in Washington, a special Civil Affairs Officer on the staff of the Australian Military Mission, to report to the Commander-in-Chief through the Directorate, especially on armistice terms and expected military government and control problems in Japan. Isles carried out this task.

In London I did some work with the Australian High

Commissioner Mr Bruce, later Lord Bruce. I worked too with Whitehall officials and the British War Office on military government generally, on Hong Kong and Japan, on the proposed British Commonwealth Force for the invasion of Japan and on efforts to achieve consultation between the United Kingdom and Australia on Japanese surrender terms and control policy.

It was close now to the end, for me, of military government days. General Blamey went north to participate in the surrender in Tokyo Bay. The question arose: would he try to carry on and demobilise the Army which had been built up under him, or would he lay down his arms?

I think he would have liked to stay on. But he had done a great job as Commander-in-Chief and carried great burdens. He had protected himself, he had remained the strong man, for the whole of the war. Chifley was by then Prime Minister, and Blamey did not get on with Chifley as well as he had done with Curtin. He decided to write the necessary letter saying he wished to relinquish his command.

Conlon and I always had an understanding between us that at the end of the war we would both be demobilised at the same time. We were in a position to be demobilised after the war ended, with Blamey's approval. We had a clear understanding that when the time came I would not be left in the Army with further military responsibilities after Conlon had returned to civil life. Conlon went himself, but he did leave me in the Army with further and new responsibilities. He did it in the following way.

In late 1945, partly through Conlon's influence on Ward and others, Colonel J. K. Murray, who was Principal of the LHQ School of Civil Affairs, was appointed Administrator of New Guinea. It was dear to Conlon's heart and to Murray's that the School should survive the end of the war and become a permanent institution of a civilian kind. It was therefore regarded by both of them as essential that someone should be selected to direct it who could achieve that result. Conlon conceived the idea that I would be that person.

He did not tell me this. Instead, he came in to the Directorate one day not long after Murray had been selected a Administrator of Papua New Guinea, and said to me that a rather awkward mistake had been made. He had typed a memorandum to be signed by the Commander-in-Chief promoting me to full colonel and sending me to Duntroon to take over from Murray at the LHQ School of Civil Affairs.

The 'mistake' to which he confessed was that this paper had got shuffled in with a lot of others that he had sent over for the Commander-in-Chief to sign, without his intending that to happen until he had discussed it with me. The Commander-in-Chief had signed it. I felt this to be a pretty serious breach of faith. Although amiable relations were restored after a time, my feelings of friendship for Conlon were scarred by it. My immediate reaction was hostile. I went home on leave and stayed there for a week or so. But ultimately I realised that somebody had to do the job and it was important to save the school; there would be people who would want to kill it; and I gave in and said I would take it on. That decision kept me for a time in New Guinea affairs and also later involved me in the South Pacific Commission. I was so engaged from 1945 to the end of 1948, when I went back to the Bar.

Conlon argued that anyone could go back to the Bar but that I owed it to myself and Murray, and to what we had all been doing, to stand by; that whether I liked it or not, that was the best thing for me to do, and accordingly he had no choice but to do what he did and tell me afterwards. If he had told me beforehand I would have refused, and then he would have found it much more difficult to put it to Blamey, since he would have had to tell Blamey at the same time that I did not want to go. Conlon said, 'You did not know what was good for you'. He claimed that what he was doing was in my interest. But there was in him an element of pleasure in deviousness as a means of exercising personal power, and realisation of this weighed with me, from that point on, to counter what had been my regard for his unusual qualities.

In October, I had to go to Duntroon to take up duties with the school. My wife and I decided that she would stay in Melbourne until the end of the year, leaving our elder girl at St Catherine's School, and go to Sydney at the same time as I would be going, since the school was to be moved from Duntroon to Holsworthy. It was moved to Holsworthy and later in early 1946 to Georges

Heights. My wife came back to Sydney at the end of the first school term in 1946. Meantime I was making the necessary arrangements for getting us settled there with our two young daughters Gabrielle and Kristin. We had no money, except a very small gratuity that one would receive on demobilisation, and housing was virtually impossible to get, but through a solicitor friend of mine we managed to buy a very small, dilapidated cottage in Roseville. My father, who in 1945 was fifty-five years old, was fit and vigorous and very much a handyman; he could do anything with tools. So before and after we settled into that house he and I — mainly he — repaired it and made it a comfortable little place.

The school, established in early 1946 as a civil body under the name of the Australian School of Pacific Administration, was housed in some Army premises on Georges Heights and later at Middle Head. I used to go in each day from Roseville to run it as Principal. I was demobilised in about April 1946 but I knew when posted to the military school in 1945 that I would have to see it through its establishment as a civil institution.

The period from demobilisation until my return to the Bar was one in which, along with my duties at the School, I spent three months in New York in 1947 as an adviser to the Australian delegation to the United Nations General Assembly, and visited Fiji and New Caledonia in 1948 as part of a site-choosing mission for the South Pacific Commission, of which I was Organising Secretary.

My wife had never been particularly keen on my postponing my return to the Bar and running the School and the South Pacific Commission. She was antagonistic to the idea of my going to New York for three months, but it was not a serious problem: she simply thought I was crazy not to go back to the Bar, as everybody else had done. After all, she thought she had married a young barrister, not a sort of minor academic and amateur diplomat.

It was while I was in the process of converting the School to civil status that I was asked by the Department of External (now Foreign) Affairs, in 1946, to help with preparations for the South Seas Conference, which was to be held in Canberra on the initiative of the Australian Government and notably of Dr Evatt, at that time Minister for External Affairs. This was the conference that founded the South Pacific Commission (the proposal had been to call it the South Seas Commission, but someone from the United Kingdom pointed out wittily that people would call it the Bubble and that would be the end of it). Our staff at the School wrote background papers for the conference.

I was later asked by John Burton, at that time Secretary of External Affairs, to undertake the organising of the South Pacific Commission. I took on this task as Organising Secretary of the, as yet, unformed South Pacific Commission together with my work as Principal of the School. The Commission had been determined upon but still awaited some ratifications from the participating Powers, the six colonial Powers of the South Pacific — Australia, New Zealand, France, the Netherlands, the United Kingdom and the United States.

When I took on the work with the South Pacific Commission I needed new premises big enough for both the School and the Commission, and additional Army buildings were made available on Middle Head.

It was because I was involved with New Guinea and engaged in organising the Commission that I was included, in 1947, in the Australian delegation to the United Nations General Assembly. Dr Evatt led the delegation. He was, in 1947, Chairman of the Palestine Committee, and the Palestine issue was the critical one of that year. In the following year he became President of the United Nations. I had seen him fairly often during the war, including once in Washington when I passed through in 1945 — he was on his way to San Francisco. It was at about that time too that I considered joining the Department of External Affairs.

The international strands in the pattern of my personal life had been appearing one by one in an unforeseen and seemingly haphazard way. I had no idea when I entered the Army that I should become involved in military government and diplomacy; my interest had until then been absorbed by national affairs, remaining essentially that of a reader and student of the international scene. By the end of the war this had changed greatly.

I had twice visited the United States when passing through to London, and had talked military government with American officers. I had been twice to the United Kingdom and taken part in military government discussions with officers and officials of the War, Colonial and Foreign Offices. I had done some work in the Post Hostilities Planning section in the Cabinet Office in London and had seen the results, in the War Office, of British preparations for talks with the Americans about armistice planning for Japan. The opportunity had fallen to me to have a number of conversations with Lord Bruce on that subject. New Guinea civil affairs planning and liaison with Ward and Blamey had led me to think about post-war New Guinea and its coming journey to independence.

To these war-time experiences were now added my activities in the Australian School of Pacific Administration and the South Pacific Commission, within which I dealt closely with representatives of the six Pacific colonial Powers. All of this work was extremely fascinating to me. It was only after a good deal of thought and serious discussion with my wife Alison that I decided to turn my back upon the attractions of professional diplomacy and not apply for a post in the Department of External Affairs.

I believe, analysing it now, my reasons were twofold. To begin with my wife was against it. She really always wished to live in Sydney. She wanted to get started on what would then be a continuous life in Sydney, bringing up a family, among people she knew, with me a success at the Bar. The war had of course interrupted most people in their chosen course, and Conlon had interfered a lot with my plans. But now everyone was going back or had gone back to the Bar, and this was what my wife had expected and now wanted me to do. She opposed my choosing a diplomatic career.

Of course we discussed all of this, and questions of where our children should grow up and be educated, and so on. I weighed my wife's opinion, as I always did. But I clearly see now that the true reason why at that point I turned my back on diplomacy was that, consciously or subconsciously, my basic intention was and always had been to get back and prove myself at the Bar, towards which I had set my course when I was eleven years old. That is why, although I was busy with the task of converting the School from a military into a civil institution and getting it and the South Pacific Commission established, and was involved in New Guinea and other dependent areas affairs, I regarded myself as only temporarily engaged with all of that. I believed always that I would return to the Bar. I had to prove to myself that I could do it.

There was perhaps a further contributing element in my attitude. I grew up with a strong sense of being an Australian, of having things to do in Australia.

In my decision when I made it, I was confirmed and supported by a conversation I had with General Blamey when I had gone to say goodbye to him in 1945. He asked me what I was going to do and I said, 'Well, I suppose, in the long run I'll go back to the Bar'. I added, 'I think I could, if I wanted to, go into External Affairs and become a diplomat'. Blamey said, 'Well, if my advice is of any use to you, I'll say this. The Bar is an independent profession. I'd go back to the Bar. If the country is ever in any serious crisis, you'll find you are well placed to be of real use'. I thought that was pretty sound advice and I have always remembered it.

So, from early in 1948, I was beginning to make my plans to return to the Bar.

8

Transition — Return to the Bar

Conlon's idea in regard to the future of the School of Pacific Administration as a civilian institution originally was—and indeed I embraced this idea and hoped it could be achieved— that the School should be converted into a true institute of Pacific studies with both research and teaching functions. But when it was determined that the Australian National University would be a post-graduate institution, the research side of such activity fell naturally within its scope. The name Australian School of Pacific Administration was chosen to indicate that the School would not have a wide Pacific studies and research role but a practical one. Nevertheless, even after that happened we both tried, although with little success, to procure additional funds for developing research activity for our own special New Guinea area.

As the New Guinea civil administration got under way people who joined it from around Conlon's orbit and the School included Colonel J. K. Murray, whom I had succeeded as Principal of the School. Murray was installed in Port Moresby as the first post-war Administrator. He had a deep and real interest in the welfare of the native people of New Guinea and was sympathetic to what he believed to be the Minister's emerging policies; he was highly thought of by Conlon.

Dr John Gunther, who had been close to us in the Directorate and worked on the tropical medicine side in the Air Force as a squadron leader, went to New Guinea as Director of Health. Gunther remained Director of Health for many years, became Assistant Administrator, and later was Vice-Chancellor of the University of Papua and New Guinea. (I invested him as a

Knight in September 1975, in the garden of the old Government House in Port Moresby to which Colonel Murray had gone as the first post-war Administrator. The investiture took place on the eve of Independence Day in Papua New Guinea, when the Australian flag was lowered there for the last time.)

The School of Pacific Administration was functioning usefully in the early post-war years, offering a two-year course approximately at undergraduate level and having some limited research functions. This represented great progress from the pre-war situation when New Guinea administration staff received little specialised preparation for their work. Among newcomers to the teaching staff of the civilian school was J. H. Wootten, a first class honours graduate in Law from Sydney. After a few years at the School he was admitted to the Bar and he and I worked closely together at the Bar and in other activities until I became a judge. He was appointed to the Supreme Court Bench and served as a judge whilst I was Chief Justice.

A research appointment was made for study and lecturing in Comparative Colonial Administration with particular reference to the French overseas territories, which then constituted the second great colonial structure in the world, of a young first class honours graduate of Sydney University, French Government Travelling Scholar and *Licenciée ès lettres* (Master of Arts) of the Sorbonne, Mrs Anne Robson, who is now my wife. We were married during my Governor-Generalship on 29 April 1975, almost thirty years later.

Anne was recruited to the staff of the School at Middle Head and worked with James McAuley in the department of Government, making field trips to New Guinea and the French territories in the Pacific. In addition to lecturing at the School she published writings on French overseas territories administration and policies. The difficulty of obtaining the material necessary for such research in Australia at that time was extreme. When the first international conferences began to be held in Australia — the South Seas Conference followed by ECAFE at Lapstone and early meetings of the South Pacific Commission, the School lent Mrs Robson to the Department of External Affairs to interpret for the French delegations. At first this was welcomed by her and by the School for the opportunity it provided of organising the proper documentary and informational basis for research in French overseas territories administration through direct contact with top level French overseas administrative officials. But the international scene itself, with the tension and variety offered by international conference interpretation, at once exercised a powerful appeal.

On the last day of the Lapstone meeting she was offered appointment at ECAFE's headquarters in Bangkok as second staff interpreter to Basil Chilikin, now Assistant Chief Interpreter of the United Nations in Europe. She could not accept this, but from then on undertook periodic overseas engagements with United Nations Agencies and other international organisations in Asia and the Pacific. The period at the School had oriented her, as it turned out, towards what was later to become an absorbing international career.

Meantime Anne was in Bangkok for ECAFE and FAO conferences early in 1949 and so was lucky enough to miss the forthcoming drama with Conlon at the School.

In May 1948 I organised the first session of the South Pacific Commission, held at the School's premises on Middle Head. Dr Evatt, then Minister for External Affairs, opened the session. I was asked if I would take the job of Secretary-General. I declined, saying I wanted to go back to the Bar. Conlon, who had returned to the Medical School to finish his course, developed a very deep desire to be Secretary-General of the South Pacific Commission, and he asked Ward to nominate him for the position. Ward was a great admirer of his. But Conlon had not realised that the war was really over: he was back at university as a medical student; he had no power of his own and no Commander-in-Chief to issue orders; there were people about who were less than his friends, especially in Canberra. He wanted to be back in the mainstream, and he thought that being Secretary-General of the South Pacific Commission would open the way for him to do again the sort of things he had done in the war-time years.

Ward nominated him to External Affairs. As Ward wanted it and an Australian candidate had to be found, at the first session in 1947 Conlon's name was canvassed. I think most of the other metropolitan Powers might have accepted Conlon. But the British did not want him. The Commission was not able to select a Secretary-General at that first session and I was asked if I would stay on for six months.

By this time my arrangements to go back to the Bar were well advanced. I had intended to move back in two stages, first limiting my connection with the School to part-time activity. I was ready to get started, and I even had the offer of a brief or two. I therefore replied that I would carry on at the South Pacific Commission only in a broad supervisory way, and they appointed me as Interim Secretary-General until the next session. In October 1948, at the second session, Australia put forward the name of Mr W. D. Forsyth, a career diplomat who was later Australian Ambassador to Vietnam, and afterwards Lebanon. He was appointed and took over the South Pacific Commission from me towards the end of that year.

When that happened, Conlon switched to an ambition to return to active participation in New Guinea affairs by succeeding me at the School. A Principal was being sought to take over from me. My own view was that he probably could not do it, not for lack of intellectual capacity, but simply because even the small degree of power involved in running a small-scale institution like that might be difficult for him to handle. But it would have provided him with a base from which to operate and, of course, he was very close to Ward, who was the Minister, and to Murray, who was the Administrator. In such a situation he could, perhaps, had he been able to run the School with a loose rein, gradually have talked his way into an interesting position, at least during the days of the Labor Government. But part of Conlon's magic had gone. I feared that he would run into trouble. However, I supported his succeeding me. After all, he had brought the School into existence, sincerely believed in its importance, was an able man and I could be wrong about the risks. The Council on which he had friends and admirers appointed him for a period of a year.

Almost every person on the staff of that School was a friend of Conlon. They came from the old Directorate or the old Military

School or were otherwise friends. They were people with whom he had many times spent hours of talking over the years. In particular James McAuley, the most influential amongst the staff, was a close friend.

To illustrate the nature of relationships I must recall the famous Ern Malley literary hoax, concocted in Directorate days by poets James McAuley and Harold Stewart. In order to ridicule avant-garde versifiers the two poets composed the 'poems' and sent them off for publication when some non-existent sister found them in some non-existent box, after the 'death' of 'Ern Malley'. Conlon was an inspiration in the sense that he regarded it as magnificent fun and urged them on. Thirty years later, recalling a talk with me at the time of the famous hoax, in an article in the January 1976 issue of *Quadrant* McAuley wrote:

> When Harold Stewart and I were ready to send off the Ern Malley poems to Mr Harris, I asked John what the legal position would be if we received money under what might be loosely termed false pretences. John laughed and said he doubted whether the law had anything to say on the point, and therefore it might unpredictably say anything, though he doubted whether there was any serious risk. (Nevertheless Ern's sister Ethel said in the letter Harold and I concocted that she didn't want to receive any financial benefit from her brother's work, just to give it a chance of being published if thought acceptable. I've sometimes wondered what the copyright position really now is, but have never pursued the question).

I remember that conversation very well. Another idea we toyed with was whether the hoax should be extended. Thought was given between McAuley and myself to whether an important public figure might be invited to write an introduction to the poems; but we decided it was too risky and idle talk along those lines was abandoned. It was wise to disclaim any interest in money — the aim was that the hoax should be public property and the poems able to be widely read and published without any fear of legal complications.

The 'poems' were published. The result was a spectacular hoax; many faces were red and the whole of literary Australia was laughing, as were many people overseas. Conlon enjoyed this whole affair enormously. He and McAuley were close friends still when Conlon became Principal of the School.

Although Conlon should have known better, having moved so much in academic circles, he set out immediately to run the School as he had run the Directorate, somewhat in the military pattern instead of the academic pattern. An atmosphere of tension built up in the School that was almost volcanic. Gradually all of Conlon's friends rebelled: they hoped and believed that the School was already, or else was about to become, a significant academic institution in the colonial studies field; they were people qualified for university-level teaching, and were working hard to make it such. Academic freedom was necessary to them, whereas Conlon was apparently seeking to administer it under a personal discipline of an unpredictable kind.

In the end McAuley led a revolt six months or so after Conlon took over. The Registrar rang me in my chambers, said there was a grave crisis at the School and asked me to go out. And he meant a crisis, there and then. The staff had had a meeting and had decided that unless Conlon left the School that day, they would take some action — I do not think it was actually expressed in the language of a strike, but in reality there was a real risk of teaching ceasing. McAuley had delivered Conlon an ultimatum, and the Registrar said Conlon had locked himself in his room and was in a state of profound depression. Conlon since the war had occasionally been subject to states of extreme gloom. I remember sitting there with him at his home sometimes — no word would be exchanged for an hour or more. Then I would say, 'Oh well, I'll go now', and I would leave.

That day at the School he let me in to see him and I said, 'What's it all about, Alf?' 'Oh,' he said, 'they just . . . they don't want me'. And I said, 'You really shouldn't be here, Alf. I think you should go back and finish your Medicine'. He said, 'I don't want to be thrown out, and I think they mean it, they just won't teach tomorrow'. He suggested that he be given six weeks to disengage and to find a means of rationalising why he was going.

The tension among the staff was so great that it was doubtful whether they would agree to the six weeks. I went out to the others and had some negotiations with McAuley. As I remember it, McAuley said, 'Well, John, he's got to go, physically, now. As far as we're concerned it can appear publicly for six weeks that he's still Principal but he must not come into the place — he must stay away'. So something along those lines was worked out and Conlon accepted it. In due course he went back and qualified in Medicine. In his last years, though his life was less dramatic than in the war-time years, he appeared happy in his medical work and his friendships.

I lost contact with the School from then on. With Conlon, too, my friendship was to be a declining one. I have indicated what I regarded as his manipulative approach to his friends: his theory of friendship that was not only manipulative but based on a philosophy of so-called therapeutic mendacity as a necessary element in friendship, as a means to the end of procuring what he personally considered to be for the friend's good. He expounded this theory of friendship to me and I rejected it.

But this did not blind me to the fact that I owed him a great deal from many points of view. He vastly broadened my horizons, inspired me to my best efforts, gave me a variety of experiences and great responsibilities for a young man. After his death some years later, I put some observations about Conlon on tape for John Thompson for his ABC series 'On the Lips of Living Men'. I should like to have the long tape but it appears to have gone. The following may be quoted:

> In his relations with people, young people in particular, but all people, he came to be indispensable psychologically to them, so much so (I had this experience myself) that one could positively feel that Alf was entering one's mind and occupying it and taking it over. One came to be dependent upon him and to need, before one acted in any field at all, to talk it over with him . . . Alf had a kind of therapeutic approach to his relationships with other people. He worked out what he thought to be their weaknesses and failings and he set out to help them to overcome these, often without their knowing it, and he had a whole theory of how far he was entitled to go in these matters. For example he had a theory (which he often enunciated to me) of mendacity, a kind of end-justifies-the-means theory . . . And he was never at any stage motivated by anything else

but a desire to bring out the best in people. Of course Alf derived very great personal satisfaction from his power, using this word in its very broadest sense, his capacity to impress and control people, and from the fact that many people of great intellectual eminence were happy to dine at his table, engage him in conversation, and respond to his advice. So that in that sense of course he was not disinterested.

On the other hand, he was not at all interested in material things. He didn't seek the outward trappings.

From 1949 and onward through the fifties my activities were centred on the crowded life at the Bar, where I devoted myself energetically to building up a practice. Before the war I had been trying to diversify the range of my work, but when I resumed full practice in 1949 I thought it was better to get going and earn a living, doing the work at hand. I did not have much choice, I had a wife and two daughters. A son was born at the end of 1949.

The remarkably challenging experiences of the forties had forced me to grow up fast. Although I started my Army experience in a reconciled, acquiescent way, the pressure of working alongside Conlon, of reacting to his stimulating enthusiasm and adjusting to his mixture of practical ideas and impractical hopes, while retaining some authentic independence of personality, produced a realistic participation in what was going on around me. Dealing with older and very experienced men, Australian and non-Australian, coming to grips with New Guinea, the South Pacific and colonialism, international travel, American and British approaches to problems relevant to us — all of these things I had tackled in a barrister-like way. I had set out to master and handle whatever brief I held.

It was all infinitely removed from my pre-war experience. Things were never going to look the same to me again. I felt stronger, better able to look after myself, more capable of making my own decisions, more able to direct the developing pattern of my life. When I looked back on the forties they seemed to confirm my basic philosophy. I had felt in a real sense in control of my life — hemmed in of course, but nonetheless conducting it in my own fashion — toughened but enjoying life and its challenges; enjoying friendship; and struggling to get my own way in many matters and in negotiations with many able people.

Like the forties, the first years of the fifties were to help strengthen my independence of spirit and aspiration.

Whereas before the war I had been strongly Labor-oriented I had, by the time I had become a colonel and gone on to the Australian School of Pacific Administration and the South Pacific Commission, in practical terms in daily life ceased to think much about Labor affairs. There had still been a Labor element in my life as I came to meet and know Labor leaders, especially Ward, but the years until I returned to the Bar were very pressing years. The world was wide, the challenge great and I was able to think of myself and my work as being non-ideological, as going on in a world in which it was possible to decide what was the best thing to do in a given situation and try to get it done.

I was rather surprised on returning to the Bar to find that despite all my experiences and, as I saw it, growth, back in Sydney I was still regarded as a Labor lawyer and still predominantly doing Labor work. Nobody had really heard much about what I had been experiencing during the war-time years at the Directorate; they were not much interested in what I had done at the School and with the South Pacific Commission. I did not become recognised as anything different from the person I was previously known to be in Sydney. My sources of work were still predominantly Labor sources of work. I always had it in mind that if the opportunity ever offered I would diversify, but that was going to take time.

Two things happened of great significance in that early period. First of all, there was the Timber Royal Commission, concerning allegations of corruption which had been made against Eddie Ward, then Minister for Transport and External Territories in the Chifley Government. I was junior counsel for Ward in that Commission; he asked for me as junior to Eric Miller, Q.C. The Commission sat for several months. Ward was completely cleared by Mr Justice Ligertwood of the South Australian Supreme Court. That was quite an important brief for me and it got me started financially. I was able as a result of it to sell my house in Roseville, and buy a rather charming timber cottage in Lindfield. We lived at Roseville for four years, from 1946 to about 1950, and in Lindfield for four years or so, until 1954.

The second happened in December 1949, just before my son was born and when we were still living at Roseville—he was born on 29 December, and I remember it was between Christmas and New Year that Laurie Short came to see me. Laurie Short was very much on the right of centre in the Labor Party. I had met him at different times over the years, one occasion being a memorial meeting held after Trotsky's murder in Mexico.

When Short called, the results had just come in of the 1949 ballot of the Federated Ironworkers' Association, of which Ernest Thornton, a leading communist, was National Secretary, and Short was convinced that it had been rigged. We started then to develop the legal investigation, which in due course, led in 1952 to a declaration that that ballot was indeed rigged. That launched me into what might be called the 'industrial groups' phase of my career.

I was still a fairly orthodox right of centre Labor lawyer, a social democrat, a little bit stiffened by experience, a little less idealistic—in fact, quite a lot less idealistic; more pragmatic and more inclined to think that if I went in for politics on the Labor side it would be, without any question, as a kind of liberal-minded administrator of a mixed-economy State. I did not see capitalism as disappearing nor socialism arriving.

Chifley as Prime Minister had the problem in politics of how to deal with communism in the trade unions. During the war, with Russia on our side, communism developed very strongly in the trade unions—in the Ironworkers' Union, the Miners' Union, the Railways Union and many others. So much so that a lot of people in the Catholic church, and hence in right-wing Labor Party circles, where there were many Catholics, were receiving warnings about it.

Ward had a reputation for being radical. He was an interesting left-winger. He was certainly on the left in the Labor Party in his ordinary day-to-day ideological attitudes. Later on, after Labor went into Opposition, I remember talking to Ward about industrial group activity and chiding him for not being more active in fighting communism in the unions, and his chiding me for the work I was doing in litigation for the industrial groups. In that context, I remember he remarked that he intended to stay on the left, adding, 'You can always move to the right, Jack' — a lot of people called me Jack, from earlier days. By which he meant, of course, that you can never move back to the left, once you have moved definitively away from it, and the time to do that, if you are going to do it at all — which I do not think he ever really intended — is at the critical and only moment. Evatt later showed that swinging from left to right and right to left could be attempted, but it did not benefit him much.

Ward, though a man of the left in Labor Party politics, was a conservative administrator. In New Guinea he could never be persuaded to take action of a significantly progressive kind. He did act to change the indentured labour system that had previously operated in New Guinea, but that was a matter he understood in terms of trade union rights. But to persuade him to agree to any progressive measures at all in colonial policy was an exceedingly difficult thing. He went on administering the Territory, broadly speaking, as would a conservative Minister. Certainly he did not seek to introduce any major change or push Murray to hasten any movement towards the acquisition of power by the indigenous people. Indeed, I remember putting it to him once that he was a conservative colonial Minister. To be called a colonial Minister was abhorrent to him — he did not think he *was* a colonial Minister. He subscribed to the view that Australia was not a colonial power by comparison with the old imperialist colonial powers — as a Government we were up there to do good. But I said to him, 'Look, you don't seem to understand that it's possible to have a socialist colonial policy. Now, there's a Labour Government in control in Britain at the present time. There are plenty of brilliant, able colonial administrators who support the Labour Government and who have a colonial policy for development of the colonies which they would regard as a socialist-oriented policy'. I had met some of them during the war-time years. I said, 'Why don't you get in touch with the British Colonial Secretary and ask him to lend you a good colonial administrator whose political orientation would be the same as your own? Someone like that would tell you how to approach it — what you should be doing to move things along'.

Ward never would follow that sort of advice. He quite explicitly said he would never ask the British to tell him how to run New Guinea—not even a British socialist. He could not believe that the British could do anything right in the colonies or that we could learn anything from them. The fact that someone was presented as a British socialist colonial expert did not impress him, he regarded them as tools of the British system.

The colonial system was of course being debated at that time, but few people if any foresaw the extraordinary speed of the coming rush to independence of so many countries. The debate itself was in any case beyond Ward's horizon. He was not a reader or leader in colonial matters and, speaking from my point of view, working with him when I was at the School between 1946 and 1948 was difficult because he had no policy destination. Murray gave him great personal support and had some broad ideas of improving the general position of the indigenous people, but it really was not pursuant to any militant Wardism—there was no such doctrine. I suppose I was rather impatient and a little restless—not quite as pragmatic as I thought I was.

It was a big enough job in New Guinea for the first three or four years trying to repair the war-time damage and re-establish the civilian administration, to set up departments of education and health and agriculture, to reorganise and staff District Services and get the territory working again. That was the task that faced Murray, in a climate of little enthusiasm from the European population for the attempts he made to give a better kind of recognition to the indigenous inhabitants. There was really little that Ward could have done in the short time before Labor went out of office in December 1949.

I did not think that Ward would make a future leader of the Labor Party, and he did not achieve any overall leadership though he was a strong and fiery debater and aspired to power. He had some factional power in the party but, in any event, the Labor split of the fifties meant that he was destined not to achieve even ministerial rank again. He died whilst still relatively young.

Apart from the Timber Royal Commission which launched me after the war and the meeting with Short which was to lead into the work with the industrial groups, a third development of consequence occurred not long after I went back to the Bar. It had to do with the Australian Stevedoring Industry Authority. Joe Hewitt, who had been a private secretary to Evatt and whom I knew, was at this time Deputy Chairman of the Authority, and Mr Justice Richard Kirby of the Commonwealth Conciliation and Arbitration Commission was Chairman of the Authority. The Authority ran the waterfront, and on that Authority as member for the union was Jim Healy, General Secretary of the Waterside Workers' Federation and a communist.

In 1949 Chifley became very much concerned about the communist leadership of the waterside workers, and he broke up the Authority and gave what had been its power in the arbitration field directly to the Commonwealth Conciliation and Arbitration Commission. Kirby was the man who, thereafter, handled the waterfront, from the point of view of wages and conditions, as settled by arbitration.

Hewitt became the Chairman of a new bureaucratic body called the Australian Stevedoring Industry Board which, generally speaking, appeared in all the cases, whether administrative or arbitral, that Kirby dealt with. Hewitt gave me regular briefs to appear for the Australian Stevedoring Industry Board before Kirby, and I did a great deal of work on the waterfront from 1949 or early 1950 onward — indeed on and off throughout the time that I was at the Bar. Sometimes big work, sometimes less important. I went through a Royal Commission into the waterfront with the brief from the Australian Stevedoring Industry Board. The Board had the task of dealing with the communist-led union and trying to keep it within bounds. Hewitt was until his death a close friend of mine from whom I learned a great deal about the practical side of communist activity in the unions.

One of the things that brought down Chifley and the Labor Party in 1949 was a rash of bad strikes in the late forties led by the communist unions. Chifley resorted to very strong methods of breaking the communist-led strikes, especially in the coalfields. Indeed, Chifley put the troops in to handle the problems that had arisen, and he took action as a result of which some leaders went to gaol.

By this time I found myself absorbed by professional and family life, as a young Sydney barrister with a growing practice and growing family commitments. Increasingly, however, my professional work had a national flavour, and this was more and more so as the years went by. I was not reconciled to the fact that my international experience appeared to be over; but it was not for some time that my horizon began again to widen and to embrace national and international concerns beyond my daily work in the courts.

9

Post-war Supply Crises;
Double Dissolution 1951;
Labor Endorsement for Lowe

During the late forties and early fifties, although busy with work at the Bar, I continued to observe with interest the passing national political parade. Some developments attracted my attention because of their constitutional significance, and in one case, the double dissolution of 1951, because it touched my own life. The others were supply issues at the level of the States.

A dissolution of the Victorian Legislative Assembly was granted on 8 October 1947 by the Governor of Victoria, Sir Winston Dugan, to the Labor Premier Mr John Cain. The Legislative Council had withheld supply from a Government undefeated in the Assembly, as a means of getting an election in which it and the Opposition parties in the Assembly could fight on the federal issue of bank nationalisation — a dramatic national issue. The Cain Government resisted, but finally gave in and accepted that it would have to resign and go to the people.

I had no reason to follow these Victorian events closely at that time. There was discussion and some constitutional authorities maintained that the Council should not have denied supply, partly because the Council members were elected on a restricted franchise. As I later learned, Sir Isaac Isaacs, who had retired from the office of Governor-General several years before, entered the debate, writing letters to the Melbourne *Age*. On 7 October he wrote: 'The matter is plain. The Council has gravely erred against the constitutional practice, and the Government is, in my opinion, not merely justified, but bound in duty to Victoria to resist it'. In his letter of 9 October he set out to make clear that he considered the Council had erred in regard not only to constitutional practice but also to constitutional law. He wrote:

'It is plain to me that the Council has "in effect" violated the Constitution in one of its most important respects. It has "in effect" altered the Supply Bill . . . it is doing indirectly what it is forbidden to do directly. That is "in effect", though not technically, a violation, and it is an evasion of the prohibition against altering the bill'.

What is meant by the phrase 'in effect' and by the concession that 'technically' there had been no violation of the Constitution? It is hard to see, if this is conceded, how there could have been a breach by the Council of constitutional law.

In a third letter, on 11 October, Sir Isaac said: 'Surely if the Council cannot insist in striking out a word, but it must be as the Assembly "may see fit", it cannot insist, except for some reason I have previously indicated, in rejecting at will, the whole Bill'. Sir Isaac is an eminent authority but his opinion did not carry the day, and to the best of my knowledge no one tried to act upon it to get a legal decision from the courts so as to frustrate the Council in its intention. The Labor Government accepted that it had to agree to a dissolution.

Sir Isaac had said on 7 October that the Government was bound in duty to Victoria to resist the Council. But the next day, 8 October, so far from resisting, the Government recognised that it must go to the people. How could it properly resist? By governing, or attempting to govern without supply? It did not apparently believe that it could properly do so. The Labor Government, presumably in the interests of the people, conceded that a complete deadlock on supply between the two Houses made an election inevitable. It was an act of statesmanship on the Premier's part to accept the inevitable; abide by the principle that if he failed to secure supply he would have to test the people's reaction to the Council's decision to deny it; and refrain from action which might force the Governor to resort to the reserve powers. His action, objectively assessed, relieved the Governor of any necessity himself to force the issue to the people.

A Tasmanian precedent was set in 1948, which I later had an opportunity to study by reference to the relevant parliamentary papers. On 8 July 1948, only nine months after the events in Victoria, the Tasmanian Legislative Council, in dealing with a

Bill to apply moneys out of the Consolidated Revenue for the year 1948–9, passed a resolution returning the Bill to the Assembly with a request that the Assembly amend the Bill to reduce the supply granted to two months' supply, 'on the understanding that the Government seek an immediate dissolution of the House of Assembly for the purpose of a General Election'.

The House then expressed its disagreement with the Council. It argued that the proposed amendment was designed to force a dissolution of the House for which the Government, having its confidence, could see no valid reason. It claimed that it had been denied supply to raise an issue in regard to the Government's support of a recent federal referendum for the transfer of powers over prices and rents to the Commonwealth. The Council denied this, saying its attitude was based upon the general loss of confidence by the electors in the Government.

The House argued, in the usual fashion, that the Council was acting unconstitutionally. It said that 'by long usage the practice has been indisputably established that Second Chambers such as the Legislative Council have no power to reject a pure money Bill such as a Supply Bill. The constitution does not contemplate that the power to reject a Money Bill shall be used in the manner in which the Legislative Council now seeks to use it, but only in specific cases where a Legislative Council does not agree to expenditure of public funds for specific purposes'.

The Assembly argued that there was no Tasmanian precedent to justify the Council's action and that if the Council had, as it claimed, the right to force an election by refusing the Government supply the whole structure of the legislature would be fundamentally altered. The mainspring of government would be transferred from the popularly elected House of Assembly to the Legislative Council which is elected on a restricted franchise.

In reply the Council said, *inter alia*:

> In the view of the Legislative Council the Act of 1926 [which gave it its power on Money Bills] leaves no room for a conventional code to continue side by side with the new legal code as to Money Bills. The position in Tasmania, from the point of view of constitutional

power, is now the same as under the Constitution of the Commonwealth, from which the Tasmanian Act was largely copied. If the Federal Senate should reject a Supply Bill, it could not be suggested it had acted unconstitutionally. The action might of course be criticised on political grounds, but its constitutional power would be undoubted for the reason that the Commonwealth Constitution is an Act of Parliament, dealing comprehensively with the powers of all the organs of government. The Legislative Council does not, by this statement, suggest that there are no practical limitations upon these powers not appearing in the Act itself. But such limitations are of a political and not a constitutional character.[1]

The power to defer supply exists equally with the power to reject.[2]

The 1947 precedent and Sir Isaac Isaacs' views were canvassed in the debate between the two Houses, but the Tasmanian Council was not deterred.

A Conference of Managers of both Houses of the Tasmanian Parliament was held and failed to reach agreement. The Legislative Council then laid the Bill aside on 15 July 1948. On 20 July the Premier, who headed a Labor Government, made a statement in the House in which he said: 'Ministers reaffirm their contention that the Council has not properly exercised with regard to the Supply Bill whatever constitutional powers it may be held to possess; it has acted against constitutional practice; and, moreover, has violated the Constitution.'

He nevertheless announced that if the Council persisted in its attitude 'the Government in the interests of the people will recommend His Excellency the Governor to dissolve the House of Assembly forthwith'.[3]

This happened and an election was held, the Government clearly thinking that in the absence of supply no alternative course could be contemplated. As in Victoria in 1947 and later in 1952, the Government in Tasmania accepted the inevitable. It is very significant that the Premier in conceding that he should go to the people said that the Government had decided to take this course 'in the interests of the people'. This act of statesmanship, as in the 1947 Victorian example, relieved the Governor of any need to decide whether in the event of a decision to govern without supply, or to try to do so, he should exercise his reserve powers to dismiss and force the issue to the people. Of course an element of electoral judgment may enter into cases similar to the 1947 Victorian and 1948 Tasmanian ones. The Premiers may have gone to the people believing they would win the election. It could hardly be said, in constitutional terms, that a Government denied supply has to go to the people only if it believes it can win but does not have to do so if it believes it will lose. It would be hard to frame a constitutional principle based upon the prediction of the electoral outcome. Dicey's attempt to do this in relation to the prerogative of dismissal and forced dissolution is now discredited. In any event the Labor Premier of Tasmania did what he did 'in the interests of the people'.

A constitutional crisis of significance occurred in Victoria in 1952. I followed this too with interest but not in detail, refreshing my memory in more recent times because of its relevance to two separate discretionary powers of the Crown. The Melbourne press on 13 October 1952 reported that Mr John McDonald's Government was expected to fall because the Labor Party had decided to refuse supply in the Upper House to any Government except one led by the Liberal, Mr T. T. Hollway, who was pledged to electoral reform for the Lower House — to a redistribution scheme. It was therefore a case of the Labor Party threatening to assist in withholding supply in the Upper House in order to force an election to achieve an important political end. Two Liberal and Country Party members of the Legislative Council had agreed to support the denial of supply so as to force an election on the distribution issue. Supply was due to expire on 31 October.

The Melbourne *Age* in an editorial on 22 October said that since the Labor Party had withdrawn its support from the McDonald Country Party Government in July Victoria's Parliament had been in a crisis, which now seemed to be reaching its closing stages. 'It is,' said the *Age*, 'scarcely in keeping with the traditional role of the Upper House to interfere with money bills. But there is precedent in the Council's 1947 action, which precipitated an Assembly election by withholding supply from the then Labor Government'. The *Age* commented that there might be historic retribution in the reversal of party relationships. The public was confronted by a Parliament 'in such chronic deadlock as to be virtually unworkable'.

The McDonald Country Party Government was a minority Government, and when Labor withdrew its support the Liberal-Country Party took its place in keeping the McDonald Government in office. The redistribution issue had caused a cleavage in the Liberal-Country Party, and Hollway led the faction in that party that was in favour of electoral reform.

The Government challenged the power of the Legislative Council, saying it had no right to unseat the Government.

Supply was blocked by the Council and the Premier decided to seek a dissolution. But, according to the *Age* of 24 October, the Governor reached the conclusion that in the extraordinary circumstances that confronted him, only an emergency Government headed by Mr Hollway was capable of keeping the machinery of government moving and ensuring supply *before the vote ran out*; and that he must act accordingly. The risk was that Mr Hollway would fail to win the confidence of the Assembly, 'thus bringing about the Government's dismissal almost before it had properly begun to function'.

The new Government was soon in office, the former Premier having been refused a dissolution and having resigned. The new Government was, as predicted, defeated on the floor of the Assembly and Mr Hollway, the new Premier, asked for a dissolution. Mr Hollway's Government and the Labor Party maintained that Mr Hollway had been commissioned to obtain supply and had succeeded. He should retain his commission as Premier for the inevitable election. The Governor had to decide whether Mr Hollway should go to the people as Premier or Mr McDonald be recommissioned.

Mr McDonald having failed to get supply had recommended a dissolution. Mr Hollway having obtained supply had failed to obtain the confidence of the Lower House. The Governor, having earlier refused the request for a dissolution by Mr McDonald, refused the request for a dissolution by Mr Hollway and asked him for his resignation, which was reluctantly given. Mr McDonald was then commissioned and the Governor granted a dissolution of the Assembly.

This precedent is important for a number of reasons. It is in significant respects different from what happened in the federal Parliament and in federal affairs in October–November 1975. It was important in that, first, it was the second precedent in recent times in Victoria, making with the 1948 Tasmanian case three modern precedents for an Upper House refusing supply. Secondly, it offered the precedent of a Governor exercising his discretion and refusing a dissolution to a Premier who advised it and who could not obtain supply, virtually forcing him to resign, as he did. Thirdly, it was a precedent of a Governor exercising his discretion to obtain supply and explore the workability of the House under another Premier. Fourthly, since it turned out that the new Premier though successful in getting supply was not able to win the Assembly's confidence, it was a precedent of the Governor exercising his discretion and refusing the new Premier a dissolution though he advised it, obtaining his resignation and recommissioning the previous Premier. All of this went unchallenged in the courts.

In the light of all these precedents it is surely difficult to argue that an Upper House does not in constitutional practice and law have the power to reject supply, whatever political motives may be involved in its doing so.

I turn now to the national scene. A constitutional issue arose in 1951 concerning a double dissolution of the Commonwealth Parliament. The Governor-General at the time was William McKell.

Mr W. J. McKell, the Labor Premier of New South Wales, in 1947 had been appointed as Governor-General. The appointment had aroused controversy. An earlier appointment to the office, that of the first Australian Governor-General Sir Isaac Isaacs in 1930, had also been controversial; but in Mr McKell's case the objection was because he came from active partisan politics rather than because he was an Australian.

I could see no reason to criticise the appointment on either score. My father, then fifty-seven years of age, was delighted to see his old apprenticeship mate in the position. I felt sure Mr McKell would be able to bring to the office the impartiality and objectivity indispensable to it. I was accustomed to seeing barristers from both sides of politics do just that on becoming judges. McKell was a barrister although not a practising one. He had been a member of the Lang Cabinet during the 1932 crisis, and later as Premier had been directly in contact with vice-regal life in the State of New South Wales. I had no doubt he would exercise his role with appropriate independence of mind, and no fear that he would put his discretions at the disposal of a Labor Government or Opposition because of his own political beliefs.

By no means everyone took that point of view, and his accession to office was attended by a significant period of press and other speculation and criticism. For example Mr Archie Cameron, who later became Speaker of the House of Representatives, along with other members boycotted Government House — a boycott which continued after he became Speaker. The top protocol list for all State banquets at Government House includes the Speaker in a position of high precedence. *Plus ça change, plus c'est la même chose.*

But McKell was to prove that as Governor-General he was in no way politically biased: he did his job objectively and well and this came to be understood and assumed by the public. By the time the Australians Lord Casey and Sir Paul Hasluck came to hold the office, the principle that impartiality could be counted on from men of integrity, irrespective of the fact that they had included politics in their careers, was clearly understood and accepted by the public at large.

To suppose that any person of quality would allow his judgment to be swayed by partisan support of former political associates when he has accepted the responsibilities of the Governor-Generalship indicates both a total failure to understand the nature of that office and an inability to grasp the concept of integrity. An extreme form of this distortion of view which I personally encountered after the events of 1975 was the complaint that I had failed to adopt a pro-Labor stance and to support those who had appointed me. Labor was the party I supported in my earlier years, but that was just as irrelevant, when in 1975 my vice-regal duty compelled me to take action in dismissing Mr Whitlam, as was the fact that I had detached myself from the Labor Party, and from direct party politics in general, more than twenty years before—after the split in the Labor Party in 1954–5. Similarly, it was irrelevant to my performance of my duties as a federal judge and as Chief Justice that both of those appointments were made by Liberal-Country Party Governments. The relevant fact in 1975 was that I had a duty to carry out as Governor-General, that is to say without fear or favour, affection or ill-will.

To be unable to grasp this principle is a sorry condition. To claim that I was a 'traitor' to the Labor Party is as ridiculous as to suggest that I should have given preferential treatment to those who appointed me. You do not buy a man when you appoint him.

When it came to the events leading up to the double dissolution of 1951 I was, as a young man, watching with a much more personal involvement than I had the supply crises in the States.

I was now increasingly engaged in important litigation in which communist leadership in Australian unions was under legal challenge. It was also under running internal political challenge at toughly fought elections inside certain unions. My membership of the Labor Party and my legal activities marked me in leftist eyes, when taken together with my known anti-Stalinism, as being of the right wing of the Labor Party, and this was so. Nevertheless the antagonisms that later led to the 1954–5 split had not up to 1951 been by any means as intense as they later became. It was understandable that a junior Labor barrister of thirty-six might contemplate entering federal politics, and contemplate it I did.

I looked around for a possible seat and soon came to the conclusion that a winnable seat was not available. Friends of mine in 'Room 32' of the Trades Hall, then the centre of power in the New South Wales branch of the Labor Party, suggested that I should stand for an unwinnable seat, thus earning an 'honest scar' in the service of the party and waiting for another day. I accepted this advice and was endorsed, somewhat unenthusiastically on my part, for the federal seat of Lowe, the sitting member being Mr (now Sir William) McMahon, who many years later became Prime Minister. He had entered Parliament in 1949 when the Chifley Government was defeated. There was no chance of my unseating him.

So it came about that when the 1951 double dissolution occurred it was to have been I who would be the candidate against Mr McMahon. In fact it was John Burton who stood.

Burton had been the Secretary of the Department of External Affairs in Evatt's later years as Minister for External Affairs in the Chifley Government. When Labor was defeated in 1949 he stayed on for a year or so under the new Minister, Mr Spender (now Sir Percy), and helped in organising the Colombo Plan, an international aid programme on behalf of south and south-east Asian countries in the initiation of which Australia and Ceylon (now Sri Lanka) played leading parts. In 1950 or 1951 he left his position as Secretary and accepted an appointment as High Commissioner to Ceylon.

Accordingly when the 1951 double dissolution occurred Burton was in Ceylon. I was dumbfounded to receive a telephone call from him from Colombo and to learn that he had decided to return home to stand in the 1951 election. It seemed to me impossible for him to get a selection at such a late date. He arrived in Darwin and in due course made a public attack upon the Government. I told Burton that I had the Labor endorsement for Lowe; that it was not in my opinion winnable, that I was not very keen to stand myself and would step aside in his favour if Room 32 agreed.

He accepted this proposal, and the two of us went down to Room 32 and discussed the idea with the Secretary and Assistant Secretary of the New South Wales branch of the party. They ultimately agreed.

Burton stood, as a result, in the election following the 1951 double dissolution. He duly, indeed inevitably, lost.

This being the background to the 1951 double dissolution and the election that followed, it can be readily imagined that I had been following the issues that led to that double dissolution with practical personal interest. There was also the intellectual interest provided by this example of the exercise of a vice-regal discretion, and of its handling between the Prime Minister, Mr Menzies, and the Governor-General, Sir William McKell.

Sir William had to consider Mr Menzies' advice that he should grant a double dissolution. I watched the build-up to Sir William's decision with attention, because I believed he had a true discretion to exercise, and I was aware that some people maintained that his long-standing Labor connections would affect his decision. At that time too I believed that if he decided in favour of a double dissolution I should be standing for Lowe. The theoretical issues involved in the 1951 double dissolution were not abstract or academic questions for me but very real political and constitutional questions affecting my immediate future as well as reflecting my past studies.

The key question in the 1951 double dissolution was whether the Senate had failed to pass a Bill which came to it, in accordance with section 57, after three months had elapsed since its first rejection or failure to pass the Bill. The Senate on this second occasion, after considerable delay, referred the Bill to a committee for consideration, and the question was whether in the circumstances it had on the second occasion failed to pass the Bill.

A very real point arose as to whether it was for the Governor-General to decide whether the Senate had failed to pass the Bill for a second time. If so, he must decide whether, in the exercise of his personal discretion, he would grant a double dissolution.

On the question of the Governor-General's discretions and his right to outside advice on the exercise of his discretionary powers the 1951 double dissolution must be examined. On this point the papers relating to it are revealing. They show that opinions were furnished to the Governor-General by the Prime Minister. These were opinions of the Attorney-General Senator John Spicer and the Solicitor-General Professor Sir Kenneth Bailey.

When in 1956 the Prime Minister tabled the documents, he said that in his opinion an occasion had arisen in 1951 warranting the making of a decision by the Governor-General that both Houses should be dissolved. However, he had advised the Governor-General that he was entitled to make up his own mind on the matter. The Prime Minister was the Liberal leader Mr Menzies; the Governor-General was a former Labor Premier of New South Wales, appointed to office by a Labor Government

The Prime Minister's words in his foreword to the documents being tabled were:

In the course of our discussion, I had made it clear to His Excellency that, in my view, he was not bound to follow my advice in respect of the existence of the conditions of fact set out in section 57, but that he had to be himself satisfied that those conditions of fact were established.[4]

In that foreword he added that 'His Excellency said that he thought section 57 spoke for itself, but he would naturally want to satisfy his own mind about the performance of the conditions'.

That statement of Mr Menzies, agreeing as it did with the general approach of Sir Samuel Griffith and Dr Evatt, was made only a little over twenty years ago. The independent discretion of the Governor-General in matters arising under section 57, as Evatt said in his *Canadian Bar Review* article[5], applies also to a single dissolution of the House. Indeed it must logically apply in some circumstances to the Governor-General's discretions under sections 5, 28, 57 and 64.

The view of Sir William McKell in 1951 was the same as that of Mr Menzies, namely that he had to satisfy his own mind. So we have Evatt's opinion expressed in 1936 and 1940 confirmed in 1951 by Mr Menzies and by a Governor-General of true Labor extraction. This had also been Sir Samuel Griffith's advice accepted by the Governor-General in 1914.

Professor Cowen in his introduction to Evatt's book went to some pains to point out that nothing in the documents relating to the 1951 double dissolution indicated that the Governor-General was not entitled to independent advice, nor was there any assertion in the Government documents of any obligation to act on the advice of Ministers.[6] In fact opinions were tendered to the Governor-General by both Law Officers. Professor Bailey's opinion, tabled in 1956 with the other documents, examined and endorsed an earlier opinion of Sir Robert Garran, a famous founding father and long-time Solicitor-General. In his opinion Garran considered 'many ways in which the passage of a Bill may be prevented or delayed'. Professor Bailey's opinion concluded as follows:

Perhaps the principle involved can be expressed by saying that the adoption of Parliamentary procedures for the purpose of avoiding the formal registering of the Senate's clear disagreement with a Bill may constitute a 'failure to pass' it within the meaning of the section. The proceedings in the Senate in relation to a Bill must I think be appraised in the light of some such principle. While therefore the preliminary question on which the Governor-General must be satisfied can properly be said to be a question of fact, its ascertainment is a matter rather of political interpretation or elucidation than the mere establishment of acts and events.

Professor Bailey is here affirming specifically that what is committed to the Governor-General for exercise of his discretion includes political interpretation or elucidation. This certainly applies in my view in the case of a dismissal of a Government having the confidence of the House of Representatives, in which case the exercise of the discretion is not examinable in a court. Such ascertainment of facts and such 'political interpretation or elucidation' as may be necessary in such a dismissal must be matters for the Governor-General's discretion. In a complex situation he has to interpret and elucidate what is the factual situation at the relevant time.

In his abovementioned foreword Sir Robert Menzies says he took the oral advice of Mr Garfield Barwick, K.C. Sir Kenneth Bailey's opinion is dated 16 March 1951. Sir Robert in his foreword, having previously said he had sent Mr Barwick a record of the parliamentary history of the Bill, stated:

> On the evening of March 15th, I also saw Mr Barwick who had, by that time, stated his opinion to the Attorney-General and the Solicitor-General after a complete examination of the records. When Mr Barwick saw me, I showed him the draft letter to the Governor-General which I had, during the afternoon, prepared. Having perused this, he advised orally that, in his opinion, the submission I was making was completely justified on the facts and in terms of the Constitution.

Having regard to Barwick's conferences with Menzies and Bailey and the opinions expressed to the effect that the Governor-General had himself to be satisfied that the conditions referred to in section 57 had been fulfilled, it is clear that the Governor-

Sir John Kerr, Governor-General of Australia, July 1974 to December 1977. (Age)

John, aged three.

John Kerr, graduate in Law, 1936.
(John Fairfax and Sons Ltd)

Alison Kerr, soon after their marriage in 1938.

*Dr H. V. Evatt and John Kerr at an Old
Fortians dinner in 1960.* (John Fairfax and Sons Ltd)

Third Commonwealth and Empire Law Conference, Sydney, 1965: the Prime Minister, Mr Menzies, John Kerr and Lord Gardiner, Lord High Chancellor of England. (News Ltd)

General, the Prime Minister, the Attorney-General, the Solicitor-General and Mr Barwick, K.C. as an independent adviser all believed that the Governor-General had this independent decision-making power.

Professor Cowen mentioned the discussion which took place in the press at the time of the 1951 double dissolution. He said:

> While these events were unfolding, the question was actively discussed in the Press. It was said that Labor members believed that the Governor-General would not accept the Prime Minister's advice, and it was also suggested that the Governor-General might seek the independent legal advice of the Chief Justice of the High Court, Sir John Latham. There was much discussion of the 1914 case when Sir Ronald Munro Ferguson had consulted the Chief Justice, Sir Samuel Griffith, who had furnished him with a detailed memorandum.
>
> In fact the Governor-General did not seek independent advice and accepted the advice of the Prime Minister, supported by the opinions of the Attorney-General and Solicitor-General. It is noteworthy that no reference was made in these documents to any obligation or supposed obligation of the Governor-General to accept ministerial advice. In 1914 Mr Cook had urged this obligation on Sir Ronald Munro Ferguson as a ground for granting the requested dissolution.[7]

It is, of course, inconceivable that the abundant speculation to be found in the press of the period was unknown to Dr Evatt. In 1951 he was deputy leader of the Labor Party. Had he felt, contrary to his published views expressed as recently as 1940, that the Governor-General had no discretion and no right to independent advice, it is hardly likely that in intellectual honesty he could have silently allowed Labor members to be canvassing the possibility of the Governor-General consulting the Chief Justice as he had himself previously said was proper. The attitude of Labor Party members in 1951 is further confirmation, if it were needed, that Evatt in 1951 was of the same opinion as he had been in 1940.

When Robert Menzies tabled on 24 May 1956 the 1951 papers, with his foreword saying that the Governor-General had the right to make up his own mind about the satisfaction of the conditions laid down in section 57, the following discussion took place in the House:

> *Mr Menzies:* I lay on the table the following paper —
>> Documents relating to the Simultaneous Dissolution of the Senate and the House of Representatives by His Excellency the Governor-General on 19th March, 1951.
>
> I have annexed to the documents a narrative of the events immediately preceding the tendering to His Excellency of the advice which I gave him.
>
> *Dr Evatt:* Does the Prime Minister intend to move that the paper be printed?
>
> *Mr Menzies:* No, it has already been printed.
>
> *Dr Evatt:* I know, but in order that the matter may be discussed, if desired, I wish to move —
>> That the paper be printed.
>
> *Mr Deputy Speaker:* Notice is required of such a motion.
>
> *Dr Evatt:* I ask for leave of the House to give notice of my intention so to move.
>
> Leave granted.
>
> *Dr Evatt:* I give notice that at the next sitting I shall move —
>> That the following paper, laid on the table of the House on the 24th May, be printed:
>> Documents relating to the Simultaneous Dissolution of the Senate and the House of Representatives by His Excellency the Governor-General on 19th March 1951.
>
> *Mr Calwell:* We shall have an interesting half hour.
>
> *Mr Menzies:* I do not need to tell the honorable members that if there is to be a debate I should like to be in it.
>
> *Mr Deputy Speaker:* Order![8]

There was thereafter no further debate on these papers and the motion foreshadowed by Dr Evatt was never proposed and debated. Mr Menzies' last remark as quoted shows how much he would have relished having Dr Evatt expounding his views on the power of the Governor-General. The backbencher Mr Whitlam, one assumes, must have followed all this attentively in 1956.

It may be unlikely today that a Chief Justice would allow himself to be consulted about whether there had in fact been a 'failure to pass' in relation to a double dissolution under section 57 because such an issue has recently been held, at least in some circumstances, to be justiciable, though on the question whether the Governor-General had a duty to make up his own mind the position could be different. But a Governor-General, as Evatt said, can in any event on such an issue, so far as his own decision is concerned, go elsewhere for advice, and this certainly applies *a fortiori* to non-justiciable issues on which he can go to the Chief Justice, if the latter is willing to advise, as well as to others.

So in 1951 my first and only active step publicly towards a political career came to nothing. I cannot say that I regretted or regret it. But 1951 was important in another way. It constituted part of my education about the role of the Governor-General, a study on which I had fortuitously embarked at seventeen years of age in the vital year of 1932. Nineteen years later I was having the experience of watching vice-regal power illustrated in a different context, with Evatt, and indeed all members of the Labor Party, in 1956 failing to bring on a debate or otherwise attempt to cast doubt on the existence of the vice-regal discretion. They expressed no disagreement in Parliament with Mr Menzies or Sir William McKell when the opportunity for such a debate arose.

10

The Great Labor Split of 1954–5; the 1955 Dissolution

The Ironworkers' Ballot enquiry that followed my conversation with Laurie Short in the last days of 1949 went on for a long time, and during its course I came to realise what the industrial groups were. The Secretary of the industrial groups was Jack Kane, Assistant Secretary of the New South Wales branch of the Labor Party, later Senator Kane, and also Federal Secretary of the Democratic Labor Party. Industrial groups were organised in many trade unions which were controlled by communists: the object of the groups was to dislodge them. It was mainly Catholics who joined industrial groups in the unions and were willing to work constantly, finding candidates to stand against communists and to endeavour to beat them in union elections. Short was not a Catholic, but most members of the groups were.

The litigation for the industrial groups was generally concerned with breaches of union rules, members of the groups being wrongfully expelled or deprived of office or rights, or wrongfully punished, or the rules being erroneously interpreted in relation to elections, candidature and the like. Orders had to be obtained to prevent or remedy these breaches.

As a person who was interested intellectually in the communist story I was opposed to a Stalinist-led Communist Party and to Stalinist activity in unions. The industrial groups litigation came congenially to me, not for religious reasons, as was the case with the Catholics, but I had read widely of the horrors and terrors of Stalinism, the purges, the appalling inhumanity of the Stalinist regime in Russia, and I was an anti-Stalinist for intellectual and political reasons.

I was willing to help. I did not realise, to start with, the degree of disciplined organisation that went into the industrial groups in these unions. But in any event I had no problems in accepting industrial group briefs. I did what the briefs required. Many people imagined I must be a Catholic to be doing so much work in these 'Grouper' cases, just as other people imagined the barristers on the other side must really be communist fellow-travellers, or communist sympathisers.

To be gradually gaining a reputation in industrial group work was far from damaging in the development of a career at the Bar. Work started to come from various quarters. In Labor Party circles however there were people like Ward who criticised me for helping the industrial groups. I said to Ward, 'If you fellows would give leadership things would be different. If you really believed in the Labor Party, you would give leadership in this. You would not leave it more or less exclusively to active Catholics. You would say, if the Labor Party is fit to run the country it is also fit to run the unions which are affiliated with it and you would give leadership to people who are setting out to defeat communism in trade unions. But you don't do it; you leave the field exclusively to Catholics, or almost exclusively so, and then you complain because it is Catholics who are carrying on the fight. It's a fight that you don't carry on yourselves and if it were not carried on by them, it would be carried on by nobody. Communist strength would grow in the unions and in the Labor Party through the unions' influence on the Labor Party.'

This approach of mine did, to some extent, adversely affect my relations with certain people. I found myself, so far as Labor supporters were concerned, being identified more and more with the right wing. In fact, I always believed in a Labor Party that had both a left wing and a right wing, that was balanced on these two wings and was therefore a coalition. Of course there are never clear-cut left and right wings. There is movement between them and people alter their position according to the issue but broadly speaking one can usually detect the two types of general position in the party—on the right or the left. Such a party is often forced, by a series of compromises such as are necessary in every coalition, to adopt a middle of the road moderate policy. This is what Chifley and Curtin were able to do: leading such a party, they were able to steer a course more or less in the centre, perhaps slightly to right or to left to keep the party stable. Once the party falls into the hands either of its right wing or of its left, it becomes difficult, as later events showed, for it to win and hold power.

By the end of 1951 we had wound up the Ironworkers' Ballot case and Short was National Secretary of the Ironworkers' Union.

Through the period of the Timber Royal Commission and the industrial groups stage I was still a member of the Labor Party. I took silk in 1953 — I was thirty-nine. On the basis of successes for the industrial groups in a number of trade unions I knew that work could come to me as a silk. I then set out to develop my practice as a Queen's Counsel. It was based initially on Labor work and on work coming to me through Hewitt for the Australian Stevedoring Industry Board. Before and after taking silk I came more and more to see that the industrial groups were organised and disciplined groups, mainly of Catholics who were associated in some other way than merely through the industrial group organisation of the Labor Party.

Nobody saw fit to expose to me the details of their organisation and I did not myself know any details except that B. A. Santamaria, a Melbourne Catholic, who later became very well known on the Australian political scene, seemed to be important in it. I had never heard the term 'the Movement', for example, until about 1954, but I knew that the Catholics in these industrial groups were always able to mobilise a lot of support, to engage in canvassing and preparing propaganda, in fund-raising and similar activities and there must, therefore, be some machine at work, somewhere. Jack Kane was a very good organiser and it all appeared on the surface to be being done through the Labor Party, but this I knew could not be fully true.

Evatt was very ambivalent about it all. He was anxious to win the 1954 election, which was the Petrov election, and I was known to have associations with the industrial groups. Evatt thought that by co-operating with the right wing and getting behind him those able to win in union elections, by building that into a coalition in support of himself, he could defeat Menzies in the election which was held in 1954. The industrial groups for their part, I have no doubt, hoped to gain some leadership support in their struggle against communism in the unions.

Before the 1954 election Evatt opened the Federated Ironworkers' Union Conference, which was a right-wing conference dominated by Short and controlled by Groupers. He also went, towards the same time, to a Sunday meeting of all the industrial groups in the Labor Party. I went to both of those meetings with him at his request, because he was uncomfortable in such circles. He believed he had made a bargain with the right wing—the Groupers—as a result of which he could and would win the national election in 1954, and he said to me on one occasion that if they let him down, if he discovered that what he thought to be an agreed co-operation turned out not to be—he never really trusted them—he would take some retaliatory action.

I was never close to Evatt again after my early days at the Bar. However, during the war-time years I often called on him to have a talk. When, after the war, having become a political figure he encountered public criticism for appearing in litigation before the High Court of which he had formerly been a justice, I defended him in letters to the press.[1] Although I still saw him from time to time and talked with him, I became less and less an admirer of Evatt the man. He was in many respects a strange person: he was very suspicious and trusted few people, if any. I found his company less and less congenial. I made no attempt after the war to continue on the basis of the old relationship of my student days and my early days at the Bar. Basically too, he did not like the work I was doing for the industrial groups, though as a leader aspiring to victory he tolerated them in the hope he could get their machine behind him in the 1954 election.

The Petrov case broke and he lost the election, but he lost it, so he always believed, not solely or even mainly because of Petrov, but because in certain electorates and in certain ways the bargain he believed he had made was not kept. He said he believed that Santamaria and those around him had moved in such a way as to prevent certain seats being won, which would have had to be won to enable him to become Prime Minister; he believed that 1954 was an election he could have won if the Labor Party had been truly united behind him. Whether there was any substance in these beliefs of Evatt I do not know.

He then launched out and made an attack on the Movement, proclaiming that it had been set up for the highly secret, highly organised infiltration of the Labor Party by dedicated Catholics; that they were not interested in the Labor Party as such but had outside interests of their own and were trying to capture the party and its machine for their own purposes; that they would dominate and control the party if they could.

This was a dramatic outburst from a Labor leader. He set out deliberately to have them excluded from the party — to have the Movement destroyed and its adherents and supporters cast out from the Labor Party forever. That was the beginning of a great split and is a remarkable story in itself. Gradually it extended to all of Australia.

In the midst of this, I came to the conclusion that I was neither a supporter of the newly emerging separatist right-wing group — shortly to become the Democratic Labor Party — nor was I any longer interested in being a member of the Labor Party itself, because it was, as I saw it, firmly in the hands of its own left wing, of which I was an opponent. Moreover I felt that a leadership which allowed such a disaster to overtake a great party was an incompetent and hopeless leadership. I could no longer identify with that party.

A number of my friends disagreed with me and believed that, as had happened in other splits within the Labor Party, the separatist group would wither away and die; that the Labor Party — the great Labor Party — would come back as a coalition of all the forces that opposed the Liberal-Country Party coalition.

My opinion was that even if this were possible it would take twenty years. The Movement was too well organised and too strong and too likely to survive; at the same time it was a Catholic organisation and could not aspire to independent political power as a majority party.

It was in this context that I found myself again in contact with one of the friends whose lives were interlaced with mine at different phases and in various circumstances. James McAuley had thrown in his lot in Catholic circles with Santamaria.

When I had known McAuley earlier it was first of all when he was in a bohemian phase at the university, in Arts, iconoclastic and gifted in subtle satire. After graduation we met often in a group to which we both belonged for an end-of-the-day drink at Usher's Hotel in Sydney, now gone, where we talked politics and debated the general problems of the late thirties and earlier forties. Along with his literary preoccupations McAuley always had pungent, realistic and practical things to say about current affairs. He has described our pre-war group as being from Labor to further left including a couple who were or had been Trotskyists. There were no Stalinists. He has said that he doubted if in those days I gave much attention to Marxism as such, or thought of it as a live option. In this he was right.

In the course of the war-time contacts of which I have written, both in the Directorate and in the Australian School of Pacific Administration, I spent a lot of time with him socially in his home and mine. A pleasant friendship developed between us.

McAuley had, early in his life, abandoned religion, but in the years after the war gradually returned to it and was ultimately converted, I believe while in New Guinea, to the Catholic faith. Shortly before that I had become the godfather to his first child who, after his conversion, was re-baptised with new Catholic godparents. Conversion calmed McAuley's soul, and as the years went by his personality matured and mellowed. After a time his poetry also reflected his new outlook and new spiritual certainty.

At the School McAuley became a close friend of Hal Wootten, who had joined the staff as a tutor. He has written that in our industrial group days Wootten and I in conversation with him enabled him to gain the essential knowledge of the relations between industrial and political power in the Labor movement 'without which Australian politics as a whole does not make sense'.

It was McAuley who in the fifties persuaded me to join the Council of the Australian Association for Cultural Freedom, of which the retired Chief Justice of Australia, Sir John Latham, was then President (and in which McAuley and I had our differences); who interested me in the Orr case[2]; and who gradually became more strongly and articulately anti-communist. His original intellectual anti-communism was strengthened by his deep commitment to Catholicism. I had met Bob Santamaria a few times, before the schism in the Labor Party, having been introduced to him through Jack Kane and the industrial groups of the Labor Party. Separately from myself McAuley came to know Kane and Santamaria and became a friend of both. He valued the high intelligence of Santamaria and his judgments and opinions and the tough, practical abilities of Jack Kane.

It must have been some time after the split, in 1955, that I was invited to a meeting in a suburban cottage in Fivedock or Haberfield, Sydney. McAuley was there and Santamaria and others.

At the meeting they were talking about the organisation of a new party that was to be established. It was to be called the Democratic Labor Party. I was asked if I would join the new party and accept a role of leadership. I said that I would not. The way those who were forming the Democratic Labor Party saw it was that Evatt must be prevented from becoming Prime Minister. It was important to prevent the Labor Party from ruling whilst it was in the hands of the left wing. I could understand their viewpoint but I could not join them because their party could not have been formed on other than a sectarian basis.

I had always taken the view that the unwillingness of people like Evatt and Ward to lead an anti-communist movement in the Labor Party was a mistake. They had, as I saw it, now been forced to produce a split in order to keep the party in their own hands and to minimise right-wing strength, so delivering it into the hands of the left wing. To spend years around the edge of a leftist party, in which communist fellow-travelling views were strong, did not appeal to me. For me that meant breaking not only with the former Groupers, but with the Labor Party itself: its right wing severed, having been destroyed by the split, the Labor Party no longer attracted me. When I affirmed that I would not be interested in DLP leadership or membership and was moving out of Labor Party politics and industrial group politics altogether, my approach was that I could not identify with the DLP; that the DLP would necessarily be a Catholic party; that as a Catholic party it would survive and would keep Labor in the hands of its left wing for a very long time. That whole scenario was not for me.

Later I was told that McAuley had been taken somewhat aback at this, he and others having thought that I might be persuaded into co-operation. McAuley, I was told, said that the way I put it—the stark, frank, realistic way in which I put it—was like being hit over the face with a wet fish. He was always a poet.

Describing this meeting, in *Quadrant* of January 1976 McAuley wrote:

> It would also have been immensely helpful to the party in its beginnings if so splendid a figure as John Kerr had joined us with all his energy, ability and influence. Since the occasion has been mentioned in the press, I will recall here that I was present when John pronounced his negative answer to that proposition. While it was disappointing to those of us who desperately needed help, his decision was not unreasonable. Kerr had a lot to throw away: would any use he could have been really have justified the sacrifice in a perfectly honorable commonsense view? It's not really a question one can answer. I think that for a while John thought I was disappointed *in him*, because he wouldn't act in a way that he felt would be merely quixotic; but I always understood and respected the difficulty of the personal decisions that many people in NSW had to make at that time.

My last regular contact with McAuley was in the years before he went to Tasmania as Professor of Poetry and later of English Literature at the University of Tasmania. Thereafter, although we remained friends, I saw him only occasionally when he was in Sydney. It was not until towards the end of his life, after I became Governor-General, that I came into real contact with him again. In Tasmania early in 1975 I saw him, together with my old friend Professor Keith Isles of Directorate days, who after being Vice-Chancellor of the University of Tasmania was in retirement.

In February 1976 I was again in Hobart, staying at

Government House with my wife Anne, who had been on friendly terms with James and an admirer of his writing when they were colleagues at the Australian School of Pacific Administration. We met James and his wife at a formal reception in Government House. We knew then that he was very sick, though given some prospect of living. This led us to visit him at his house, as a long-standing friend of both of us whom we would perhaps not see often again.

McAuley knew that death was imminent. Later in 1976 he was in Sydney for medical treatment, and I saw him sometimes at Admiralty House. He was at that time particularly concerned and distressed about what he viewed as the serious decline in tertiary and secondary education in Australia. In so far as his physical state permitted he remained active and positive in his concern to the end of his life.

In general he was calm and indeed serene as death approached. His friendship with Santamaria had, he told me, continued. It was during that period, when I would have sought to be of comfort to him, that he was of great comfort to me. At the worst period of the 'rage' and the protests whipped up during 1976, he offered me the moving contrast of his intellectual lucidity, his felicity of expression, our long-standing and many-faceted friendship and our respect for each other's differences of approach and opinions.

McAuley had, however, no influence upon any aspect of the constitutional crisis of 1975, during which period I had no communication with him. Nor did I discuss the problems of those days with any of the former industrial groupers or with anyone in or around the DLP.

McAuley wrote in *Quadrant* in June 1976 that I told him at his home after the crisis that the period leading up to my decision was the loneliest and most difficult in my life because I could not consult anyone at all. This is true. In that article he said he was amazed to hear in December 1975 that it was common talk in the Canberra press gallery that he had been the guiding influence in my decision. This was false and he said so. He wrote: 'It is on this firm foundation of the utterly ludicrous that history began to be constructed'.

In his June article he commented on the fact that before 11 November 1975 'wiseacres were saying that Kerr was too weak to take any drastic action'. He wrote: 'Subsequently, therefore, since wiseacres cannot be wrong and the left is always right, an explanation had to be found why Kerr acted with such decisive effect. The political legend would not read aright unless he acted not on his own judgment but under some behind-scenes influence'.

McAuley was in hospital when the 1975 crisis unfolded. He published in *Quadrant* of January 1976 a cover-story in which he retraced our long friendship over the years. His memories substantially accord with my own. In the article he defended me calmly and rationally against detractors. Of my break with Evatt he said:

> The break with Evatt has been adduced as discreditable conduct. Evatt as a politician veered wildly and sharply from left to right to left, and he was in the middle of trying to execute another swift turn to the right when time ran out for him. What was one supposed to do in order to maintain integrity . . .? Evatt was a man with whom a break was practically inevitable. Anyway, it was Evatt who dumped Kerr, in fact.

What McAuley says is substantially true. Evatt wanted no more co-operation with me nor I with him, although occasional civilised contacts continued after he became Chief Justice of New South Wales. I would question the term 'dumping' since I was seeking no further relationship with Evatt. I did not regard myself as either dumped or dumping. A friendship had simply died.

McAuley went on to refer to Conlon, whom also I had been accused of deserting:

> Then there is the question of the later relations with Conlon. Towards the end of the war many of us already felt that Alf had lost control of himself and was skirting disaster. For a period after the war he became Principal of the Australian School of Pacific Administration which he had created. I was on the staff as lecturer in Government. It became painfully evident that the magic touch had

gone, both the spellbinding powers and the operational judgment. Members of the staff who had not known the Conlon of the great days frankly said they could not see the justification for the legend. Students in the courses — men at that time already with experience in New Guinea administration — obviously regarded his manner of presiding over the School with scant respect.

McAuley recounts, from his own view of it, what has been called 'the strike':

> In the tense period that followed it was John Kerr who spoke up and convinced Alf that he must quit. John's greater experience in confrontations and hard decisions enabled him to carry through a difficult task on our behalf and retain the capacity to deal personally with Alf on later occasions without obvious embarrassment. I never really got over the emotional trauma of having made the move, which I continued to believe was the necessary and right one; my relations with Alf thereafter always had a degree of embarrassment (as well as disillusion) from my side, though Alf sucked his pipe and was as cheerful as ever in later encounters.

There was, as I have said, a break with Conlon from about 1948 onwards in the sense of an assertion of psychological independence on my part. It was not a break in friendship: we remained friends till his death. We still visited one another's home. I visited him in hospital after his stroke. I was of course present at his funeral and afterwards at a big gathering of his friends.

McAuley's reflections continued:

> I have a legal friend who is close to John Kerr, and when we occasionally meet he likes to ask me what is my view of whatever is the latest development in John's career. We went through our ritual when the appointment to the Governor-Generalship was announced. We recalled that so many people over the years had expected John to become Prime Minister one day. We agreed that one reason why this didn't happen was because John lacked ruthlessness. He could never eat people for breakfast or wield the bloody axe. He is in fact a soft-hearted person who greatly dislikes taking part in the infliction of hurt on anyone, though in the end he will do what a commonsense practical judgment seems to require as right and necessary.

Rereading McAuley's words as I write this, I am reminded that on one occasion months before November 1975 the then Prime Minister said to me, 'Everyone tells me that if things had worked out right you would have been in my job'. He added, 'My opinion is, John, that you would never have made it. And the reason why you wouldn't have made it is that you are not ruthless enough'.

Some people did idly say to me over the years that the Prime Ministership was within my grasp—my failure to move politically may well have been due to a lack of ruthlessness, but political ruthlessness is one thing and carrying out a duty which one has undertaken is another—even when one has the regret of knowing it may have seriously adverse effects upon other people. Judicial life demands this and so it can be—albeit rarely—with the Governor-Generalship.

Reviewing in his mind our intertwined life stories McAuley concluded his article:

> Thinking over all this, as I lay in bed, I concluded that John Kerr probably would act in the way he soon after did. He would enjoy the opportunity for a grand dramatic moment: he would appreciate the opportunity, such as few Governors-General are given, to enter the history books. But he would not make his decision for these reasons, nor for any partisan reason, nor in any callous disregard of the effect his decision may have on individuals. He would have genuinely sought to discharge the duty of his office in the light of the law and good sense. I also think that Whitlam didn't understand Kerr at all, and thought he was being clever in making that nomination.

The decline of the Labor Party was strongly in evidence at the time of the 1955 dissolution of the House of Representatives, which furnished a further example of the exercise of a vice-regal discretion, by Sir William Slim. The dissolution was rather unusual in that the House had been in existence for only eighteen months—half of its term.

Mr Menzies was at that time strongly in control of his party and of the House of Representatives. He wanted to bring the House and half-Senate elections into line at simultaneous elections, and had economic arguments to support his request for

153

a dissolution. It seemed to me that his real reason was the distinct political advantage he might gain by dissolving early. The Labor Party was in disarray, Evatt's leadership was poor and the subject of internal conflict, his reaction to the Petrov enquiry and a famous letter he wrote to the Foreign Minister of the USSR, Molotov, all put the Labor Party on the wrong foot and made the time most propitious for Menzies to go to the people.

The Prime Minister set out to persuade Sir William Slim that he was entitled to an early dissolution, and Sir William granted it. It would be extremely difficult to justify refusing a dissolution to a Prime Minister who has the confidence of his party and of the House of Representatives and who is able to provide reasonable grounds for his advice. This does not mean, of course, that no discretion in the matter resides in the Governor-General, and Mr Menzies' handling of the situation recognised this. But in the absence of countervailing circumstances of a most unusual kind, a Governor-General would almost inevitably accept the advice given. Ironically enough Evatt himself, in his 1940 *Canadian Bar Review* article, expressed the view that in the very circumstances that were to arise in 1955 the Governor-General has *no* discretion and must act on the advice to dissolve. Menzies accepted a marginal discretion, as do I. However the matter is viewed, Evatt was a victim in 1955 of the doctrine he had expounded.[3]

I had no reason to follow this dissolution issue closely at the time: I saw it as an occasion for the exercise of the discretionary powers of the Governor-General, though one in which he had little real room to move. I have since had the opportunity to learn what happened between Sir William Slim and Mr Menzies at that time. Sir William undoubtedly saw himself as exercising a marginal discretion. The papers involved are personal and confidential and as yet unpublished. Nevertheless I had the benefit of this background knowledge when I was confronted by very similar circumstances in late 1977. In 1955, being interested in the discretionary powers of the Crown I merely noted the occasion as one for their exercise.

At that time my observation of events bore rather on the depth of decline of the Labor Party. I felt, with some real regret, that I was being proved right in my prediction. Although no longer a supporter of the Labor Party, I believed that a strong opposition was necessary for the health of the nation's political life. I remember an occasion when Lord Casey, then Minister for External Affairs, said to me at lunch how unfortunate from the country's point of view it was that the Labor Party was so weak and disorganised and obviously unable to provide an alternative Government.

From this time forward my contacts with Evatt came to an end except for an occasional casual meeting. There was no quarrel. There was a break. Contact virtually ceased from the time of the schism in the Labor Party in 1954–5. Nonetheless I realise that my life would have been different had I never known him. I remember always his spontaneous and generous help to me, an unknown student, at a vital time in my youth. His advice, his direct and indirect influence helped to mould my career. His thinking and writing as an eminent constitutional lawyer were of great value in my intellectual development.

In a taped interview recorded by John Thompson I gave some impressions of Evatt — in 1968, long after the Labor split and long before I became Governor-General. I include here extracts from the transcript as it stood in its original form (subject to correction of minor slips) for its interest as a live commentary, even though it may re-traverse to some extent material in the main text:

What was he like to deal with during the war?

Well, to deal with during the war, that was the time when I first began to see that it wasn't all the charming liberal. That was the only side of him that I knew. He could, of course, be extraordinarily charming, and personal relations with him whilst that was the mood were extremely good and in the early part of my contact with him when I was a very young man and he was talking about this and that he was always very charming, no problems at all. On the contrary, he was psychologically and in many other ways very forthcoming and helpful to me. But in the war-time years one saw, perhaps because of the stresses and strains, the first signs, I did anyhow, of the other side . . . of difficult personal relations, often insult and thrown out comments of a cruel and unnecessary kind, not even mainly to me but with others . . .

155

The Santamaria thing, this was a direct sort of difference of opinion between yourself and Evatt, wasn't it?

Oh, no. Now let's get this very clear. You see, the whole problem of Catholicism is very heavily mixed up in this now. I'm not a Catholic. Evatt was not a Catholic. I came into it, really, professionally to start with. I was in a whole series of cases, in which what was undoubtedly a Catholic-dominated, right-wing faction in trade union movements was having considerable success, as a result of organisation, the organisation being provided by what later came to be called the Movement . . .

Now this leads one, if you're talking about Dr Evatt, into what I consider to be the heart of the matter. The Labor movement has always consisted of a right wing and a left wing, and leadership of the Labor movement always has depended, if it's to be successful, on trying to ensure that those factions, those wings, are more or less even in strength and that the coalition between the two is built and controlled by a leader who can make quite sure that neither one nor the other dominates.

What was really happening with the right wing was that it was getting greater and greater strength and there was the feeling that it was controlled from outside the party.

Now my criticism of Dr Evatt, Mr Ward and others in those days was that they allowed the thing to happen. I had conversations with both of them, in which I put the point of view to Dr Evatt and to Mr Ward, that if they wanted to keep the party balanced, and a proper coalition situation possible within the party, there had to be leadership given to anti-communist movements, by the leaders, by Evatt and by Ward. They had to give leadership and provide the machinery and do what the politics of the day required. And if that had happened, I think the situation would have been different . . .

Would you feel looking back on him that you liked him on the whole? Is it hard to say?

Well, I did like a lot about him, but I disliked a lot about him and because of the constant recollection of earlier days when I was a Law student, I was always inhibited psychologically in reacting too strongly to that part of him which I didn't like as the years went by. I'd always felt controlled to some extent by earlier well-remembered occasions.

With the exception of McAuley, with whom I had contact for

a time in the Association for Cultural Freedom, and who over many years was editor of the Association's journal *Quadrant*, I saw little, after the split, of those in the DLP. At that 1955 meeting, when the DLP was in process of being organised as a political party, I had announced a decision which had been crystallising in me from the time of the great split. From then on my life was entirely different from what it had been. I was free.

Return to New Guinea Interests

I was out of politics altogether by 1955 and was building up my practice as a silk. I had good sources of work from the right-wing unions and on the waterfront; and I started to get work from employers, in arbitration matters, and from the Menzies Government and Commonwealth Government instrumentalities. Work also came from the State Labor Government. I moved without planning it in any detailed way out of Labor Party politics altogether and into what some people have called a pragmatic position in which I was interested in issues as they appealed to me, irrespective of party politics, and in consolidating and expanding my practice.

I wanted to be more of a generalist and ultimately I did achieve this. I put aside New Guinea; I put aside the Labor Party; and I worked hard and did well.

We bought a fairly large house at Turramurra in 1954 and we lived there for twenty years; all the children grew up there; and we were still living there when I was appointed Governor-General. It was a lovely old house and a happy place to live.

From 1954 or 1955 on, having turned my back on politics and elected life in Sydney and at the Bar, my horizon perhaps began to seem more confined than I found entirely satisfying. I had had no direct interest in New Guinea since I left the School of Pacific Administration. Then, in 1957, James Plimsoll asked me, exploring the question for the Australian Institute of Political Science, if I would present a paper for the Institute's Summer School in January 1958 on the subject of New Guinea's future. I agreed; and began then, really for the first time since 1948, to think again about New Guinea.

My paper expounded the idea—it was too late—of a Federation of Melanesia. The idea was that Dutch New Guinea and Australian New Guinea should be brought along to a common political future, with the British Solomons, as one State. We had already amalgamated German New Guinea, later the mandated and then the trust territory under Australian tutelage, with Papua which had previously been British and had become an Australian territory: to bring Dutch New Guinea and the British Solomons into one State with them would have resulted in all of those peoples, of common racial origin, common general culture, common background, becoming one political unit.

In 1957 when Mr Casey was Minister for External Affairs, the Dutch entered into a joint agreement with Australia to develop the two territories so as to leave open to them the prospect of ultimate political union. The Dutch were trying to bring on very rapidly an elite capable of combining, so it was hoped, with an emerging Papua New Guinea elite, and of working together with them. This the Dutch wanted, in part, because they knew that they had to withdraw and they preferred that future for New Guinea to any alternative.

I accepted this as a possibility at the time. It ought I suppose to have been clear that it was not possible; there was no time left. Indonesia had not been following, so far, a strong line on Dutch New Guinea but fairly soon after 1958 it became clear that the Indonesians simply would not tolerate any future for Dutch New Guinea except as part of Indonesia. It should also have been clear that when it came to the point neither the United States nor the United Kingdom, nor anyone else, would wish to stand in their way. When it came finally to an issue there was no other political and practical alternative but for Dutch New Guinea to become part of Indonesia. I came later to agree with that point of view.

I used the occasion of the Summer School and nine tenths of my paper to think out my view, in 1958 terms, about where New Guinea was heading and what its future might be. An idea that was being put forward at that time was that New Guinea should become a seventh State of Australia. I opposed this.

I took the view that New Guinea would, in fact, be independent within a relatively short number of years. Many people believed we had decades in which to bring New Guinea on to maturity and ultimate self-government. I felt strongly that there would be no holding New Guinea independence back for an indefinite period of time, and that we should have to educate an indigenous elite to take over from the Australians. The pressure for this, internationally and in New Guinea, would I felt be strong. I believed that our own interests also required this since we obviously could not afford to underwrite the future of New Guinea at Australian standards, and underwriting it at lower standards would have been bound to cause problems. The islanders had to take responsibility themselves although we would help. This meant independence.

Independence I believed would come much more quickly than most people thought, but I also realised the burdens of trying to run New Guinea as an independent country. They would in political and economic terms be considerable; and a serious problem would exist of a possible break-up and internal struggle. While not unaware of the difficulties I nevertheless thought not only that independence would come speedily, but that it should. In fact Papua New Guinea became an independent country in September 1975, seventeen years after the 1958 Summer School. Very few people present at the Summer School would have predicted such an early outcome of the movement to independence. In 1958 it had not in any real sense begun, and I would have myself thought that it would take longer than it actually did. The majority would have said much longer.

The policy advocated by some, of uniform development aimed at bringing the native people throughout the whole of Australian New Guinea through primary education to literacy, holding back for the time being substantial activity in secondary education and tertiary education, would have demanded an infinitely more gradual timetable. A more vigorous policy of secondary education was undertaken in the late fifties; tertiary education did not come until the middle of the sixties. Advocates of the policy of uniform development took the view that if that policy were not adopted there would be a risk of something like brown fascism, with an elite taking over and becoming the new bosses in a regime of possible oppression in which the ordinary people of New Guinea might suffer. The latter had to be protected, because of our trusteeship, from that possibility. One should not, it was urged, bring on an elite.

That danger had of course to be recognised, but it was too late for any colonial country to have the luxury of such a long perspective. By the late fifties, countries were becoming independent in Asia and Africa, unready though some might be thought to be, and it was necessary in Australian New Guinea to produce an elite to whom one could hand over power, doing one's best to provide stable political institutions in time. It is not possible here to discuss the dangers of economic and political instability as seen in the fifties, sixties and early seventies nor to assess what has happened since independence.

Various points of view were put forward in 1958 at the Summer School and papers at that school stimulated the debate on New Guinea. That is only twenty years ago. Everything leading to independence being attained in 1975 happened since then. I became and remained actively interested in New Guinea affairs from 1958 until I became Chief Justice.

Some years later Sir Norman Cowper, Chairman of the Australian Institute of Political Science; Mr Peter Hastings, a leading writer on New Guinea affairs whom I had come to know as a result of my 1958 paper; Sir John Crawford, in turn Director of the School of Pacific Studies and Vice-Chancellor of the Australian National University; Mr Stephen Rich, a business man with New Guinea interests; and I, produced the idea that there should be a Council on New Guinea Affairs which would encourage debate in Australia on the future of New Guinea. At that time we were not interested so much in encouraging debate in New Guinea itself about the future of New Guinea because there were hardly any indigenous people able to participate.

There had previously been formed, with the help of Sir John Crawford, a kind of business consortium for conducting business activities in New Guinea which would at the same time be advantageous to the country. Much the same people as were involved in that were represented by Stephen Rich in the little group to which I have referred. Crawford, Cowper, Hastings, Rich and I went to Canberra and had a meeting with the

Minister for Territories, Mr Paul Hasluck, at which we proposed forming a Council on New Guinea affairs. The Council was to be financed substantially by the business interests that had made up the consortium. But it was to be given complete freedom to develop its own approach to the New Guinea debate. Naturally, there was criticism of it as being created in the interest of the business community. That was not the fact.

The Council on New Guinea Affairs was soon formed under the chairmanship of Sir Norman Cowper. Peter Hastings, who had been with Consolidated Press, became full-time director of the Council. I took the view, which I would also apply in the Industrial Relations Society, that the first thing to do was to establish a journal. A journal proves that an organisation exists and provides it with a much wider audience than a relatively small membership.

The journal speaks for itself; it was an important and influential part of New Guinea history. It existed for ten years and throughout its lifetime Hastings remained editor, combining this with his responsibilities as director of the Council and convenor of seminars.

In the Council on New Guinea Affairs we ran seminars on economic policy, constitutional matters, politics, all the problems related to decolonisation. People from the appropriate academic disciplines and professions and from all sides in Australian politics took part.

The Council on New Guinea Affairs, through the journal and seminars, became significant. After a time it became obvious that the debate in Australia, which was aimed at interesting Australians in what their attitude should be to an emerging New Guinea, to independence for New Guinea and to other related matters, needed to embrace more and more indigenous New Guineans. Articulate and impressive indigenous people were appearing and were going to count. Seminars were in the main moved from Australia to New Guinea and more and more local people took part in them; the journal took on more of the character of a journal for debate by and between indigenous people as well as debate between them and Australians. The dialogue between Australians and the local intellectual and other leaders undoubtedly contributed to the remarkable speed of political development in those years.

As time passed I narrowed my own participation more and more to the constitutional and legal issues facing New Guinea. Several papers that I wrote on these aspects of New Guinea affairs were published during that period.[1] I felt that the discussion was becoming inevitably more political; parties and unions were being formed; debates were going to take on more of the quality of political controversy and it might be difficult for me, as a judge, to be involved. Certainly that was so after I became Chief Justice. I resigned from the Council and I have not written nor taken any active part in New Guinea affairs (except on the occasion of the Independence celebrations and once before then, as Governor-General) in the last few years.

The Council's money started to dry up after a couple of years and Hastings had to give up his position as full-time director, going back to journalism but remaining a member of the Council and part-time convenor of seminars and editor of the journal. We ran it more or less on a voluntary basis, without much money at all. The journal shows exactly how things moved from quarter to quarter in the realm of discussion and ideas.

Since I shall be referring later to the Law Council of Australia as one of the organs of corporate professional legal life that absorbed a dominant part of my activity from 1960 to 1966, I may mention here the interest taken during those years by the Law Council in New Guinea affairs. I suppose this flowed in part from the fact that I was myself active in both areas.

While I was Vice-President and President of the Law Council of Australia two facets in particular of New Guinea's emergence drew the Law Council's interest. The Council accepted the view that the profession in Australia had a duty to do something towards bringing into existence an indigenous legal profession in New Guinea; that we should be recreant to our trust as lawyers if we showed no interest whatsoever in the emergence there of such a profession. The second concern had to do with a law school in New Guinea.

How to get an indigenous profession? There were no lawyers. Someone had to go to the secondary schools of Papua New

Guinea and encourage children in their final year to consider the law as a career. At that time, the only way they could study law was to come to Australia and enrol in an Australian law school. Whilst all this was going on, a Royal Commission, the Commission on Higher Education in Papua and New Guinea, was held to study the proposed establishment of a University of Papua New Guinea. There were two schools of thought about whether it should from the outset include a law school, or not.

The Royal Commission, one member of which was John Gunther, wanted to know the opinion of the Australian profession, so the Law Council of Australia was asked for its views. The Council formed a small committee including myself and Wootten, who was not a member of the Law Council but was co-opted, and the President, Mr Bruce Piggot, from Tasmania. I was Vice-President at the time. We looked at this problem. We came down strongly in favour of having a law school, from the beginning, in the University of Papua New Guinea.

One ground for this conclusion was that law schools in Australia were all oriented to a highly-developed commercial society, whose school system provided a flow of people capable because of their experience and way of life and the families they grew up in, and because of the nature of Australian society, of understanding the complicated property and other law and the legal system of a developed country. One could have a law school which would be run at the same standard of academic excellence, but which would be oriented towards the way of life of Papua New Guinea. Certainly, commercial law and criminal law and company law and the rest would need to be studied, but in the context of the situation in a developing country, the existing customary law and the hundreds of different communities involved, each with its own way of conducting its affairs. The clash of cultures between New Guinea and Australia as it expressed itself in legal problems would need to be taken into account and studied.

We came down very strongly too on the side of establishing a law school which would be of the same standard as Australian law schools, just as a faculty of Arts or a faculty of Science in Papua New Guinea would approximate to the standards of a faculty of Arts or Science in Australia. But it would be built to the needs of the local people, and would produce a legal profession whose practitioners would have understood what they studied because it related to their society, instead of trying to study in depth our local Australian law, from which their local law differed, most markedly in the case of customary law in the villages.

Our view prevailed. The Law School was set up from the beginning as part of the university. The Law Council of Australia was involved in two ways: we helped to recruit promising people in Papua New Guinea and provide them with the opportunity of meeting lawyers in Australia, living in their homes—to recruit students for the legal profession who would find law a possible way of life. We tried also to see that facilities for legal teaching would exist in their own country. As to lawyers, my view was that any country reaching independence needs lawyers not only to go into private practice but, more importantly, to staff the judicial branch of Government and to take positions in administration, business and politics. Even half a dozen, a dozen, twenty trained lawyers can make a big difference in a newly emerging country.

In the economic field there was, as always, ample room for disagreement; ample room for different theories about how much of the economy should be in private hands and how much should be developed with State participation and to what extent more indigenous businesses should be encouraged. All sorts of economic questions were discussed in seminars and from all points of view, by people with many different opinions. But the Council itself under its constitution could not as a body have any views or seek to impose any policies of its own upon New Guinea. For it to do so would have destroyed the whole exercise.

We were interested, of course, in everything that could conceivably be of concern to that territory. We were interested in Australia's relations with New Guinea at the time and in the future, and in the relations New Guinea might be likely to develop with other countries. New Guinea when it reached independence would have its own foreign policy. But everybody had different views and theories on these matters. There was no Council view or theory of what might be New Guinea's relations with other countries. So far as I was concerned, although I had been originally interested in the idea of Dutch New Guinea, later West Irian, becoming with what was then our end of the island a single State, I did not in the Council have any personal concern with or about Indonesia-New Guinea relations.

In the Council on New Guinea Affairs Peter Hastings was a leading figure. It is I think true to say that out of his connection with the Council he developed a deepening and widening interest in Indonesia as well as in New Guinea. He was a writer whose special fields apart from Papua New Guinea, as the years went by, were Indonesia and Malaysia, and he travelled extensively through these countries as a reporter and writer. He published widely and kept closely in touch with relations between Australia, Indonesia and Papua New Guinea.

Of the country at that time, one knew that it had some hundreds of different languages and thousands of village communities sometimes quite isolated from one another. Often they were only lightly touched, if at all, by the culture of the western world as imposed mainly by Australia and the Australian legal system. Some villages, of stone age culture, had had contact with Europeans for only a few years. The published proceedings of the Council, while recognising the continuity and importance of existing local cultures of a complex and long-standing kind, reflect the concern of the members about these conditions as a basis for an independent country in the modern world.

My interest in indigenous legal systems and methods of dispute settlement in Papua New Guinea is expressed in a number of my published papers and articles particularly in the Roy Milne Memorial Lecture *Law in Papua and New Guinea*[2] which I delivered to the Australian Institute of International Affairs in Townsville in 1968. In it I touched upon the contact between the indigenous forms of society and their dispute settling procedures on the one hand and the Australian legal system on the other.

I followed closely the development of the discussion about a Constitution for an independent Papua New Guinea during the years leading up to 15 September 1975, when Independence Day was celebrated for that country. By then I was Governor-General of Australia and had the opportunity to read our policy documentation as events unfolded, both before going to Por

Moresby for the Independence celebrations and afterwards. It was striking to see the new country adopt the British Honours system. More important was its decision to become a monarchy, with a Westminster-style government though with severely limited vice-regal powers.

There is not much purpose in making a comparison here between the powers of the Governors-General of Australia and Papua New Guinea, but I may mention a paper I wrote in 1969, in which I considered the relationship between a Governor or President and a Prime Minister of a future independent Papua New Guinea. What I wrote in 1969 reflected the extension of my old interest in the reserve powers to newly emerging countries. In the journal *New Guinea* in an article 'Wanted a Constitution — before it is too late', I wrote as follows:

> The classic Westminster system, either by conventions or by rules written into the Constitution, provides for a Prime Minister under some circumstances to be entitled to a dissolution of the legislature, and under others for him to be bound to resign to enable another government, with the confidence of the legislature, to be commissioned. Whether the rules governing these matters can or should be fully set out in the Constitution even in its early stages of evolution is a difficult problem. Attempts have been made to do this in many constitutions of newly independent Commonwealth countries, but it is not possible here to discuss the complexity and difficulties of the policy and drafting problems involved.
>
> The principles of collective ministerial responsibility and collective resignation, if the legislature's confidence is withdrawn, are an important part of the Westminster system, but it is difficult to think that these principles will work properly in the absence of a strong single party or a sound party system. In an unstable legislature, jockeying for position among Ministers and the formation and re-formation of uneasy coalitions can destroy the 'collective' idea or prevent it emerging.
>
> If both the Governor (or President) and the Prime Minister are indigenous persons and if both are elected by some direct or indirect means, difficult questions of power relations between them are inevitable even under the Westminster system which normally envisages a strong Prime Minister and a relatively weak Governor or President.

All of these matters require the most careful thought, especially if the expected political base in the House of Assembly is likely to be undisciplined by a single party or a strong and workable party system.

If the political base in the legislature is unstable and governments are likely to be often defeated in the House, the Westminster system is very hard to work. This could easily be the case, in the absence of a developed party situation, especially when regional interests express themselves in the legislature on different political and economic issues.

The question inevitably arises whether the Westminster system or some modification of it is the best one for New Guinea. If it is to be persisted with in the evolution of a New Guinea Constitution then one of the difficult problems requiring careful and continuous discussion will be *the expression in the Constitution of the rules for selecting the Governor-President and the statement of his powers in respect of the dissolution of the House, the obtaining of alternative governments in some circumstances on the defeat in Parliament of a government in office, and the dismissing of a Prime Minister either because of loss of confidence in the legislature or because the machinery of parliamentary government is threatened with disruption by the Prime Minister's improper conduct.* One problem which is dealt with in some new Commonwealth constitutions is the power of the Governor-President where the Prime Minister is defeated in the House and refuses either to resign or advise a dissolution.[3]

It can be seen that relations between the Governor-President and the Prime Minister in a future independent New Guinea, operating under the Westminster system, were concerning me, including the power of a Governor-President to dismiss a Prime Minister. Needless to say I never contemplated being myself directly involved in such a situation in Australia, with rules in many respects unwritten to govern the position. I was in 1969 writing in a theoretical way. I did not call this article of mine to mind in 1975 but came to rediscover it, with interest, in 1976.

It was a great experience for me as Governor-General to make an extensive tour of Papua New Guinea early in 1975 as a vice-regal farewell, and later in the year to be present as Australian Governor-General at the Independence celebrations. To watch the lowering of the Australian flag for the last time there was very moving. It was a grave and momentous ceremony. In the presence of H.R.H. Prince Charles representing Her Majesty the Queen of Papua New Guinea, the Australian flag was handed to me by the first Governor-General of Papua New Guinea, Sir John Guise. In his speech to the silent assembly he said, 'We are lowering the Australian flag—we are not tearing it down'.

So ended my long-time association with that country. It is unlikely that I shall ever be in close contact with Papua New Guinea again, as I was in varying ways from the early war-time forties until the flag came down in 1975.

12

Crowded Years

Apart from the revived interest in New Guinea my life in the latter fifties was largely a technical legal life. But as the decade moved on, I found myself increasingly involved in the affairs of the profession after having become, in about 1955–6, a director of Counsel's Chambers Limited. Barristers' chambers had become virtually unobtainable in Phillip Street and we built Wentworth Chambers, and later demolished old Selbourne and incorporated the new Selbourne Chambers as a mirror half of the Wentworth building. We moved into Wentworth in 1957. Barwick was the Chairman.

During the last years of the fifties, my wife Alison said to me, 'Don't you think you are living far too narrow a life, compared with the way you used to live — devoting yourself exclusively to the law?' I said, 'Well, as you see it, politics is out. What is there to do?' She said, 'You are starting to get interested in New Guinea again, there must be other things'. I realised I was perhaps in danger of finding myself in a cul-de-sac by the narrowing of my interests, and I started to broaden out into a great number of different activities and organisations. From the late fifties until my appointment to the Bench in 1966 my life, crowded with activity on professional, family and community levels, was lived at a racing tempo. An active life at the Bar is itself a night and day affair. The responsibilities of office in a number of organisations were added to those of a strenuous practice which took me to many corners of Australia — to scenes ranging from the steel mills of Newcastle and Wollongong to cattle runs like Brunette Downs in the Northern Territory, to waterfronts everywhere, to shipyards in Whyalla and down mines in Broken

John Kerr is congratulated by his daughters, Mrs Gabrielle Kibble (left) and Dr Kristin Johnson, and his son Philip after being sworn in as Chief Justice of New South Wales in June 1972. (John Fairfax and Sons Ltd)

Sir John shakes hands with former Liberal member for Parramatta, Mr Nigel Bowen, after swearing him in as a Supreme Court judge in July 1973.
(John Fairfax and Sons Ltd)

The Governor-General, Sir Paul Hasluck, invests Sir John as a Knight Commander of the Order of St Michael and St George at Government House on 18 April 1974.
(Canberra Times)

Sir John meets the press at his Turramurra home on the day of the announcement of his vice-regal appointment. (John Fairfax and Sons Ltd)

Sir John, Governor-General designate, and Lady Kerr arriving at Canberra airport on the eve of his investiture. (Canberra Times)

The Prime Minister, Mr Whitlam, watches as Sir John is sworn in as Governor-General on 11 July 1974. (Canberra Times)

Hill; and through the great range of city-based industries. My practice introduced me in those years to the great sweep of Australian primary and secondary industry and gave me a strong feeling of the exciting vastness and potential of my country. It was a practice with nation-wide aspects as was my work in the councils of the profession.

In 1960 I was elected to the Bar Council. I had had some experience on the Council earlier when asked temporarily to fill a casual vacancy during Barwick's last presidency. I had to stand as a silk, under the system we had for electing the Bar Council — there were five silk and a larger number of junior members. Everybody is elected by the Bar as a whole, but there could be only five silk.

Then began a period from 1960 until I went on to the Bench in 1966, during which I devoted myself with great energy to the affairs of the Bar and of the legal profession in general.

Barwick was Chairman of Counsel's Chambers Limited until he became Chief Justice in 1964. This included the period after he entered politics in 1958 and became Liberal Attorney-General and later Minister for External Affairs. Although as an articled clerk I had briefed him in the thirties I was never close to Barwick in the days before the war when I was closest to Evatt. After I returned to the Bar and especially when on the Board of Counsel's Chambers Limited I came to know him better. Although I did not follow him into active party politics, I recognised in him a great leader of the Bar both professionally and in its organisation. He briefed me occasionally when he was Attorney-General and, in Counsel's Chambers and generally, we were friendly. In due course I was to hold the presidency of the New South Wales Bar Association and the Law Council of Australia as he had done.

Nigel Bowen, Q.C. (now Sir Nigel Bowen, Chief Judge of the Federal Supreme Court), was the first President of the Bar Association under whom I served for an extended period as a member of the Bar Council. Bowen succeeded Barwick as the Liberal member for Parramatta when the latter became Chief Justice of the High Court of Australia in 1964. He later held successively the portfolios of Attorney-General, Minister for

Education and Science and Minister for Foreign Affairs. After the Whitlam victory in 1972 he left politics and became a judge in the Supreme Court of New South Wales while I was Chief Justice, moving later to become Chief Judge of the Federal Supreme Court.

Bowen's Vice-President in 1960 was Leycester Meares. In due course I was the number three of the five silk and I became Meares' Vice-President after Bowen's period ended. In 1964 I became President myself. Meares later became a judge of the Supreme Court of New South Wales and also served with me on that court during my Chief Justiceship. With his energetic, creative and forceful personality he has achieved a great deal within the profession and in public service. He is now Chairman of the National Advisory Council for the Handicapped, established in 1974, and of the Australian Bravery Awards Committee — and a close and trusted friend of many years' standing.

Meares and I played a part in forming the Australian Bar Association — a federal body of the Bar, where before had existed only the Bar Associations of the States. Meares was the President and I a Vice-President. In the early sixties also I was elected Vice-President of the Law Council of Australia — the umbrella organisation to which all solicitors' bodies and barristers' bodies belong and constituting, as it were, the national cabinet of the legal profession in Australia. I became Vice-President of the Council with the succession to the presidency assured.

The Third Conference of the lawyers of the British Commonwealth and Empire was to be held in Sydney in 1965 and I chaired that Conference. We had lawyers from all over the British Commonwealth — Asians, Africans, Canadians, New Zealanders, and a powerful group from the United Kingdom including the Lord Chancellor Lord Gardiner and the Attorney-General, now the Lord Chancellor, Lord Elwyn-Jones. Australians were there in big numbers. It was a very successful conference.

In the Law Council from 1964 we were also planning — it came into existence at the conference in Canberra in 1966 — the Law Association for Asia and the Western Pacific known now as Lawasia, of which I was the first President.

Meares and I made a partnership in the Bar Council. We were activists: we believed in change, in developing the communal life of the Bar, and in developing the right of the Bar to express opinions about matters of significance—matters affecting lawyers and the law such as law reform, problems of fees and ethics, day-to-day problems in the courts. We were interested in all matters affecting the profession, including co-operation within it, and the ability to produce change in the law relating to procedures and the methods of administering justice. That became a dominant interest of mine from those days forward, which as Chief Justice I was able to develop actively. Another area was building up the Bar Association as a community. In the Bar building of Wentworth and Selbourne Chambers we developed a club-like atmosphere. Counsel's Chambers Limited had designed into the building a library, a common room and a dining room, and large numbers of the Bar lunched there together every day. Our communal affairs at the Bar grew strongly.

From the late fifties to mid-sixties my surplus energies poured out also into a number of community activities which were apart altogether from my work for the legal profession. These included the Council on New Guinea Affairs, the Industrial Relations Society, the Association for Cultural Freedom, the New South Wales Marriage Guidance Council, the New South Wales Medical Board and two theatrical bodies—the Phillip Theatre and the Marian Street Theatre in Sydney. Some reference to these activities may be made to round out the picture of the widespread and public character of my life. Everyone having any contact at all with me then could not help but know that I was conducting a busy all-round practice, playing a role of leadership in a powerful profession, displaying a detailed and constructive interest in New Guinea and engaging in a wide range of community activities.

One body which I helped to found was the Industrial Relations Society, a New South Wales organisation originally, though later similar bodies were formed in each State and federated into the Industrial Relations Society of Australia. I was the second president of the New South Wales Society and the first national president in the formative stages of the national body. In the Society representatives of unions and employers, government officials, academics and members of the professions joined to discuss industrial relations. A journal of some quality was published and discussions and conferences were held. The debate was usually lively and vigorous. Sir John Moore, now President of the Conciliation and Arbitration Commission, was a successor of mine in the national presidency.

Meetings of the Society brought together people who were all directly involved in one way or another in handling industrial problems, and who were concerned to improve their understanding of industrial relations. My own involvement with industrial relations extended over my years as a barrister and later when I became a judge of the Commonwealth Industrial Court. The Society took up much of my time and was an outstanding interest of mine until I went on to the Bench.

The Association for Cultural Freedom, to which James McAuley introduced me and of whose executive I became a member in March 1957, also engaged my activity. Sir John Latham, then retired as Chief Justice of Australia, was President of the Association when I joined it, and my successor as Governor-General, Sir Zelman Cowen, was President at the time when his appointment to vice-regal office was announced.

Although setting some store by the Association I withdrew from it after a time because of a concern in my mind that its attitude was too much a hard-line anti-communist one. My view was that the Association should be trying to attract the interest of social democrats and Labor supporters who could be induced to see more clearly the advantages of the liberal philosophy and to be more resistant to leftist-to-communist tactics and ideology.

I decided to resign from the executive because I felt there was little chance of my view prevailing and I was so busy that I did not have the time to devote to pressing my approach with little hope of success. Instead, however, persuaded by a group within the executive to test the position, I agreed to be nominated for the presidency when Sir John Latham retired. I did so, standing against an old friend and client Dr Lloyd Ross. He defeated me at a meeting of the executive in October 1961. Although I tried for a

174

time to stay with them I ultimately resigned altogether because I could not persuade them to follow a softer line.

Dealing with this matter in his article in *Quadrant* of January 1976, McAuley wrote:

> John Kerr stood for the presidency but was not elected. Subsequently he transferred his energies to other activities. The difference of policy or emphasis involved in his not getting majority support was within a very small band. Kerr's slightly 'softer' line probably flowed from the differences of attitude and orientation created by the Labor split even among people who were fundamentally in agreement. Once again there is no basis for complaint. This is just one of the normal incidents that occur in organisations.

I should say that McAuley and I were on opposite sides on the issues involved. Richard Krygier, the Secretary, who was with McAuley and against me, wrote in the *Australian* of 3 August 1976 that it was true I had had my differences with the Association for Cultural Freedom. 'They were', he said, 'about differing assessment of some people and events. Looking at it from hindsight I would admit that Sir John has proved more right than I have'. He added that these differences had never led to any personal squabbles.

While I was a member of the Association Hal Wootten and I made an investigation of the legal proceedings that Professor Sydney Orr, having been dismissed from the Chair of Philosophy in controversial circumstances, brought against the University of Tasmania claiming wrongful dismissal. Orr lost the case. Later there was a great public controversy about whether there had been a miscarriage of justice and whether alleged fresh evidence warranted some kind of reopening of the matter. The Association was considering whether it should intervene on Orr's behalf.

We decided upon legal grounds that no case existed for a reopening. We so advised the Association, which did not intervene. The executive which considered our report was presided over by Sir John Latham. Former members of the old Directorate of Research and Civil Affairs were active on both sides of the Orr case. Many academics supported Orr and at one

175

point a black ban was imposed on the filling of the Chair of Philosophy. Important questions of academic freedom and security of tenure were said to be involved and the case provoked strong feelings among many academics. Old friends split on the issue, Conlon and Professor Wright being pro-Orr and Keith Isles, McAuley and I being against joining the battle on Orr's behalf. This issue takes me back for a moment to Conlon and, again, I feel it best to let McAuley speak:

> The second stage of John Kerr's later dealings with Alf was the Orr affair. I'm not going to recount in detail here why he and Hal Wootten, originally at my instigation, read the transcript of the Orr case in order to advise the Australian Committee for Cultural Freedom (as it then was named) whether or not there was ground for the Committee to declare that the Court's decision was clearly wrong and that Orr's case should be espoused. In the event they advised that there was no ground for such a recommendation to the Committee, and having examined the material along with them I agreed—though my original expectations were quite otherwise. Subsequently, Alf Conlon decided to become active on Orr's behalf. All that this seems to show is that people differed on the Orr case. Some people, no doubt, want to pretend that there was no room for legitimate disagreement, but that's their problem.[1]

I cannot undertake an examination of the Orr case here. Later the whole matter took a new turn in which I was not involved and about which I developed no views. The case was big in academic circles and produced much bitterness; but I had by then passed on to other problems and interests and, as far as I can remember, except for opposing the black ban on the Chair, I had little if anything to do with the later stages of the controversy.

In 1967 the partial funding of the World Congress for Cultural Freedom by the CIA broke into the news in much the same way as happened with the Asia Foundation and indirectly with Lawasia.[2] By then I was no longer on the executive of the Association for Cultural Freedom and had no contact with its handling of the problem. I had never known anything about CIA funds getting, through the World Congress for Cultural Freedom or indirectly, to the Australian Association. McAuley, however, described the situation in *Quadrant* of May–June 1967:

The world now knows that the C.I.A. many years ago decided to contribute funds in covert support of a large number of activities which it judged to be valuable . . . The organisations carried on their legitimate and valuable activities without awareness on the part of their members that they were partly indebted to the C.I.A. There was nothing to make them aware, because they were not being manipulated or subjected to pressure: in this respect the C.I.A. showed itself commendably enlightened.

There were some resignations here and overseas and also some embarrassment within the group producing the magazine *Encounter* for the English Congress for Cultural Freedom, leading McAuley to say that his brief summary 'of embarrassment suffered by very eminent people who were engaged in producing the outstanding intellectual magazine of the English-speaking world is a sufficient indication of the damage which the C.I.A.'s well-meant blundering has caused'.

McAuley concluded by saying:

> In sum, therefore, my comment on the recent disclosures about former C.I.A. contributions to the Congress for Cultural Freedom is that the C.I.A. made a well-intentioned blunder and placed those whose independence they meant to respect in an embarrassing position. *Quadrant* will, however, continue to light its own path with such illumination as its joint editors and its contributors can supply.

My handling, as President of Lawasia, of the similar problem of CIA indirect support of the Asia Foundation (which helped Lawasia) was along the same lines as were followed by the Association for Cultural Freedom. Lawasia had indirectly suffered from the CIA's 'well-intentioned blundering' so far as indirect and covert partial funding was concerned, but in no other way.

The Australian Association for Cultural Freedom published *Quadrant* and, for a time, a magazine called *Free Spirit*. It brought lecturers to Australia and conducted seminars and discussions. I derived genuine intellectual stimulus from its activities whilst I was on its executive.

In 1961–2 I was president of the New South Wales Marriage Guidance Council, having been previously chairman and a member of its executive for a few years. This arose directly out of a deep interest of my first wife, who had trained as a social worker and who, beginning in the fifties, did part-time voluntary marriage counselling for the New South Wales Marriage Guidance Council. She was a successful marriage counsellor and frequently presented records of her cases in lecture and discussion form to assist in the training of students. She interested herself too in the general affairs of the Council.

When Barwick was introducing his important reforms to the Divorce Law under the Matrimonial Causes Act of 1959, I attended on Barwick with the Director of the Council, the Reverend W. G. Coughlin—'Cog' as he was known to everyone —to advance the case for subsidising recognised marriage counselling bodies. The arguments were successful and a number of bodies, religious and secular, working in that field have benefited since that time.

Pressure of affairs forced me to move out of this work after 1962 but my wife continued as a counsellor until interrupted by an illness in 1965. After a time she was able to resume and worked with Life Line until my appointment as Governor-General.

The Phillip Street Theatre, opposite my chambers, produced witty satirical revues. I often went to its shows with my wife. I became involved professionally with it when the Director, Bill Orr, was suddenly dismissed by the Board of the Co-operative which ran the theatre. Orr was very strongly supported by the full-time staff and by actors and actresses who had played at the theatre, which helped to promote many careers that have prospered in show business.

Joyce Grenfell, who was about to open there in a one-woman show, was told there would be a strike that night of theatre staff, and protesting pickets would be in the street. The show could not go on. Miss Grenfell received this with understanding and aplomb. In the evening actors and actresses paraded up and down outside the theatre with placards, and arriving theatre-goers were surprised to find that the show was not going on, though a strike was. As the evening progressed the Board capitulated. Some members resigned and I was invited to become the new Chairman. For a time I enjoyed all the bustle and creative activity of show business from behind the scenes. During my days as Chairman the premises in which the theatre operated had to be demolished and new premises found: the theatre moved to Elizabeth Street. After a time I had to give up the chairmanship as other activities crowded in.

In later years I was concerned with the establishment of the Community Theatre, later called the Marian Street Theatre, in Killara. Alexander Archdale, the actor, was the original moving spirit in this venture and devoted himself with great energy to getting the theatre established. I was a member of the Board for a few years in the middle sixties and had the experience of helping to solve the almost overwhelming difficulties of starting a new theatre in the suburbs — on the North Shore of Sydney.

These were all zestful activities but I found less and less time for them as the sixties moved along and my work for the various bodies of the legal profession absorbed me more and more. This brings me to Lawasia and the Third Commonwealth and Empire Law Conference.

A major achievement of the Law Council during my period with it was the foundation of Lawasia. Through the Council we initiated the association, within a single international body, of lawyers from the whole of the region covered by ECAFE — the United Nations Economic Commission for Asia and the Far East, since 1974 ESCAP, the Economic and Social Commission for Asia and the Pacific — spreading from Iran and Afghanistan down through the Indian sub-continent, through South East Asia and Australasia, out into the Pacific to Fiji, up through the Philippines, Vietnam, Korea, Taiwan and to Japan. That was a most exhilarating enterprise and led to extensive travel throughout Asia.

In 1964, a year before the Commonwealth Conference, I went with my first wife to Kabul in Afghanistan as representative of the Australian Government at a seminar of the United Nations Division of Human Rights (I was in private practice at the Bar at the time). I used the opportunity to visit a number of other countries, including Pakistan, India, Malaysia, Singapore and Indonesia. My object was to meet the lawyers of those countries with a view to learning whether they would be interested in some co-operative exercise with Australian lawyers in establishing an Asian Law Association. In the Law Council we felt that there would be a lot to gain by having a regional association of their own for the lawyers of the Asian–Pacific area.

This idea was new to them and was received reasonably well from the outset. Other Australian lawyers, as they travelled from Australia to Asia, had conversations with lawyers in different countries.

At the Human Rights seminar in Kabul I floated the idea that an international legal body for Asia would be a valuable thing. The seminar covered, geographically, the very area that would be covered by the Law Societies and Bar Associations in which we were interested, while ideologically an international law association in the region could by its very existence give some help in underpinning the basic notions of human rights in Asia with which the seminar was concerned.

Discussing this with some of the leaders of that seminar, I was told that I could get the seminar to record its approval of the development of such an idea provided I could get unanimous support, and this was achieved.

It was necessary to fund this body. We had first to finance the founding conference in Canberra, which was held in 1966. In the period after the Kabul trip and after my visit to London in the course of organising the Commonwealth Conference, we started correspondence with the Bar Associations and Law Societies in the region, and also with American foundations, in an attempt to attract funds for the enterprise.

Gradually support developed for the idea amongst various Asian groups of lawyers. But such an enterprise needed money, and I made contact with the Ford Foundation. We had quite detailed correspondence and I was able to put forward a convincing argument in favour of a completely autonomous body to which Foundation aid could be given without any strings attached.

There was no chance of finding the money in Asia, and in those early days there was no chance of getting any subsidy from the Australian Government. I reached the point where the Ford Foundation had agreed in principle to underwrite the project for two or three years, when suddenly there was a change. A new President of the Ford Foundation was appointed who introduced a new and more stringent financial policy: the blue pencil was put through a number of projects that had been approved previously and one of them was ours.

We were then on the brink of having the conference organised: our invitations had gone out to Asian lawyers of each country and this was a disaster for us, but we were told by the Ford Foundation that if we got in touch with the Asia Foundation, which had headquarters in San Francisco, it would probably be able to do a rescue operation for us, at least to get the first founding conference funded.

Dr Heydon Williams was President of the Asia Foundation, and by telephone conversation with him and some correspondence, I managed to get the funds from the Asia Foundation to enable us to have our founding conference in Canberra. From then on the Asia Foundation has funded Lawasia to some extent, and in varying ways.

At the founding conference of Lawasia I was elected its first President. At the time, I was still President of the Law Council of Australia, but a rather unusual thing had happened: just before that conference I had been appointed to the federal Bench, and it was unprecedented for a president of the Law Council of Australia when appointed to the Bench to be invited to remain on as President of the Law Council. The Law Council, however, took the view that as the Lawasia foundation conference had been largely prepared under my guidance they would like me to stay on for the time being and run that conference. I agreed not to resign as President of the Council until after the conference ended. The founding conference was broad enough in its approach to cover all lawyers—judges, academics, practising lawyers, government lawyers. As a judge—a new judge—I presided and they elected me first President of Lawasia.

At that conference we had French-speaking lawyers from Iran and South Vietnam. This meant we had two official languages and needed French interpretation. My present wife Anne, who was by that time well established in Europe and elsewhere as an international conference interpreter, interpreted for us as she had done for the Australian Government at the South Seas Conference and later for the South Pacific Commission. She had in the intervening years acquired a wide international practice, and been elected to the governing body of her profession, the *Association internationale des interprètes de conférence* (AIIC), Paris, of which she was the first and until 1975 the only Australian member. Shortly after her election she was appointed Regional Assistant to AIIC for the Far Eastern and South Pacific area. In the years 1965–75 she was active as a consultant to Governments and to many international bodies including in our area the Asian Development Bank, on multilingual conference interpreting services.

At that Canberra conference I met again some of the leading lawyers from Asia with whom I had had conversation in their countries. In that way my relationship with the lawyers of Asia developed. I had thus by now made contact with the lawyers organised in their professional bodies in the United Kingdom, and the lawyers organised in their professional bodies in Asia. Although I had been to America several times, I had not as yet made direct contact with the organised professional bodies in America.

An article I wrote and which was published in the proceedings of the Lawasia founding conference explains why we adopted the policy we did as to the range of countries that would be invited, through their lawyers, to participate in it. We decided to limit its scope to Bar Associations and Law Societies from countries that were members of ECAFE and of the United Nations.

Lawasia started out by being in fact a non-communist group of Asian lawyers. We concluded in 1966 that the form of organisation we were most likely to succeed in getting established would be one limited specifically to lawyers from member countries of the Economic Commission for Asia and the Far East. If we stuck to that, we should get a body formed.

The Asia Foundation at no stage attached any strings to anything we did. They gave us money for projects, which we proposed; they underwrote for a time some of our administrative expenses. They never suggested that we should follow some particular line or some particular ideology. They agreed that the rule of law is a good thing, a strong legal profession is a good thing, and talk between lawyers is a good thing. Research and conference discussions and getting to know one another are all desirable. This was commonly accepted by everybody including the Asia Foundation and on that basis they agreed to provide us with funds.

There was a lack of enthusiasm for American finance among some lawyers in India; nevertheless that did not prevent India from joining. In Pakistan too there was not a lot of enthusiasm for American money; arguments about this among Pakistani lawyers were, I think, quite an important factor in preventing them in the early days from joining. The problem would, I believe, have been overcome had it not been for the internal political troubles that developed in Pakistan and led in time to war. In Japan too there were problems at first which for a time delayed that country's joining. While there doubtless was, in some cases, suspicion about relying on American funds, there never was any particular criticism of the Asia Foundation itself in the early years.

All of this led to my becoming known in America as the President of Lawasia, and in 1967 I was invited in that capacity to be the guest of the American Bar Association at its annual conference in Hawaii. I was a judge at the time; the Government gave approval for me to leave Australia for the purpose and I spent two or three weeks in Hawaii. I went first to San Francisco and met for the first time the people running the Asia Foundation.

I had contacts with top people on the permanent staff of the Foundation who were located in offices in San Francisco. From there I went on to the American Bar Association where I met many American lawyers, some of whom I already knew because as presidents of the American Bar Association they had previously come to Law Council conferences in Australia.

In 1967 a story broke that the CIA — the Central Intelligence Agency — had been part-funding the Asia Foundation. This came completely as news to all of us. We took up the matter with the Asia Foundation and were given assurances then that this part-funding activity had come to an end. The CIA apparently had a policy of picking out groups whose activities it regarded as a contribution to the general fight against communist ideology. They maintained that this aspect of their activity was designed to provide — secretly, as seems clear — an input of funds to various bodies which they thought were opposing communist ideologies and supporting liberal philosophies and ideologies.

It was a big story at the time and it affected a number of organisations. I do not remember which came first — some kind of injection of CIA funds flowing through to the various Associations or Congresses for Cultural Freedom or an injection to the Asia Foundation. We were simply not in a position to take funds from the Asia Foundation any longer if it were being funded by the CIA, irrespective of whether the CIA was attaching strings or not, because one could not live in Asia with a body that was to any extent funded, directly or indirectly, by the CIA. The whole question had to be discussed with the Asia Foundation. They took the view that they could not continue on the basis of receiving, even though without strings, CIA funds, and they assured us that that CIA funding was cut out completely.

The matter was discussed at the next council meeting of Lawasia, which was held in Kuala Lumpur. Everything was gone into very thoroughly there, and it was agreed to accept the assurances of the Asia Foundation that they were free of this contact. Thereafter Lawasia grew with the help of the Asia Foundation on the financial side, and I believe that the association between Lawasia and the Asia Foundation still exists.

The legal profession in many Asian countries is not rich, in the sense that the professional bodies, as distinct from some individuals, are not rich. Membership fees from the constituent bodies to Lawasia had to be kept low. But those that could afford it were encouraged to make a higher contribution and Australia, as the moving body, responded. Membership fees alone however were of course insufficient to finance Lawasia's activities.

We also had provision for constituent members of umbrella organisations to join, such as the New South Wales Bar Association and the various Law Societies. Seven Australian regional Law Societies joined and paid fees. There was provision for individual membership, and Australian lawyers became members in considerable numbers. It never was a massive organisation with a vast membership, but there were some funds that flowed in from membership contributions, corporate and individual; and each time we had a conference the host country would provide certain facilities and financial subsidy to make the conference in that country a success. Moreover the Asian Development Bank funded a number of quite important and expensive research projects for us because it covered the same area as ours.

An attempt to link me personally with the CIA by referring to that former tenuous indirect link, unknown to Lawasia and to me, between the CIA and Lawasia through the Asia Foundation, was made as part of the hostile campaign that followed the 1975 crisis. In repudiation, a letter was written to the newspapers signed by Mr Justice Wootten, who was Secretary-General of Lawasia from 1967 to 1973, and by Mr Geddes, who succeeded him as Secretary-General, dealing with this whole subject. The letter set out the resolution of the trustees of the Asia Foundation when in 1967 they issued a statement referring to contributions that had been received from private sources. They said:

> The Trustees wish to state that in the past they have also knowingly received contributions from private foundations and trusts which have been recently named as having transmitted Central Intelligence Agency funds to private American organisations. The Trustees' independent decision to accept funds from these foundations and trusts in no way affected the Foundation's policies and programme.
>
> All contributions to the Foundation from whatever source were accepted on the condition that the expenditure of such funds was to be left to the discretion of the trustees without any interference and that the funds be used solely for the Foundation's declared purposes.

At Kuala Lumpur in 1968 the minutes of that meeting reported me as having spoken as Lawasia President. I quote:

> The President said that whatever may have been the position in the past as to the Asia Foundation, Lawasia had never been affected. The Foundation had done nothing but provide us with finance.

It had provided us with money for various purposes and had expressed no views as to the policies we should follow.

The President said that he had been in touch with Dr Williams, the President of the Asia Foundation, and had the latter's personal assurance that the Asia Foundation did not now receive and has not for some considerable time received directly or indirectly any financial assistance from the CIA.

After some discussion, the President said that the consensus of opinion was that Lawasia should maintain its present relationship with the Asia Foundation unaltered. This policy was adopted unanimously.

But in Japan, in India and in Pakistan, and in some other places, there was suspicion of the money that came from the Asia Foundation.

After I became Governor-General I was asked to be Patron of Lawasia. The advice I had from the Australian Government was that there was no reason why I should not be Patron of this international legal body, and I accepted.

The first Secretary-General of Lawasia was Paul Toose. He devoted himself vigorously to the foundation of Lawasia. He is now a judge of the Supreme Court of New South Wales. Hal Wootten was the second. Wootten had travelled very widely in Asia and he worked very hard for the organisation.

Lawasia worked in close association with the Asian Development Bank to produce a set of books on the law governing securities and investment in different Asian countries. It produced other publications and published a journal. But its greatest value lies in the conferences it holds where Asian lawyers can get together. These have so far been held in Kuala Lumpur, Manila, Jakarta, Tokyo and Seoul. I presided at the first three; then an Indonesian President S. H. Soelisto took over from me.

Over the years, in the late fifties and the first half of the sixties, approaches were made to me to consider Liberal candidature in New South Wales and at the federal level. I thought seriously about these approaches. In summary I should say that on mature reflection I was not interested in New South Wales politics nor in the Senate. Had I been attracted at all it would have been to candidature for a seat in the House of Representatives. As things happened a number of factors prevented me from making any move in that direction until the serious illness of my first wife in 1965 closed it off as a possibility. By the time she had recovered I was on the Bench.

During that period I developed real friendships with prominent Liberals just as I retained friendship with some Labor Party members. There was nothing secret about this; all my friends who knew about my general way of life knew about these friendships. The Liberal approaches made to me were always on the basis that top leadership positions could be open to me.

It was in late 1964 or early 1965 that I had my first long conversation with the then Prime Minister, Mr Menzies.

I had two reasons for being in Canberra. One was that I was conferring with the Attorney-General's department and the Government lawyers on some industrial matter on which I was briefed at the time. The other was to see the Prime Minister and endeavour to get financial help from the Government for the 1965 Commonwealth and Empire Law Conference, which was in need of subsidy. The Conference was to be held in Sydney, and I did receive a promise of Government help.

I had been given the usual sort of appointment which was expected to last twenty minutes or so, in the morning. It so happened the Prime Minister was either very relaxed or very free of commitments—because the conversation went on for more than half an hour and he was showing no signs of wanting me to go. We moved away from the practical purpose of my visit to broader political questions, and ranged fairly widely across the field. We ended up in the little room next door, where he dispensed drinks after Cabinet meetings, or so I understood. He invited me to fly to Sydney that afternoon with him on the VIP aircraft—he was going up to make a speech at the University of New South Wales—but I was tied up with the legal matter and I could not go.

In the conversation—we had been talking about his run of power and his leadership of the party—I ventured to say, 'You must admit, Prime Minister, that you have had a lot of luck'. He did not take kindly to that, at all. He said, 'Luck! What do you mean "luck"?' I said, 'Well, if you had been able to pick the leader of the Opposition yourself, you could hardly have picked someone more to your liking for that role than Dr Evatt'. He burst out laughing. He said, 'Oh, you call that luck'. I said, 'Unless you did actually pick him, it must be luck. After all, you have been dealing for ten years with a split Labor Party, led by Evatt. I don't of course assert that you split the Labor Party, but Petrov and other things must have helped Evatt to make up his mind to split it. The split, from your point of view, was luck'. He said, 'Yes. If that's what you mean by luck, I can see that I have been lucky'.

On a visit to London in 1964 to attend a conference of the Law Society of England and Wales I used the opportunity to do some preparatory work for the Third Commonwealth and Empire Law Conference, which I was to chair in Sydney in 1965. One question which arose had to do with the proposed establishment of a Commonwealth Court of Appeal. The Bar and the solicitors of the United Kingdom wanted, as did the Lord Chancellor, to have the subject discussed at the first general session of the Conference. The proposed Court of Appeal was to replace the Privy Council and the House of Lords as a final Court of Appeal for the Commonwealth, including the United Kingdom. The Australian profession was opposed to this idea, as was I. I felt it would be difficult for the British profession to give up their ancient appellate institutions for a multi-racial court of final appeal. Nevertheless I received assurances that the idea was accepted.

The proposal had no chance of adoption. To make it the centrepiece of the Conference was to risk racial questions getting mixed into the debates at its most public initial session. I persuaded them that it should be played down and discussed at an ordinary, later, working session as one among several topics to be simultaneously discussed in different groups. There was some support for it but not much and the idea petered out. National independence was by then too strong to give such a proposed court a chance of adoption.

I admired the British for supporting the proposal but at the same time harboured the thought that they could safely do so as they must have foreseen the idea was doomed to failure.

In due course Mr Menzies addressed the opening of the 1965 Commonwealth and Empire Law Conference, where other speakers included the British Lord Chancellor, Lord Gardiner, whom I had met in London in 1964 just after the Wilson Labour victory.

As the delegates began to arrive for the Conference, an eminent lawyer from an African country stated publicly that he would not attend the opening ceremony because the Minister for Justice from Rhodesia was to be present. I attempted to negotiate with him to change his mind or to achieve a compromise. This was on the eve of the opening ceremony which was to be addressed by the Prime Minister of Australia.

On the day of the opening I was sitting in my pew at the pre-opening church service in St Andrew's Cathedral. I was about to read one of the lessons when a message was passed to me to telephone the Solicitor-General (then Mr Anthony Mason, Q.C.) urgently. I read the lesson, then managed to efface myself in the direction of a telephone. Mason told me the Prime Minister was about to land at Mascot and would be at the Town Hall in half an hour for the opening ceremony. He wanted an assurance from me that no African leaders would walk out from the opening. I had to be ready to give him this assurance on his arrival or he might not be willing to address the Conference opening session at all.

I went back to my pew and sat out (it is the only word) the rest of the service. Then I went next door to the Town Hall and met the Prime Minister on his arrival. I told him that I had personally no doubt there would be no boycotting and no walkout but I could not give an absolute assurance or undertaking. There was as I saw it, however, no real risk. He was relaxed and said, 'Kerr, I just wanted to be certain you had really thought about this and I shall rely on your judgment. Naturally I do not want political headlines on the racial issue on such an occasion. Don't worry, we'll go ahead if you feel reasonably sure about how things will turn out.' In fact there was no incident and it was a brilliant opening ceremony.

During the crowded years of the late fifties and early sixties, in addition to participating in the affairs of a number of organisations I gave expression to my interest in various questions, including questions of concern to those organisations, in papers and addresses many of which were published in journals. These show that I was devoting myself not only to leadership and administration of the bodies in which I was participating but to making a contribution in the areas of ideas. It is not possible to give in a book of this kind a detailed outline of the views I held and wrote about but for anyone interested I set out in an appendix a list of published and unpublished papers and addresses, including some prepared during my Governor-Generalship.

My wife suffered a sub-arachnoid haemorrhage in 1965 shortly before the Conference. She was paralysed on the left side and was substantially out of action for a couple of years. It took her two years of hard work with physiotherapy to get back to reasonable well-being. She did not achieve full freedom of movement. She had thereafter a minor limp and a minor weakness of the left hand but in due course she returned to all her activities: she began marriage counselling again and lived a full social life.

This meant that politics was almost certainly impossible for me. I had during the sixties been tempted to submit myself in the Liberal interest. This was a very delicate question for me. But in 1965 I came to realise that it was not going to be possible for me because of my wife's health. I realised that although I had made plenty of money I had spent a lot. We had some insurance, but if anything were to happen to disable me my wife would not be as well provided for as I should wish. I therefore decided I would take the next offer of appointment to the Bench that was made to me. I had been asked if I would accept appointment to the Supreme Court Bench in the late fifties, in Labor Government times, but I had preferred to remain at the Bar. The next offer was, in fact, made by Mr Snedden, then Commonwealth Attorney-General and now Sir Billy Snedden, Speaker of the House of Representatives, who offered me appointment to the Commonwealth Industrial Court and to the Supreme Court of the Australian Capital Territory, which I took. From 1966 on I lived the life of a judge until I accepted the Governor-Generalship. I needed to be sure of a pension for my wife.

Elevation to the Bench largely ended my personal role within the organs of the legal profession, although as I have said I maintained some activity with Lawasia and in the Papua New Guinea legal and constitutional debate. In the New Year Honours list of January 1966 I received the award of Companion of the Order of St Michael and St George for my services to the legal profession in Australia.

I had welcomed, from the late 1950s on, the reopening to me of the world scene as the international and legal strands in my life became interwoven within the international affairs of the legal profession. I had enjoyed my contacts and friendships with leading lawyers of the third world, of the Commonwealth and the United States, and was glad to have been made an honorary member of the American Bar Association and life member of the Law Society of England and Wales. Tracing the international legal pattern in my life forward towards the present time, I attended in August 1977 the World Peace Through Law Conference in the Philippines to receive the award as World Lawyer 1977 for 'contributions to the rule of law and the legal profession'. The others to receive World Awards were Lord Wilberforce, Lord of Appeal in Ordinary and member of the Judicial Committee of the Privy Council; Professor Kisaburo Yokota, formerly Chief Justice of Japan; and Maître Adolphe Touffait, former President of the Cour de Cassation of France and now a judge of the Court of Justice of the European Community. Looking back over my choices and decisions of the 1940s I found I had not after all, in rejecting diplomacy for the Bar, turned my back on the international scene, but was to approach it again by many engaging paths.

13

Judicial Life

When the Attorney-General Mr Snedden approached me in 1966 with the offer of appointment to the Commonwealth Industrial Court and to the Supreme Court of the Australian Capital Territory, he mentioned that there was a policy dating back to Sir Garfield Barwick's day as Attorney-General that there should be a new Commonwealth Superior Court with a wide range of federal jurisdiction, which would absorb the Commonwealth Industrial Court and the Federal Bankruptcy Court. Its status would be aligned with that of the State Supreme Courts. This should, he believed, be achieved within twelve months. He wanted mine to be an appointment made with the new wide-ranging work of the proposed court in view. In accepting, I was influenced both by personal reasons already explained, and by the fact, of which I was already aware through my Law Council interests, of the policy of setting up the new court.

Over the years, as things turned out, my main judicial work federally was on the Commonwealth Industrial Court and the Supreme Court of the Australian Capital Territory. This was because there were changes in policy affecting the proposed new court.

When Nigel Bowen succeeded Billy Snedden as Attorney-General he remained a supporter of the established policy, and in 1967 appointed Mr Justice Gibbs, now Sir Harry Gibbs of the High Court of Australia but then a Supreme Court judge in Queensland, to become Judge in Bankruptcy, with a view to his joining the new court. He wanted Gibbs to go, with me, to what was to be the general division of the court when it was established. However, when Anthony Mason, Q.C. (now Sir Anthony Mason, a justice of the High Court of Australia), went to the Court of Appeal in New South Wales and R. J. Ellicott, Q.C., succeeded him as Solicitor-General, Ellicott turned out to be opposed, at that time, to the idea of the new court. He failed to persuade Bowen to abandon the policy, but when in 1969 T. E. F. Hughes, Q.C., became Attorney-General Hughes agreed with Ellicott that the Commonwealth should not establish the court. This left Gibbs and me in an awkward position as we had accepted appointment when the established policy was otherwise. The position changed fairly soon in the case of Gibbs, who was appointed in 1970 to the High Court of Australia. It was somewhat later, in 1972, that I became Chief Justice of New South Wales. When, finally, the new Federal Supreme Court was recently established, Bowen (now Sir Nigel) became its first Chief Judge.

In the meantime I occupied myself, in addition to ordinary judicial work, with three administrative enquiries for the Federal Government. The first of these was an enquiry into the federal system of administrative law—a review of the situation as to administrative decisions affecting the rights, property and liberty of individuals. Other members of the committee which, under my chairmanship, conducted this enquiry were Anthony Mason, then Solicitor-General of Australia, and Professor H. Whitmore, an expert in administrative law. Later, when Mason went to the New South Wales Court of Appeal, he remained as a member of the Administrative Review Committee and Ellicott, the new Solicitor-General, was added to it. The Committee had a secretary but no staff and we did the work ourselves whilst continuing with our ordinary work.

The intention was that this enquiry should not delve in great detail into the departments concerned, although it was necessary to some extent, but should deal with general principles: what system of administrative law should the Commonwealth have; what kind of administrative tribunals should it have; what should be done about an ombudsman; should there be some kind of general Council of Tribunals as a permanent body to keep under review the tribunals and their jurisdiction; what kind of appeal should there be from administrative decisions; what kind of law and procedure should exist as regards the review of administrative decisions, both judicially and administratively. This meant that we had to consider the literature on the subject, systems of administrative law in some other countries, and in a broad way our own federal administrative structure. We had to produce a series of general propositions about what reforms should be introduced in our system of administrative law and the structure of review of administrative decisions.

Our report was then made the subject of a more detailed investigation in the relevant departments by a committee under the chairmanship of Sir Henry Bland. A related committee, on prerogative writ procedures, was chaired by Mr Ellicott, Q.C. Most of the general principles and structure that my committee originally recommended were adopted and became law some years later when Ellicott, having entered politics meantime, was Attorney-General. Dr G. D. S. Taylor, Director of Research of the Administrative Review Council[1] and former senior lecturer in Law at Monash University, recently published an article in the *Australian Law Journal* under the title 'The New Administrative Law', in which he wrote:

> The history of administrative law reform in Australia has as its watershed the Kerr Report. The ensuing legislation reflects strongly the ideas of that Report. Where the Bland or Ellicott Committees differed from the Kerr recommendations, the latter have, almost entirely, prevailed.[2]

His article concluded:

> The new administrative law already necessitates substantial changes in university administrative law courses. It requires the learning of new law by the practitioner and a change of emphasis from review to appeal. The new administrative law is geared to promoting good and efficient decision-making in government and to meeting the interests of citizens in our ever more complicated society. Judged by this measure, the new administrative law will be to a large extent in advance of that in the United Kingdom, New Zealand, Canada, the United States, and even France. Eventually it is hoped that the Commonwealth will have a comprehensive

original, coherent and above all practical system of administrative review.[3]

The second enquiry was into the unbelievably cumbersome and indeed almost incomprehensible system of pay and the financial conditions of the Armed Forces of Australia. I chaired a committee which produced the series of reports which now provide the basis of a simpler, more modern and more equitable system of remuneration for the Services. Just as the first enquiry gave me a chance to look at the bureaucracy in the light of broad administrative principles, the second provided an opportunity to examine the work of the Armed Services. It involved me in wide travel throughout Australia and took me to New Guinea, Malaysia, South Vietnam (where the war was in progress), the United States and the United Kingdom.

In the course of my Governor-Generalship when as Commander-in-Chief of the Armed Forces I had many official appearances at Services occasions, servicemen of all ranks and arms referred with appreciation to the 'Kerr report' on pay. I had been particularly concerned with improving the status and lot of NCOs and was invariably well received within their ranks. But all levels had, I think, benefited. Three or four days before leaving Yarralumla on retirement from my office as Governor-General I was present at the wedding of my senior aide Captain Warner. In lighthearted conversation with one of his senior officers I said, 'Have you by any chance heard of a document known as the Kerr report?' He snapped to attention and said, 'What page, what line, sir?'

The third enquiry was into parliamentary salaries at federal level. This gave me detailed knowledge of the work of our legislators. I recommended, amongst other things, the establishment of a permanent Remuneration Tribunal for parliamentarians. This has been set up.

These three investigations, covering as they did aspects of the bureaucracy, the Parliament and the Armed Services, not only provided valuable general experience which benefited me in my work as Governor-General, but also left me with a feeling of some satisfaction at having contributed in a developmental way in the three fields covered. This was in due course supplemented by my concern with judicial administration, especially after I became Chief Justice of New South Wales. My published papers on that subject must be taken as rounding out the account of my general governmental experience as it is reflected in the reports of the enquiries. Other writings relevant in this context are my 1974 Garran Oration *The Ethics of Public Office*, and a paper on *The Bureaucracy and Society* delivered at the Summer School of the Australian Institute of Political Science in 1972.

Except during the Armed Forces enquiry I was engaged at the same time with ordinary judicial activity on the Bench. When one comes to the Bench from the hurly-burly of the Bar, it is necessary to adopt a different mental approach. Judicial life imposes restraint in one's tendency to interfere with the flow and conduct of a case. Judges should be, relatively speaking, silent; they should try not to get down on to the floor of the courtroom; they should restrain their understandable desire to cross-examine witnesses because that is the job of the people down in the well of the court. Partly because of an element in my own personality — I tend to believe that whatever is, is best — when I left the Bar for the Bench I really left it. I did not have any feelings of never-ending nostalgia for the old way of life. Of course I remembered it and I had loved it all; but I had become a judge. I probably talked a bit too much, but I did not feel any psychological embarrassment about the transition. My years on the federal Bench were of course, like all the others, very busy years, and there is no need here to retrace my judicial activity. One case however may perhaps be mentioned since it has a certain relevance to later events.

The Clarrie O'Shea case came before me in the Common-wealth Industrial Court. There was a system under which if there were a strike, the employers could bring a case to the Industrial Court for an order that the union should cease to be involved directly or indirectly in the strike, and that order, if made, became binding on the union itself. If there was later evidence that the union had continued to be involved in the strike, proceedings could be brought for contempt of court against the union, for breach of the order or injunction that had been previously issued. The Court could and very frequently did then impose a fine on the union. That system operated for years and, by and large, the unions paid the fines.

A big industrial issue, however, arose. A decision had been made in the Commonwealth Arbitration Commission fixing certain levels of remuneration on the basis that over-award payments previously made were absorbed into the award rate, and the employers were no longer expected to pay those over-award rates in addition to the new award rate. Unions everywhere defied the decision and the Australian Council of Trade Unions supported them in their defiance. There were a great many cases in which unions were fined in disputes arising over that judgment. A good deal of resentment developed in union circles about the constant fining. There was a growing feeling that the fines should not be paid and that the whole penalty system was unfair and should be abolished.

It was in that atmosphere that the Clarrie O'Shea case came before me for hearing. It was not directly connected with the issue of the absorption of over-award payments, but it so happened that the union of which O'Shea was the Secretary had allowed a considerable amount to accumulate in unpaid fines imposed on other issues, and the Commonwealth Government felt it should do something about this. One cannot have a system in which fines are imposed but not paid. No judge likes to be involved in a fiction of imposing fines that are not being collected and, of course, the Commonwealth did not like that either.

So it decided it would set out to collect those unpaid fines by attaching the assets of Mr O'Shea's union. To do that, one had to find out what assets the union had and where they were. The method was to issue a summons under the Arbitration Act calling upon O'Shea, as Secretary, to come to court and tell the court what assets the union had and where they were, so that processes could be instituted to appropriate those assets to the extent sufficient to satisfy the fines.

Two or three times, O'Shea received the summons to appear in court and did not turn up. As a result of one of those failures to attend, a case was brought—since the matter did not involve contempt of court in the face of the court—before a Full Bench of the Industrial Court. O'Shea was fined for refusing to appear. He did not pay that fine.

It was obvious, in the general atmosphere of the day, that opposition to the penalty system was building up in the union movement. This led me to think about what might be the next likely development in the O'Shea case. I remember going down to Melbourne to court one morning by plane from Sydney and saying to myself, 'I think Clarrie O'Shea will turn up today. And if he does he will probably refuse to answer any questions. If that is to happen, what should I do?' Just turning this over in my mind as to the various possibilities that were open to me, I said to myself, 'One possibility is that he will come along fully intending to get himself convicted of contempt of court and get himself sent to gaol. Should I gratify that desire on his part which obviously would operate as a signal for the trade union movement, or should I try to think of something else to do?' That was the state of mind in which I went into court — it was an open mind but I was well aware of what might happen.

Clarrie O'Shea did turn up that day and there was a large crowd of men who were outside the court, demonstrating. Inside, everything was handled with calmness and politeness by O'Shea and by everyone else. He went into the witness box and, when asked if he wished to be sworn, said that he did not and that he challenged the authority of the court to deal with his case. In due course he was asked the fundamental question, 'Do you or do you not intend to bring the books which you have been ordered to bring or to answer questions?' O'Shea said that he did not, that he refused to produce them and to answer questions.

I then directed that O'Shea be arrested and charged with contempt of court. The court was adjourned for half an hour so that he could be properly charged and I told him he could ask for an adjournment and to be represented. When the court resumed he was charged and evidence was given as to his contempt. He said he did not want an adjournment or to be represented. He argued that his union had been unjustly fined in the first place and he was protecting the funds of his union and particularly the working people against the viciousness of the penal clauses. I told him this raised a matter of reform of the law which he would have to deal with elsewhere. Whilst the law was what it was it had to be administered.

O'Shea said that if he answered questions truthfully he would have to say where the union's funds were and he would not do that.

My judgment was short, as follows:

Clarence Lyell O'Shea, I find you guilty of contempt of court committed in the face of the court. I find the charge that was orally preferred against you proved. Every week in this country judgment debtors — that is what your organisation is in this respect — are called upon by orders of courts to attend to be examined as to their assets. The same applies every week to secretaries and other officers of limited companies that operate throughout this country. The general administration of the laws of this country, not only in cases like this one but in many, many cases requires that a court order should be obeyed. Trade unions and trade union officials do not enjoy any special exemption under the law. Judges have a duty to administer the law as it stands. People who choose, by what is fashionably called nowadays civil disobedience, to defy the law do so on their own responsibility and must take the consequences. You have frankly said you have deliberately — and having thought about it in advance — refused to answer these questions and by way of defence from the floor of the court you have said your reason for doing this is that if you were to answer the questions truthfully, as you say you would do if you were to do it at all, you would in fact disclose what the assets of the union are and where they are. Because you are unwilling to do that you have deliberately, and without any doubt in your own mind about it, committed contempt of court. You have refused to accept any opportunity to purge your contempt and you have seen fit to seek no legal representation or to ask for any adjournment to enable your position to be further thought about by someone on your behalf.

If you choose to defy the court as you have deliberately done, for some special reason of your own in order to make some protest about what the law is, then you must take the consequences just as other citizens, young and old, must do; and if you seek to have the law reformed you must do this by other processes that have nothing to do with this court or what is going on in this court today. Whilst the law remains in its present form, it must be carried out and the court has a positive duty to see that it is.

You have, as I have said, deliberately defied the court. You have refused to be orally examined and you have refused to produce the books which I previously directed you to produce when I ordered you to do so in this court.

In those circumstances, Clarence Lyell O'Shea, I have no alternative but to order you to be committed to prison, there to be detained until you shall make to the satisfaction of the court proper answers on your oral examination or until the court should otherwise order.

When I did that, I knew the result would inevitably be to raise in a very big way the whole question of what was going to happen to the penalty system. Obviously, although O'Shea was not being imprisoned because his union had not paid fines, the distinction in the mind of the ordinary person is a very difficult one to draw. He was of course being imprisoned because he would not say where the union assets were. The last thing that can be done, many think, is to imprison trade unionists for breaking the law in pursuance of what they consider to be their duty to their union, even although that had happened under Labor Prime Minister Chifley with some trade union leaders when the big strikes were on in the late forties. Things blew up in a big way and nobody was willing to pay any fines. The whole penalty system collapsed. It was not that it was repealed, but it was no use employers bringing cases any more; it was no use the court making orders any more because there was a blanket refusal to pay any fines. The Clarrie O'Shea case, while not the cause, marked the death of the penalty system, as one foresaw it must.

In my preparatory thinking about what I should do my simple position was this: I was a judge; I had taken an oath of office; I had a duty to perform. If the consequences of performing it were, socially and politically speaking, to be difficult for somebody else, for the Government or the employers; if ultimately through social and political power and pressure the whole penalty system were to collapse, that was outside the judicial process. If we have contempt of court proceedings and if the law is that people must answer the question they are asked in court, then the judge's duty is quite clear. This happens in all courts all the time. In the O'Shea case the Commonwealth Government set the process in motion by a decision to try to collect the fines unpaid by O'Shea's union. Once this happened a situation was precipitated in which the penalty system would collapse.

The process of dealing with people for contempt of court operates throughout the judicial system. If policy makers believe they can make that contempt system apply also in the vast contentious area of industrial relations, it is a matter for the legislature: the legislature believed it could be done. It imposed judicial duties and responsibilities on the judges; the judges carried out those responsibilities and ultimately the whole system fell not because the judges failed to carry out the duty imposed on them but because the unworkability of the system caused it to fall into disuse—cases ceased to be brought.

If anyone were to believe that in some naïve way I sat and sent Clarrie O'Shea to gaol not foreseeing what the results would be, he would be wrong. If anyone thought that I sat and sent Clarrie O'Shea to gaol because I was some kind of reactionary instrument of a ruling class or of some oppressive Commonwealth Government, as has been suggested since 1975, he would be equally wrong. I simply carried out a duty imposed on me or any other judge who might have happened to be sitting, by the law as it stood and by the judicial oath. I would not have treated the O'Shea case at such length had it not recently been used as some evidence of conservative bias. The case received great publicity and was therefore widely known long before Mr Whitlam recommended me for the Governor-Generalship.

I followed closely what happened after my O'Shea decision. The fines owed by the union were paid by somebody who had won the lottery and walked into the Registrar's office and laid the money on the table. The Registrar took it and, as a result of that, the Commonwealth decided that the fines having been paid there was no further basis for pressing on with the summons to find out where the union assets were, and came into court and withdrew the summons. That having been done, I released O'Shea. There was no further basis upon which he could or would be held.

In the meantime I had heard that he had a heart condition and was concerned about that. I made enquiries from the Registrar with a view to being sure that all precautions were taken to see that he had whatever medication he would normally be having or anything that he needed.

The O'Shea case illustrates the point that the judicial oath requires an honest decision 'without fear or favour'. If I had not sent O'Shea to gaol, the penalty system would have collapsed because I failed to do my duty. Instead it collapsed because the penalty system had proved to be unworkable. If changes in law, including constitutional law, are necessary, Parliament or in some cases the people must make them.

When in 1972 I was offered appointment as Chief Justice of New South Wales I had no difficulty at all in deciding that I would accept. The New South Wales Chief Justiceship is one of the most important judicial posts in Australia; there was said to be a big administrative job to be done because the court was suffering from certain tensions in the aftermath of introduction of the New South Wales Court of Appeal; many judges of the New South Wales Supreme Court and many members of the Sydney Bar were my personal friends; and for domestic reasons it would suit me because instead of travelling I should be at home and I knew my wife would prefer that. When the Attorney-General rang me up and asked would I accept the Chief Justiceship if it were offered, I did not need to think about it overnight; I simply said yes.

My appointment was well received in the press and much detailed material was published about my life, including my wide-ranging activity of the sixties. Gavin Souter setting out my life story in the *Sydney Morning Herald*[4] wrote of my role in building and strengthening institutions, which he regarded as a substitute for real politics in my life. The *National Times* wrote:

> In choosing Mr Justice Kerr for the State's top legal position the New South Wales Cabinet has picked a man of outstanding breadth of community and international experience rather than a candidate whose life has been spent in the narrower confines of the New South Wales Bar.[5]

All of this was in 1972. The thorough examination of my life by major organs of the media at that time makes it truly difficult to understand how, after the dismissal of 1975, so much rubbish could have been written and spoken, and apparently believed by some, about totally imaginary activities alleged to have been mine—plotting and spying and skullduggery—and about a partisan pro-Labor stance which I was alleged to have had a duty towards former personal friends to adopt, when all the facts of my life—withdrawal from Labor Party attachments twenty years previously, and over those twenty years a life so crowded day and night with public activities as to leave little enough time for drawing breath, let alone for lurking about with a cloak and dagger, even had I the figure for it—had been so thoroughly, so publicly, and so recently canvassed.

The story of the twenty years from 1954 to 1974 has received scant attention from the media and others in all that has been written about my life since 1975. I include it in this book so that people may form their own view of what in reality, not fiction, were the activities and achievements filling that productive and responsible time in my life. I have no doubt it was the record of those years that led to my being invited to become Governor-General—not the slender story of my Labor days a quarter of a century before.

Appointment as Chief Justice of New South Wales is appointment to a very important position in the State. The Chief Justice is almost invariably also the Lieutenant-Governor: in the absence of the Governor it is he who replaces him and who administers the State. I became Lieutenant-Governor when Sir Leslie Herron died, and this happened at a time when the Governor was overseas. Sir Leslie had been administering the State at the time of his death and I at once took over, carrying on for a month or more until the Governor arrived back. On one or two other occasions I administered the State in the Governor's absence. During those periods I did not sit in criminal cases because the prerogative of mercy that may be exercised by the Governor in such cases would make it anomalous to carry the dual role. The experience I had, limited though it was, gave me some insight into vice-regal office, although of course there are many considerations that apply to the Governor-General that do not apply to vice-regal office at the level of the States.

The Chief Justice also is, in a sense, the head of the State judicial system. That does not mean that he has power to administer courts other than the Supreme Court; but he presides over a court to which there regularly come, apart from the wide range of matters within its own jurisdiction, appeals from those other courts. Within New South Wales the Supreme Court sits at the apex of the judicial system.

The Chief Justice does not have within the Supreme Court any executive power that is given to him by legislation. He is only *primus inter pares*. But the judges accept that he must administer the court, with their co-operation.

In the old days when there were only eight or nine or ten judges the court virtually administered itself. But a court of thirty-six or so judges, as it was when I was there, does not administer itself. The Chief Justice has then both an administrative and a diplomatic task. At the time of my appointment there were differences of opinion between some of the judges and tensions and difficulties connected with the Court of Appeal. One of the main problems had to do with precedence amongst the judges. The passage of time, retirements and a slow healing process gradually caused these tensions to disappear, especially as new appointments were being made. Summing up my career recently in his *Portraits of the Chief Justices* a biographer, J. M. Bennett, wrote:

> It was during his tenure that the Supreme Court Act, 1970, took effect with its many alterations to procedure and administration. There were also constant problems to be overcome concerning the Commonwealth-State Law Courts Building then in course of construction. The Chief Justice found it an ideal time to constitute the Executive Office of the court, better enabling the judges to cope with ever growing administrative burdens, and for the same purpose to institute an effective judicial committee system. 'The Chief Justice', said Mr Justice A. R. Moffitt, President of the Court of Appeal, 'by force of his personality has achieved these results accompanied by an atmosphere of goodwill'.[6]

One or two innovations of my period at the Supreme Court are perhaps worth stressing. We introduced a Chief Executive Officer, at a senior level in the Public Service, to cope, under the

Chief Justice, with matters of an administrative kind. This was in my view—not all judges would necessarily have agreed—an extremely useful appointment. When I recently visited the Court the same officer was still there, working under my successor as the principal administrative officer of the court.

An extensive system of judicial committees was introduced. Because I wanted all the judges to have a feeling of participation in the running of the court, I established eight or nine different committees to deal with particular matters: one, for example, to run the library under a new active policy; one to help in legal education. There were committees of the judges of the various divisions of the court; and there was, overall, a Chief Justice's Committee which was the cabinet of the court and which would meet regularly every few weeks, perhaps more frequently. In that cabinet all the court's business would be discussed and gone over and finally recommendations would be made by that committee to me as Chief Justice. I had to give leadership in it; it was the main committee of the court and, generally speaking, if I really wanted something to happen and was persuasive enough, the committee would ultimately agree to it. Sometimes the debate would go on for weeks, sometimes for months, sometimes there would be immediate agreement. But if I felt that the judges really did not want a particular thing then I did not push it. Certainly nothing was ever introduced, as far as I can remember, without the approval of the main committee.

The committee activity was, I think, an important innovation, and appeared to be welcomed by the judges. It created a sense of being members of the Supreme Court of New South Wales and of helping to run it, rather than of being isolated individual judges coming to court at nine o'clock in the morning and going home after the day was over to write their judgments. They became identified with the actual policy of the court and helped to form it.

Another activity of particular interest to me concerned the preservation of the old Supreme Court building.

Back in the sixties it had been decided there was to be a common building to house the Supreme Court of New South Wales and the federal courts. It was to be built fronting on to

King, Macquarie and Phillip Streets — opposite the old courts and opposite St James' Church.

The Supreme Court judges were never very happy about sharing a building with the federal judges. There were a lot of problems over that and some of the earlier plans had to be discarded. I was a federal judge at that time and I was on a committee of other federal judges to look after the federal side.

The plan involved pulling down the old Supreme Court building and leaving St James' Church standing as an island opposite the new building. The old building included two courts which had been originally designed as part of Greenway's overall plan, which included St James' and the Barracks building on the other side of Queen's Square. Those two courts were first occupied in 1827, three years after the Supreme Court of the colony was established, and had been in constant occupation by the Supreme Court ever since. In 1974 I presided as Chief Justice over the 150th anniversary celebration of the foundation of the Court. Lord Hailsham, formerly Lord Chancellor of the United Kingdom, was our guest of honour and delivered an oration. I had the enlivening experience of discussing questions of judicial administration with him on television one evening.

Another part of the building, the stone part on the corner of St James' Road and Elizabeth Street, had been the old Registry Office. It was built in the mid-1850s; the Banco court was added in the 1890s. A lot of messy building had taken place over the years to join these three segments together. Nobody seemed to care in the early 1960s about the fact that the whole thing was going to be pulled down. I was Vice-President and President of the Bar Association; we did not really apply our minds to it, nor did the solicitors, nor the planners, architects, nor anyone else. National heritage questions did not yet loom so large in the public consciousness in those days as later. The Supreme Court building had become an old warren and would need careful restoration to bring various parts of it back to a form which would express the history of the court as part of our inheritance.

The heart of the matter is that the old court is the centre of the legal precinct. It is precisely because it has always stood where it is that the legal precinct has grown up around it. Gradually over

206

the years the barristers, who used to be in houses and cottages and terraces around, moved into sets of chambers; old Denman Chambers, old Selbourne and old University Chambers came to be occupied in the vicinity of the court by the barristers.

Later on, modern buildings were built: the new Wentworth and Selbourne; and the Law Society erected its building in that precinct. Then the Law School, which had been in University Chambers, could no longer be housed there, and after a big battle as to whether it should move to the campus or not, it was decided, over a lot of opposition, to keep it downtown. The new enlarged Law School was built immediately opposite the Supreme Court. Across the road, over on the other side of Queen's Square, the District Court and the Industrial Commission were established. Soon the District Court is to have a large new building nearby.

The plan visualised, first, pulling down the Supreme Court and sacrificing the Greenway courts and the other parts of the Supreme Court which between them constituted the history of the contribution by the early Government Architect Francis Greenway to that part of Sydney; and secondly, leaving a great open area in which St James' Church would have stood as an island.

I discovered that planners and architects were beginning to feel some concern about the destruction of this Greenway building, and I started to think about it myself after I became Chief Justice. I came to the conclusion that the court buildings — not all of them but the better parts — should be saved. They could be put to good use for the criminal jurisdiction of the Supreme Court of New South Wales which would thus maintain its continuous occupancy dating from 1827.

So I found myself engaging in the struggle to preserve it. There was a gradual building up of interest by planners, architects and the National Trust; I argued the case strongly in a document which received a fairly wide circulation; the lawyers — Bench, Bar and solicitors — gradually reviewed their attitude to it; and ultimately the forces for preservation, restoration, renovation prevailed. The better parts of the building will it seems remain as part of the Supreme Court and for use by the District Court according to decisions to be made as needs reveal themselves.

One further interest of mine over the years in judicial office is gradually bearing fruit. In Australia in recent years, largely due to the initiative of Mr Justice Fox acting with the support of Mr Justice Meares, Justice Roma Mitchell, Sir Stanley Burbury, myself and others, there has been a movement to establish judicial conferences. Federal and State Supreme Court judges now meet regularly to discuss problems of judicial administration and judicial work. Similar Australia-wide conferences of District and County Court judges are held. I gave this movement strong support and worked hard with the others to make it a success. During my term as Governor-General my wife Anne and I entertained conference groups of both jurisdictions at Yarralumla. In the vast distances of Australia judges had previously seen little of one another interstate, and had little chance of sharing and comparing their experience. Nowadays that is changed. Only benefit can flow from such contacts.

There is, I believe, a chance that an active, more broadly based Institute of Judicial Administration may be formed and may operate to keep all problems of judicial administration under review. I pressed hard for this in my later years as a judge and especially when Chief Justice, and should greatly like to see a healthy Institute of Judicial Administration operating. Some day the Commonwealth and the States may act to foster means of bringing at least the judges, and I would hope the magistrates and others interested in judicial administration, into constant productive contact, with great advantage to the judicial system in Australia. These things take time to achieve. I hope to see a serious institutional attack of an intellectually co-operative kind, with real judicial participation, on the complex problems of our court system and of judicial administration.

In July 1974 I ceased to be Chief Justice and became Governor-General. In the New Year Honours List I had been awarded a knighthood in the Order of St Michael and St George. Looking back over my eight years of judicial life, I had no regret at not having followed the political pathway; and certainly no premonition stirred in me that I was yet to have a role in a great political drama of our history.

14

Forsey — the Power of Dismissal and Forced Dissolution; the Rubber Stamp Theory

It was during 1975 that I read the great work *The Royal Power of Dissolution of Parliament in the British Commonwealth* by the eminent Canadian constitutional authority Senator Eugene Forsey.[1] Sir Zelman Cowen wrote of it in 1967: 'This book . . . is the most elaborate study of this important reserve power so far written . . . Readers of *The King and his Dominion Governors* should certainly take account of this fuller study'.[2]

Eugene Forsey is still alive and vigorous in his seventies; although we have not met, I feel that I have come to know him personally through our correspondence and telephone talks since the 1975 crisis. His main book is out of print, but in 1976 he generously sent a copy which had belonged to his mother, presenting it to the library in Government House, Canberra. He has also published a book of collected essays called *Freedom and Order*. A copy arrived on my desk early in 1976, inscribed 'with respect and admiration, from Eugene Forsey' — a message greatly valued.[3]

My correspondence with Senator Forsey since 11 November 1975 shows him, as do his writings, to be a lively and stimulating man, with a deep interest in the special subject of the reserve powers of the Crown. While his name is naturally less familiar to the Australian public than is Dr Evatt's, his work and reputation are well known to constitutional scholars throughout the world.

Senator Forsey graciously offered me permission to quote from his personal letters. On 29 July 1976 he wrote he had

> been much distressed by the blackguardly behaviour to which you have been subjected. I am surprised that any Australians could behave in so disloyal and so unsportsmanlike a manner.

On 2 March 1977 he wrote:

> I am glad to hear that the 'rage' has subsided. I hope it will not be revived. It is too bad that partisanship can make people so stupid. For the life of me, I still cannot see what you could have done except what you did.

The rage had indeed subsided by that time, and an attempt by some to revive it in February 1978 was I believe a failure.[4] Senator Forsey went on:

> I do not think I have changed any of the views I expressed in the two books. If I have, it is certainly only in some detail so minor as to have escaped my recollection.

Since 11 November 1975 Forsey has been following a great deal of what has been published in Australia about the crisis. One point in particular, made in a letter to me of 13 September 1976, is that the article of Professor J. Richardson 'The Legislative Power of the Senate in Respect of Money Bills' published in the *Australian Law Journal* seemed to him 'to dispose completely of the contention that the Senate has no right to reject Supply'.[5]

Soon after news of the Australian happenings of 11 November reached Canada Senator Forsey wrote a letter to the Toronto newspaper *Globe and Mail*[6] containing the following passage:

> Your editorial on the Australian constitutional crisis (A Bonus Election issue for Mr Whitlam — Nov. 17) appears to rest on the belief that 'in the monarchies of the British Commonwealth . . . the Crown is expected to exercise' its 'sovereignty only on the advice of its selected advisers'.
>
> Ordinarily, yes: but not always. 'The Queen can do no wrong.' Therefore, the Crown must always have a minister who will take responsibility for its actions. In other words, the Crown cannot act without advice. Normally, that advice is the advice of the Government in office, which, again normally, has a majority in the lower House of Parliament. But circumstances can arise in which the Crown has an undoubted constitutional right to refuse the advice of the Government (even if that Government has a majority in the Commons), and find other Ministers who will tender different advice. The authorities for this are legion. They include, very notably, Sir Ivor Jennings, at pp. 412–16 of his Cabinet

Government, 1969, and, in Canada, Dawson and Ward, Government of Canada, 5th edition, p. 162.

From what I have been able to discover, in the newspapers and in official documents from Australia, there is strong ground for believing that recent events in that country were such as to justify Sir John Kerr's exercise of his undoubted 'reserve power' of dismissal.

Later in the letter Forsey said:

> In view of all the circumstances, I should be much interested to know what you think the Governor-General should have done, and why you apparently believe that submitting the whole question to the people was wrong.

From my correspondence with him I know that this authoritative writer remains of the same view about events in Australia in October–November 1975 as he was from the time he first heard of them. The opinions he expressed after the Australian crisis of 1975 have to be borne in mind when considering what Mr Byers, Q.C., said in a 'draft opinion' made available to me on 6 November 1975. In that 'opinion' he referred to the subject of dismissal of Governments and forced dissolutions and I discuss his views later in the book.[7]

Although Evatt and Forsey appear to have been in many respects very different personalities, both were able to reconcile belief in socialism or social democracy with belief in the discretionary powers of the Crown. Donald Creighton, in his introduction to Forsey's collected essays *Freedom and Order*, says that the two major intellectual enthusiasms of Forsey's career were his constitutional traditionalism and social radicalism.[8] He refers to Forsey's deep interest in labour problems and vigorous socialist faith, which however did not disturb his belief in the British constitutional tradition.[9]

Creighton continued his portrait:

> His socialist faith, as well as his position as Director of Research for the Congress of Labour, has focused his attention on social questions and labour disputes. His historical knowledge and his firm belief in the significance of history for modern politics has led him into innumerable debates and controversies . . .
>
> As a historian and political scientist, Eugene stands quite alone in

Canada. His combination of scholarly and literary qualities is unique. His historical traditionalism and social radicalism form an incomprehensible mixture which completely baffles most Canadian critics . . . If only there were more Canadians like him![10]

In this introduction, we get a picture of Eugene Forsey as a notable and engaging figure on the Canadian scene—a picture which is constantly borne out by the book itself. In his preface to *Freedom and Order* Forsey says that after he returned to Canada from Oxford in 1929 he became 'notorious' for his socialist opinions and activities; but that his views on constitutional matters remained unimpeachably traditional. He writes: 'I do not say "orthodox", for I was already preaching what was then the heresy on the reserve powers of the Crown, which now seems to have become orthodoxy.' This was written in 1974.[11]

The Royal Power of Dissolution of Parliament has a foreword by the eminent authority J. A. R. Marriott, who described its nature:

> The author concentrates attention upon a single point: the power of the Head of the State, King, Governor or Lieutenant-Governor, to dissolve Parliament *proprio motu*, or to grant or refuse a dissolution to his responsible advisers.

He added that it is clear

> that the King is entitled to appeal from Cabinet to Parliament. This would naturally involve the resignation of the Cabinet and the appointment of a Minister, if not a Ministry, willing to accept responsibility for the King's action. Should Parliament support the outgoing Ministry, the King would be compelled, sooner probably than later, to appeal from Parliament to the 'political sovereign', the electorate. This is evidently a right and duty which must be cautiously exercised. For an obvious reason. Were the electorate to endorse the policy of the displaced Ministry the authority of the King would necessarily be weakened, his dignity impaired.

Marriott later summed up:

> It all boils down to this. Save under very exceptional circumstances the King can appeal against his responsible advisers to Parliament, or against Parliament to the electorate, only if he can induce an alternative Minister to accept responsibility for the step contemplated.[12]

Marriott's foreword must be kept in mind when reading Forsey's book. It is impossible to read it, and especially its last two pages and fail to appreciate that Forsey accepted the power to force dissolution but only negatively, preventively; never as a means of bringing about some positive end desired by the King himself or his representative.

In his work Forsey deals at several points with the subject of what he calls 'forced dissolutions'. The final section of his book, 'Conclusions', treats this subject very directly. He says:

> It is probably safe to say that under modern conditions forced dissolutions will take place only if the Crown considers them necessary to protect the Constitution or to ensure that major changes in the economic structure of society shall take place only by the deliberate will of the people.[13]

In a footnote to this paragraph Forsey says: 'It is now scarcely conceivable that the Crown or any of its representatives would force a dissolution on such grounds as were given in New Brunswick in 1856'. Forsey discusses the New Brunswick case:

> In the spring of 1856, Parliament being then two years old, the Lieutenant-Governor tried to induce the Fisher Government (Liberal) to advise a dissolution on the question of the repeal of the Prohibition Act which, he claimed, was not being enforced. The Government at first refused, but when the Lieutenant-Governor insisted, the Provincial Secretary, Mr Tilley, one of the chief supporters of prohibition, agreed to countersign the proclamation. He did so, under date of May 21, leaving the date for the return of the writs blank. The Lieutenant-Governor then dismissed the Ministry, and the Gray-Wilmot Government then took office and issued a new Proclamation, May 30.[14]

When Forsey points out[15] that this New Brunswick case appears to have been the only one in the overseas Empire in which a forced dissolution occurred because the Crown (i.e. the Lieutenant-Governor) insisted on a dissolution and dismissed Ministers in order to procure others who would tender the desired advice, he makes it clear his reference to the Crown's insisting on a dissolution is a reference to a positive personal desire of the Crown, i.e. the Lieutenant-Governor, which led him to dissolve. The New Brunswick case was thus in Forsey's terminology a single instance of a 'true' forced dissolution. But he gives many other examples of what is now generally called forced dissolution — that is, dissolution forced upon a Government for constitutional reasons and not because the representative of the Crown personally wanted it:

> Ministers were not dismissed because they refused to advise dissolution [i.e. a dissolution the representative of the Crown personally wanted]; they were dismissed for quite other reasons, and dissolutions granted to their successors because they could not hope to carry on government with the existing Lower House.[16]

This passage shows that there are a number of precedents for dismissing a Ministry which has a majority in the Lower House and granting a dissolution to its successor because it could not carry on government with the existing Lower House.

Forsey's vivid mind conjures up various examples of unusual situations in which the Crown's powers might validly be engaged to force a dissolution. There could be disagreement about some of the situations that he sees as justifying a forced dissolution, and hence argument about the rightness or wrongness of a particular decision. I am myself prepared to take my stand on the ground that a Government cannot be expected to be allowed to govern without parliamentary supply, insisting despite the denial of supply on refusing either to advise dissolution or resign.

Forsey's conclusion to his book could not have been written if the Crown were powerless to do anything but what the Prime Minister permitted. In order to understand the passage, which clearly asserts a power to dismiss and force a dissolution in some circumstances including, for example, where the Crown considers it necessary in order to protect the Constitution, one must examine Forsey's references to this matter in other parts of his book.

Early in the book Forsey says that throughout the Commonwealth as it then stood (1943), except Eire, 'the King or his representative may, in law, grant, refuse or force dissolution of the Lower House of the Legislature'.[17] He points out that in Australia the Governor-General may in defined circumstances dissolve both Houses. He then goes on to say: 'In legal theory the discretion of the Crown is absolute (though of course any action requires the consent of some Minister), but the actual exercise of the power is everywhere regulated by conventions'. He asks: what are these conventions? Evatt had asked the same question in 1936 and had pleaded for them to be codified as law.

The reference to the need for consent of some Minister is — in the case of a forced dissolution and in those cases where there is dismissal of a Government having a majority in the Lower House, followed by dissolution — a reference to the need to find a Minister who, even though he does not have the support of the Lower House, will accept political responsibility for the dissolution, accept a commission and take the issue to the people.

Forsey, after discussing some views of Evatt, says:

> It might be added that the absence of any clear rule, or the misunderstanding of whatever rules do exist, combined with the obscurity of the subject and the democratic electorate's ignorance of such matters, is a positive invitation to unscrupulous demagogues to play fast and loose with the Constitution.
>
> Nor is this all. The enormous increase in the power of the Cabinet, and especially of the Prime Minister, raises the question whether the reserve power of the Crown to force or refuse dissolution may not be one of the few safeguards against dictatorship by 'the leader of the junta wielding for the moment the power of office'. If, for example, a Cabinet with a majority in both Houses tried to use that majority to prolong the life of Parliament indefinitely, a forced dissolution would be the only constitutional means of preserving the rights of the people. On the other hand, there may be times when, for the preservation of the Constitution and the rights of the people, it will be essential for the Crown to refuse dissolution.[18]

(In Australia the Constitution limits the life of a House of Representatives to three years.)

In 1932 in New South Wales the dissolution was produced, after dismissal of a Government having a majority, because the Governor believed the Government was acting illegally and because it would not cease acting illegally. Neither then nor in 1975 was there a personal vice-regal motive. The dissolution of November 1975 occurred for a mixture of reasons. First it was preceded by the dismissal of a Government. That dismissal was due to (a) the inability of the Government to obtain supply, (b) its declared intention of governing without supply, and (c) the unwillingness of the Government either to recommend dissolution or to resign. The dissolution that followed was not 'forced' in the sense used in the New Brunswick case but it was inevitable because Mr Fraser, having accepted a commission to form a Government, did not have the confidence of the House of Representatives and conceded he did not have it. The dismissal and his acceptance of the commission forced him because he did not have the support of the House to advise dissolution, having accepted responsibility for the dismissal, in order to put to the people the question of the propriety of what he had done (a) in denying supply, (b) in accepting responsibility for the dismissal of the Whitlam Government and installation of a caretaker Government, (c) in advising dissolution. The dismissal in these circumstances produced a necessary and inevitable dissolution of the House. The dismissal did not occur in order to satisfy any personal desire of mine. It was due to the Prime Minister's refusal to advise dissolution when he could not obtain supply and to his insistence upon continuing to govern without supply, whereas his duty was to resign or advise dissolution. The dissolution in fact, for special reasons, took the form of a double dissolution and this was based on further special considerations.[19]

Evatt's approach is referred to by Forsey:

> On forced dissolutions overseas, Evatt makes only one comment, and that by implication. A Governor faced with the question of giving or withholding assent to a bill prolonging the life of Parliament, which might be 'nothing less than [an attempt] to cheat the electors of their right to control the Legislature . . . an impudent attempt to thwart their will by a coup d'état under the forms of law', might have to refuse assent. Clearly, this might result in the resignation of the Cabinet and assumption of office by an alternative Government prepared to take the responsibility for the early dissolution deemed necessary by the Governor.[20]

In his chapter 'Critique of the Opinions of Constitutional Authorities', Forsey discusses opinions of other text writers. He then puts his own position in the light of that examination:

216

On the Crown's right to force dissolution, as on its right to refuse, there is considerable difference of opinion. The term 'forced dissolution' is applied to one which takes place not at the wish of the Cabinet but of the Crown itself. The element of 'force' is most clearly evident when the Cabinet of the moment will not accept responsibility for dissolving Parliament, and is dismissed to make way for a new Cabinet which will . . . If the Crown's rights in the matter do not extend to dismissing a Cabinet which refuses to advise dissolution, there clearly cannot be a 'forced dissolution' in any sense . . . The real problem, therefore, is whether the Crown can force dissolution by dismissing a Cabinet which refuses to give the desired 'advice' and finding a Cabinet which is willing to do so, and if so, when.[21]

All this proceeds on the basis that the power to force dissolutions is not absolute. Whether it is proper to force a dissolution depends on the circumstances and about these there may be disagreement. Indeed any exercise of the power will probably produce argument and disagreement, precisely because it is a discretionary power. But it is evident that the discretionary power exists where the constitutional situation requires a dissolution and the Government will not advise it. It is also evident that there is a power of dismissal of a Government having a majority, in constitutional circumstances demanding this course, followed by a dissolution. The latter type of dissolution is analogous to a forced dissolution.

Senator Forsey holds views about the rubber stamp theory which are identical with my own. He expresses his views in an essay in *Freedom and Order* entitled 'The Crown and the Constitution'. This essay was written in 1953, a year in which two provincial legislatures in Canada had prolonged their own lives. The courts ruled that this was legal. Forsey commented:

This is clearly a grave threat to democratic government. Yet, as Mr Justice Hope pointed out in 1943, the provincial constitutions provide only one means of protection: the reserve power of the Crown to refuse assent to such bills, or to force dissolution, and bring on a general election.

Many people will object that there is no reserve power; that the Crown is just a rubber stamp for the Cabinet, or that if it isn't it ought to be.

The first objection is nonsense. The Crown undoubtedly has some power to refuse a Cabinet's advice. It has done it, often. The most conspicuous example is in relation to requests by Cabinets for dissolution of Parliament, that is, for a fresh general election.[22]

It is essential to keep clearly in mind, when recognising as everyone must that the power of the Governor-General to grant or refuse a dissolution truly exists, two important points. First, the argument is often framed, as Forsey is doing here, in the way necessary to refute absolutely, as so clearly can be done, the rubber stamp theory; this is done simply by demonstrating the existence of a discretion or power to refuse. Secondly, the power to refuse is merely the obverse of the power to grant, which is the aspect seen in the great majority of cases. Very often it is the case that in the then existing circumstances there is a duty to grant a dissolution and no room or little room for the exercise of a discretion to refuse; this is clearly illustrated by the 1955 and 1977 dissolutions of the House of Representatives.

Forsey goes on to demolish the rubber stamp theory:

Moreover, the rubber stamp theory has been decisively re-pudiated by statesmen of all parties, notably Wellington, Peel, Aberdeen, Russell, Derby, Disraeli, Gladstone, Salisbury, Courtney, Asquith, Lloyd George, Simon, Churchill and Attlee in Britain, and by Macdonald, Mackenzie, Blake, Cartwright, Laurier, Meighen and King in Canada. Mr Churchill's and Mr Attlee's statements are particularly noteworthy. On March 29, 1944, a Labour member, Mr Price, accused Mr Churchill of 'claiming for the Executive power to dissolve Parliament and go to the country.' He replied: 'I never said anything of the sort. I must make it absolutely clear that it does not rest with the Prime Minister to dissolve Parliament.' Mr Price attempted to brush this aside with: 'That, of course, is the law, but in actual fact the advice comes from the Prime Minister.' Mr Churchill replied: 'This is one of the exceptional occasions when the Prerogative of the Crown comes into play and where in doubtful circumstances the Crown would refer to other advisers. It has been done on several occasions. I must make it absolutely clear that it does not rest with the Government of the day. It would be most improper on my part to use any language which suggested that I have the power to make such a decision.' Mr Attlee, in February 1952, in an article on the death of King George VI, was equally clear and emphatic: 'The monarch has the right to grant or refuse a Prime Minister's request for a dissolution of Parliament which involves a general election. This is a very real power. It means that there is always someone other than a party leader who is available to take action in critical times'.[23]

This last clear statement, by the former British Labour Prime Minister Clement Attlee, was repeated by him in 1959. It appeared in the *Globe and Mail* of 26 August 1959, and Professor Roger Graham (Meighen's biographer) reprinted it with Attlee's explicit permission, in his *The King-Byng Affair, 1926: A Question of Responsible Government* (1967).

Later Forsey says:

Among writers on the Constitution, Austin, Hearn, Todd, Dicey, Anson, Low, Marriott, Keith and Ramsay Muir have all emphatically asserted the existence of a reserve power; Keith, indeed, devoted a large part of his later works to discussing it, and elaborating his celebrated theory of the Crown as guardian of the Constitution. Lowell, Jenks, Jennings, Chalmers and Asquith, and even Laski, all admit a greater or less degree of such power. Dr Evatt, who speaks with particular authority, as a former judge of the Australian High Court, a former Commonwealth Minister of External Affairs and Attorney-General, as the present Leader of the Australian Labor Party, and as a distinguished writer on the Constitution, has devoted a whole book to explaining the nature and necessity of the reserve power.

Unquestionably, then, the power exists. Unquestionably also, it is a power to be exercised only in very special circumstances. Ordinarily, the Crown does, and must, follow the advice of the Cabinet in office. Many eminent statesmen, and most writers on the Constitution have considered that there were occasions when it ought not to do so. But many ordinary people feel there must be no exceptions whatsoever; that the only safe rule is to insist that the Crown shall invariably accept the advice of the Cabinet in office, regardless of circumstances.[24]

The author in the following pages gives a number of concrete examples to show that what many ordinary people feel is not safe doctrine is nevertheless correct. Having set out his examples which warrant careful study he concludes with a vigorous repudiation of the rubber stamp theory:

> In every one of the cases described, the rubber stamp theory is an affront to common sense and results in a monstrous perversion of democratic government. Yet some people persist in maintaining that exercise of the reserve power in such cases would be 'undemocratic'.[25]

He later goes on:

> As both Dicey and Lord Oxford have pointed out, the reserve power cannot be used arbitrarily or against the will of the people. The Crown cannot act without the advice of Ministers. If it refuses the advice of the Ministers in office, and they refuse to back down, it must find other Ministers who will take responsibility for the refusal; and the new Ministers must secure the support either of the existing Parliament or of a new Parliament.
>
> The reserve power is, indeed, under our Constitution, an absolutely essential safeguard of democracy . . .
>
> It is the rubber stamp theory which is undemocratic. *It makes existing governments irremovable except by their own consent.* Such a doctrine is a travesty of democracy. It delivers every Opposition gagged and bound into the hands of its opponents. It delivers the people gagged and bound into the hands of any jack-in-office. The jack-in-office may, of course, loosen the gag and the ropes. He may loosen them so much that we don't realize they're there. But he can tighten them again whenever he pleases, and as tight as he pleases. This is not democracy. It is despotism; more or less benevolent, perhaps, for the moment; but despotism none the less.[26]

Forsey demonstrates that even Mr Mackenzie King did not support the rubber stamp theory, in an essay entitled 'Mr King and Parliamentary Government' published in 1951:

> This is notably true of his theory of the Crown. Two facts about it are unmistakable. First he did *not* believe in the 'rubber stamp' theory. In the 1926 crisis, he said three times, once in the House of Commons and twice in his opening campaign speech, that there would be circumstances in which the Crown would be justified in refusing dissolution. He also said, before the vote on the Robb motion, that if Mr Meighen's Government were defeated, and did not resign, the Governor-General should dismiss it, and he himself

would take responsibility for the dismissal. This is about as far from the 'rubber stamp' theory as anybody could get.[27]

Forsey's essay sheds further valuable light on the position of Ministers and their relationship to the Crown and to Parliament:

> In 1931, he [Mackenzie King] declared: 'The cabinet is a committee of the House of Commons; any power it has is derived from the members who sit in this house.' This is not so. Mr Ilsley, then acting Prime Minister, stated the correct doctrine in 1945: 'The authority of the government is not delegated by the House of Commons; the authority of the Government is received from the Crown . . . His Majesty's advisers are sworn in as advisers to the Crown. The government is responsible to parliament . . . but that is a different thing from the doctrine that the government is a committee of the House of Commons or that it exercises authority delegated by the House of Commons. That is not so.' No one has ever effectively challenged what Mr Ilsley said.[28]

In his paper 'Constitutional Monarchy and the Provinces', published eleven years ago in 1967 and republished in *Freedom and Order* in 1974,[29] Forsey gives us the true flavour of his constitutional philosophy:

> The Crown is the embodiment of the interests of the whole people, the indispensable centre of the whole parliamentary democratic order, the guardian of the Constitution, ultimately the sole protector of the people if M.P.s or M.L.A.s or ministers forget their duty and try to become masters, not servants. The Crown's reserve power to refuse the advice of ministers when that advice imperils the Constitution still remains, as Lord Attlee reminded us in 1952 and 1959; and if parliamentary government is to survive, it must remain.

When Forsey talks about the Crown being the guardian of the Constitution or having a role to prevent the Constitution from being imperilled, or when he talks about forced dissolutions taking place to protect the Constitution he is, as I understand him, using these concepts of guardianship, of protection of the Constitution, of preventing it from being imperilled, in a sense different from the way in which we refer, for example, to the High Court of Australia as being the guardian of the Constitution. The courts guard the *law* of the Constitution, keeping all within their legal powers and declaring invalid action going beyond legal constitutional power. Forsey is not talking about this. He is referring to an area of decision making for the guardianship and protection of the *whole* Constitution, not just that part of it which consists of constitutional law. He is talking about 'the whole parliamentary democratic order', part of which rests not upon law at all but upon convention and customary usage. It is an area of decision making in which the reserve powers may be engaged, and in which decisions will generally be non-justiciable. It is an area in which the Constitution, in the sense in which Forsey is using the word, can be, in proper cases, guarded by the Governor-General. The decisions he makes, as Professor Bailey remarked in the opinion he gave in 1951, may properly be said to involve not only matters of fact but also matters of political interpretation or elucidation.[30]

In 1975, Mr Whitlam had his commission from the Crown, not from the House of Representatives. He had the confidence of the House but he was answerable to the Crown and not entitled to keep his commission in all circumstances, whatever happened, merely on the ground that he had the confidence of the House. He held power subject to his observance of the basic principles of the whole parliamentary democratic order. The Crown, or in Australia the Governor-General, has both the legal and the real power to dismiss in certain circumstances and it is not possible to say that the power of dismissal is non-existent, whatever a Prime Minister or Government does, merely because that Minister or Government retains the confidence of the Lower House.

Mr Whitlam moved outside the proper principles and asserted a power to remain in Government without going to the people, even though Parliament would not grant him supply. In such circumstances the Governor-General can use his admitted power of dismissal, which is not a mere notional legal power but a real power, a reserve power of the Crown. That is what I did.

15

The Loan Affair and Justiciable Issues

In my first six months after taking up office as Governor-General two policy matters arose which illustrated the proper approach of a Governor-General to justiciable legal issues on which he disagrees with the legal advice given to him. The first had to do with the joint sitting of the two Houses of Parliament held early in the second half of 1974 and the second had to do with the $US4000 million loan affair. The second was the more significant and I shall deal with it first. Both of these examples illustrate a principle in operation which requires that a Governor-General should accept advice, although he believes it to be erroneous in law, in cases where the courts can if necessary correct anything that in law has been wrongly done.

Contrasted with this situation is the very rare kind of situation which arose late in 1975, in which personal discretionary decisions of a Governor-General cannot produce a justiciable issue.

By a purported Executive Council meeting of Friday 13 December 1974 the Minister for Minerals and Energy was appointed as an agent of the Commonwealth Government to borrow for temporary purposes a sum not exceeding four thousand million US dollars. I was not present at that Executive Council meeting. Nor was the Vice-President of the Executive Council, and neither of us had approved of the holding of the meeting nor called it. The first time I heard of the meeting was early the following morning, 14 December 1974. The business conducted was very important but I had not heard anything at all about that business before the meeting was held. Before relating the facts I shall discuss the legal issues.

The Federal Executive Council is established by section 62 of the Constitution to advise the Governor-General in the government of the Commonwealth; but executive decisions are in practice made by the Cabinet or by individual Ministers and come, when necessary, to the Governor-General in Executive Council for final formal approval. This is given at meetings called as and when required and attended usually by the Governor-General and only two or three of the Ministers, all of whom are members of the Executive Council.

Questions arise as to whether the meeting of 13 December was a valid meeting of the Executive Council. Professor Geoffrey Sawer has examined closely, in his book *Federation Under Strain*, a number of legal problems involved in the calling of Executive Council meetings, and many matters of practice associated with the work of the Executive Council. He appears to be of the view that, as a matter of interpretation, only the Governor-General or the Vice-President can call a meeting of the Council.[1] This is the legal situation as I always saw it and as accepted in practice.

Sawer discusses whether the Senior Member of the Executive Council present can call such a meeting; and says it is arguable that any suggestion that such Senior Member has been appointed with such a power may fail, because the appointing instrument may have to nominate a particular person as deputy.

The form of appointment of Vice-Presidents of the Executive Council in use at the relevant time was:

> In pursuance of s. 126 of the Constitution and of Clause 6 of the Letters Patent relating to the Office of Governor-General, I hereby appoint . . . . Vice-President of the Executive Council, to be my Deputy to summon Meetings of the Executive Council, and in the event of my inability to be present to preside over meetings of the Executive Council and signify approval of the proceedings of such meetings. If, for any reason, the Vice-President of the Executive Council is unable to attend, the Senior Member of the Executive Council who is present is hereby authorised to exercise the authority herein vested in the Vice-President.

My view of the legal result of this was that if the Vice-President is unable to attend a meeting already properly called either by the Governor-General or the Vice-President, then the Senior

Member present at such an already properly called meeting may exercise the authority vested in the Vice-President to preside at such a meeting and signify approval of its proceedings, always assuming, of course, that the Governor-General is unable to be present. Sawer, in examining the right of the Senior Member present to call a meeting as opposed to presiding and approving proceedings says, correctly as I believe, that

> it seems more likely that the intention was to give a Senior Member only the power to preside and to approve in the absence of the Governor-General or Vice-President through inability to be present at a meeting which one of *them* has called.[2]

An attempt by a Senior Member present to call a meeting would lack validity because he has no such power, and probably also for the additional reason mentioned by Sawer that such a power may only be given to a nominated particular person. In any event my legal assumption was, on December 14, and is, that only the Governor-General or the Vice-President may validly call a meeting. The Vice-President in December 1974 was one of Mr Whitlam's Ministers, Mr Frank Stewart.

Sawer deals with the meeting of 13 December 1974 on the basis that it may not have been a valid meeting because it was not called by the Governor-General or the Vice-President or because the delegation of the power to call a meeting to the Senior Member is invalid. The purported meeting of 13 December 1974 was in my view invalid. Sawer says that if this were so 'it is doubtful whether the Governor-General could subsequently validate it'.[3]

I was asked, as I shall relate, to approve of the holding of the meeting after it had been held, and was advised that I could validly so approve. I was advised by the Prime Minister to do so and I did. If my own view and the trend of Professor Sawer's reasoning are sound it may well be that what I thus did, upon advice, was invalid and had it been tested in the courts this might have resulted in invalidation of the decision. It was never tested and the point became an academic one. It was however one to be left to the courts. For this reason I expressed no view to Mr Whitlam as to the validity of the meeting.

Professor Sawer has said that

> it would be safer in such circumstances to arrange for the business at the meeting of doubtful validity to be repeated in its entirety at a subsequent properly called and constituted meeting, if necessary and legally possible making any relevant appointments etc. retrospective.[4]

This is in my view correct, but the firm advice given was that I could validate the meeting by an approval of the holding of it, given after it was held; and this I did, thereafter signing the Minute on the advised basis that it would then be valid. I was told that it was not practicable to bring the Ministers together again: Parliament was now in recess until the following February, the Ministers had dispersed and Mr Whitlam himself was leaving for overseas.

Before relating events in detail there is one further threshold point to be mentioned. Professor Sawer has pointed out that even if the meeting of 13 December were invalid and had not been validated by anything I had later done

> this does not necessarily invalidate the authorisation of Mr Connor, because that was not an 'appointment' under s. 67 of the Constitution requiring the interposition of the Executive Council. It was an exercise of the general executive power in s. 61 of the Constitution, under which the Governor-General could act on the advice of ministers not necessarily meeting in Executive Council . . . the meeting was a meeting of ministers who had ample legal authority to consider the matters they did consider and to advise the Governor-General to give the authorisation he did give.[5]

The professor's view was, however, that it was of no legal significance that the Ministers and the Governor-General may have been mistaken in thinking that they were carrying out these activities in an Executive Council setting.[6]

The point made by Professor Sawer was never raised with me by the Prime Minister. The matter was dealt with, in all discussions concerning it, on the basis that a decision of the Executive Council, as such, was necessary for the business in hand.

What happened, in fact, about this meeting was a great shock to me. I found it very disturbing that business of such importance could be handled in the way this was handled. It worried me deeply that when the facts of the meeting became public they could cause serious confusion in the public mind about the role of the Governor-General. I believed the decision would produce invalidity for procedural reasons. There were also reasons of substance: the loan was said to be 'for temporary purposes', whereas a loan of the kind contemplated, if negotiated, could not be for temporary purposes according to my view of the law. But if the decision were acted upon, any resulting loan of the kind which was in mind could be invalidated by the court. My deepest concern was not a legal one, because the court could attend to legal matters. It was related to a question which was forming in my mind as to whether the proper attitudes were being adopted to the Governor-General and his functions.

The unvarying practice had been to give the Governor-General full information on matters of State. I had had no reason to suppose that Mr Whitlam would seek to adopt a rubber stamp approach to my office. Yet when I later learned more fully of the circumstances surrounding the loan meeting I began to wonder whether a first approach to such an attitude might be that the Governor-General could be increasingly ignored and on occasions forgotten rather than being kept fully informed as Governors-General had been in the past. I had no wish for the vice-regal office to be diminished during my period in it. I had a duty to assess whether such a process was unfolding adversely to its true nature and quality.

On this point however it did not seem to me that the issue was one on which I could usefully now take a stand. The courts could remedy the legal errors which I believed had been made. I decided I should put the affair down to experience and learn a lesson from it. The lesson was that I might need to be mindful of the risk of rubber stamp attitudes in the future.

I shall now discuss what happened in more detail, indicating the practices that have normally been followed in the affairs of the Executive Council and the departures from them in regard to the meeting of 13 December 1974. For this purpose I shall assume, as everyone did at the time, that a valid meeting of the Executive Council was necessary.

The Executive Council is in existing practice an important constitutional instrument. Government is now so complex and governmental decisions so voluminous that it is quite impossible for all the business that goes through the Executive Council to have been considered in advance by Cabinet and to have been the subject of Cabinet approval. Consequently there are very many decisions which as a matter of practice come direct to the Council over the signature of a Minister. His Minute is submitted for Council approval accompanied by an explanatory memorandum. The Ministers decide what matters they wish to submit. Very often approval is obtained in Council for the execution of legal instruments of various kinds.

A great deal of the business coming to the Council, countersigned by a Minister, is routine and generally results from departmental recommendation. It is important to distinguish those items which are routine from those which are not, because the Council has a safeguarding role to play for the Prime Minister, the Cabinet and the country. In ordinary circumstances the Prime Minister and the Government expect the Council to play this role and it does.

In order to assist the Executive Council there is a Secretary to the Executive Council who handles the administrative work of preparing for Council meetings. All business passes through his hands. If further information appears to be necessary he discusses the matter with the appropriate department and endeavours to obtain it.

Certain practices have been developed to help the Council in its safeguarding role. As a matter of routine the Secretary is normally able to inform the Council in each case whether the matter has been to Cabinet and, if not, whether the Prime Minister knows about it, approves of what is being sought and is of the opinion that it need not or should not go to Cabinet. The Prime Minister does not often attend Executive Council meetings but the Council needs to be informed of his knowledge and approval of important business.

If the matter has not been to Cabinet and there is no indication of the Prime Minister's knowledge or approval the Council can and sometimes does, depending on its view of the matter, decide to defer its consideration of it. It can happen, and it has, that after deferral the item of business never comes back to the Council or comes in a different form.

The Council is entitled to be shown that the proposed decision has been properly considered and is lawful, being supported in appropriate cases by the considered legal advice of the Attorney-General. It should appear to be consistent with Government policy.

Sir Paul Hasluck in his Queale Memorial Lecture examined the ordinary working of the Executive Council. He said:

> In presiding in Executive Council in this way a Governor-General is both a watchdog over the Constitution and laws for the nation as a whole and a watchdog for the Government considered as a whole (whatever Government may be in power). He does not reject advice outright but seeks to ensure that advice is well-founded, carefully considered and consistent with stable government and the established standards of the nation.
>
> Various steps are open to him. He can ask questions. He can seek full information. He can call for additional advice on any doubtful issue. In a matter of major importance he may suggest to the Prime Minister that an augmented meeting of Executive Council be held to consider all aspects of a question or, perhaps better still, suggest that the matter be discussed in Cabinet, if there has been no discussion already, so that the recommendation to Executive Council is certain to be the agreed view of his Executive Councillors.

I accept these opinions of Sir Paul as applying to ordinary Executive Council affairs and meetings. But when there is a matter before the Council and it involves a legal point which is justiciable, and when that point is covered by the advice of the Attorney-General and the Ministers present are the Prime Minister, the Attorney-General himself, the Treasurer, and the Minister specifically concerned, all identifying themselves with that advice and so informing the Governor-General, the latter has no real alternative but to accept the firmly tendered advice and the determination of the Ministers to proceed to a decision upon it. The Governor-General cannot be his own lawyer in handling business passing through the Executive Council. If a legal point involved is justiciable, provided it is not clearly

229

unarguable, the Council should proceed to its decision and leave the point to be decided by the courts. Some believe that even an unarguable point, if justiciable, should be left to the courts. This is especially so when the Prime Minister knows about the matter and approves of the advice, *a fortiori* if he is at the meeting. If no legal point arises, Ministers can force a decision through if they are determined to do so.

Moreover, it is not possible for the Governor-General to insist upon a matter going to Cabinet if the Prime Minister has decided that it will not and the Ministers present accept that point of view. It is obviously better, generally speaking, for a proposal to be supported by a Cabinet decision, if it is important, but there may be policy considerations leading to a decision by the Prime Minister to take it direct to Executive Council. The Governor-General can seek to dissuade him and the Ministers present but he cannot insist upon Cabinet consideration and decision before action is taken in the Executive Council.

Both of these points have to be remembered in considering the loan affair.

I was informed of the Executive Council meeting early on 14 December 1974 in a telephone call from the Prime Minister. I had never seen the Minute nor the explanatory memorandum for the business dealt with. My Official Secretary Mr David Smith was also totally ignorant of the matter. It was a complete departure from established practice not to inform Government House that a meeting might be necessary, and give information of the matter which might be dealt with, thus ensuring that the Governor-General would have an opportunity to call the meeting, to be present and to be informed in advance as to the subject-matter.

I attended an official engagement at the Sydney Opera House on the evening of 13 December, with members of my staff including the Official Secretary, and we travelled to Sydney for the purpose on that day. Had I known of the possibility of a meeting and its business I would have been in Canberra, ready to preside if the meeting went forward. When we returned to Admiralty House after the Opera Mr Smith received a message to ring an official in Canberra, but was unable to make contact with him until about two in the morning. It was then that he first learned a meeting had been held. He told me of it early on Saturday.

At about eight in the morning of 14 December the Prime Minister rang me up at Admiralty House. He said that on the previous night after a long discussion it had been necessary to hold an urgent Executive Council meeting in Canberra. The Prime Minister Mr Whitlam, the Deputy Prime Minister and Treasurer Dr James Cairns, the Attorney-General Senator Lionel Murphy and the Minister for Minerals and Energy Mr Rex Connor had been present. The Prime Minister said that the circumstances were most exceptional, and as it was the middle of the night it was decided not to wake me up for advance approval of the holding of a meeting in my absence but to call me in the morning to get my approval, after the event, of what had been done. He advised that I should give this approval by signing the Minute.

There had in fact been preparations by officials during Friday for a possible meeting. On Saturday morning 14 December the Prime Minister did not tell me this and I did not know it. I do not know now when these preparations began. In normal practice it is not when a positive decision is made to have a meeting that Government House is notified, but when it becomes apparent that a meeting may be necessary. The Secretary of the Executive Council would normally act at that time. On this occasion he did not.

To hold a meeting in special circumstances in the absence of the Governor-General is not unusual, though the practice is of course to ask in advance for his approval. My own practice was to attend and preside whenever possible.

The Prime Minister said that he and the other Ministers at the long meeting had discussed an urgent and important matter and were in agreement about what should be done. An immediate meeting of the Executive Council at which all of those who had participated in the earlier ministerial discussion would be present had been in his and their view necessary to finalise the matter because of its urgency, and because they were all breaking up for Christmas and he personally was leaving for overseas that same day. They had all signed the Executive Council Minute. He appreciated that it was unusual to ask for approval for the meeting afterwards but urged that the special circumstances and the urgency warranted this course. He said that if I would have been prepared to give approval in advance I could do so afterwards, though it certainly was unusual to ask for it. His advice was that the circumstances warranted my giving such approval and signing the Minute.

I can imagine that in a moment of great crisis a sudden meeting might be needed in the middle of the night without the possibility being anticipated. If this were the situation the Governor-General should be awakened and his approval obtained. But on 13 December the facts were such that I could have been told in Canberra or later in Sydney. Preparations were going on for the meeting, as I later discovered, some time before I left for the Opera. If I had been told of the possibility I could and would have either stayed in Canberra or come back from Sydney in time for a late 'middle of the night' meeting. I once flew down during the night from Katherine in the Northern Territory — some 3000 kilometres — for what was expected to be an important Executive Council meeting. I often changed plans in order to be present at meetings. Under our scheme of things in Australia the Governor-General has played a not unimportant part in presiding at the Executive Council.

The Prime Minister told me that a special messenger was on his way from Canberra to Sydney with the Minute and the explanatory memorandum.

As a result of my talk with him I assumed the matter was most urgent and important and that it had not been to Cabinet. The four key Ministers concerned accepted full responsibility for the decision to authorise Mr Connor to negotiate for the $US4000 million loan. The taking of the decision by the Prime Minister and his colleagues was a guarantee that their action was in their view consistent with general Government policy. Any attempt by me to force the matter to Cabinet would I believed have been fruitless and interpreted as an intrusion into politics. My conclusion was that the Prime Minister wished to confine the matter to the Ministers who had signed the Minute and not to widen the political discussion.

I was told that the loan, on the Attorney-General's advice, could be regarded as a loan for temporary purposes and did not need to go to the Loan Council. The Prime Minister indicated in general terms what the purposes were, that he and the Ministers had accepted the Attorney-General's advice and that the signature of the Attorney-General on the Minute was evidence of his policy opinions and his legal opinion. My view, even before looking at the constitutional provisions, was that the purposes mentioned by the Prime Minister did not seem to be temporary and that the Attorney-General's advice was probably wrong. I said to the Prime Minister that the purposes did not seem to be temporary to me. He replied that the Attorney-General believed that the point was arguable.

I received the Minute and the explanatory memorandum by courier at about nine o'clock that morning. The explanatory memorandum stated:

> The Australian Government needs immediate access to sub-stantial sums of non-equity capital from abroad for temporary purposes, amongst other things to deal with exigencies arising out of the current world situation and the international energy crisis, to strengthen Australia's external financial position, to provide immediate protection for Australia in regard to supplies of minerals and energy and to deal with current and immediately foreseeable unemployment in Australia.[7]

I had, since the Prime Minister's call, looked up the constitutional provisions and confirmed my earlier impression as to the law. I did not make a detailed constitutional study but had little doubt that the purposes of such a contemplated loan could not be regarded as temporary. However the legal point would, I believed, in relation to any actual negotiated loan, be a barely arguable one and the point would certainly be justiciable. Confronted by the signatures of the Ministers who had decided to act on the Attorney-General's advice I felt that their legal error, if the authority were acted upon and a loan negotiated, would have to be corrected in the courts.

Professor Sawer has said that the authority was to raise a loan for unspecified temporary purposes. Leaving aside procedural questions as to the validity of the meeting, and looking at the substance of the decision, he commented:

> It might seem in terms of practical reality unlikely that so enormous a loan could possibly be for a temporary purpose, but there is no legal impossibility about it and hence on this score also the Governor-General's approval to the document had to be regarded as completely valid in law.[8]

I understand Professor Sawer to mean by this that it was unlikely it would be possible in practice to devise and negotiate a loan within the terms of the explanatory memorandum which would in truth be for temporary purposes, but that that was not a matter which it lay within my responsibility to decide.

Professor Sawer then examined the evidence in relation to the actual loan later contemplated. I did not in giving my approval, on advice, at the time I signed the Minute know the details of the actual loan later the subject of negotiation, but from 14 December 1974 onwards believed that only a loan of that general kind would be negotiated under the authority and that such a loan, if negotiated, would be invalid. Professor Sawer has said:

> The actual loan contemplated was for twenty years, payable as to capital and accumulated compound interest at the end of that period. Taking the terms of the loan and the purposes mentioned in the explanatory memorandum accompanying the Minute to the Governor-General, it is difficult to see how it could be a loan for temporary purposes, whatever meaning is attributed to that mysterious phrase. It is clear that among the main activities contemplated were the development of mineral resources, whether by direct Commonwealth acquisition and exploitation or investment in existing enterprises, and that this involved a programme likely to extend over many years.[9]

My personal opinion was to doubt its validity but pursuant to the doctrine that justiciable legal questions should be left to the courts for decision I did not act upon any legal opinion of my own and did not explore fully by personal examination the legal arguments arising. Professor Sawer, in discussing this doctrine of justiciability, has made the point:

> The position is illustrated by the situation in which Sir John Kerr

had been placed by the Connor loan case, discussed in chapter 5. There were obvious legal questions arising from the authorization to Mr Connor, but they were readily capable of judicial resolution at the suit of interested parties; it was a clear case for accepting the advice of ministers and leaving legality for the courts.[10]

On 14 December I spoke directly to the Solicitor-General, Mr M. H. Byers. I knew that the Prime Minister did not in general agree that I was entitled to direct advice from the Law Officers, but the matter was so urgent and so worrying that I felt I should have some confirmation of the legal consideration given to the matter. The Solicitor-General by telephone confirmed that the Attorney-General had advised the Ministers that the loan contemplated could be regarded as for temporary purposes. He said that he thought the Attorney-General's view was an arguable or tenable one. I spoke to the Prime Minister and told him what I had done about the Minute and what the Solicitor-General had said. He raised no objection to the initiative I had taken in speaking to the Solicitor-General.

I shall now indicate the considerations which I had in mind in deciding to sign the Minute after approving of the holding of the meeting.

The position as I saw it was that the meeting had been held, its business had been important and urgent, the senior Ministers who had decided the matter had dispersed, urgent action was apparently needed, no element of policy controversy was known to me. In considering whether I should sign the Minute I was faced by the fact that the rule which required that I should be asked in advance for approval to holding the meeting in my absence had not been observed, but to refuse to sign and thus force another meeting in the circumstances described to me would cause extreme difficulty. I asked myself the following questions:

(a) Would I if awakened in the middle of the night in the circumstances as outlined to me have given approval for the meeting?
(b) Had I been there and had the Ministers unanimously and firmly recommended the proposal, backed by the Attorney-

235

General, would I have accepted the recommendation and signed the Minute?

The answers to these questions were, I concluded, 'yes' in both cases.

I was confronted by a solid political and formal decision made unanimously by the Prime Minister, the Deputy Prime Minister and Treasurer, the Attorney-General and the Minister for Minerals and Energy, backed by the Attorney-General's opinion; their obvious view was that the matter need not go to Cabinet and that it was urgent; and the decision was based upon an explanatory memorandum indicating policy intentions which were put forward as the true reasons for the loan. It seemed to me, as a matter of personal judgment, that the proposal could run into serious legal, and probably serious political trouble, but the Prime Minister was quite explicit in his advice and was fully identified, as a moving party, with what had been decided.

It has to be remembered that my role of signature and approval did not involve personal approval but approval based upon conventions including the convention that I would act on ministerial advice in the normal case. Some of the conventions are directed to ensuring that I should receive unanimous advice, consistent with Government policy. These conventions were satisfied in the instant case. One convention is that in urgent cases where it is not convenient for the Governor-General to be present the Executive Council may meet in his absence, and had I been asked for approval for this, in advance, by a telephone call late at night I would have agreed. I came to the conclusion that in these circumstances it would have been absurd to insist on another formal meeting of the Executive Council to decide everything again in my presence. If the advice that I should not insist on another meeting resulted in invalidity this question too would be for the courts.

I considered whether it was an occasion on which I would have resorted to the 'advise and warn' doctrine on the policy and politics of the matter, at least so far as the Prime Minister was concerned. Normally policy and politics are not for the Governor-General; but on rare occasions, if he judges it to be useful and practical, he can suggest further thought about a matter. On this occasion I concluded that, even if present, I would not have resorted to this doctrine, faced by political unanimity and no known controversy. At the meeting an absolutely firm political decision had been taken and any attempt to change it would have been fruitless. There was no value in my volunteering political advice which had no chance of being accepted. Recourse to the 'advise and warn' doctrine is exceptional and a matter of prudent judgment. My judgment was quite clear in this case — on the Saturday morning I considered but at once rejected it. I have since read the controversy in the press and the suggestions that behind the political and administrative scenes there was much difference of opinion about the proposal. If this were so and had I known it at the time, I think it would have confirmed me in my view that I should not intrude into the policy and politics of the matter.

In all of these circumstances I decided that the sensible thing to do was to excuse the lapse by which I had not had an opportunity to be present at the meeting and by which my prior consent to its being held had not been obtained, and to sign the Minute.

At an Executive Council meeting at which I presided on 7 January the decision made on 13 December was rescinded.

On 28 January I presided at a further meeting of the Executive Council which was attended by Mr Connor, the Minister for Minerals and Energy, and by the Attorney-General, Senator Murphy. This re-established the original decision except that the amount was changed from $US4000 million to $US2000 million. I was told that the reasons for entering into the new decision were the same as those previously canvassed. Senator Murphy in answer to a specific enquiry from me said that he was of the legal view that the loan could be entered into and legally justified despite the provisions of the Constitution and the Financial Agreement, on the basis that the loan was for temporary purposes; that he had so advised at the previous Executive Council meeting and he was still of the same opinion. He said that his advice accordingly was that the Minute should be approved relying on his legal opinion and because it was the policy of the Government as expressed by the four Ministers who had previously been involved, including the Prime Minister. Mr Connor confirmed this. Although there was no detailed statement about the immediate availability of money on loan, the whole impression was one of urgency because he wanted to get on immediately with action on the authority of the Minute. I came to the conclusion that in this situation it would be useless for me to try to discuss policy and of no relevance what my own legal opinion might be. Clearly any suggestion that the matter should go to the whole of Cabinet would have been fruitless.

On 20 May 1975 the decision of 28 January was rescinded at a meeting of the Executive Council. At that time I was absent from Australia on State visits to Fiji and New Zealand. Some months later — on or about 20 October — the Vice-President of the Executive Council Mr Frank Stewart spoke to me on the telephone about a problem he had in connection with that meeting, at which he had been present. I listened to what he had to say but concluded there was nothing I could do to help him resolve his problem.

I now turn to justiciable issues connected with the 1974 joint sitting of the Parliament.

Early in my Governor-Generalship, as I have made clear, I realised that legal points should be dealt with judicially if they were justiciable. When it came to issuing a Proclamation calling a joint sitting of both Houses soon after I took up my office it seemed to me that what had happened about the Petroleum and Minerals Authority Bill had not satisfied the requirements of section 57 of the Constitution, and that the Bill had not provided a proper legal basis for the 1974 double dissolution, though there were five other Bills which did. Sir Paul Hasluck had accepted legal advice to the contrary and had included a reference to the Petroleum and Minerals Authority Bill in his double dissolution Proclamation. I was advised to include it with the other five proposed laws in my joint sitting Proclamation. I sought legal advice, through the Prime Minister, as to whether I was bound to do this. I received advice that I was. Ultimately I decided that I should act upon the overall legal and political advice tendered to me and include the Bill in the list of proposed laws which the joint sitting might deal with and vote on, although my own view was that any resulting Act would be invalid. It was later held by the High Court that the Petroleum and Minerals Authority Act, passed by the joint sitting of 1974, was invalid because the provisions of section 57 had not been complied with in its case. The Court also held that there was no need to list any of the six Bills in the Proclamation, but that doing so was surplusage and did not invalidate the Proclamation.

I have not discussed in close detail the intricate legal problems, nor the political, economic or financial problems of the loan affair. These are for others. I have given the reasons for my actions. The affair had a real effect upon me because I could not see a good reason why the ordinary practices relating to the Executive Council had been departed from. Despite preparations for a meeting on 13 December the Governor-General had not been brought into the matter; and I pondered on the reasons why this was so. It seemed to me that what had happened ought not to have happened and that it could perhaps be a warning of the risk that the reality of the Governor-General's office might be by-passed and refuge taken in the rubber stamp assumption. I was very much concerned too that what I had had to do might be misunderstood by many in the community as indicating that I myself was indifferent to important government business and subscribed to the rubber stamp theory. Certainly this was not true.

If I had been present at the meeting of 13 December, I could have tried to get in writing the legal advice offered by the Attorney-General, although I would have accepted his oral advice if he had persisted with it. By the time the meeting was concluded in my absence and the decision of 13 December 1974 firmly taken and recorded upon oral advice, it was too late in practical terms to get written advice. I had no doubt that the Ministers wished to act on oral advice. It would have been interesting for history to have the extended written argument of the Attorney-General on this point. Perhaps it could be said that when it came to the meeting of 28 January 1975 I could have asked the Attorney-General for written advice. My judgment was that the Ministers had acted once on the oral advice and that this was a matter on which it was profitless for me to run violently into a brick wall. I decided that as they and the Prime Minister and Deputy Prime Minister had clear-cut views there was nothing I could do about it. I had been in office only six months and was learning fast what was possible and what was not.

As the loan crisis built up during the middle months of 1975 I worried about the lack of knowledge in the community about what had happened. Some criticism was made in which it was said I apparently preferred to be at the Opera than at a very important Executive Council meeting. I had at that time to remain silent. As new problems emerged in the second half of 1975, especially towards the end of September and afterwards, I ceased to worry so much about what had occurred in December 1974, but began to think very carefully indeed about where my duty might lead me if a supply crisis developed. The loan affair was to lead, in mid-October, to the resignation of Mr Connor, which was treated by the Opposition as one reason for denying supply in that it was said to provide evidence of extraordinary and reprehensible conduct by the Government. In its resolution denying supply on 16 October the Senate relied *inter alia* upon 'the overseas loan scandal which was an attempt by the Government to subvert the Constitution, to by-pass Parliament and to evade its responsibilities to the States and to the Loan Council'.[11]

I had learned some lessons from the loan affair, and as the supply crisis deepened in the latter part of the year I knew that I should need to keep a very watchful eye on events. The warning I had received left me somewhat changed in my attitude as to the vigilance that might be necessary to my office and its duties. I did not intend to deal with any crisis which might involve exercise of the reserve powers acting automatically as a rubber stamp for whatever the Prime Minister might advise; and I stiffened myself against the need to be ready to make an informed and neutral assessment should critical discretionary matters arise for my decision.

16

July to October 1975

The atmosphere in which the drama of the blocking of supply unfolded is well evoked in material written in the press of the period. An appropriate starting point is the Bass by-election in June 1975, held to fill the vacant seat of former Labor Minister and Deputy Prime Minister Lance Barnard, who had resigned to become Australian Ambassador to Sweden. It was commonly held, as shown by the press, that the result of that election was something of a disaster for the Government. The campaign was strongly fought by Mr Whitlam and Mr Fraser. Mr Fraser took the offensive on federal issues, and the Prime Minister took up the challenge. The swing of seventeen per cent away from the Government and the gallup polls of the time were interpreted by the media as meaning that the Government was not in good electoral shape in July.

Soon afterwards the headlines in the press turned to the dismissal of Dr James Ford Cairns on 2 July. One element in his dismissal, and in the transfer of Mr Clyde Cameron from the Ministry for Labour and Immigration to Science and Consumer Affairs not long before, bore an ironic relationship to the drama of November. To understand these dismissals it is necessary to have section 64 of the Constitution at hand. It reads:

> The Governor-General may appoint officers to administer such departments of State of the Commonwealth as the Governor-General in Council may establish. Such officers shall hold office during the pleasure of the Governor-General. They shall be members of the Federal Executive Council, and shall be the Queen's Ministers of State for the Commonwealth.
>
> After the first general election no Minister of State shall hold office

for a longer period than three months unless he is or becomes a senator or a member of the House of Representatives.

I had an appointment to receive the Prime Minister at 8 p.m. on 2 July 1975, at which time I knew he intended to advise the dismissal of Dr Cairns from his portfolio as Minister for the Environment (to which he had earlier been translated after resigning as Treasurer). I was at dinner when at about 7.30 p.m. my staff received a telephone call from Miss Junie Morosi, private secretary to Dr Cairns, requesting me to talk to him on the telephone. It was not difficult to guess what he wanted to speak about and I did not wish to have a conversation with him before speaking with the Prime Minister. I sent him a message that I was at dinner and that if any need to talk arose I would let him know. He at once rang back through Miss Morosi to say he knew from the Prime Minister what the latter's advice to me was to be and he asked to be heard before I made any decision.

I believed then, as now, that a Minister has not the right to be heard by the Governor-General before being dismissed under section 64 of the Constitution. A similar request had been made the month before when the Prime Minister obtained the dismissal of Mr Cameron from his portfolio. Mr Cameron had refused to resign as Minister for Labour and Immigration. The Prime Minister was at the time engaging in a reshuffle of some of the portfolios in his Ministry. I was advised by him to terminate Mr Cameron's commission under section 64 and this advice was supported by appropriate legal and constitutional opinion. A letter was received from Mr Cameron by the Prime Minister whilst he was talking with me — it was delivered to him by hand in my study. Mr Whitlam offered me the letter to read but I elected not to read it. Mr Whitlam however told me that Mr Cameron had argued that I was not entitled to dismiss him on the advice of the Prime Minister without hearing him. I took the view that I had the power to dismiss Mr Cameron, because that was the Prime Minister's advice and consistent with the legal and constitutional position as set forth in the supportive documentation and legal advice. I also took the view that I should not hear Mr Cameron, because I could not put myself in

242

the position of being at the same time the recipient of conflicting political advice from the two Ministers. Accordingly I exercised my legal powers on the Prime Minister's advice and dismissed Mr Cameron without hearing what he wanted to say. The Prime Minister advised me to do this and I agreed with his advice.

When Mr Whitlam arrived on 2 July and the expected advice was tendered to me, together with the advice that I should not hear anything from Dr Cairns, I acted in accordance with the same legal and constitutional principles. I had Dr Cairns informed that I had received certain advice from the Prime Minister and that in the circumstances I could see no point in having discussions with him.

The actions of Mr Cameron and Dr Cairns, in asking me to hear them before I came to a decision, were consistent with the view that I had a personal discretion and did not have to act on the advice of the Prime Minister. They were, of course, right about that but wrong if they believed I was bound by law to hear them. I was legally entitled but not bound to hear them. Amongst other considerations I felt that the Prime Minister had to take personal responsibility for the dismissal of his Ministers.

I did not know whether Mr Cameron or Dr Cairns had taken legal advice. Certainly neither challenged my decision in court.

Some have, I understand, said that Mr Whitlam taught me the nature of my dismissal powers under section 64, later to be used against him and his Government. In reality I well understood those powers. But I found it intriguing that two experienced Ministers like Mr Cameron and Dr Cairns apparently aspired to be heard by me before I made a decision on the Prime Minister's advice.

The advice tendered to me by Mr Whitlam, on legal and constitutional grounds, that a Minister has no legal right to be heard before being dismissed under section 64, applies to the Prime Minister just as to Ministers generally. When later I came to the decision that he and his Ministers should have their commissions withdrawn by action under section 64, the *law* applicable was the same law that he and I had previously agreed should be applied to Mr Cameron and Dr Cairns. In dismissing

Mr Cameron and Dr Cairns I was exercising my legal powers on the Prime Minister's advice. In dismissing Mr Whitlam and his Government I was acting at my own discretion, but the law applied in all three cases was the same. There is no legal right to be heard before a dismissal under section 64.

However — whereas in dealing with Mr Cameron and Dr Cairns I decided that they had no legal right to put a case to me against dismissal and that I was under no moral duty to hear anything they might wish to say since I believed I should follow the Prime Minister's advice — when it came to the termination of Mr Whitlam's commission and those of his Ministers, Mr Whitlam nonetheless had an opportunity, as I shall reveal, to put a case to me had he any wish to do so. Instead, his reaction was to attempt to take a different, a drastic and dramatic course.

By early July speculation was growing that Mr Fraser, who had said previously that the Government should be permitted to see its time out unless extraordinary and reprehensible circumstances demanded that it be brought down, might use the Senate's power to block supply when the Budget was presented.

On 4 July, the *Canberra Times* published an editorial in which it discussed the nature of the Governor-General's powers and duty. This was I believe the first, or one of the first, occasions in 1975 when points of the kind made were publicly put forward. This early reference to vice-regal powers which were to be engaged by the supply crisis was made in the context of developments in the loan affair. The editorial said:

> The ultimate guardian of the Constitution, of the rule of law, and of the customary usages of the Australian Government in a time of crisis is the Governor-General, who has certain clear powers to check an elected government. He normally acts on the advice of his Ministers but there are occasions when he need not seek or accept that advice. He could, for good and sufficient reasons, revoke the commissions of a Prime Minister or of other Ministers. It is within his power to take steps that could lead to a dissolution of the Parliament and to a general election. The good government of Australia, especially at a time of grave economic disruption, is the only thing that counts and the most extreme steps to ensure this must be taken if there is no other way.

The *Canberra Times* is one of our leading newspapers, widely read in political and administrative circles. After 4 July presumably its opinions quoted above received some attention and evaluation at top political level.

What was said in the editorial was to become relevant in the supply crisis, but it was not relevant to the loan affair. Having regard to what happened when the powers were exercised in November it can readily be imagined what the reaction would have been if they had been exercised in July, or at all, in connection with the loan affair. All questions arising in that affair were justiciable and appropriate for the High Court to deal with. Two academic lawyers, Professor L. R. Zines and Professor Geoffrey Lindell, after the publication of the *Canberra Times* editorial wrote to the editor saying that the branch of government whose prime duty is authoritatively to determine the law is the judiciary, and that even in cases of 'plain illegality' the availability of judicial remedies would be a very relevant consideration.

In opening the annual conference of the Australasian Law Schools Association at the University of New South Wales on 25 August 1975 I referred to all of this, including the views of the two academics, saying that the question remained whether there were any circumstances in which either on a legal or other issue 'the Governor-General may or should precipitate a crisis for Parliament or the electorate'. In this opening address I remarked that it had been 'an interesting first year for a Governor-General who is a lawyer'. In saying this I had in mind the joint sitting but in particular, of course, the loan affair. I added, 'I have been serving an interesting apprenticeship'. My address, made to a large audience of academic lawyers presumably of all shades of political opinion, was a clear indication that at the end of August my mind was engaged on the question of the reserve powers.

My records show that by the end of July I was considering that an election could take place before the end of the year. We should know, I thought, by the end of October or at least the first week in November. My view then was that the Prime Minister would, if supply were blocked, ask for a double dissolution, and an election would take place about the first week in December.

In August the Budget was introduced. Mr Fraser said that although it would be criticised no election would be precipitated unless some unexpected and serious change occurred. On 25 August, at Admiralty House, the Prime Minister said to me that an election could occur early in December if supply were denied. This was no longer his approach in September and thereafter.

By 12 September I had come to the tentative conclusion that the Prime Minister believed that if forced to a general election on the Budget the loss for his party would be great, with a possibility that the Opposition would end up in control of both Houses. I did not think he was in a mood to go quietly to an election.

On the morning of 12 September the press carried a story to the effect that Mr Whitlam was going 'to tough it out'; that his attitude was: only the House had the political right to decide about the Budget; if the Senate refused to pass it, the Prime Minister would not accept that as a ground for coming to me for a dissolution of the House of Representatives or a double dissolution, he would simply say that the responsibility for funds running out must be borne by the Opposition. He would send the Budget back to the Senate and if necessary would do so again and force them to block supply more than once. Then there would be a battle in the country about who was responsible for the ensuing mess. So the theory ran.

The Papua New Guinea Independence Day celebrations took place in Port Moresby in September 1975—Independence Day was 15 September. I was in Port Moresby for the ceremonies, and so too were Mr Whitlam, Mr Fraser and Mr J. D. Anthony, leader of the National Country Party.

In Port Moresby on 15 September the Prime Minister told me that he was thinking he might, if the Senate rejected the Appropriation Bills, present them to me nevertheless for assent, with advice that the Senate had no legal power to reject them. This discussion took place at an Independence Day reception. I parried this by saying that if he did that there would be an uproar but doubtless the High Court, assuming that I did assent, would hear immediately a case to declare the resulting 'Acts' invalid. He agreed.

The Government did not take this course and I was never

confronted by the problem of whether I would assent to the Bills or not. If they had been sent to me early after a deferral of supply, with legal advice that the Senate had no power over money Bills and advice from the Prime Minister to sign them, my difficulties might have been less intense than they would have been had it occurred, say, in early November. It was an academic question as things turned out. Nevertheless it was a worrying one until it was resolved.

The Prime Minister put to me in Port Moresby another point of importance: he said on 15 September that if I were, at the height of a crisis, to contemplate terminating his commission at a time when salaries were not being paid, he would have to tell me that Mr Fraser would not be able to get supply either, because new legislation would probably be necessary and it would not pass the House of Representatives. He recognised, however, that it might be legally possible for Mr Fraser to have the Bills revived and passed in the Senate. The Prime Minister said that, as he saw things, people who were left unpaid would have to rely upon a promise for a while. The conversation was very significant indeed because it showed the Prime Minister had already in mind the possibility of my contemplating his dismissal, and was pointing out difficulties he believed would stand in my way. It showed too that he was already entertaining the notion of attempting to govern without supply if it were blocked.

Meanwhile in Australia the debate was proceeding. On 15 September the *Financial Review* had an editorial, 'Exit the Marquess of Queensberry', which contained the following passage:

> If the Senate (or more correctly the Opposition through the use of its numbers in the Senate) chooses to exercise the power by knocking over the Budget the question arises as to what happens then.
>
> The Opposition, quite naturally, expects Mr Whitlam to drive out to Government House and seek an election.
>
> But Mr Whitlam has said to hell with that. He said on Friday: 'One can say there is no obligation by law, by rule, by precedent or by convention for a Prime Minister in those circumstances which are threatened, to advise the Governor-General to dissolve the House of Representatives and have an election for it'.

The editorial continued:

> Mr Whitlam is quite right. There is no constitutional compulsion on him to seek an election for the House of Representatives should the Senate reject the Budget.
>
> The decision on what flows from rejection of the Budget is entirely for the Prime Minister. He has various options, from doing nothing, to seeking a single dissolution, a double dissolution or even bringing forward the Senate election due before next June.
>
> Mr Fraser has described Mr Whitlam's remarks as arrant nonsense, and said that if Mr Whitlam fails to call an election after rejection of the Budget the Governor-General could be forced to sack him.
>
> Undoubtedly Sir John Kerr has the power to do so, but that is another question altogether.
>
> If and when Sir John Kerr decided to revoke Mr Whitlam's commission and call an election the nation would be in the grip of a raging constitutional crisis and today's major issue of economic management would play second fiddle in the campaign.

This amounted to acceptance of the view that in extreme crisis I had the power to revoke Mr Whitlam's commission. The *Financial Review* is very widely read in political circles.

In passing I may recall that the prediction that economic issues would play second fiddle to constitutional issues proved to be false. In the election campaign in November–December 1975 the economic issues were not displaced by the constitutional issues. Both were very important.

In the *National Times* of 15–20 September 1975 an article by Mr Andrew Clark stated:

> The message is that Gough Whitlam will play it hard. If the Budget is rejected he may advise the Governor-General that there is no reason to call an election. This would result in the Government machine coming to a halt.
>
> However, the Governor-General—in this case the Labor-appointed Sir John Kerr—has wide discretionary powers. If he decides that the system of government is in jeopardy he has the power to ignore the Prime Minister's advice and issue writs for an election.
>
> There are also precedents for his commissioning the Opposition

leader to form a Government. However, Mr Fraser's Government would be short-lived, as the tightly disciplined Labor majority in the Lower House would defeat him on the first vote.

Mr Clark, although he did not at that time appear to grasp the complexities of a dismissal followed by a dissolution, accepted the fact of wide vice-regal discretionary powers.

In the same issue of the same weekly Mr John Edwards wrote:

> Ultimately the Governor-General, Sir John Kerr, will have to do something for the peace, order and good government of the Commonwealth. He would ask the Prime Minister over, and tell him that there has to be an election — either for the House, or a half Senate, or a double dissolution of both Houses.

As things turned out I did not do this. My reasons appear in the coming chapters.

In the *Sydney Morning Herald* of 23 September Professor P. H. Lane, Professor of Law at Sydney University, quoted the distinguished constitutional lawyer Sir Harrison Moore as saying:

> A check upon the Ministry and the Lower House lies in the fact that the Upper House might in an extreme case refuse to pass the Appropriation Bill, and thereby force a dissolution or a change of ministry. These are the conditions recognised by the (Commonwealth) Constitution.

Lane also quoted Mr J. R. Odgers, the Clerk of the Senate, as saying in his book *Australian Senate Practice*:

> A Senate, which correctly interprets the mood of the electorate, has a quite remarkable annual opportunity — by refusing to join in the grant of Supply — to bring about the dissolution of the House of Representatives and the resignation of the Government.[1]

Lane then himself says:

> One may regard the practice and the writers as evidencing 'the customary usages of Australian Government' to cite the former Governor-General's criterion for legitimate government. And in these customary usages one would find a duty on a Prime Minister to dissolve when the Senate refuses Supply.

Mr Peter Bowers in the *Sydney Morning Herald* of 20 September had written:

> Mr Fraser may be undecided, but not so Mr Whitlam, according to the Prime Minister's advisers.
>
> Mr Whitlam, his advisers say, has decided that he has no practical alternative to sitting it out if Supply is blocked.
>
> His argument is that the Government has nothing to lose by literally going for broke. If he were to agree to an election for the House of Representatives or a double dissolution of both Houses, the Government would be annihilated, losing possibly 20 or more seats.

Mr Bowers then outlined 'the constitutional scenario Mr Whitlam's advisers are scripting of events that would follow the denial of Supply'.

He concluded:

> It would be a breathtaking gamble of Whitlamesque proportion but anyone who thinks Mr Whitlam is bluffing, does not know the man.
>
> He has lived dangerously all his political life.
>
> . . . He is being pushed into a corner by Mr Fraser. Whitlam at bay is a very dangerous stag.

In the *Australian* of 18 September an article had appeared written by Mr Graham Williams. He mentioned the possibility that the Governor-General might dissolve the Lower House himself. This possibility, he said, was quite plausible. He quoted Professor Sawer as saying:

> Mr Fraser could form a government simply for the purpose of advising the Governor-General to dissolve the Lower House and call an election;

and as being of the opinion that it would be much better from Mr Whitlam's viewpoint if he himself called a double dissolution.

> 'That way Mr Whitlam would have the chance of gaining control of both Houses.'

In the emerging public debate the following comments from Mr Williams, although containing complimentary references, are to the point:

Sir John, the brilliant Q.C. and former judge, is likely to be put in the very tough spot of deciding key constitutional issues if the Government is trapped in a corner by a hostile Senate.

Sir John is a big man. A formidable intellect. A generous personality. In the looming constitutional impasse, he will need all these qualities in large measure.

He, more than anyone else, may become the man of the moment.

It was quite impossible for anyone to read the press of the second half of September without having it driven home that the Governor-General in a great crisis has a power of dismissal and dissolution. Nor could it be imagined that either of the leaders would fail to assume that I must be watching the unfolding of their policies in full awareness of what they might involve for me.

By 30 September it was evident to me that the Prime Minister, as then advised, was no longer taking the view that he could present to me Appropriation Bills which had been rejected by the Senate, and ask for royal assent. The Attorney-General said to me on 30 September that he was of the clear view that the Senate had legal power to reject the Appropriation Bills, and that such Bills must be passed by the Senate before they could be put before the Governor-General. Nevertheless I thought it possible there might be a later change of mind.

Among possibilities being canvassed in late September was that if the Senate rejected the Appropriation Bills Mr Whitlam would take the view that the Senate should be the House to face the people, and as a half-Senate election was soon due that was what he might recommend.

There were difficulties for him in this tactic. He perhaps might have derived some advantage from such an election if held in, say, early October, though that would have been an unusually early time to hold it. There would then have been time to have it over, before money came near to running out if there should be a denial of supply. It would have been unsatisfactory if the non-Labor Premiers had advised their Governors not to issue the writs until much later: the election would then have had to be held piecemeal. Moreover there was a very real doubt as to whether the Government would derive any advantage from such an

251

election. Nonetheless the Prime Minister seemed to me at that stage to be keeping his mind open about an early half-Senate election, at which four new Senate positions would be filled for the first time, two each for the Australian Capital Territory and the Northern Territory.

In September whilst considering a half-Senate election the Prime Minister observed that if he could get through until after a half-Senate election was over he would re-present the Appropriation Bills to the Senate. If they were rejected again he would then probably advise a double dissolution, but he said that the ensuing election would not take place until February 1976. This idea, which would have meant attempting to govern for two to three months without supply, did not last long if it were ever seriously intended. In fact the Prime Minister let the chance of an early October half-Senate election pass him by and did not come for it until 11 November.

On 29 September, long before the crisis came to issue, the half-Senate election being a matter of public debate, I asked the Prime Minister what he would do for supply whilst awaiting the half-Senate election should he want to have one. He said, first, that particular Appropriation Bills relating to certain matters would be presented to the Senate and some of these would doubtless be passed, but he accepted the position that other Appropriations would inevitably not be agreed to, if the Opposition finally made up its mind to refuse full Appropriations. He conceded that for the period up to December, if the Opposition remained solid on this point, the Commonwealth would be unable to meet all its obligations.

I asked him whether he thought that Mr Fraser would grant him temporary supply until after such a half-Senate election. Whilst thinking this might be possible, he was very doubtful about it. He realised that there would be a profound constitutional crisis when the money first started to run out — in early November, he said — but he also declared he would certainly not recommend a double dissolution of the House of Representatives and the Senate. On the contrary he told me he would call for a vote of confidence from the House of Representatives and would argue to me that he was entitled to retain his commission for as long as he held the confidence of the House of Representatives, despite his failure to obtain supply.

Here again it was clear that Mr Whitlam had it in his mind that he might have to argue for the retention of his commission. But by the time the critical moment arrived he had apparently abandoned any idea of arguing a case, and taken his stand on his claim that although denied supply he could continue to govern as long as he had the confidence of the Lower House, and that I had no alternative but to let him do as he liked.

October unfolded amid intensifying public debate. On 10 October 1975 an article by Mr Bruce Juddery appeared in the *Canberra Times*. He wrote:

> It is generally assumed that, in the event that the operation of the Commonwealth Government was to run the risk of total collapse, the Governor-General could by-pass the Prime Minister (his chief regular source of advice on these matters) and call either a House of Representatives or a double-dissolution election, in order to settle the issue.

The writer opened up the question whether I would be entitled to seek outside advice and quoted Sir Paul Hasluck's opinions. He wrote:

> Sir John may be wondering if he can seek such external advice off his own bat—or if it is tenable only when offered by the Prime Minister.

Mr Juddery went on:

> Conceivably he could invite Mr Fraser to take over the Government, then wait until he, inevitably, was forced to recommend a dissolution of at least the House of Representatives.
>
> But the whole point of the exercise, it is pointed out, is to ensure Supply. And Mr Fraser has an even thinner chance of doing that in the present Parliament than has Mr Whitlam.

Despite inaccuracy in the final prediction this was an example of the serious public examination of the Governor-General's role that was taking place.

Then came a new public drama with the resignation on 14 October of the Minister for Minerals and Energy, Mr Rex

Connor. Shortly before that broke, I had a conversation with the Prime Minister in which he told me that if supply were denied he would not go to an election of the House, or of both Houses, but would carry on without supply. He said he intended to destroy forever the power of the Senate to refuse supply. In the course of the conversation I said to him, on the subject of governing without supply, 'Do you think that is the wisest course? Wouldn't it be better to go to an election even if you lose? Your opponents will have a difficult time next year if they win, and provided we do not have chaos over supply you would have a very good chance of coming back as Wilson did in England. You are still young and, even if you lose now, if you play your cards right you could easily have a second term as Prime Minister.' In saying this I was going as far, as Governor-General, as I could prudently go in the exercise of my right to 'advise and warn'. The Prime Minister rejected this approach out of hand. He said he would never be forced into an election by the Senate denying supply.

This was one of the first conversations in which an implacable element began to appear in the Prime Minister's approach to the potential crisis. He made it clear that my suggestion was not discussable and never would be. He confirmed it in a further conversation with me on 14 October, when he was at Government House for the swearing-in of Mr Connor's successor as Minister for Minerals and Energy. On both occasions my suggestion was rejected out of hand and very forcibly — the manner in which it was done was one of the circumstances which led me to foresee there would be no compromise on his part. From that time forward my opinion was that he was beyond the reach of any argument of mine, or even discussion. Everything he said publicly, or privately to me, thereafter strengthened me in that view.

The political background to Mr Connor's resignation, which was closely associated with the loan affair, is well known in Australia and constitutes another chapter in the political disputation of that time. The resignation was taken up by the Opposition as providing the extraordinary and reprehensible circumstances which Mr Fraser had said would justify the denial of supply, although when it came to the point in mid-October he based his decision to defer supply not only on the loan affair including Mr Connor's resignation, but on the Government's total record.

By 15–16 October the Prime Minister, in response to Mr Fraser's decision to defer supply, decided on the policy that was widely described as 'toughing it out'. He said in the middle of October that the Senate must reject supply outright, not defer it, before he would call an election of any kind. He told me on 16 October he would not be out to Yarralumla on the crisis for some time.

Mr Fraser, on the other hand, took the view according to his public statements that I had ample power, before chaos developed too far, to dismiss the Government and produce an election.

I know that one Minister was worried about the policy of 'toughing it out'. His approach was that it would be better for the Prime Minister to accept the inevitable, go down if need be to defeat in an election and start laying the foundation for a return to power in due course. He was very worried about what would happen if step by step we moved into chaos, and concerned that there could be violence in the streets.

Nevertheless in mid-October it was reported that Caucus supported the Prime Minister's tactic of strongly resisting the denial of supply and refusing to recommend a dissolution of the House of Representatives, whilst asking in due course for a half-Senate election.

The stage was thus set for the final confrontation, with all the constitutional possibilities being publicly examined and debated including the Governor-General's power of dismissal of the Government. Privately too—from barbecue to beach, from congress ante-room to club—it was said to be increasingly rare to hear any other topic discussed. On 16 October, the day on which supply was deferred by the Senate for the first time, Mr Don Whitington in an article in the Melbourne *Herald* brought out into the open the possibility of my own recall. He said:

> It is conceivable that Mr Whitlam's advice would be that the interests of the Australian people could be best served by giving the

Royal Assent to the Supply Bill regardless of the Senate's rejection, and that any other course could lead to poverty, hardship and perhaps even civil disturbances.

The Governor-General could reject that advice and seek some other solution.

What is little known, however, is that the Prime Minister would still hold the final ace.

The Prime Minister has the power to dismiss the Governor-General in the event of disagreement. It is a power he almost certainly would not use, but it is still a power he, or any other Prime Minister, possesses.

Coming events were to shed some light on the question of whether the power would have been used in extreme circumstances.

Graham Williams in the *Australian* of the same day, 16 October, said:

> Sir John's role in the looming crisis will be of utmost importance. For the Government's funds will soon begin drying up in various departments—and by mid-November there will be no money left to run the country.

This prediction was interesting, while not entirely accurate as to timing. Although in some areas money would run out earlier the complete drying up of funds 'to run the country' would not occur until the end of November.

He quoted Professor Colin Howard as saying that it was 'fanciful' to suggest that Mr Whitlam would ask me to assent to the Budget after it had been rejected by the Senate—'a proposition floated some weeks ago by government ministers'. Professor Howard, he said, was of the view that 'There's no doubt the Governor-General does not have the power to assent to a bill which has not passed both Houses'.

Mr Williams continued:

> Another possibility is that Sir John will refuse to accept the advice of the Executive Council. He will feel that he must act to resolve the constitutional crisis.
>
> And he can do this by terminating the commission of the Prime Minister—in effect throwing him out of office, as the Governor of

256

N.S.W. Sir Philip Game did to the N.S.W. Premier, Jack Lang, in the 1930s.

On the same day the *Sydney Morning Herald* carried an article by Mr Ian Hicks quoting opinions of Professor Lane, who said:

> The leading writers in the field accept the refusal of Supply by an Australian Senate as machinery to bring a Government to the people.

Professor Lane was quoted as saying:

> Let's stop all this humbugging about convention and law and the done thing, and all this hysteria about crisis and anarchy and civil war. This is a perfectly respectable machinery which, if followed through, just means that the Government is put before the people and the electorate might say 'give them a fair go' or 'they've had a fair go; give us a new Government'.

The Professor supported his arguments with the views of eminent constitutionalists of the past 'and an odd couple — Mr Whitlam and the former Senator Murphy — from the present'.

Professor Lane is quoted by Hicks as saying that 'there is no question that the Governor-General has a discretion, a personal discretion. Evatt said so in his book, *The King and his Dominion Governors*'.

Mr Hicks then asked Professor Lane, 'What might Sir John do if an impasse arose?' The Professor answered:

> He would simply dismiss the Whitlam Ministry, call in the Leader of the Opposition and ask him to form a Government. The Fraser Government would be defeated immediately on the floor of the House and would ask the Governor-General for a double dissolution.

My purpose in quoting from the press of the period up to the morning of 16 October is to make it clear how the discussion was developing publicly. Anyone who followed it could not fail to note that many people believed I had a power of dismissal and might exercise it. They were speculating; but the question of the exact nature of my powers was one which no one involved in the looming crisis could ignore. The press writers, whatever their views, were putting everyone upon enquiry as to the nature of the

Governor-General's powers and his likely reaction to unfolding events. Mr Whitlam could not ignore the possibility of his own dismissal; and I could not ignore the risk that a more compliant Governor-General might in certain circumstances be substituted for me, my own commission being withdrawn, and the crisis being exacerbated by the consequent involvement of the Queen.

On the night of 16 October, before a State banquet at Government House in honour of the Prime Minister of Malaysia, Tun Abdul Razak, in my study in the presence of the guest of honour and his wife, Mrs Whitlam and my wife, Mr Whitlam in referring to the crisis, which had broken that day with the Senate's deferral of supply, said to me with a brilliant smile, 'It could be a question of whether I get to the Queen first for your recall or you get in first with my dismissal.'

We all laughed.[2]

17

The Deferral of Supply

My wife and I had been invited to make an official visit to Canada during 1975 and this was, with the Prime Minister's agreement, to take place in November. We were also to go to the United Kingdom to be received by the Queen, and at the Prime Minister's request to make a State visit to Eire. The absence was to be of four or five weeks and arrangements had been made long before the supply crisis.

On 15 October 1975 the leader of the Opposition announced the intention of the Opposition to delay Appropriation Bill (No. 1) 1975–6 and Appropriation Bill (No. 2) 1975–6, which had been passed by the House of Representatives. These Bills, amongst other things, appropriated moneys for the ordinary annual services of government.

It was impossible on 15 October to foresee what might happen, but once the leader of the Opposition had spoken I came to the view that the situation, as it developed, might require the presence of the Governor-General. There were a number of possibilities depending upon what the Opposition actually did and how the Government responded. One was the possibility of an election. I therefore spoke to the Prime Minister and put it to him that in view of what the leader of the Opposition had said I should cancel my overseas trip, since it was possible a crisis might develop over supply. The Prime Minister agreed. (In the result we went to England in late December 1975 to report to the Queen, after the elections, when the Labor Party was in Opposition. The State visits to Canada and Eire had meantime of course to be cancelled. The trip was criticised by some Opposition elements; but it was in fact a substituted trip, taking the place of the one approved by Mr Whitlam, and made at a time when the value of reporting to the Queen was far greater, having regard to the crisis and the dismissal, than it would have been had the crisis not occurred.)

On 16 October the Senate decided that the two Appropriation Bills be not further proceeded with until the Government agreed to submit itself to the judgment of the people. The resolution in respect of each Bill was that:

> this Bill be not further proceeded with until the Government agrees to submit itself to the judgment of the people, the Senate being of the opinion that the Prime Minister and his Government no longer have the trust and confidence of the Australian people because of—
>
> (a) the continuing incompetence, evasion, deceit and duplicity of the Prime Minister and his Ministers as exemplified in the overseas loan scandal which was an attempt by the Government to subvert the Constitution, to by-pass Parliament and to evade its responsibilities to the States and the Loan Council;
> (b) the Prime Minister's failure to maintain proper control over the activities of his Ministers and Government to the detriment of the Australian nation and people; and
> (c) the continuing mismanagement of the Australian economy by the Prime Minister and this Government with policies which have caused a lack of confidence in this nation's potential and created inflation and unemployment not experienced for 40 years.[1]

On the same day the House of Representatives adopted a resolution as follows:

> 1. This House *declares* that it has full confidence in the Australian Labor Party Government.
> 2. This House *affirms* that the Constitution and the conventions of the Constitution vest in this House the control of the supply of moneys to the elected Government and that the threatened action of the Senate constitutes a gross violation of the roles of the respective Houses of the Parliament in relation to the appropriation of moneys.
> 3. This House *asserts* the basic principle that a Government that continues to have a majority in the House of Representatives has a right to expect that it will be able to govern.

4. This House *condemns* the threatened action of the Leader of the Opposition and of the non-government parties in the Senate as being reprehensible and as constituting a grave threat to the principles of responsible government and of Parliamentary democracy in Australia.
5. This House *calls upon* the Senate to pass without delay the Loan Bill 1975, the Appropriation Bill (No. 1) 1975–76 and the Appropriation Bill (No. 2) 1975–76.[2]

In this chapter I shall be quoting extensively from the debates in the House of Representatives. Although the Senate had the power to block supply it was in the House, where the two leaders were, that the real drama was enacted. Proceedings in the Senate reflected the drama in the House. It is not my intention to give the parliamentary history of the crisis but to remind people of the mounting atmosphere of strain and anxiety of those days.

In the House of Representatives on the previous day, 15 October, Mr Fraser had asked the Prime Minister whether he would 'resign decently in the interests of the political health of Australia'. Mr Whitlam's reply included the following statement:

No newspaper will support any idea that the Senate should reject a budget, but they now suggest that I should relieve the Leader of the Opposition of his dilemma; that I should put him out of his misery by having a double dissolution. I am sorry. This is a matter which he will have to solve himself. He will have to tell his followers to do the unspeakable, the unprecedented, the reprehensible, of rejecting a Budget. If a Budget is rejected there is very likely to be an election of one sort or another. It would of course be quite improper for me to foretell the advice which I would tender to the Governor-General in those reprehensible and extraordinary circumstances.[3]

A question was asked the same day by the leader of the National Country Party, Mr Anthony, as follows:

Has the Prime Minister yet become aware of the fact that the people of Australia have lost confidence and trust in him and his crumbling Government? Does he know that the majority of Australians are sick and tired of the smell of scandal that hangs around his Government and that they no longer believe that he and

261

his Government are capable of governing or fit to govern? I again ask the Prime Minister will he do the decent thing and resign.[4]

Mr Whitlam said in his answer:

> The Government should be that party or parties with the majority in the House of Representatives. The Australian Labor Party has a majority in the House of Representatives . . . It will be my duty to tender advice to the Governor-General to issue writs for a House of Representatives election before 9 July 1977.[5]

On 15 October Mr Fraser asked the Prime Minister whether he recalled 'saying on 1 October 1970 in Parliament that we all know that in the British Parliament the tradition is that if a money Bill is defeated the Government goes to the people to seek their endorsement of its policies'. (Mr Fraser said it was 'quite plain that the Prime Minister was referring to a rejection by the Senate as well as by the House of Representatives'.)

Mr Whitlam's reply included the following remarks:

> If a money Bill were rejected in this House I would go to the Governor-General. If the Government were defeated on a vote of confidence in this House I would go to the Governor-General . . . it is the Government formed in this House and answerable to this House that determines financial matters . . . However much the honourable gentleman may squirm he will be the guilty man if this practice which has endured for three-quarters of a century, and this practice which is observed throughout the world today, is broken. I will not let him off the horns of his dilemma. He could not carry a motion of no confidence in the Australian Government in this House.[6]

The battle was thus joined in the Parliament on 15 October. It was on the same day that Mr Whitlam in Parliament made his uncompleted quotation, already referred to, from Sir Robert Menzies' 1932 letter to Sir Philip Game[7]; thereby revealing that he had been making a study of dismissals of Governments and conceding without question the existence of the vice-regal prerogative and his awareness of it.

On Saturday 18 October I had another talk with the Prime Minister. I found his attitude had hardened considerably. He said he would advise no election of any kind whatsoever. An early half-Senate election would have involved a departure from that policy.

The Prime Minister said again that he was determined to break the Senate's power, which enabled it at its whim to force an election of the House of Representatives by denying supply. He had reached the conclusion that in October we had come to a great moment of history such as happened in the United Kingdom in 1909–10. He had, he said, finally and irrevocably decided never to take the House of Representatives to the people because the Senate denied it power to govern by cutting off money. He would not do this in October–November, nor the following May, nor ever.

Of course in 1909 Asquith took the opposite view and did take the Commons to the people when the Lords denied supply. It can readily be imagined what an uproar, what an extreme constitutional crisis would have arisen if Asquith had tried to govern Great Britain without parliamentary supply.

Mr Whitlam seemed to me to be in an exuberant, even a euphoric mood on 18 October. In the same conversation he said to me, 'You are in the position of George V.' My riposte was, 'But you are not in the position of Asquith. You cannot pack the Senate.' He asserted that the only solution was a political one and he could and would prevail.

Already that day the Prime Minister was talking of finding a way of getting the banks to lend to everyone to whom the Commonwealth owed money — public servants, troops, police, contractors and so on — the amount owed. He said that by this means, if the technique were legal, and he was confident that it was — though it was subject to further examination — he could defuse the issue: no one, or almost no one, would suffer, and Mr Fraser would be outmanoeuvred. The crisis would, he argued, be no real constitutional crisis, because despite denial of supply he would still be able to govern, and there would be no excuse for me to demand evidence from him that he could get supply, and no excuse for removing him and sending for someone willing to advise an election.

From the tone of this conversation I clearly felt that no comment or suggestion from me would be welcome; and this was the climate, from the second week of October onward, of all my conversations with Mr Whitlam regarding his intention to govern without supply. I was being *told* what the Prime Minister intended to do. The impression I had received a few days earlier in conversation with him[8] was strongly reinforced.

I never again felt I could *talk* to the Prime Minister about his policy on supply. When later he permitted, though without enthusiasm, discussion to take place about a compromise involving a half-Senate election[9], it had to proceed on the assumption that capitulation by Mr Fraser and grant of supply were irreducible conditions.

I said to the Prime Minister at this time, 'You say you intend to break the power of the Senate to force the Lower House to the people. You can do that only by getting a constitutional amendment or by breaking Mr Fraser.' He said, 'I cannot get a constitutional amendment but I can and will break Fraser, if my party stands behind me and it will.' I replied. 'What about his?' He said, 'It will break.'

I have mentioned earlier the State banquet for the Prime Minister of Malaysia, held at Government House on the night of 16 October. A few days before that dinner I had raised with the Prime Minister the question of my having a talk with Mr Fraser with a view to ascertaining how serious things were. This was before the actual deferral of the Appropriation Bills. I had in mind that it would be important to be able to assess possible future developments in a realistic way, and that neutral discussion could help. At first the Prime Minister said he could not agree to my proposal, but on a later occasion he said that although he could not agree to an official call on me by Mr Fraser he thought an informal chat at the Tun Razak dinner would be appropriate. By the time that dinner took place, however, Mr Fraser had the day before publicly crossed his Rubicon.

At the dinner I had an informal, short conversation with Mr Fraser in which he reiterated his public position without qualification. I gained the impression that he was well aware of how much he had at stake. This was not a discussion intended to explore possibilities of compromise, since I had no agreement from the Prime Minister for such a move, nor had I made any such suggestion. At no time did I contemplate giving Mr Fraser, nor through him the Senate, advice of any kind.

There was, during the crisis, speculation about such action on my part. On 19 October the Sydney *Sun–Herald* printed an article setting out some views attributed to Professor Howard of Melbourne University and Professor Sawer of the Australian National University, both of whom were said to have strongly suggested that I should assume the role of mediator or conciliator between the two leaders to resolve the deadlock.

Professor Howard was quoted as saying:

> The Governor-General is the only person left with sufficiently high office, and who is not identified with either party, to resolve the situation;

and as having expressed the view that the Constitution was not yet in danger—in which case the Governor-General would be virtually forced to intervene—

> but if the train of events that has been set in motion continues uninterrupted then it will be in grave danger.

Professor Sawer was said to have supported the call for me to mediate.

Whether the views of the two professors were accurately reported or not I do not know. In my view, the Governor-General cannot take an independent initiative of a political kind, as he would be doing if without the Prime Minister's approval he sought to mediate between the parties or their leaders. No advice could be given me by Mr Fraser nor could I offer him advice.

This view is expressed, in terms of the Sovereign, in a memorandum written by the Prime Minister of the United Kingdom Mr Asquith, as follows:

> It is not the function of a Constitutional Sovereign to act as arbiter or mediator between rival parties and policies, still less to take advice from the leaders on both sides, with the view to forming a conclusion of his own.[10]

In an editorial of 20 October the *Sydney Morning Herald* wrote:

> It is quite wrong for Mr Fraser to imply that Sir John Kerr will

shortly intervene by calling for a House of Representatives poll. It is equally wrong for the Prime Minister to imply that Sir John Kerr will do what Mr Whitlam tells him to do. There are proper channels by which advice may be tendered to the Queen's representatives; they should be followed.

On 21 October I had a long talk with the Prime Minister. Among other anxieties I had increasingly, as the tension in the community built up, been worried that the Governor-General might appear, though it was the reverse of true, to the people of Australia as being indifferent to the grave crisis in which they were caught. I had until then done nothing of a public character. It was not my intention at that time to take any constitutional action. But the growing expression of the point of view that the Governor-General should mediate, or intervene to help produce a solution, forced me to consider the need to give the public some evidence of my very deep concern.

When talking to the Prime Minister that day I said that it seemed to me the crisis, though very serious, was still a political crisis — it had not yet crossed the threshold into a true constitutional crisis because the Senate had only deferred the Budget, not rejected it, and money had not started to run out. The Prime Minister said that even if money were to run out he believed he had a solution available with the help of the banks, backed by Commonwealth guarantee (he was at that time thinking in terms of guarantee by the Commonwealth, although in the event he asked the banks to provide credit without guarantees) which would enable him to carry on, but that this possibility was not then public. I listened to all of this and thought about it.

I suggested that the Prime Minister should agree to my seeing, with public knowledge, the leader of the Opposition in order to assess whether he was determined to cross from a political to a constitutional crisis. He would do this, if he were going to do it, by ultimately producing a rejection of supply, either by active rejection or by continued deferral up to the point when the money was about to run out and breakdown was imminent.

The Prime Minister agreed to my seeing the leader of the Opposition, in order to do my best to ascertain the likely course of future events. Accordingly I invited Mr Fraser to call, which he did on the evening of 21 October.

Our conversation lasted more than an hour. I first explained to him why I had invited him to call. The Prime Minister had agreed that, although I was not entitled to any advice from Mr Fraser, I could see him and ascertain from him what he said were the facts of the situation facing the country, as well as his view of the likely future situation as time passed. I told him the Prime Minister had agreed that I was entitled to know what his view was about where we were heading.

Mr Fraser said that a firm decision had been made to deny supply, that this would be persisted in to the end, that whatever the press said or predicted the Bills would be deferred as often as they were presented and the Prime Minister would have to face the country. I asked him about the solidarity of the coalition attitude and the likelihood of defection. His answer was that the Senate and the coalition would be firm and constant on deferral of supply. In view of the current discussion on the difference between deferral and rejection of supply I asked him why deferral had been chosen. He said that supply had been deferred so that, should it come to a dissolution, he would be able to guarantee supply by passing the Appropriation Bills immediately. I told him not to assume that I accepted the Ellicott thesis[11] but he responded to this by saying that, if the Prime Minister tried to govern without supply — and he certainly would be forced into that position — he (Mr Fraser) would need to be in the position of being able to guarantee supply although the Prime Minister could not. I had in my mind at that time, though I did not mention it to Mr Fraser, the discussion between the Prime Minister and myself in Port Moresby when Mr Whitlam said to me, 'Fraser would be no more able to guarantee supply than I would because new legislation would be necessary and it wouldn't pass the House'. He had recognised, however, that it might be possible for the Senate to revive the Bills which had already passed the House and pass them in the Senate.

Mr Fraser's attitude in this first talk with me and until the end was that deferral was not a sign of weakness due to internal problems with some senators, but a deliberate and unanimous tactic designed to leave him flexibility of action. Mr Fraser did not at any time attempt to give me any advice. He simply told me that he and his supporters were firmly determined to deny supply by deferral, to keep their options open, to operate on the broad basis of the Ellicott thesis and to await events. I gave Mr Fraser no indication whatsoever of my reaction to all of this except when I said he should not assume that I would act on the Ellicott thesis. This was the state of affairs at the end of my first talk with Mr Fraser. No discussion of compromise or of any alternative attitude on his part was raised by me or by him.

Mr Fraser believed at that time that there already was a serious constitutional crisis. The attitude of the two parties in his view made such a crisis inevitable and he considered that we were now in presence of that crisis. The talk therefore could not go further in any real sense. However, from the point of view of the vice-regal office I was glad to have been able to give the Australian people some evidence of my deep concern. There was a great deal of media discussion about my talk with the leader of the Opposition.

A rumour in press circles immediately spread, on the night of 21 October, to the effect that I had summoned Mr Fraser to reprimand him in some way or other. When he was confronted by the rumour, he felt, understandably, that merely to say 'no comment' would leave the impression that the purpose of the meeting had indeed been to reprimand him. I authorised him to say that was not so and that this could be confirmed by enquiries at Government House. Enquiries were made and the press the following morning did not carry in any significant way any such implication.

Despite all the suggestions in the press, including editorials, that I should mediate, or even adjudicate, there was no way in which, of my own initiative, I could assume such a role. The two leaders were set upon their courses and unless one or other party weakened, the clash would come constitutionally within quite a short time, by early November. On 22 October this was what I believed.

The press asked on that day whether they could have an account of what had happened the day before. It was pressed upon my Official Secretary that the situation was of such gravity for Australian citizens in general that there should be some explanation as to why they could not be told what had occurred. Whilst sympathetic to their anxieties I could not as Governor-General make public statements about a political situation. But I always held the view that I would speak when it became possible.

The newspapers on 23 October reported certain remarks made the previous day by Mr Fraser on television and radio programmes. He had, it seemed, been asked if the Governor-General had legal authority to request the Senate to pass the supply Bills. He was quoted as replying that he would need legal advice on that but he doubted very much that I had. He was then asked how the Opposition would react if I took this course and he apparently said, 'We would obviously look very closely at any request from the Governor-General because I have very high regard for the office. Any decision made by the Governor-General would obviously be a decision we would follow.'

Earlier he was, it seems, asked on radio if he would accept my advice. His reported reply was, 'If he gives a decision we would respect and accept it absolutely. If he gives advice we would give the greatest possible weight to it because of the respect we have for the office and the man.'

This was treated by most newspapers as a sign of retreat, being taken to mean that the Opposition would go along with anything I decided. At first blush, it was a surprising statement; on examination it was ambiguous. Mr Fraser would have been fully aware that I had no status or duty to give political advice to the Senate and therefore was hardly likely to do so, while the Prime Minister had lately been stating to all comers that I must in all circumstances do what he advised me. I could not, even if I had wished, give a ruling binding upon both parties. Nevertheless on the afternoon of 23 October Mr Fraser was reported to have issued a challenge to the Prime Minister to abide by my advice and to show the same respect for my office and for me as he had done. He is supposed to have said, 'I challenge him to indicate that he will accept any decision and give weight to any advice the Governor-General may give him.' He denied that his remarks of the previous day were a sign of backing down. The afternoon press immediately pointed out that Governors-General are not permitted to give advice of a political character.

As already made clear I had no desire, or intention, to give political advice to either side. Whether Mr Fraser gained any points by his tactical exercise is for others to assess.

I come now to the Ellicott thesis. On 16 October Mr Ellicott, Q.C., a shadow Minister in the Opposition Cabinet, had issued a press statement which was in effect a legal opinion on the powers of the Governor-General. I read it as published in the press but, after it had become public property, for the sake of accurate knowledge asked my Official Secretary to obtain an authentic copy.

The document, which I read with care, implied that, there and then, I had a duty, 'in the proper performance of' my role, to receive certain explanations from the Prime Minister as to 'how he proposed to overcome the situation' resulting from a 'refusal by Parliament of supply'. It stated:

> In the current situation now facing us [i.e. on 16 October 1975] the Governor-General, in the performance of his role, would need to know immediately what steps the Government proposes to take in order to avert the problem of it being without supply in the near future, so endangering the maintenance of the Constitution and of the laws of the Commonwealth. He is not powerless and the proper exercise of his powers demands that he be informed immediately on this matter. The Prime Minister should inform him on his own initiative. If he does not, the Governor-General would be justified in sending for him and seeking the information.

That is to say that Mr Ellicott believed all of this could and should happen immediately upon a first blockage of supply.

Mr Ellicott then set out certain things which I was, according to him, entitled there and then to know. Depending upon what answers and information I received,

> the Governor-General . . . is entitled to and should ask the Prime Minister if the Government is prepared to advise him to dissolve the House of Representatives and the Senate, or the House of Representatives alone as a means of ensuring that the disagreement between the two Houses is resolved.

If the Prime Minister refuses to do either it is then open to the

Governor-General to dismiss his present Ministers and seek others who are prepared to give him the only proper advice open. This he should proceed to do.

This statement of Mr Ellicott's view will later lead naturally to a consideration of Mr Byers' views. My objection to what Mr Ellicott had to say was his claim that I had certain rights and duties which I should exercise there and then (i.e. on or immediately after 16 October); that there and then the Prime Minister had a duty to give me certain information; that unless I got certain reactions I had a duty within the immediate future after 16 October to take the action he urged.

On the question of timing I found myself in disagreement with Mr Ellicott. Professor D. P. O'Connell, Chichele Professor of Public International Law at Oxford University, wrote in *The Parliamentarian* in January 1976:

> It has also been said . . . that politicians should be allowed enough time to 'bluff it out': that Mr Whitlam should have been given the opportunity to see if a Liberal Senator would cross the floor on the issue of Supply, so as to give the Government its majority, or if Mr Fraser's resolve would weaken.

Much could happen politically in the weeks after 16 October and I disagreed with Mr Ellicott as to what I or Mr Whitlam should do at the time when Mr Ellicott's document came forward.

Professor O'Connell went on:

> This is a matter of judgment as to the gravity of the situation and the plausibility of these considerations in the circumstances. Only the Governor-General was in the position to make that judgment.

I thought it desirable at this point to ask Mr Whitlam for an opinion from the Law Officers. I told Mr Whitlam that I did not agree with Mr Ellicott when he said the Governor-General had a duty to act immediately, but that in view of the publication of Mr Ellicott's document I should like to have the opinion of the Law Officers on the propositions set out in it. He agreed to get such an opinion on his own behalf and said he would probably pass it on to me. As with all legal advice from the Law Officers he claimed it was a matter for his discretion whether he would pass it on to me.

I had no right, so Mr Whitlam had several times said, to ask the Law Officers direct for their advice. In asking for this opinion I reflected that if the Law Officers were to go so far as to say that there was nothing left of any substance of the reserve powers of the Crown, it would be contrary to my own view, and it would not have followed that in an extreme constitutional crisis I would have accepted their opinion. However, as will be seen, I never received the joint opinion I had asked for, but only a 'draft opinion', signed by Mr M. H. Byers, the Solicitor-General, but that signature being struck off by Mr K. E. Enderby, the Attorney-General.[12] I received it on 6 November having asked for it on 21 October.

On 21 October Sir Robert Menzies entered the debate. He made a public statement on that day dealing in the main with the constitutional position of the Senate:

> As is well known, I have, for a long time, abstained from entering into any current political controversy. But the circumstances today are such as to compel me to break that silence. For, quite simply, I think more nonsense is being talked about the constitutional position of the Senate than I can comfortably listen to, or read.
>
> If we desire to know what are the powers of the Senate over money Bills, we find them expressly set out in the Constitution. The draftsmen of the Constitution included these provisions because they knew (and this is a matter of historical fact) that the smaller States i.e. smaller in population, would not vote for federation unless they had some protection given to them in the Senate and they got it. And they still have it.

Sir Robert set out section 53 of the Constitution[13] and went on:

> While the Senate may not itself amend what we call 'money Bills', it can pass them, or reject them, because these are the powers of the House of Representatives in respect of the same measures.
>
> Let me repeat, the Senate may not amend these measures, but it may reject them, or, of course, in the ordinary course of debate, it may adjourn them.
>
> It would be absurd to suppose that the draftsmen of the Constitution conferred these powers on the Senate with a mental reservation that they should never be exercised.
>
> Now, nobody has any doubts about this legal position. Mr

Whitlam had no doubt about it when he was Leader of the Opposition, nor did Senator Murphy, as he then was, when he asked the D.L.P. Senators to join with Labor in throwing out a financial measure. All that has happened is that Mr Whitlam is now Prime Minister and, as I know from experience, Prime Ministers become a little frustrated if the Senate carries a vote against them. But this does not settle the arguments of constitutionality. The Constitution's meaning does not change according to the direction from which Mr Whitlam and his Ministers look at it.

Now let me go on from there.

I do not believe that the Senate ought as a matter of political judgment, to exercise its powers in every case.

I think that in the interests of stability of government it would be wrong for the Senate, for example, to reject supply for the sole reason that it did not like the financial measures and had the power to reject them.

Everything depends on the circumstances. For a Government, fresh from the people, with a victory to be challenged in the Senate under section 53, would be, in my opinion, wrong. Not illegal, no, but politically wrong.

But these are not the circumstances today. The Government has, in the last 12 months, itself put up a record of unconstitutionality and, if it is not too strong a word, misconduct on a variety of occasions.

He then set out some political opinions which are not relevant here and with which I was not concerned. Thereafter he said:

This, if there ever was an occasion, was one when the Senate ought to have exercised its undisputed right to defer or reject financial measures involved in the Budget.

All these things are so simple to anybody who (like myself) has been both legally and politically familiar with the Constitution and its workings that I have been astonished to discover that the Opposition is now being treated, not as a body authorised to check malpractice by the Government, but as itself guilty of violating and defying the Constitution!

I cannot imagine that any competent lawyer would agree with this view. But a lot of people will, if it is sufficiently pushed into them by a variety of people in the Government, aided and abetted by some elements in the media.

Sir Robert then expressed some views about the propriety of the Prime Minister seeking from me a half-Senate election. I set out these opinions for completeness but as events developed my own thinking on this subject moved along a broader path. Sir Robert said:

> Finally, and I would say this with unfeigned respect for the vice-regal office, I think it would be a singular piece of impertinence on the part of the Prime Minister to go to the Governor-General, whose reputation is high, and who understands these things very well, and ask him for a premature 'half Senate' election, calculated and designed, hopefully, because of the recent legislation about Senators from the Capital Territory and the Northern Territory, to give the Government control of the Senate for a month or two, in which time, of course, all their legislation which now has been attacked in the Senate, could be carried, with permanent (and I think damaging) effects on the Australian political structure. To offer advice to the Governor-General on the lines that have been hinted at would, I think, be both improper and insulting. There is no legal principle that permits a wrongdoer to profit from his own actions.[14]

In the period up to 24 October there was speculation about the possibility of some senators weakening. However, when the House passed two new Appropriation Bills, identical with the earlier two that had failed to pass the Senate, a motion was again adopted that the Bills be not further proceeded with until the Government agreed to submit itself to the judgment of the people. The motion went on to refer to the same matters as were contained in the Senate's motion of 16 October. This second deferral took place one week after the first.

Some things said and done in the House of Representatives during that week are worth recalling. On 16 October Mr Whitlam moved a motion noting Mr Fraser's statement of the previous day that supply would be denied in the Senate with the object of forcing an election of the House, and noting also that on 15 October the leader of the Opposition in the Senate announced that the Opposition parties in the Senate would delay the Bills. The motion, *inter alia*, condemned the threatened action of the leader of the Opposition and of the non-Government parties in the Senate 'as being reprehensible and as constituting a grave threat to the principles of responsible government and of Parliamentary democracy in Australia'.

In his speech on the motion the Prime Minister said:

> The Leader of the Opposition announces with some pride that departments are running or will run short of funds. Of course they will run short of funds. The Leader of the Opposition is refusing to pass the Appropriation Bills in the Senate which provide for the ordinary, annual services of the Government. He will be responsible for bills not being paid, for salaries not being paid, for utter financial chaos, and this will continue as long as the Leader of the Opposition refuses to allow the Senate to pass the Supply already authorised by this House, the people's House. And now, like a pyromaniac he dances around the fire. He will get burnt.[15]

One theme of this speech of the Prime Minister was to be much reiterated by Labor leaders. He said:

> There are compelling reasons why the Opposition cannot be allowed, in an unscrupulous grab for political power, to shatter the principles that have stood for 75 years. Appropriation and Supply Bills can originate only in this House and the Senate may not amend them for the ordinary annual services of the Government. Responsible government on the Westminster model, upon which our system of government is founded, requires absolutely that the people's House — this House — through which the Government is chosen, should hold financial paramountcy over an Upper House. The convention has been clearly established that the Senate, which has no power to originate or amend money Bills, shall not block or reject them either.[16]

Mr Fraser joined issue with the Prime Minister on this approach and quoted earlier statements of the Prime Minister in the House. He said:

> I wish to quote no more eminent a legal authority than the Prime Minister himself when he was in another place using other clothes and adopting other principles. This eminent legal authority, the Prime Minister, said in this Parliament in 1970:
>
>> 'If the motion is defeated, we will vote against the Bills here and in the Senate. Our purpose is to destroy this Budget and to destroy the Government which has sponsored it'.

He was making it quite plain that he would use the powers of the Senate to defeat the Government. Again he said on another occasion on another Bill:

> 'Any Government which is defeated by the Parliament on a major taxation Bill should resign. This Bill will be defeated in another place. The Government should then resign'.

He said:

> 'This Bill will be defeated in another place'.

By another place he meant the Senate. This eminent legal authority was asserting the power and the right of the Senate.[17]

In the same debate the Treasurer, Mr W. G. Hayden, said that the leader of the Opposition had pushed the country to the brink of the most serious constitutional crisis since Federation:

> It is no exaggeration to assert firmly and with a great deal of concern that the economy of this country, if the present course of action which the Opposition has set in train is pursued, will get out of hand, that there will be a major economic collapse, that a substantial number of enterprises in the corporate sector will fail, that there will be an upsurge in unemployment and generally that there will be the worst deepening of the recession that we have seen at any time since the great Depression of the 1930s. Let us look at the effects of this course of action which the Opposition has set itself upon. It is true that about 60 per cent of what is covered by the Budget in fact is automatically appropriated by existing forms of legislation, but of the other 40 per cent a considerable amount of money is involved and a very wide range of people in this economy—in this social-economic system—will be dependent for their success, for their capacity to sustain themselves in the near future, on the flow of money which comes from the passage of the Appropriation Bills. I refer to the suppliers of goods and services to the Government and the suppliers of goods and services to people who serve the needs of government, community agencies, States and overseas governments.[18]

In this and other statements in Parliament the Treasurer and other Ministers described how very serious indeed would be the social and economic chaos that would arise if the money supply were cut off. The political hope doubtless was that by describing this coming chaos they would deflect the public mind from the

276

fact that it would in reality result both from the Senate's blocking of supply and from the Government's policy of governing without supply; and at the same time that the Opposition would be deterred from maintaining its stand. But from my point of view responsible statements of Ministers on the situation into which the country was heading were very valuable. The Minister for Housing and Construction Mr J. M. Riordan and the Minister for Defence Mr W. L. Morrison on 21 October gave details of what would happen in their departments. Mr Riordan said:

> Within three weeks the Government will not be able to meet its commitments in respect of certain works and construction . . . by the end of December it will be completely unable to meet its commitments in the field of construction . . . some pretty horrific consequences not only for the building and construction industry but also for employees in the industry and for the economy generally . . . .[19]

Mr Morrison said:

> . . . the defence preparedness of Australia would grind down . . . Maritime and air surveillance of the Australian coastline would cease . . . As of 30 November salaries and allowances to all members of the armed forces would cease. They would have either to be stood down or go on leave without pay . . . .[20]

I was not involved in the politics of denial of supply or deciding to govern without it but I did have to assess the likely consequences to the country if the confrontation continued.

On 21 October the House passed a motion to the effect that the Senate's action in delaying the passage of the Appropriation Bills 'is not contemplated within the terms of the Constitution and is contrary to established constitutional convention'. The House asked the Senate to reconsider and pass the Bills without delay.

In the debate on this motion Mr Whitlam made a reference to the press 'proprietors' and the Governor-General:

> The proprietors are having second thoughts [about the denial of supply]. So should the Leader of the Opposition. So should his supine followers. The conditioning which the Leader of the Opposition and the proprietors sought to impose upon the public last

week, and indeed for weeks before that, they now seek to impose upon the Governor-General himself. There have been those long months of conditioning by the political, the business and media interests who have never been prepared to accept the legitimacy of an Australian Labor government. Now we are seeing a fresh phase in this exercise. Now we have the headlines: 'Will Sir John Kerr act?' and 'Fraser says Kerr must sack PM'. Where will this intimidation stop? I find it thoroughly depressing that the honourable member for Wentworth (Mr Ellicott), a former Solicitor-General, one who discharged his office with distinction and impartiality, lends himself to this disgraceful episode.[21]

In his concluding remarks Mr Whitlam said:

> Let me place my Government's position clearly on the record. I shall not advise the Governor-General to hold an election for the House of Representatives at the behest of the Senate. I shall tender no advice for an election for either House or both Houses until this constitutional issue is settled.[22]

Statements like this made publicly and to me confirmed my belief in an irreversible attitude by Mr Whitlam against an election.

Mr Fraser again quoted Mr Whitlam's earlier statements in Parliament about the Senate's powers over money Bills. He went on to quote Sir Robert Menzies, saying:

> I shall quote another authority, who spoke in a different context to this eminent Prime Minister. Before giving the authority let me read the words because they were said in relation to the Parliament of a State where the same systems apply. They are:

> > 'The Legislative Council in rejecting three Supply Bills had used the power conferred upon it to be exercised in extraordinary circumstances . . . The Legislative Council of Victoria cannot originate a money Bill, but it may reject such a Bill, including a Supply Bill. It may suggest amendments but it has no power to make them. Surely it is a curious argument to say that a power deliberately specifically conferred on the Upper House is in no circumstances to be exercised. I agree that such a power should be used only in extraordinary circumstances'.[23]

Mr Fraser then quoted the London *Times* as saying:

> The Senate's Opposition majority has vetoed the Budget, leaving

the Government without supply. In a parliamentary democracy the inevitable result should be an appeal to the electorate for its verdict. But Mr Whitlam does not accept the validity of the Opposition tactics in the Senate. Mr Whitlam now says democracy is in danger. It is not in danger providing he holds a general election.[24]

The leader of the Opposition concluded:

Then he (Mr Whitlam) makes a charge against us. This is his own charge — a charge against himself of trying to bully the Governor-General. What more outrageous proposal could the Prime Minister have made? Everything he said on 'This Day Tonight' and in this Parliament was as a direction to the Governor-General. That is not something that ought to occur from the Prime Minister or from anyone else. The Governor-General has responsibilities under the Constitution. We in the Opposition have a place under the Constitution as part of the processes. The Constitution is not only for a Prime Minister. Once he has lost the capacity to govern because money is cut off he has then lost the capacity to stay in his present place.[25]

On the television programme referred to, Mr Whitlam had given the following replies:

Q. Must Sir John Kerr accept your advice, whatever advice you gave him?
A. Unquestionably. The Governor-General takes advice from his Prime Minister and from no-one else.
Q. And must act on that advice?
A. Unquestionably. The Governor-General must act on the advice of his Prime Minister.
Q. There is no tolerance here? He must do . . .?
A. None whatever . . . There is no question that the Queen or her Viceroy must accept the advice of the Prime Minister.

In the same debate Mr Anthony said of Mr Whitlam:

His statement last Saturday in which he said 'The Governor-General will take advice from me and from me alone' was an act of intimidation of the Governor-General. The Governor-General certainly should listen to the Prime Minister. It is his duty to get advice from the Prime Minister, but it also is his duty to get advice from the greatest constitutional advisers of this country.[26]

279

Mr Alan Reid, in his book *The Whitlam Venture*, refers to charges made by each side against the other of attempting to 'impose upon', 'intimidate' or 'bully' me:

There were the psychological blitzes by Whitlam, to whom the ALP was leaving virtually sole management of the affair, and by the Liberal-CP to brainwash the Governor-General into accepting as proper and demanded by both circumstances and the Constitution the opposing courses they were advocating.[27]

On 21 October Mr Ellicott, Q.C. spoke:

Every day the Prime Minister delays the closer he puts the people of this country and the public servants in peril. The Constitution provides a process that can be followed. That simple process is for the Prime Minister to get into his car, go out to Yarralumla and sit down and discuss the matter with the Governor-General. There is only one piece of proper advice for him to give the Governor-General, and that is to dissolve this House or to have a double dissolution. There is no question about that. There is no question whatsoever that that is the proper thing for the Prime Minister to do. I have little doubt that he will not do it. We know that by the way he has been going on here and on television — the irrational stance, these eyes that flash in defiance of the Australian Constitution. That is what is happening. Day after day it has been happening. He is implanting fear into our people when there is no need for fear. The Prime Minister has it clearly in his hands to go to the Governor-General at any time, to give the right advice and let us go off to the people. That is all we are asking. We are not asking for the seats opposite. What we are asking is that this dishonest government go and account to the people.

As I said before, I will not let a stone be unturned until the Government goes to the people. But in the whole of that I will stick to what is proper and what is right. Nothing that has been done so far on our side is not proper, is not right. The Governor-General clearly has a power to dismiss his Ministers. The Prime Minister says, 'The Governor-General has to do what I say'. If I wanted to I could quote 10 or 15 leading constitutional authorities. They are all quoted in Dr Evatt's book. They are all there. The Prime Minister knows they are there. They all say that the Governor-General has a reserve power in these circumstances. What a terrible disgrace it would be if the moment has to come in our country when the Governor-General is even forced into thinking about asking the Prime Minister to hand in his commission. There is no need for this embarrassment to the Crown. The Prime Minister is the one who is guilty in these circumstances. He is the one who is leading this Government, who has allowed this shadow of dishonesty to descend upon it, and he is the one who must take responsibility for the burden that the Australian people are apparently at his hands going to bear.[28]

The Loan Bill 1975 had been deferred with the Appropriation Bills and on 21 October the House passed a motion that the Senate's action was contrary to the accepted means of financing a major portion of the Defence Budget of the country. The Senate was asked to reconsider and pass the Bill without delay.

The Minister for Defence Mr Morrison led the debate for the Government. He gave details of the enormous impact lack of funds would have on the Armed Forces. There would be no fuel. The Army would be immobilised. The Air Force would be grounded. The ships of the Royal Australian Navy would have to tie up. These and many other grave results would follow.

On 22 October in the debate on Loan Bill 1975 (No. 2) Mr Frank Crean said he would clarify a remark he had made in a television interview the previous Sunday evening. The clarification was as follows:

> I was asked by Mr Alan Reid, the questioner: 'As a hypothetical case, if both sides stay firm, how is the deadlock resolved?'
> I replied: 'I think that is a difficult thing.'
> I would stress again that it is a difficult thing. The situation can be resolved by calling off the numbers in the Senate. It is not going to be resolved by this House and the Labor Government backing down on what it believes are its fundamental rights. I went on to say: 'In my view what is happening is unconstitutional.'
> I believe that what is happening is unconstitutional. I went on to say: 'Now if it continues, there certainly have got to be unconstitutional things done to stop the system from breaking down.'
> Upon reflection now, instead of the word 'unconstitutional' I should have used words like 'unusual things', 'unconventional things' or 'unprecedented things'.[29]

In the same debate Mr John Howard on behalf of the Opposition made the point:

I think it is of some significance that during the series of debates we have had in this chamber during the past week on a matter involving constitutional considerations to my knowledge we have not had one contribution in any of those debates from the Government's principal legal adviser, the Attorney-General.[30]

In a further debate on the Appropriation Bills on 28 October the Prime Minister said:

The Leader of the Opposition is leading the breach of all conventions: the filling of casual vacancies for the Senate; the deferment and, if he dares to attempt it, the rejection of money Bills by the Senate; the rebuff by State Governments to the Governor-General when he makes the request for the issue of Senate writs for their States. Like Canute the Leader of the Opposition will lose. He will lose because my Government will stand resolute in its determination that the Budget already twice approved by this House shall pass. The Government will not stand idly by while the Leader of the Opposition seeks to destroy the conventions of the Constitution. He will lose because the people's House is where governments are made and unmade and in this House my Government stands strong and secure. This government is not only justified in maintaining its position; it would be failing its duty if it did not do so. The Government, any elected government, having and maintaining a majority in the people's House, the House of Representatives, must be able to govern. This principle is of fundamental importance for all future governments and Prime Ministers and for all Australians, present and future.[31]

In the same debate Mr Ian Sinclair, speaking for the Opposition, collected together the various earlier statements in Parliament by Mr Whitlam and Senator Murphy supporting the Senate's power to deny supply. To Mr Whitlam's statements in the House previously quoted, I add what Senator Murphy said on 18 June 1970 (quoted by Mr Sinclair):

The Senate is entitled and expected to exercise resolutely but with discretion its power to refuse its concurrence to any financial measure, including a Tax Bill. There are no limitations on the Senate in the use of its constitutional powers, except the limitations imposed by discretion and reason.[32]

Mr Fraser said in the same debate:

There is a deliberate reason why the Senate is choosing to defer, as opposed to reject, the Appropriation Bills. If the measures were rejected, with the irrational nature of the Prime Minister (Mr Whitlam), the Prime Minister and this Government would leave those measures rejected until after an election with consequent harm to many thousands of people. While the measures are deferred it is within our power to resurrect those measures once it is known there is to be a House of Representatives election. That is the reason for deferral. It is the reason we stay with deferral.[33]

I have quoted only a few of the statements made in the House, as a means of recalling to mind the nature of the parliamentary confrontation. Some day a full parliamentary history of the crisis will doubtless be written.

Turning now to some of the things said in the press, on 21 October Professor Julius Stone proposed a moratorium for a period of time to be agreed, with agreement to the holding of an election for the House of Representatives at the end of that period 'be it six, nine or twelve months'.[34]

In the course of his article Professor Stone referred to the sure prospect, in the absence of a moratorium, of paralysis of government itself for a period which might last months. He said:

Even in terms of the role and powers of the Governor-General they [i.e. the two sides] need to ask themselves whether they should really stultify that high office by facing its bearer with impossible choices.

Mr Whitlam insists that the Governor-General will have to follow the advice of his Ministers; the Opposition insists that the Governor-General will need to be satisfied that the Ministers advising him are in a position to ensure continuity of Government (which means continuity of Supply) without illegal recourses.

Perhaps circumstances are conceivable in which the two sides should compel the Governor-General to a choice which, whatever the principle he tries to act on, the inescapable effect is to align himself with one party viewpoint or the other.

Surely circumstances do not yet compel that unhappy course. These rather indicate that the good offices and mediation of the Governor-General be availed of to work out the terms of the moratorium of which I have spoken.

On 24 October the *Australian* published an editorial under the heading 'Decision Rests with Kerr'. The writer concluded:

> Mr Whitlam proclaims that he will 'never surrender'. Mr Fraser, on the other hand, declares that the Liberal-Country Party coalition is resolute. Sir John is a man of the people with a distinguished background in the law and he will have available to him men of good will in all the highest places of the land. But, in the end, it is his decision alone.

On 24 October also, the Prime Minister said in a press statement that 'steps have been taken to ensure that wage and salary payments will be maintained through the supply period, that is until the end of November' and that 'it is likely that in addition to wages and salaries most other essential payments can also be wholly maintained until the end of November'.

An admirable summing up of the state of affairs was given in a letter written by Sir Norman Cowper, a leading Sydney lawyer who for many years was Chairman of the Australian Institute of Political Science, and with whom I had worked on the Board of the Council on New Guinea Affairs. The letter was published in the *Sydney Morning Herald* of 29 October under the heading 'Essentials of the Political Crisis':

> When all the rhetoric and rodomontade are brushed aside, the essential matters are clear enough.
>
> (1) The cardinal rule is that the Governor-General acts in accordance with the advice he receives from the man who commands a majority in the House of Representatives — the Prime Minister.
>
> (2) If in extraordinary circumstances he rejects that advice, his only course will be to dismiss the Prime Minister, send for the Leader of the Opposition, commission him to form a ministry, and grant him a dissolution, at least of the House of Representatives.
>
> (3) The present Prime Minister's claim that the removal of a government from office before the end of the term for which it has been elected would be a blow to Parliamentary government and democratic institutions is manifestly untenable. Indeed, the power of removal (the reserve power of the Crown) may be the only safeguard against the destruction of democracy. A government which finds its

management of a country disastrous and a rising tide of public opinion against it may in its determination to remain in office resort to illegal actions which are the negation of democracy; and only the exercise of the Governor-General's power to dismiss it will save the country from an unconstitutional dictatorship.

(4)   If the Prime Minister were dismissed, but his party won the ensuing election, the Governor-General's office would be in jeopardy and, no doubt, the Queen would be asked to recall him and replace him by someone nominated by the (former) Prime Minister. Furthermore, salutary warnings would have been given to future Oppositions and Governors-General as to the unwisdom of forcing an election against the wishes of the elected Government.

(5)   If, however, the result of the election were victory for the former opposition party, the actions of the Governor-General would have been vindicated, and the present spate of talk about alleged conventions would be seen to be of little force or value.

(6)   In view of (4) and (5), a Governor-General could not be expected to reject the Prime Minister's advice and dismiss him unless he was satisfied:

(a)   that the business of government had broken down and the continuance in office of the Prime Minister would result in administrative chaos, flagrant breaches of the Constitution and other illegalities, and

(b)   that it was highly probable that the votes of the people at the ensuing election would uphold his action.

It was because these conditions existed in New South Wales in 1932 that Sir Philip Game was able to dismiss Mr Lang and restore orderly government to the State.

(7)   The Executive Council minute purporting to authorise the borrowing of a huge sum for 20 years for grandiose schemes of long-term mineral development as being a borrowing 'for temporary purposes' was a flagrant breach of the Financial Agreement which is part of the Constitution. In my view, however, this does not by itself satisfy condition (a) above.

(8)   The rejection or deferral of Supply is undoubtedly within the power of the Senate under Section 53 of the Constitution, but it is a power to be exercised only in very exceptional circumstances.

(9)   The circumstances alleged as exceptional are: incompetence in the management of the economy, the breach of the Financial Agreement, dismissal of Ministers for misleading Parliament and, generally, inept and dishonest government. Whether these circumstances exist to such an extent as to justify the confusion, hardship and breakdown of orderly government which the refusal or deferral of Supply will entail is a question which I would answer no, but which the Opposition has answered yes.

(10)   If it persists in holding up Supply it may force the dismissal of the Government but will run the grave risk that its actions will antagonise public opinion and lead to the loss of the ensuing election. There is, perhaps, some indication that this swing against the Opposition has begun.

(11)   On the other hand, the continued refusal of Supply may put the Government in such difficulties that it cannot carry on without committing gross illegalities and flouting the Constitution, in which case if the Governor-General were reasonably assured that the people would support him, he might well decide to dismiss the Prime Minister and force an election.

(12)   Other possibilities are:

   (i)   That the Prime Minister, believing that the refusal of Supply has caused a revulsion of opinion in favour of the Government, will himself advise a dissolution;
   (ii)   that the Opposition, deciding that the revulsion of opinion has prejudiced its chances at an election, or that the consequences of refusal of Supply are too damaging to the economy or inflict too great hardship on the whole community, decides to pass the Supply bills; or
   (iii)   that a compromise will be reached.

For a constitutional lawyer, it is the most interesting confrontation since Federation.

Although inconsistent in some details with my own views — an instance is its assumption that in the decision to resort to the reserve powers a forecast of the likely electoral outcome should be a significant element[35] — the letter gives a lucid analysis of the situation that existed in late October.

Regrettably the letter had, two years later, a minor unfortunate sequel to which I must refer here, parenthetically, since it directly concerned my own conduct. The misrepresentation involved — which was certainly due solely to a brief sliding of memory on the part of a distinguished elderly gentleman — was publicly corrected soon afterwards. I may here add my own rebuttal.

In the *National Times* of 4–9 October 1977 Andrew Clark wrote an article, based on an interview with Sir Norman Cowper, under the title 'Kerr, Menzies, Barwick — an Establishment View'. In it, Mr Clark said that Sir Norman, after his letter of 29 October 1975 was published, was contacted by Mr Peter Hastings. Clark reported Sir Norman as saying to him:

> Peter told me that Kerr was very impressed with my letter. He thought I had shown great acuity. That was the way he (Kerr) expressed it. Peter used to ring me every two or three days and give me a ball-by-ball description of the game. Peter urged me to see Kerr, and said he was anxious to talk to me.

The statement in this paragraph, made by Sir Norman to Mr Clark, is, as will be seen, quite wrong, and he corrected it later. Mr Hastings corrected it also, and was reported in the same article as having done so. The *National Times* of the following week, 31 October–5 November 1977, published a letter from Sir Norman in which he said:

> I am concerned that Andrew Clark's very good account . . . may have given a misleading impression on one crucial point. Contrary to what I told him in our first interview, I had only one conversation with Peter Hastings regarding the constitutional crisis and that was after Mr Whitlam's dismissal.

I had no discussion about the supply crisis with Sir Norman Cowper or Mr Hastings before 11 November 1975.

By the end of October 1975 the opinion polls were showing a pro-Labor and anti-Opposition trend.

The House passed the Appropriation Bills for the third time on

29 October. As November approached I was assessing the degree of firmness in the Senate's attitude. While I was still of the view that action such as Mr Ellicott had urged had not as yet become appropriate, I was very seriously studying my powers, authorities and duties under the Constitution.

I was also considering whether I could do anything at all to help produce a compromise. It seemed to me, in the light of the public discussion, that there was a possibility the Opposition might want to find an opportunity for retreat, and that if they could save themselves from any risk of a half-Senate election producing a hostile Senate before all the new senators could take their seats on 1 July 1976, they might grant supply. I did not believe that they should or should not or that they would or would not, but simply that they might. I knew Mr Whitlam believed that the Senate would break; and a compromise proposal about timing of a half-Senate election might be so designed, if there were a movement towards breaking, as to make this in public terms a little easier for the Opposition. Perhaps they might come to think they had painted themselves into a corner, or to put it another way — both expressions were being used — want to get off the hook: many people were saying this and I myself considered it a possibility. A compromise proposal which I had in my mind would, I thought, by offering a way out, at the same time test the degree of strength in their stand.

On 30 October I put these thoughts to Mr Whitlam and later, with his permission, saw Mr Fraser and sought to explore his attitude to the possibility of grant of supply on the condition of a half-Senate election delayed until the following May, with an. undertaking that the Senate would not meet before 1 July 1976. Neither leader showed much interest and the initiative came to nothing. I at no stage indicated to either leader any attitude of mine as to the rightness or wrongness of the policy being pursued by either party.

As things turned out, in the weekend immediately following 30 October the coalition parties in their top councils decided upon a different compromise as being the farthest they would go. They would not grant supply for a late Senate election; they would grant it for a half-Senate election at any time, provided it was accompanied by an election for the House. I was told of this on 3 November.[36]

Mr Fraser did not at any time ask me for advice, nor even imply that he would welcome or consider it. Nor did I at any time give him the impression that any advice to him or to his parties or to the Senate would be available from me. Whereas the Governor-General cannot take advice from, nor advise, the leader of the Opposition, the doctrine in relation to the Prime Minister, that the Governor-General may 'advise and warn', permits the giving of some advice, but has its limitations in practice. A wise man would not be volunteering it often.

It is possible to test the different position as regards the leader of the Opposition by looking at the problem of the Senate's attitude to supply. It was suggested publicly that I could, and perhaps should, have advised Mr Fraser that the Senate should grant supply. To have done this would have been to interfere directly in the Senate's business, problems and politics. It would have been equally out of the question to advise Mr Fraser against his supply policy or to advise him in favour of it. It was essential for the Senate to take full responsibility for any decision it made.

On 30 October also, Mr Whitlam approving, I spent a short time with the Treasurer Mr Hayden. I told him that I should need to be informed how government was to be financed, and that the legality and practicability of any proposals would be of importance. Mr Hayden was to see me again in the near future. Until this time the Government had given me no information whatsoever about the financial situation. I had had to ask for it.

We had now reached the end of October and were about to enter a vital week. Mr Whitlam's position was crystal clear. There would be no retreat and no surrender by him. I never again returned to my early suggestion, made before the first deferral of supply, that if supply were denied he should consider going to the people, with the real prospect, if he lost, of living to fight another day. In view of his reiterated determination to govern without supply I had to accept that this would be his course. If he wanted to change his position he would have to say so; and I did not see this happening. Mr Fraser too, despite the trend in opinion polls and notwithstanding speculation in the press, showed no sign of backing down. The atmosphere among press and other media commentators was rather that it would be Mr Fraser who would retreat; that Mr Whitlam would not. I was myself, over the first weekend in November, being forced to the conclusion that neither would give in and that the following week would bring the climax.

18

The Week Before

Mr Fraser and I had a conversation at his request and with Mr Whitlam's approval on 3 November in my Melbourne office. When Mr Fraser arrived he told me at once that he and his senior colleagues, both federal and State, had met during the weekend 1 and 2 November and had agreed on their supply policy. As I understood it the meeting had been at top level with federal and State parliamentary and organisational leaders present. It was a meeting designed to settle, in a way binding on all concerned, a final coalition policy for the crisis.

As a result of decisions made at that meeting he would offer a compromise to the effect that supply would be granted if the Prime Minister would agree to hold an election for the House of Representatives at the same time as any election held for the Senate. Mr Fraser said he felt obliged to tell me this before releasing the proposal to the press, having regard to our previous conversations. He said that this would allow the Prime Minister to have an election as late as May, and that would give everyone time to assess the Hayden Budget in practice and also the developing economic issues.

Mr Fraser said that this was as far as the Opposition parties were prepared to go and that if it were rejected they would unfailingly stand firm on the refusal to pass supply. I saw the Prime Minister half an hour later at Government House, Melbourne, before a pre-Melbourne Cup reception. I told him what Mr Fraser had said. He indicated that he had already heard the substance of Mr Fraser's press statement but that he would have nothing whatsoever to do with any election for the House of Representatives. He said he would never advise an election for the House of Representatives until he himself was ready to do so, and certainly not at the behest of Mr Fraser or the Senate.

Mr Whitlam told me that the only way an election for the House could occur would be if I dismissed him. The expression he used was: if I were willing 'to do a Philip Game'. This revealed him to be taking into account the possibility that I might exercise the reserve power. Being, I suspect, of the opinion that I would probably not be strong enough to do it, Mr Whitlam was using an expression which, as both of us I am sure recognised, carried the implication of the unpleasant consequences to myself in controversy and obloquy if I did. I made no comment.

The Prime Minister stated in the House of Representatives on Melbourne Cup Day, 4 November 1975, that

> the Government is discussing with the banks the provision of credit for its employees and suppliers for the amounts the Government will owe them but will not be able to pay them if the Budget Bills are not passed this month. Honourable gentlemen will appreciate that it is not possible to pursue such discussions today with banks whose headquarters are in Melbourne. Honourable gentlemen opposite seem to have some apprehension about the use of section 70B of the Audit Act . . . the Government is not using that section because it applies to the Reserve Bank, the Commonwealth Trading Bank and the Commonwealth Development Bank. Clearly the Government expects that all banks will cooperate in relieving hardship to persons who would ordinarily be paid by the Australian Government but who could not be paid by the Australian Government because of the unprecedented and reprehensible actions of the Opposition which, in the Senate, has three times deferred debate on all of the Budget Bills. It is well known, of course, that if the Senate were allowed by the Leader of the Opposition to vote on the Budget Bills they would be passed.[1]

On 4 November the banks were invited by the Treasurer to attend a meeting in Canberra on the sixth to discuss provision of credit to employees and suppliers of the Government.

It is interesting to note that this was the first approach to the banks for a meeting. The exercise being proposed was most complex, involving consideration of important and difficult legal and constitutional questions and questions of proper banking practice, assessment of the impact of what was proposed on the depositors, customers and creditors of the banks, problems of liquidity of the banks to undertake what was asked of them without reducing the normal availability of their funds to their usual clients, complex administrative and staffing problems and many others. To prepare for and mount such a service would take time and even if it were possible, legal and prudent, all of which were at the least doubtful, vast effort and substantial time would be necessary.

The fact that the Government, having delayed in approaching the banks until 4 November, did so then must be seen as indicating that the Government no longer believed denunciations would necessarily suffice to deter the Opposition, and was now facing up to the real risk that the Senate would stand firm and supply not be available.

In the House of Representatives on 4 November the following questions and answers provide some of the atmosphere of crisis.

> Mr Fraser asked: 'Does the Treasurer know in which areas of Government activity the Government's money supply will be first exhausted? Will he give this information to the House?'
> Mr Hayden answered: 'This involves an extensive and complex exercise which has not been totally completed by the Treasury Department. As to when, or even if it is tabled in this Parliament, that is a matter for decision by the Government.'
> Mr Fraser also asked: 'I ask the Treasurer: What powers does the Government propose to use to by-pass the Parliament in obtaining an alternative supply of funds? What legal basis is there for these powers? What opinions have been obtained concerning their legality?'
> Mr Hayden: 'No steps would be taken which would by-pass the Parliament. Anything that was done would be done legally, would be done within the Constitution and would be done with the approval of a decision of Parliament.'[2]

In the House that day a question was asked which had reference to Mr Fraser's compromise proposal of 3 November: had Mr Whitlam seen the reports about 'a proposal to end the Budget deadlock'? Was the proposal acceptable? Mr Whitlam in reply said he gathered one of the proposals was that he should inform the Governor-General that in six months he would advise him to issue writs for a House of Representatives election. He said: 'This is a most diverting proposal. When I advise the Governor-General to issue writs for an election for the House of Representatives I shall do it at a time of my own choosing.' Mr Whitlam also said he gathered there was 'some proposition that the Leader of the Opposition . . . should himself give advice to the Governor-General as to when there should be elections for the House of Representatives — a very novel proposition.'

Mr Whitlam then spoke of his attitude to a half-Senate election:

> When there will be an election for the Senate depends on various factors. I notice that honourable gentlemen opposite have become quite distraught at the prospect that there might be an election for the Senate at the usual time in November or December before the new senators take their places in July.[3]

Mr Whitlam said he was not persuaded that he should advise a Senate election in 1975. He still wanted to look at the matter.[4]

On 5 November Mr Whitlam moved in the House a motion which was later passed and which *inter alia* denounced the Senate's actions and called upon the Senate to pass the Appropriation Bills. Mr Whitlam in his speech referred to the compromise proposal of Mr Fraser. He said:

> It is clear that they are prepared to go to any lengths to prevent a half-Senate election. We now find the Leader of the Opposition offering a 'compromise' — that the Senate Opposition will allow the Budget Bills to pass if the Government agrees to a general election for this House to be held by the middle of next year. The blackmail, of course, is still there. The only difference is that the time for the payment of the ransom has been generously extended![5]

In the same speech this statement was made:

> Let me make my Government's position clear yet again. I shall not advise the Governor-General to dissolve both Houses at the behest of this tainted Senate.[6]

And later:

Time is rapidly running out for the Opposition in the Senate to end this crisis honourably by passing the Budget before innocent people are made to endure personal hardship.[7]

And:

The Budget must pass, and it will pass. While it is not my intention, or desire, to provide needless fear or alarm, we must be quite clear about the consequences of the continual refusal to pass the Budget. This refusal is already damaging the business community, threatening the normal life of the nation and endangering the delicate process of economic recovery. As I have said before, there can be no surrender to the Senate on this issue. The fundamental principle of democracy is too important. I call on all honourable members to condemn the actions of the Opposition in the Senate. I call on that Opposition to pass the Budget without further procrastination, without further delay.[8]

Mr Fraser, in reply, said:

The Government now says that it will govern without Supply. How? Why? The Parliament is not entitled to know. The country is not entitled to know. But the Government is going to govern without the Budget, it claims. This Parliament is entitled to know but the Treasurer (Mr Hayden) does not even know when present Supply will run out. If he does know, he keeps it secret for himself. Is the Government going to use Section 9 of the Banking Act and give special directions to the trading banks requiring them to open special accounts to meet the bills of the Commonwealth? Is it going to use Section 8, 9, 10, 11 or 87 of the Reserve Bank Act and the powers it has under that Act? Is it going to use, by some secret and diverse means, Sections 32, 62B or 70B of the Audit Act and use control of the banking system without appropriations by this Parliament? It needs to be remembered that if directions are given to the banks under these powers or any part of these powers, not backed by Appropriations through the Parliament, it is the deposits of the banks and the assets of the banks that are ultimately at risk. We need to know the answer to these particular questions, but the Prime Minister sits back and refuses to answer questions in this House.[9]

Then:

What nonsense, humbug, deceit and deception is involved in the heart of this Government. Now the Prime Minister, in the last and most desperate act of all, seeks to govern without the Appropriation Bills. By what device is he going to do it? By what device is he going to take this country on the first significant but important step towards dictatorship in ignoring the Parliament and making parliamentary appropriation quite irrelevant? This is the greatest threat to democracy since the foundation of this federation. Partly because of the nature of this threat, partly because of the nature of this Prime Minister, we, with completely unanimous support, made a reasonable and responsible proposal on Monday which would have enabled the people of Australia to vote. It would have provided a reasonable and proper solution to this problem.[10]

The events of 6 November were to make that day a critical point in the unfolding of the crisis. On that day my certainty became much greater that collision was coming; and evidence I received confirmed for me the true nature of its consequences for the country.

On 6 November the Senate sent a message to the House after its deferral of the Appropriation Bills on the same day. It had decided that the Bills be not further proceeded with until the Government agreed to submit itself to the judgment of the people.

It will be remembered that the Prime Minister when talking to me earlier had referred to a scheme which he said had been evolved to give guarantees to the banks under section 70B of the Audit Act, to enable them to lend money to members of the public service, the defence forces, Commonwealth contractors and others. Later he told me that section 70B need not be used. As to the Commonwealth banks, he said they might need directions from the Government on the policy of underwriting the scheme and, if they did not agree, an Executive Council instruction might be necessary. My information from the Prime Minister on 6 November was that a legal scheme was being evolved not dependent on section 70B.

On that day I saw the Prime Minister at Government House, having previously seen Mr Fraser with his approval. I saw Mr Fraser in what I expected might be a final attempt to see whether he was prepared to consider the late Senate election idea now that his compromise of 3 November had been rejected. I was not particularly hopeful that he would be willing to consider the idea any further. When I spoke to Mr Fraser he made it clear that he and his colleagues were not interested in a late Senate election unless it were accompanied by a House election. This did not surprise me. When I put the idea to him it was with two conditions laid down by Mr Whitlam: one, Senate elections in all States on the same day, and two, the proposed new preferential system for Senate voting. These Mr Whitlam had told me would have to be agreed to before he would even consider the idea. Mr Fraser was not interested at all. He said the terms he had already announced were final. He said that the Senate had shown its firmness and would continue to do so; that he realised he could not advise me but felt he should say that if I failed to act in the situation which existed I would be imperilling the reserve powers of the Crown forever; he accepted that the discretion was mine but inaction on my part, with supply running out, the Senate firm on deferral, and the Government asserting a right to govern without supply, would destroy the reserve powers.

I did not then or at any time give Mr Fraser any indication of the development of my own thinking on the reserve powers except for my earlier comment, already mentioned, in relation to Mr Ellicott's document.

I told the Prime Minister during my talk with him that day that Mr Fraser was not interested in the late half-Senate election except with a House election at the same time. The Prime Minister said he probably would advise a half-Senate election on 13 December, which was the last practical day on which an election could be held before Christmas. After my conversation with the Prime Minister on 29 September about the possibility of getting temporary supply for a half-Senate election[11], he never returned to this question and was never able to tell me he could get temporary supply for such an election. It was clear that if the Prime Minister so advised and I acquiesced, and if the Senate stood firm — there being no guarantee of temporary supply for a half-Senate election — the election would be held after money had run out, as it would by 30 November. If on the other hand the reserve powers were to be exercised and a general election produced before Christmas, 11 November would be the last day for decision. To wait longer would mean having a caretaker Government until probably February at least, which because of the conditions in which such a Government operates[12] would mean virtually interrupting the government of the country for a period of two months or so, and must obviously be avoided.

I had no doubt, after these two conversations, that the leaders were on the point of collision. I knew on 6 November that I would have a weekend of very serious private deliberations which I intended to undertake alone.

On the decisive day of 6 November when the Senate denied supply for the third time and I had the talks referred to above with Mr Whitlam and Mr Fraser, I also had discussions with Mr Hayden, the Treasurer, and Mr Enderby, the Attorney-General.

From discussions in Parliament, as confirmed by Mr Hayden, I knew that nearly sixty per cent of the expenditure of the Government was already covered by special appropriations (some $11,000 million) and over forty per cent (some $9,000 million) was to be financed by the blocked Appropriation Bills. The latter covered salaries and allowances including pay of the Defence Forces and many administrative and other ordinary annual services. Also covered were capital works and services, payments to the States and other items.

The Supply Acts 1975–76 had, in the normal way, provided moneys which would be covered later in the year when the annual appropriations were voted, and which were required meantime for expenditures from 1 July to 30 November 1975. This was an interim measure, passed earlier in the year to cope with expenditure pending the passing of the Appropriation Bills, which when enacted would displace the Supply Acts. In general the Supply Acts did not cover cost increases between 1 July and 30 November, and the money they provided had in some cases run out. In the case of the RED Scheme[13], for example, the Supply Act appropriation was fully expended early in September. Accordingly had things been normal a supplementary provision would have been needed for this period. Economy measures had been initiated to conserve funds remaining under the Supply Acts appropriations.

Sir John and Lady Kerr arrive for the Father of the Year dinner in Sydney in 1976. (John Fairfax and Son Ltd.)

Shortly after taking up office, Sir John granted a joint sitting of Parliament: 6–7 August 1974. (Canberra Times)

Sir John with the Prime Minister of Papua New Guinea, Mr Michael Somare, during a State visit in April 1975.

On the steps of Parliament House, 11 November 1975: the Governor-General's Official Secretary, Mr David Smith, ends his reading of the Proclamation dissolving Parliament with the words 'God Save the Queen'. (Australian Consolidated Press)

Mr Whitlam: 'Nothing will save the Governor-General!'
(Australian Consolidated Press)

Mr Fraser leaves Parliament House for Yarralumla during the peak of the crisis.
(Canberra Times)

The new Fraser Ministry leaves Government House after being sworn in by the Governor-General. (From left) Mr Fraser, Mr Phillip Lynch, Senator Reg Withers, Sir John Kerr, Senator Ivor Greenwood, Mr Ian Sinclair and Mr Doug Anthony. (Canberra Times)

The scheme proposed to the banks provided for the issue of certificates acknowledging the indebtedness of the Government and certain of its authorities to employees and suppliers; the borrowing from banks by those receiving the certificates of the amount specified in them, and the assignment to the banks of the debt referred to; and an announcement by the Government of an intention to provide recompense, at a common rate of interest agreed to. The Government's principal Law Officers had advised that the scheme could survive legal and constitutional challenge.

Many people and organisations however would not be covered by the scheme. Those who would suffer included students, cultural and other organisations, recipients of foreign aid, locally engaged staff overseas, overseas suppliers, and recipients of Medibank benefits.

Mr Hayden handed me a document prepared for my information. He told me that the scheme would be very messy indeed. It would, the document said, be a major administrative undertaking—a most imperfect, costly and inconvenient substitute for normal arrangements. Participation of the banks would be essential. The scheme would require an appropriation by Parliament to meet the interest liability of the Government in respect of loans made by the banks.

Our conversation proceeded on the basis that by the end of November funds would not be available for salaries if the Appropriation Bills were not passed. Mr Hayden stated that there would be insufficient funds available for the Public Service/Defence Force pay day of 11 December 1975. So 27 November 1975 would be the last real pay day for public servants and members of the armed forces.

Further, appropriations under the Supply Acts for expenditures in addition to wages and salaries would become exhausted. Some were already, on 6 November, exhausted and most would become exhausted soon after the end of November. The amounts likely to be still available from the Advances to the Treasurer to the end of November would cover only a small proportion of requirements from there on, until they too ran out.

In the light of Mr Hayden's document of 6 November 1975 I find it hard to understand how in the House of Representatives in

February 1978, within the context of attacks made upon me in Parliament by the Labor Party during which *inter alia* I was accused of dishonesty in dismissing the Whitlam Government, Mr Hayden was able to say to the Parliament:

> The Prime Minister suggested that in 1975 the Government of the day placed the Governor-General in a reprehensible position, forcing him to dismiss that Government. The simple fact, which he has forgotten, is that the Government of that period had at least seven weeks supply with which to conduct the affairs of Government ... I am just talking about a simple practical fact, namely that the Government of the time had at least seven weeks supply lawfully available to it to conduct the affairs of this nation.[14]

Seven weeks from 11 November would have taken the country to 30 December, over the Christmas-New Year period. I find this statement strangely inconsistent with the statements and the document presented to me by Mr Hayden on 6 November 1975. It is my view that what Mr Hayden told me, and set out for me in his document of 6 November 1975, was true. I acted on what he said, and on what other Ministers said in the House, within the context of my knowledge of the Supply Acts, which provided moneys up to 30 November 1975, and my knowledge of the remuneration system.

I did not discuss the legal and constitutional issues with Mr Hayden but I had serious doubts as to the legality of the scheme; I believed the banks would have very grave doubts and would certainly seek legal advice. The clear impression I formed, apart from the great administrative burdens and cost of the scheme and its failure to cover the whole field, was of its inadequate, inappropriate and, from the point of view of the law as it governed the banks' activity at least, probably illegal nature. It hardly seemed possible to me that the banks could reach a decision to accept the scheme, if they ever did, without long delays. They would need time to consider their policies and to study administrative problems. Their depositors, customers and shareholders would be very nervous and the scheme might be challenged legally. My belief was that the private banks would not feel able to participate and would not. I had no knowledge, however, before 11 November of their actual attitudes or of the legal advice they were getting.[15]

By this time I was concerned about the extent to which I could take the scheme into account in making decisions of my own. It was clear that if Mr Whitlam asked for a half-Senate election supply would run out in the course of the campaign unless temporary supply were granted. The first pay day without pay would have passed before election day; and if any makeshift banking arrangements had got launched at all, which was I believed extremely doubtful, they would be in their inadequate infancy during the last fortnight of a Senate campaign. From my talks with Mr Whitlam and Mr Fraser there was no indication whatever that temporary supply would be available for a half-Senate election. The election being on 13 December, if sought and granted, there would be not only the predicted chaos resulting from lack of supply but the troubles and alarm associated with inaugurating such a scheme. All of this was on the assumption that the Senate stood firm and I could hardly, at that stage, make the opposite assumption that it would not. I could not gamble. I did not discuss my own thoughts with Mr Hayden but he may have concluded that I was very worried as I believed him to be.

On that same day—6 November, the day when the Government first conferred with the banks—Mr Enderby handed me a document, signed neither by him nor by Mr Byers, headed 'Joint Opinion'. He took his pen and added the word *draft* to the heading. So there was the Government, already embarked upon the arrangements to get money from the banks in order to by-pass the processes of Parliament, and no signed opinion of either of the Law Officers was being offered to me in support of the legality of what was being done, but merely this unsigned draft.

The document stated that the Government would announce the introduction of legislation to enable it to pay interest to the bankers and would give an undertaking, subject to legislation being passed, to pay interest at a rate to be struck. The opinion also stated that the banks would be encouraged by the Government's promise to introduce the necessary legislation, passing of which would ensure that their interest would be paid.

It seemed to me extremely unlikely that the Senate would pass such legislation whilst it was continuing to block supply. If it were going to do that, thus aiding a scheme of governing without supply, it might just as well grant supply.

The unsigned 'Draft Joint Opinion' expressed the view that no provision of the Constitution would be infringed by the scheme. No money was to be withdrawn from the Treasury.

> The constitutional provisions relating to Parliament's control over expenditure by the Executive are observed in letter and in spirit. Nor does the proposal contemplate nor allow the doing by indirection of what may not be done directly. The proposal and its effectuation are, in our opinion, clearly constitutional.

The 'Draft Joint Opinion' also expressed the view that public servants could assign arrears of pay by way of mortgage, as the scheme envisaged; and that the scheme would be largely applicable to members of the armed forces and the police force.

It seemed to me to be quite likely that the banks would receive different legal advice. Further it seemed likely to me that they would require an agreement with binding legal force, to pay interest and other costs — for what that was worth, since even at the point when the courts would have given them a judgment, where would the money come from to satisfy such a judgment, without parliamentary appropriations? Constitutional uncertainties might easily lead the banks not to agree to join in the scheme, their legal advisers so advising them. I could myself see many legal and constitutional questions to which the banks might want answers. Certainly I should take into account what was being attempted with the banks, but only as one factor among the many which, taken together, would shape the way in which my discretion must be exercised.

At that same time I received from the Attorney-General an 'Opinion', bearing Mr Byers' signature only, dealing with the reserve powers. Mr Enderby said he was giving me this document, with the Prime Minister's approval, as 'background'. He said it contained Mr Byers' own views subject to final discussions between him and the Attorney-General. This document became public, by some means, after 11 November and was widely misunderstood, first as being a true joint opinion of the Law Officers, and secondly as repudiating the existence of the reserve powers of the Crown. It is the only document I received in response to my request to the Prime Minister for a joint opinion from the Law Officers about the views of Mr Ellicott. It is dated 4 November. The position had changed very significantly by 6 November, when I received it, as compared with 16 October when Mr Ellicott issued his press statement. The time factor, as a matter to be taken into account, was very important and it had profoundly altered.

Even now, Mr Byers' document was not put to me by the Attorney-General as being Mr Byers' final opinion. In my presence, Mr Enderby struck out Mr Byers' signature on the document, and changed the heading to incorporate the handy word *draft*. Furthermore the document was couched in the plural, using the word 'we' instead of 'I' because it was intended to be an opinion to which the Attorney-General would also subscribe; but he did not.

Yet this is the document that has been widely quoted as being a joint opinion of the Law Officers.

I treated the document as an indication of the probable views of Mr Byers. I could not know what might be the content of any final joint opinion should one ever emerge; and none ever did.

Mr Byers told me during the caretaker period that the document did represent his views. I shall accordingly now treat this 'Draft Opinion' as setting out Mr Byers' opinion, but not Mr Enderby's opinion which was never given to me. But of course I had no means of knowing even that it was Mr Byers' actual, final opinion until after 11 November. I must say that to receive, on 6 November, from the Attorney-General of Australia, on two crucial areas of policy and at a critical time, those two unsigned, inconclusive draft 'opinions' was not particularly helpful. I found the lack of properly provided assistance deeply disquieting.

Mr Byers, referring to Mr Ellicott's statement, said the latter's view was 'that His Excellency is legally obliged to take certain steps because of, and as a result of, the current dispute between the House and the Senate'.

In paragraph 5 Mr Byers says:

The question thus is whether the deferring of supply by the Senate solely to procure the resignation or, failing that, the dismissal of the Ministry as a step in a forced dissolution of the Representatives compels His Excellency to dissolve that House. The existence, nature or extent of the Governor-General's reserve powers of dismissal or dissolution in other circumstances does not arise. On those questions we express no opinion. By forced dissolution we mean one occurring 'when the Crown insists on dissolution and, if necessary, dismisses Ministers in order to procure others who will tender the desired advice': *Forsey: The Royal Power of Dissolution of Parliament in the British Commonwealth, 1943, page 71.*

In paragraph 9 Mr Byers says:

The Senate's resolution indicates an intention to defer passage of the Appropriation Bills until either the Ministry resigns or the Governor-General acting against its advice dismisses it and, upon advice of Ministers in a minority in the Representatives, dissolves it. The Ministry has not resigned and will not do so.

This last statement is particularly noteworthy. It confirms, in this unexpected place, what I otherwise knew from Mr Whitlam's statements. Its inclusion in the document handed to me by the Attorney-General was significant: Mr Byers' opinion was prepared by him on the basis of instructions that the Government would not resign, and the Attorney-General in handing it to me made no disclaimer of those instructions. Mr Byers also takes for granted that there will be no advice from the Government for a dissolution, as he also states that the only alternative to resignation of the Ministry is forced dissolution:

That leaves only a forced dissolution. *Dr Jennings (Cabinet Government, 3rd ed. 1969)* observes (at p. 403) that 'No Government has been dismissed by the Sovereign since 1783', and points out that there was no dismissal in 1834 of Lord Melbourne's Government (pages 403–405). Dr Forsey (*The Royal Power of Dissolution of Parliament, 1943*) says that 'In the overseas Empire there appears to have been only one instance of this: New Brunswick in 1853'[16] (page 71). The passage continues — 'The dissolutions in Newfoundland in 1861, New Brunswick in 1866, Quebec in 1878 and 1891, British

Columbia in 1900, Queensland in 1907 and New South Wales in 1932, like the British dissolution of 1807, were not true forced dissolutions. Ministers were not dismissed because they refused to advise dissolution; they were dismissed for quite other reasons, and dissolutions granted to their successors because they could not hope to carry on government with the existing Lower House'.

In paragraph 10 Mr Byers says:

We have referred to forced dissolutions only to indicate that their very rarity and the long years since their exercise cast the gravest doubt upon the present existence of that prerogative.

This statement is surely inconsistent with Forsey's views as quoted in Chapter 14[17], and in making it Mr Byers seems to me to have misunderstood Forsey. Forsey, in the passage quoted (paragraph 9), is saying that in the overseas Empire the 1856 New Brunswick dissolution appears to have been the only 'true' forced dissolution — a 'true' forced dissolution being one where a dissolution is forced upon a Government at the Governor's personal wish, for his own personal reasons. Nowadays of course no Monarch or Governor would contemplate such a course. I agree with Mr Byers that a forced dissolution of the New Brunswick kind is very rare indeed and now almost inconceivable. The other dissolutions discussed by Forsey, like the modern New South Wales example I have quoted, are forced dissolutions because they followed inevitably upon a dismissal — Ministers being dismissed, not to satisfy the personal wishes of a Monarch or his representative, but for 'quite other reasons'. Whether a verbal distinction is or is not to be made in referring to the one type of dissolution as a 'true' forced dissolution is quite irrelevant to the existence, in other cases, of the prerogative of dismissal with consequent dissolution. To my mind this does not cast any doubt whatever on the existence of those powers.

Moreover, this is the only area of those powers — the New Brunswick type of case — on which Mr Byers appears to cast doubt. Forsey's letters to me after 11 November 1975 show that he still believes the power of dismissal and consequent dissolution exist and also that they were properly exercised by me.

Paragraph 12 puts the point that dissolving the House of Representatives is done on the advice of Ministers with a majority in the Representatives, and says:

> The only exception presently material is the doubtful case of the forced dissolution. In such a case the Crown in dissolving has acted upon advice of a minority Ministry.

There is, however, no doubt at all about the power to dismiss a Government having a majority, seek other Ministers and accept their advice to dissolve.

Mr Byers came to the conclusion that the Governor-General was not, in the situation which then existed, constitutionally *obliged* immediately to seek an explanation from the Prime Minister of how he proposed to overcome the situation. He also said (paragraph 16) that if the Prime Minister were 'unable to suggest measures which would solve the disagreement between the Houses and left the Government without funds to carry on' it would not be the Governor-General's *duty* to dismiss his Ministers. Paragraph 17 states:

> We do not suggest that, should a case exist for his intervention, His Excellency in considering the course he will take must disregard the fact that the Senate's deferring or refusal of supply will impede the business of Government. We do suggest that His Excellency is not confined to a consideration of that fact. He may consider others. After all the constitutional provisions but recognise that the Ministry holds office during His Excellency's pleasure (section 64) and that he may dissolve the Representatives before the expiry of its term (sections 28 and 5); they do not, considered alone, afford any guide as to the circumstances when the extreme and abnormal reserve powers of dismissal of a Ministry and consequent dissolution of the Representatives should or may be exercised or even that they still exist. This is the field of convention and discretion.

Mr Byers says (paragraph 18) that it is not correct to treat the exercise of those powers as *demanded* when refusal of supply is threatened or when it occurs. In paragraph 20 it is stated that the mere threat of or indeed the actual rejection of supply neither calls for the Ministry to resign nor *compels* the Crown's representative thereupon to intervene.

Mr Byers considers the Senate's power to block supply (paragraph 28). The question he discusses is whether the Senate's power is untrammelled, that is, one which may in point of law and constitutional practice be exercised whenever and for whatever reason commends itself to the Senate and whatever the consequences. Such an untrammelled power would include an exercise undertaken solely to determine the Representatives' term. Mr Ellicott, Mr Byers says, assumes that the Senate has such untrammelled power over supply. Paragraph 29 states:

> For if the Senate's power to reject is subject to any restraint, that restraint is not in words imposed upon the power which section 53 contains and thus must be found in a practice or convention which would then become a factor offsetting the weight that would otherwise attach to a denial of funds and the hardships necessarily thereby involved without a forced dissolution. None such is suggested. The power which Mr Ellicott assumes in the Senate must, therefore, be one legally and conventionally untrammelled.

I have always believed the power to be untrammelled[18], and did not agree with arguments in the opinion which sought to show the contrary.

I am concerned here and was in October–November 1975 with the power to dismiss a Ministry and thus to force a dissolution. I agree with Mr Byers that a Governor-General is under no legal compulsion to exercise these powers: this is of the essence of a discretionary power. My reading of Forsey did not enable me to agree with Mr Byers' statement in paragraph 10 of the opinion, that the rarity of forced dissolutions and the 'long years' since exercise of these powers cast doubt upon the present existence of the power to dismiss. Forsey and Evatt had taught me the opposite.[19]

As I have said, my correspondence and conversations with Forsey since the crisis amply confirm my understanding of his writings. His statement that he could see nothing that I could have done other than what I did makes it clear that Mr Byers' interpretation of Forsey's thinking is mistaken.

That day, 6 November, marked a decisive point in my approach to the crisis.

The Government's banking exercise showed that we were facing the real prospect of money running out. (By 11 November no beginning had been made on the scheme to get money from the banks; the banks had not even agreed to participate; and no other plan for financing government existed.)

In the crisis I was entitled to real information, help and advice, but I was not receiving them. I prepared therefore to cope with the situation myself.

The discretions I might have to exercise were my own and I had now the duty of thorough analysis and conclusive thought. There was no escape from the historic personal decisions I must make as Governor-General. The week preceding the decision of 11 November moved forward from its early intense activity into a period of intellectual review of the considerations on which I must found my decision. Many factors were to be weighed and balanced which had in various ways been present in my mind as the crisis unfolded, but after that day I had to lift them to the foreground, face them squarely and determine where I stood on each. By the evening of 9 November I had made up my mind as to what I must do if the two leaders were still in deadlock when 11 November came up, inexorably, on the calendar.

An unfounded assertion which has been made since 11 November 1975 is that I 'deceived' Mr Whitlam and other Ministers — that I set out on a deliberate course of deception, aimed presumably at inducing them to believe that I would not exercise any reserve power which I had as Governor-General, whereas I intended to do so.

That charge is totally without foundation. The simple fact, as must be clear from the preceding pages, is that although throughout the weeks as the crisis mounted I was thinking hard about it in all its aspects and with all its implications, it was not until the end of that day of 6 November that I knew I must make up my mind as to any action to be taken by me, and follow that decision through.

Mr Whitlam was not naïve. He was well versed in constitutional matters. I could not conceive that as a lawyer he believed the reserve powers to be non-existent. At no time, for my part, did I say or do anything which could imply that I did not believe in their reality. My request for an opinion from the Law Officers on Mr Ellicott's statement of 16 October was an indication of my interest in the existence of the reserve powers. It has been claimed that when I asked for the opinion of the Law Officers on the Ellicott document I referred to it slightingly. I did not. I disagreed with Mr Ellicott's views on timing and said so, but I wanted the Law Officers' opinion on what he said about the reserve powers, the duty to exercise them and the timing of any such exercise.

I have already mentioned the following occasions on which Mr Whitlam gave clear evidence of his awareness of the reserve powers:

(1) his statement to me in Port Moresby on 15 September 1975 that if I were, at the height of a crisis, to decide to terminate his commission when salaries were not being paid he would have to tell me that Mr Fraser would not be able to get supply either;[20]

(2) his statement to me in my study in the presence of Tun Abdul Razak and others, on 16 October, that it could be a question of whether he got to the Queen first for my recall or I got in first with his dismissal;[21]

(3) his statement to me on 18 October that he might find a legal way to get the banks to lend money to those to whom the Government was indebted, which would enable him to govern without supply and so take away any excuse I would otherwise have for removing him and sending for someone willing to advise an election;[22]

(4) his statement to me on 3 November, while he was still maintaining publicly that I had always to act on his advice, that the only way an election could be obtained was by his dismissal, if I were willing to 'do a Philip Game'.[23]

From all of these statements it was obvious Mr Whitlam accepted that I had the reserve powers and might conceivably exercise them. He never questioned me on my views. Since his statements made it plain that he was well aware of the reserve powers and of the risk he might run by his policy, I had no reason, nor impulse, to volunteer a statement to him of what he clearly knew. I believe, quite starkly, that if I had said anything to Mr Whitlam about the possibility that I might take away his commission I would no longer have been there. I conceived it to be my proper behaviour in the circumstances to stay at my post and not invite dismissal.[24] I elected, as the only neutral and intelligent course to follow, that I should keep silence about my thinking unless and until I decided I must act.

If Mr Whitlam or any other Minister was deceived he deceived himself.

Mr Whitlam, to take only two examples, made the charge of deception seven times in seven successive sentences at a book launching in Australia on 22 March 1976[25]; and on a television programme in London in July 1976 stated that I had given no indication to him or his Ministers that I was contemplating the possibility I would take away their commissions, and went so far as to say, 'He in fact led us to think he was supporting the course of conduct we took.'[26]

This last charge too is totally false. I believe that nothing I said or did could lead the Government to think that I supported the course of conduct it took — namely attempting to govern without supply. I remained scrupulously neutral as to the political wisdom of the parties, not supporting nor opposing either the Senate's denial of supply or the Government's counter-strategy; and I kept my own counsel as to the constitutional rights and wrongs of what was happening until I had decided what must be done.

As to Mr Whitlam's complaint that I gave no indication I was contemplating recourse to the reserve powers, I say simply that when I was in a position to tell him what I intended to do I told him, leaving him an opportunity to indicate to me what his response would be. From the time when Mr Whitlam began publicly to hammer the theme that I had no choice but to adopt his advice he disqualified himself from being offered a running account of the development of my thinking, until such time as it had crystallised in a way which might affect him positively. The Prime Minister has no claim to be made privy to the Governor-General's inmost mind. My clear belief was that Mr Whitlam, being fully aware of the reserve powers of the Governor-General, was concentrating on techniques to ensure that I would not bring them into play. I knew that failure to invoke the reserve powers in a situation calling for their use would be destructive of those powers. Mr Whitlam was not entitled to receive a running report on how I was wrestling with the problem he had set. Any guesses he made on this he made on his own responsibility.

It could perhaps have been different if he had asked me. I should have had to think very carefully about what I should tell him of the shape of my developing thought. But he did not ask. Mr Whitlam's failure to ask my view of the reserve powers must, I have always believed, have been deliberate avoidance. How natural it would have been to open up the question with me, if he had wanted to know. He never did ask that or any other question on what was going on in my mind.

So I remained silent about my thought processes. I hoped that a compromise might be found but it was not. Lawyers frequently try to help contending parties to reach agreement. In much the same way I had tried, within the limits of my office. By 6 November I saw that it was almost certainly a vain hope. Lawyers, and I believe most people, understand that if compromise fails, the person with the power to resolve the issue by decision is called upon to decide. So it now was to be with me.

19

Supply—Power to Deny, Responsibility to Obtain

Having on Thursday 6 November decided to review all the elements in the situation in order to bring my thinking to a conclusion, I turned first to the Senate's powers over supply, these being an important foundation on which other elements rested.

In my view the Senate has clear legal power to block supply, and no convention stands in the way of its doing so. I had never doubted this throughout the crisis and in my final thinking saw no reason to change my view.

Section 53 of the Australian Constitution is, I believe, a true example of legal codification, in a limited field which is left to conventions under some constitutions. It would seem to me rather strange to argue that a legislative code could be displaced or modified by conventions. The advocates of codification, having succeeded in getting some conventions legally codified, would be surprised were they to find these legal rules confined or restricted by new uncodified conventions. Sir Kenneth Bailey is clearly of this view.[1] Also as Sir Robert Menzies wrote in his statement issued on 21 October 1975: 'It would be absurd to suppose that the draftsmen of the Constitution conferred those powers [to reject or adjourn supply] on the Senate with a mental reservation that they should never be exercised.'

It is equally strange to assert that they could be destroyed, not by constitutional amendment but, after the Constitution was enacted, by the development of an unwritten consensus.

The Solicitor-General Mr Byers, in the 'draft opinion' handed to me on 6 November by the Attorney-General, discussed whether or not there is a convention which operates as a restraint upon the Senate's legal powers. He said that if such a restraint existed it is not to be found in the words of section 53 of the Constitution but must be found in a practice or convention which would then become a factor offsetting the weight otherwise attaching to a denial of funds. I did not and do not believe that any such 'offsetting' factor exists. Mr Byers said further that Mr Ellicott assumed the Senate had a power to block supply which was legally and conventionally untrammelled, and wide enough to permit its exercise solely to determine the Representatives' term. In my view, Mr Ellicott was thoroughly well-founded in assuming this. If the legal power to block supply exists in the Senate, political motives for doing so are legally irrelevant. Judgment of political motives is a political judgment and no concern of the Governor-General.

The law on the matter will appear from what follows. Section 53 of the Constitution reads:

> Proposed laws appropriating revenue or moneys, or imposing taxation, shall not originate in the Senate. But a proposed law shall not be taken to appropriate revenue or moneys, or to impose taxation, by reason only of its containing provisions for the imposition or appropriation of fines or other pecuniary penalties, or for the demand or payment or appropriation of fees for licences, or fees for services under the proposed law.
>
> The Senate may not amend proposed laws imposing taxation, or proposed laws appropriating revenue or moneys for the ordinary annual services of the Government.
>
> The Senate may not amend any proposed law so as to increase any proposed charge or burden on the people.
>
> The Senate may at any stage return to the House of Representatives any proposed law which the Senate may not amend, requesting, by message, the omission or amendment of any items or provisions therein. And the House of Representatives may, if it thinks fit, make any of such omissions or amendments, with or without modifications.
>
> Except as provided in this section, the Senate shall have equal power with the House of Representatives in respect of all proposed laws.

By section 1 of the Constitution the legislative power of the

Commonwealth is vested in a federal Parliament which shall consist of the Queen, a Senate and a House of Representatives.

By section 58 of the Constitution a proposed law, to be presented to the Governor-General for the Queen's assent, must first be passed by both Houses:

> When a proposed law passed by both Houses of the Parliament is presented to the Governor-General for the Queen's assent, he shall declare, according to his discretion, but subject to this Constitution, that he assents in the Queen's name, or that he withholds assent, or that he reserves the law for the Queen's pleasure.

My opinion of the meaning of section 53, from which I conclude that the Senate has the power to refuse or refrain from granting supply, coincides with that expressed in 1976 by Professor J. E. Richardson in his article 'The Legislative Power of the Senate in Respect of Money Bills'.[2] At all times I acted upon the assumption that the Senate has the power to refuse or refrain from granting supply, and I refer the reader to Professor Richardson's article for an examination of the reasons, unanswerable to my mind, why that opinion is correct. Professor Richardson's argument is closely reasoned and cannot in justice to him be summarised here but it should be read and studied. His view, and mine, is that the Senate has the legal power to block supply. He demonstrates that no constitutional convention exists to limit this power. He appears, however, to accept the possibility of a convention emerging, saying that 'if a convention is to emerge it will have to flow from a consensus of opinion . . .'. Professor D. P. O'Connell in *The Parliamentarian* of January 1976 said:

> Although it was widely canvassed, the theory of a constitutional convention on the subject of Supply in Australia is not readily sustainable. For a constitutional convention to arise which would, in effect, alter the intendment of the written text of the Constitution there would have to be a practice to that effect supported by a general consensus. While it is true that the Senate had not previously rejected Supply, the constitutional theorists had never previously propounded a theory on the basis of this self-denial which was explicable by political circumstances.[3]

I find it difficult to see how a convention can arise in the teeth of the written words of the Constitution. In any event it has not arisen, as the two professors agree.

When section 53 was put into the Constitution the United Kingdom Parliament Act of 1911 had not been enacted and the legal powers of the House of Lords in relation to all matters, including supply, were the same as those of the House of Commons, though constitutional conventions were said to limit them. The Lords denied supply in 1909 and precipitated a crisis of great significance. This in due course led to the passing of the Parliament Act of 1911 which took away the power of the House of Lords over money Bills and truncated its powers in all other matters, leaving it only the power to delay legislation for two years, later reduced to one year. Since the 1909–11 crisis in the United Kingdom no amendment has been made to the Australian Constitution to limit the powers of the Senate in the way in which the powers of the Lords were limited.

Although the confidence of the Senate is not necessary for the survival of a Government, and its rejection of ordinary legislation will not bring down a Government, its failure to grant supply can produce that result by making government impossible. There is a sense in which a Government must retain the 'confidence' of the Senate to be able to continue in government. It must have the confidence of the Senate expressed by the passing of supply by the Senate.

It is commonly believed that originally the Senate was meant to be the States' House and that the States, through it, could impose their will upon the federal Government by rejecting its legislative proposals if they saw fit. The development of the party system after 1901 changed this situation because, through party discipline, it could normally be ensured that if the Government, having the confidence of the House, also through its party support controlled the Senate, it could enact its legislative programme. Party loyalty, sentiment and discipline would normally prevail over State sentiment and loyalty.

Nevertheless it could happen and it has happened that power has been in different hands in the two Houses and, as the founding fathers expected, the Senate could and would exercise

315

its powers on all kinds of subjects to reject or amend Bills passed by the House. The Senate was from the beginning intended to be an Upper House with great power — one which could be kept in line by the Government of the day only if the Government held a majority in the Senate. The Constitution had therefore to deal with the problem of how to resolve deadlocks between the two Houses; and this was done by section 57. The presence of section 57 shows that the Senate was not intended to be a tame House and that a Government would, across the whole range of its legislative policy, be dependent upon Senate acquiescence. The Senate's position, in relation to supply and generally, is totally different from that of the House of Lords. The philosophy of the Parliament Act of the United Kingdom cannot be found in the Australian Constitution.

The Senate, then, possesses and has frequently exercised great powers. Whatever may have been the original philosophy in relation to the Australian Upper House, it is clear that the heavy weighting of representation in the Senate in favour of the States with smaller populations means that the party or parties controlling the House of Representatives may not be able to control the Senate, since parties and policies appealing to majorities in the smaller States may be different from those achieving victory and acceptance in the House.

In Australia this system has meant that Australians are quite accustomed to Government legislation on all kinds of subjects being rejected or amended in the Senate. It is in this setting of a powerful Senate, responsive to the interests of the smaller States within a federal system, that the question of supply has, as a matter of law and politics, to be considered. There are no grounds for arguing that the House of Representatives, repeatedly called 'the people's House' in the 1975 crisis, is entitled to assert its legislative will over the Senate in any legislative field. The Senate, constituted as it is and with the powers given to it, has always been regarded as part of the federal bargain.

This does not mean that the Senate's powers are impregnable. They could be changed by referendum but only by referendum. Since 1975 some people have argued that the Constitution should be changed by an amendment which would ensure that if the Senate denies or refuses to grant supply for, say, thirty days, there should be an automatic double dissolution. But unless some such change is made by constitutional amendment the Senate can deny supply without necessarily itself being forced to the people. For obvious political reasons the Senate is unlikely to take such a course unless a very serious political position has developed. It is bound to be a rare occurrence.

My opinion, that the Senate has untrammelled power to refuse or withhold supply, was I believe the accepted view until the propaganda and argument of October-November 1975.

Professor Sawer in his book *Federation Under Strain* accepts the view that the Senate has the power to reject and hence to defer money Bills.[4] He also considers the question whether the Senate broke a constitutional convention by using the power to reject supply as a weapon for compelling the resignation of a Government having the confidence of the House of Representatives, and the holding of a general election. Sawer states that in early October it seemed to him and to seven other constitutional law teachers that something might be 'saved' of the 'conventions' concerning Senate restraint in sending Governments to the people. They wrote to the press urging that a failure to accept such a convention might have disastrous effects upon the working of the Constitution. Sawer said in his book that he had had some hope that such a letter would itself 'help to establish such a convention, if it did not actually exist'.[5]

Events unfolded and Professor Sawer concluded:

> Although it is now well established that the Senate has and will exercise a power to compel a Government with a Representatives majority to hold an election, so long as the power to reject or defer supply exists, it is equally probable that the power will not be used capriciously.[6]

Sawer's phrasing of this point is very significant. He asserts that the denial or deferral of supply by the Senate *compels* a Government with a Representatives majority to hold an election. This is a direct rejection of the alleged power and right of such a Government to govern without supply.

317

My own opinion, as I have stated and on which I acted, is that there never has been a convention to prevent the Senate denying supply. Although one can understand the attitude of those who hoped there was or hoped to be able to create one or to strengthen the claim that one ought to exist, Professor Sawer is reconciled to the fact that no such convention exists in fact.

On 30 September 1975, in judgments handed down in *Victoria v the Commonwealth*[7], four High Court judges expressed by way of *obiter dicta* opinions which take the same view of the Senate's powers. Barwick C.J. said that the Senate is a part of the Parliament co-equal with the House of Representatives except only for the limitations set out in terms of the first three paragraphs of section 53. Gibbs J. said that the Senate can reject any proposed law, even one which it cannot amend; Stephen J. said that the Senate can reject outright any Bill, even a money Bill; and Mason J. said that, apart from the limits on Senate power expressly stated in section 53, the Senate and the Representatives have equal legislative power. Barwick C.J. in his letter to me of 10 November 1975 also expressed the view that the Senate can reject or refrain from granting supply.

It is appropriate to quote from these judgments.

> Barwick C.J. said: 'The Senate is a part of the Parliament and, except as to laws appropriating revenue or money for the ordinary annual service of the government or imposing taxation is co-equal with the House of Representatives. Bills may originate and do originate in the Senate. Section 53 makes it abundantly clear that the Senate is to have equal powers with the House of Representatives in respect of all laws other than those specifically excepted. The only limitations as to equality of the powers of the Senate with those of the House of Representatives are those imposed by the first three paragraphs of that section, to the terms of which the limitations must be confined.'[8]

> Gibbs J. said: 'Clearly the Senate retains the power to amend any proposed law in any case that is not within the specific prohibitions imposed by s. 53. The power of the Senate to reject a proposed law — a power implicit in its position as one of the chambers of a bicameral legislature — is left untouched by s. 53 so that the Senate may reject any proposed law, even one which it cannot amend.'[9]

> Stephen J. said: 'The Senate, except as to money bills, possesses

legislative power in no way inferior to the House, it has full power of initiation, rejection and amendment of Bills coming from the House and even in the case of money bills has the right freely to request amendments or to reject outright. These powers, unusual in a modern upper house, reflect the Federal character of our polity.'[10]

Mason J. said: 'In the exercise of its powers under s. 53 the Senate deliberates upon proposed laws initiated by the House; its power to pass or reject them is unconfined by s. 53 or any other provision of the Constitution; and its power to otherwise deal with them is also unconfined save in so far as contrary provision is made by the exceptions which, as I have said, have no application to this case.'[11]

I was aware of these judgments in October and they were available to all concerned with the crisis. Indeed they were incorporated in Hansard in some detail, including the above passages, at the request of Mr Fraser on 30 October.[12]

A contrary legal view was expressed by Sir Richard Eggleston in two letters to the *Age* newspaper, one on 27 October as the crisis was nearing its climax and one on 5 December, after the Government had been dismissed and Parliament dissolved, during the election campaign. Professor Richardson's article of 1976[13] and the High Court judgments quoted in my view amply demonstrate the error of Eggleston's opinion.

Sir Richard Eggleston's first letter raised nonetheless in my mind the spectre of my conversation with Mr Whitlam in Port Moresby, when he had spoken of the possibility of sending the Appropriation Bills to me for royal assent even though they had not been passed by the Senate.[14] Although both Mr Whitlam and Mr Enderby had discounted this as a possibility[15], it crossed my mind that, Eggleston having laid the ground for an argument that the Senate had no power to reject or defer, the Government might use this as a basis for by-passing the Senate and sending the Bills to me for the assent. What the Prime Minister and the Attorney-General had said to me about the law was inconsistent with Eggleston's opinion, but I had to entertain the possibility that the Prime Minister might change his mind, embrace the Eggleston approach and upon it base advice that I must assent to the Bills. In the tense days of November this added a further problem on which I must be ready with my decision.

319

I should be acting invalidly if I were to give the royal assent to Appropriation Bills which had not passed the Senate. The proposition to the contrary was in my view plainly wrong. But I had to consider what I should do if confronted in early November by such advice from the Prime Minister.

Could I regard the point as unarguable in the light of the Eggleston opinion? Was there any way of getting a High Court decision in advance of giving the assent? How long would it take to get a decision once the issue was before the High Court, assuming it to be, as it clearly was, justiciable?

In the event, although the Eggleston opinion was discussed in the House, the Government's policy on that point happily remained unaltered.

The Constitutional Review Committee 1958, of which Mr Whitlam was a member, assumed that the Senate had the power to deny supply and proposed a means for overcoming the deadlock which denial of supply could produce. It thus did not hold the view that a supply Bill did not have to pass the Senate, nor the view that a convention existed which would prevent the Senate at all times from exercising its legal power to deny supply.

I recall here the well-known statements made in Parliament by Mr Whitlam and Senator Murphy, confirming the Senate's powers and referred to constantly during the October-November period.

Mr Whitlam, in the House, on 12 June 1970 said:

> Any government which is defeated by the Parliament on a major taxation Bill should resign . . . This Bill will be defeated in another place [the Senate]. The Government should then resign.[16]

Mr Whitlam, in relation to the 1970–71 Appropriation Bill, clearly indicated a view that the Senate could 'destroy' a Budget and by this means 'destroy' a Government sponsoring such a Budget. He said:

> Let me make it clear at the outset that our opposition to this Budget is no mere formality. We intend to press our opposition by all available means on all related measures in both Houses. If the motion is defeated we will vote against the Bills here and in the

Senate. Our purpose is to destroy this Budget and to destroy the Government which has sponsored it.[17]

The only way 'destroying' a Budget could produce destruction of the Government would be by forcing it to the people. This result, Mr Whitlam must have believed, had necessarily to follow from denial of supply by the Senate.

In the Senate on 18 June 1970 the then Senator Murphy said:

> For what we conceive to be simple but adequate reasons, the Opposition will oppose these measures.
>
> In doing this the Opposition is pursuing a tradition which is well established, but in view of some doubt recently cast upon it in this chamber, perhaps I should restate the position. The Senate is entitled and expected to exercise resolutely but with discretion its power to refuse its concurrence to any financial measure, including a tax Bill. There are no limitations on the Senate in the use of its constitutional powers, except the limits imposed by discretion and reason.[18]

These statements not only were confirmatory of the Senate's legal powers and of their untrammelled nature, but also were of considerable significance on the duty of a Government which is denied supply or has an important taxation measure rejected by the Senate.

The Whitlam Government itself had upheld, and always during the crisis acted consistently with, the principle that the Senate's concurrence was legally necessary to obtain supply. If the Government believed, as it claimed in October-November 1975 (contrary to the Whitlam-Murphy opinions of 1970) that the Senate was fettered by a convention that it could not deny supply, one would imagine that breach of such a convention would have led a frustrated Government to fall back upon the legal argument, if it believed it to be valid, that in any event section 53 gave the Senate no legal power to reject or defer supply. But this it never did. It never sought to precipitate a legal issue for the High Court on this point.

The Senate was, then, entitled legally to act as it did, and no convention stood in its way.

There is a second issue, equally fundamental, in relation to supply. It is the responsibility of the Government to obtain the money without which it cannot carry on its activity. It must obtain this money from the Parliament.

The fact that money Bills must originate in the House of Representatives and that the Senate cannot amend them means that the Government has the effective power to settle the appropriation policy it wishes to pursue: it determines how much money it wants and for what purposes. The Government has in addition the responsibility of obtaining the money necessary for the ordinary annual services of government. It is committed to meet the salaries of public servants and police and defence forces and the other obligations of the Crown. It is from the Parliament that necessary money must be obtained, it is Parliament that has to vote the Budget; and Parliament, under the Australian Constitution, consists of two Houses.

The Government has two separate relationships: one, with the Parliament from which it has to obtain the money it wants; and secondly with the Crown, because it is the Crown's Ministers who constitute the Government and to whom the Crown has to look to ensure that moneys are provided to enable government to be carried on.

A Government is not a committee of the House of Representatives.[19] Ministers are sworn in to serve the Crown. They have to be or to become members of Parliament and they have to retain the confidence of the House of Representatives; but they are the Queen's Ministers with duties to administer her government, the departments of State within her executive. The executive power of the Commonwealth is vested in the Queen and is exercisable by the Governor-General.[20] Members of the Government are appointed by the Governor-General and, so far as the Constitution is concerned, hold office during his pleasure.[21] The Constitution does not mention the Prime Minister nor the Cabinet as such. When Ministers are appointed and accept office to administer departments of government they do so knowing that money must be found for the ordinary purposes of government and for other purposes, and their responsibility is to get it.

Responsible government is what makes all of this work in

accordance with the classic Westminster system. Although responsible government is not mentioned in the Constitution, the system works because of conventions which, if observed, ensure that it will; because of section 61 and the extension of that section to embrace the prerogative powers of the Crown; and because of other constitutional provisions. The system of responsible government in Australia embraces and includes the discretionary powers of the Crown—of the Governor-General—just as it embraces and includes the Cabinet system, the role of the Prime Minister and the notion that a Government must have the confidence of the Lower House—all of this despite no specific mention of any of it, except the powers of the Governor-General, in the Constitution.

Section 61 reads:

The executive power of the Commonwealth is vested in the Queen and is exercisable by the Governor-General as the Queen's representative, and extends to the execution and maintenance of this Constitution, and of the laws of the Commonwealth.

The 'laws of the Commonwealth' include the common law and hence the prerogative.

A primary, indeed *the* primary duty of a Government is to ensure the provision of supply to the Crown. The Crown cannot tax the citizens. Only Parliament can do that, and the Crown cannot draw moneys for the purposes of government from the Treasury without Parliament's approval: under section 83 of the Constitution no money shall be drawn from the Treasury of the Commonwealth except under appropriation made by law. Accordingly the raising of much of the revenue and the spending of money from the Treasury are both in the control of Parliament and not of the Crown or the Government. Vast sums are necessary to enable the Crown to carry on the complex executive government of modern times; and it must obtain those sums from Parliament. This duty is a fundamental one without which government could not be carried on and would break down.

It is contrary to the customary practice' in Australia, and could open up dangerous possibilities, for a Government in power to say, 'We shall find some other way of financing government, by-passing Parliament.' For example, suppose — and this is hypothetical in the extreme — a foreign power undertook to underwrite the funding of an Australian Government to which supply had been denied by Parliament, could this be tolerated?

This cautionary example is not, of course, to suggest that any foreign component whatsoever entered into the financial arrangements being proposed by the Australian Government in late 1975.

Professor Sawer in an appendix, 'Arrangement for paying Government Creditors, November 1975', to his book *Federation Under Strain* discusses what he understood to be the arrangement the Government sought to make with the banks. The plan was never officially announced in a public way but Professor Sawer has deduced its structure very convincingly. I quote a passage which mentions some of the objections that existed against entering into the arrangement. Sawer writes:

> However, while it is unlikely that any prosecution could have been successfully launched against members of the government for making the agreement [with the banks] in question, there were more detailed legal and practical objections to entering into it, probably more pressing in the case of the non-government than in the case of the Commonwealth banks. The banks were being asked to accept a business risk. If the ministers were correct and the Senate likely soon to cave in, this risk would be small, but what if the ministers were wrong? The plan might prove to be inadequate to meet the need; litigation might obstruct and delay its carrying out even if in the end unsuccessful. The Governor-General might in a short time have been compelled to the action he took on 11 November, on what I consider the justifiable ground of the widespread illegality caused by leaving a great many debts unsatisfied. If in consequence the Liberal-Country Parties had still been returned at a general election, it could not be assumed that they would regard themselves as bound by the Labor Government's promises to the banks. It might reasonably be assumed that no responsible government would fail to reimburse the banks for the amounts actually advanced to government creditors, but the interest and expense payments would be another thing; indeed, if the crisis and the negotiations had gone much further, it is likely that the opposition leaders would have been compelled to

declare their attitude on the extent to which they would honour any commitments made by Labor. It is possible that the interest and expenses promised were in any event inadequate having regard to the novelty of the proposal and the difficulty of estimating its administrative consequences. In the case of government creditors other than the public service, legal difficulties could arise both under the Constitution and under State legislation such as that concerning assignment of book debts, if the creditors were to be required to assign their claims. Apart from the administrative burden which operating the plan might impose on bank staffs, there could be inconvenience and loss for regular customers because 'working for the government' meant less time for them. These are only fairly obvious difficulties. I suspect that for these reasons alone, and probably the practical banker could point to others, I would have advised the non-government banks not to agree. The directors of the non-government banks were in the position of any directors of commercial companies, owing fiduciary duties to their corporations and their shareholders, and answerable for failure to act with due prudence.[22]

Professor Sawer, reflecting well after the event, said that it does not appear that the Government at any stage proposed to use its powers under the various Acts to compel either the Commonwealth Banks or any non-Government bank to join in the plan. He went on:

> So far as is known, the Commonwealth banks would have been prepared to try the plan for a limited period, though it might have been administratively impossible for them to carry on unless one or two other substantial banks also agreed; so far as is known, no non-government bank had agreed to the scheme by 11 November and it is unlikely that any would have done so.[23]

I acted on this same assumption that it was unlikely that any of the private banks would do so. The circumstances were such that I could not delay to be confirmed in this opinion, but I had no doubt that it was well founded.

As to the Government banks Professor Sawer said that a court may imply from the powers of their boards some duties of a fiduciary character, analogous to those of the director of a commercial bank, and 'if asked I would have strongly advised the boards to obtain a written direction from the Treasurer under s.11 of the respective Acts'.[24]

Professor Sawer says that 'it is likely that one or more of the opinions of barristers about the plan were transmitted to the Governor-General by the non-government banks or other parties on or about 11 November, too late to have any influence on his actions'.[25] I knew nothing of the banks' attitudes or legal advice received by them before I acted on 11 November. Two legal opinions did arrive at Government House: the first, accompanied by a letter dated 12 November, arrived on 12 November; the second, accompanied by a letter dated 19 November, arrived on 20 November. Both opinions were signed by counsel on 11 November. Neither caused me to have any doubt about the views I had formed.

Even on the most favourable assessment it seemed to me most unlikely that the non-Government banks would participate, and on that basis it would be very difficult for the Government banks to carry the whole burden. Had they been left unsupported in this way it might have been difficult for the Government to give them a direction. In exercising my discretion to act on 11 November, there being in my view compelling reasons to wait no longer, it did not seem to me that the opportunity for a general election in 1975 should be lost on the unlikely possibility of the scheme becoming operative, especially having regard to its defects and inadequacies and very doubtful legality. It must also be kept in mind that this was the only scheme put forward by the Government. Except for it no money was going to be available. I took the scheme into account but did not think that I should be deterred from acting on 11 November by the bare possibility of the dubious banking exercise getting haltingly off the ground. This exercise could not be regarded as fulfilment of the duty to obtain supply.

If unable, because of a valid exercise of the Senate's power, to fulfil its primary duty to the Crown of obtaining supply, a Government must advise dissolution or resign. Because the government must be carried on, a deadlock over supply is too serious especially in modern times to be dealt with under the provisions of section 57, which would require many months to elapse and an election to be held at the end of that period for both Houses. A Government would be unlikely to choose resignation because by advising dissolution it would retain the advantages of being in office when fighting the subsequent election. If however, being unable to provide the Crown with the money to carry on government, it refuses to recommend an election or resign it precipitates a very serious issue for the Governor-General, and courts dismissal.

It can be taken for granted that the reserve powers of the Crown are better never used and to force their use could weaken the vice-regal office, although this will not necessarily follow. One reason why there should be dissolution and an election, or else resignation of the Government, when supply is blocked in Australia by the Upper House, is to avoid facing the Crown with the burden of forcing dissolution and an election through withdrawal of a Government's commission. Wise statesmanship requires action by the political leaders which will avoid ultimate recourse to the reserve powers. The supply crises in Victoria in 1947 and 1952 and in Tasmania in 1948 show the conventions properly working. But in Australia in 1975 this convention of responsible government was being discarded.

The Senate's action and Mr Whitlam's reaction are discussed with insight in the following passage from an article in the English journal *The Economist*, which reflects very clearly my own understanding of the duties of a Government:

> The argument about what Mr Whitlam should have done once the Senate had taken this action comes back to convention, rather than constitutional texts. The governor-general contends that the same basic convention applies in Australia as in Britain. If a prime minister cannot secure the supply of money he needs, he has a duty to resign or to accept a new election. If a British prime minister refused to do either of those things after his government had failed to get a finance bill through the House of Commons, resorting to arguments that the opposition majority had been 'stacked', it would presumably be the duty of the Queen to show him the door. The only difference in Australia, in Sir John Kerr's view, is that supply depends on the confidence of two houses rather than one. The same basic principle holds good: if a prime minister cannot get his money

from the representatives of the people, he should step down. Significantly, it is a principle that Mr Whitlam himself seemed inclined to accept before he tasted office. In a speech to parliament on June 12, 1970, he declared that 'any government which is defeated by the parliament on a major taxation bill should resign'.

The cleanest way out of the impasse would have been for Mr Whitlam to call a new election himself. He chose not to do that, although his slumped popularity in the opinion polls has recently revived a good deal, showing that some Australians have their doubts about Mr Fraser's and the Liberals' manoeuvres in the Senate. Instead, Mr Whitlam pressed for a half-Senate election in which he could have gambled on winning a one-man majority in the upper house. This presented the governor-general with only two options: to let the country lumber through several months of political uncertainty and economic chaos, while vital services went unmanned and civil servants unpaid; or to appoint a caretaker prime minister who could secure the supply of money to the government and was prepared to put the matter to a general election. He handed the decision back to the people . . .

It can be endlessly disputed whether Mr Fraser or Sir John Kerr moved at the right time, or on the right issue. The politicians will no doubt give their answer according to what happens on December 13th. But there is a much deeper issue at stake: the survival of a system of checks and balances. A society in which the government of the day can do almost anything it likes with the support of a transient majority in a single assembly is more vulnerable to the abuse of power than one in which government is circumscribed by counter-vailing institutions such as a strong upper house.[26]

Just as in the United Kingdom a Government which cannot get supply from the House of Commons because of, say, a crossing of the floor by some members, must recommend an election or resign, so in Australia there could be no question, in the case of denial of funds by the Representatives, of governing without supply to force House rebels to break and recross the floor. Where two Houses hold the purse strings, the same is true in the Upper House. In neither case can it be appropriate or necessary to wait until the money actually runs out on the chance that someone may break. Supply must be secured before this dire result occurs.

20

The Queen and
November the Eleventh

I considered next the position of the Queen in relation to the Australian crisis.

The Governor-General reports regularly to the Queen. There are no rules about how often or in what detail reports are to be made: the duty is simply to send despatches which keep Her Majesty informed.

The supply crisis of 1975 was a crucial event in Australia and as it unfolded the Queen had been receiving full reports on what was happening.

In a letter which was made public and which I quote in full later[1], the Queen's Private Secretary Sir Martin Charteris (now Lord Charteris) on 17 November 1975 wrote to the Honourable G. G. D. Scholes as follows:

> Her Majesty, as Queen of Australia, is watching events in Canberra with close interest and attention, but it would not be proper for her to intervene in person in matters which are so clearly placed within the jurisdiction of the Governor-General by the Constitution Act.

This letter reveals that the view held in the Palace was that the powers I exercised on 11 November were powers committed to me by the Constitution. Evatt and Haldane have already been referred to on this point.[2] Lord Haldane is quoted by Evatt as indicating that section 61 of the Constitution has

> put the Sovereign in the position of having parted, so far as the affairs of the Commonwealth are concerned, with every shadow of active intervention in their affairs and handing them over, unlike the case of Canada, to the Governor-General.[3]

329

This is my view and the view upon which I acted. I did not tell the Queen in advance that I intended to exercise these powers on 11 November. I did not ask her approval. The decisions I took were without the Queen's advance knowledge. The reason for this was that I believed, if dismissal action were to be taken, that it could be taken only by me and that it must be done on my sole responsibility. My view was that to inform Her Majesty in advance of what I intended to do, and when, would be to risk involving her in an Australian political and constitutional crisis in relation to which she had no legal powers; and I must not take such a risk.

Had the Queen been told, there would have been nothing legally that Her Majesty could do about the crisis except conceivably to offer advice. But then it could be claimed that the Monarch, although having no legal power to act, had failed to remain aloof and had become embroiled in the political and constitutional confrontation in Australia. On the other hand to do nothing, having once been informed of my intentions, could also have resulted in criticism of the Monarchy.

The founding fathers in their wisdom had decided to relieve the Monarch of such responsibility and risk of criticism. In drafting the Constitution they had seen fit to give all the prerogative powers relevant to handling a supply crisis and its resolution to the Governor-General. As I had been placed in the position of being the only person with the appropriate constitutional powers, it was clear to me that I must, in the circumstances, bear the brunt of what was coming. Inevitably the use of the reserve powers would be controversial and it was my duty to the Monarchy, as I saw it, that full accountability for what might have to be done should be accepted by me. In this way I could hope to protect the Crown in Australia from any serious risk of being weakened by events.

I was fully mindful of what Professor Bailey had said in his introduction to the first edition of Evatt's *The King and his Dominion Governors*. He said that

> any exercise of the reserve powers by the Crown must inevitably involve the King or his Dominion representative in the assumption of very heavy personal responsibility, to his advisers, to Parliament,

December 1975: Sir John attending the RAAF graduation ceremony at Point Cook.
(Herald and Weekly Times Ltd)

Chief Inspector Barry Brown and police officers guide the vice-regal car through a demonstration in Melbourne. (Age)

Yellow paint was thrown over the vice-regal car during one of the most violent demonstrations in Melbourne. (News Ltd)

Sir John officially opens Parliament on 17 February 1976. The President of the Senate, Senator C. L. Laucke, looks on. (Canberra Times)

One year later: 11 November 1976—the Prime Minister, Mr Fraser, and Sir John at the National War Memorial Remembrance Day ceremony. (Canberra Times)

Sir John and Lady Kerr with the Queen and Prince Philip during their 1977 Australian tour.

The 19th Australian Legal Convention, Sydney, 1977: (from left) the Prime Minister, Mr Fraser, President of the Law Council of Australia, Mr D. Ferguson, Sir John Kerr, and the Chief Justice, Sir Garfield Barwick.
(Sydney Opera House Trust)

and to the people. It will inevitably entail unpopularity in some quarters. This is a serious matter even in the case of the Sovereign. But it is an absolutely vital matter in the case of a Governor, who is a temporary officer, and who now, it appears, holds his office upon the advice of his own ministers.[4]

Two risks had to be guarded against. On the one hand, the Queen could become involved in our crisis if she were asked to recall me when I was in the process of dismissing Mr Whitlam or threatening to do so. Equally, she could become involved if she had advance knowledge of my intention to exercise the reserve power.

As has been made clear from the writings on the subject there is always a risk of recall if a Government feels threatened by a possible exercise of the reserve power of dismissal — of recall, followed by a more convenient appointment. My recall would have been of use to Mr Whitlam only if followed by speedy appointment of someone who would let him govern without supply.

It has been suggested that the Queen would not have been bound immediately to accept the Prime Minister's advice, however urgent, that I be recalled and replaced by someone of his choice — that she could have delayed a decision until properly satisfied in writing of the reasons for recall and perhaps, although not bound to do so, could have heard anything I might wish to submit on the subject. But the country and its institutions would have been placed under almost impossible stress if I had availed myself of any such hypothetical period of delay before dismissing Mr Whitlam. The advice to the Queen would, I had no doubt, be so strong that any period of delay must indeed be short and any action of mine speedy if it were to be fitted into such a period. Merely to state this problem is to indicate how passionately divisive it would have been in the community, already in a precarious state of insecurity and agitation.

I have heard it said also that the Queen could if so minded have exercised some kind of 'reserve power' to refuse to take the advice of a Prime Minister seeking to dismiss a Governor-General at a time when the Governor-General was intending to dismiss the Prime Minister. I seriously doubt that such a reserve power

331

exists. In any event its exercise, if it does, would certainly have greatly exacerbated the crisis, and could hardly have failed to draw a great weight of controversy immediately upon the Queen herself.

Mr Whitlam himself subscribed to the view that all the powers of a legal and prerogative kind devolve upon the Governor-General under the Constitution. He believed that under our Constitution the Governor-General is a viceroy. It was a mistake however if he thought that I was *his* viceroy.

An opinion of the Solicitor-General Mr Byers, given to me by Mr Whitlam in another connection, demonstrated that the Queen's powers have been handed over to the Governor-General by the Constitution. What was under consideration by him at the time was whether instructions could be given by the Queen to the Governor-General as to the exercise of his powers. His opinion, and I agreed with it, was that the executive power of the Commonwealth exercisable by the Governor-General under chapter II of the Constitution (including the power of dismissing Ministers under section 64) and also the powers relating to dissolution of Parliament conferred by section 5 and section 57 could not be made the subject of instructions from the Queen. Professor Sawer says that 'the Queen could not have appointed Mr Whitlam as Prime Minister, nor could she have dismissed him. Neither would any direction of hers to the Governor-General on such matters have had any legal force, whether before or after 11 November 1975'.[5]

As the Queen could not validly give me instructions as to how I should exercise my powers under section 64, I must not burden her with prior knowledge of my actual intention to act under that section. In this way, and only in this way, would Her Majesty be kept above risk of involvement in what happened.

For all of these reasons I deemed it my duty to exercise my powers on my own responsibility, to refrain from letting the Queen know in advance, and to act with utmost speed if it once became clear that Mr Whitlam would not only persist in governing without supply but would involve the Monarchy by seeking my recall.

21

Final Thoughts

In this last period I had to take into account my assessment of the attitudes of the two leaders. Mr Whitlam's attitude is evoked by the historian Francis West[1]:

> What Mr Whitlam said after 16 October 1975 when the Senate indeed failed to pass Supply was that he would 'crush' or 'smash' this 'vicious' and 'tainted' House . . .
>
> He spoke of 'my' viceroy and said that the Governor-General would do as the Prime Minister told him, that the Governor-General could act only on his advice . . .
>
> Mr Whitlam said he would 'tough it out'. In the course of the next twenty-five days he talked . . . of 'destroying' Mr Fraser as, he said, he had destroyed his predecessors as Leaders of the Opposition.[2]

The pattern of attitudes to me of the Prime Minister was marked by his public stressing of the theme that I must unquestionably do his bidding and the private reminders to me of the risks I would run if I opposed him. I do not mean to imply that there were any warlike words. It was all politely and smilingly done. But in his determination to win, over institutions and opponents, I had not the slightest doubt that if he felt the need the Prime Minister would seek to have me recalled before I could dismiss him.

Both men were, I felt, staking all on winning the vital game. Neither was in my opinion bluffing. I felt that, on the one hand, Mr Fraser feared I might not have the strength to do what he believed my duty required, but intended to put me to the test. On the other hand Mr Whitlam, I thought, believed his will was paramount and that I would not take the one step that could stop him. Mr Fraser was perhaps worried that this might be true, but his determination, as I saw it, was to ensure that the Senate held; to put the problem firmly in the Governor-General's basket, and to keep it there.

The public statements of both leaders during the last few days before 11 November indicated that both were holding fast. I gave Mr Whitlam and Mr Fraser no indication of my reaction to the course events were taking. Mr Fraser was not entitled to know my thoughts, and Mr Whitlam, by his publicly announced and privately stated attitudes, had left me under no obligation to tell him how my thinking was developing. If he deceived himself by misjudging me, I had no duty to give him a different analysis of my character.[3]

Further questions to be squarely looked at in the last days included the timing, the basis and the nature of a dismissal if it had to take place.

Some have said that my decision of 11 November was premature.

The decision was mine and therefore the responsibility was mine.

There was about to be massive default in the Commonwealth's enormously complex set of legal obligations. I had the legal power to prevent this by dismissal. I was quite satisfied that if the Senate held firm these illegalities would occur, and that proposed banking arrangements were unsatisfactory and would fail.

I had no doubt about the irreversibility of Mr Whitlam's attitude, and as to this I let the record speak. Anyone who believes there was a reasonable possibility that Mr Whitlam could have been induced to change his mind is welcome to his opinion but it certainly was not mine.

As to Mr Fraser, the Opposition and the Senate, some people claim that there might have been weakening on their side, but the meeting of 1–2 November in my view had provided a firm top-level policy decision. Responsibility for it was widely spread in the councils of the Opposition parties. If there was any possibility of defection I could not know of it and I had to deal with realities as I could best assess them.

I had the legal power to act. I also felt fully able to rely on the constitutional dicta and principles concerned with

'Constitution preservation' — that is, preservation of the constitutional complex of law and usage. I had an active duty, by the exercise of my powers under the Constitution, to preserve it by preventing the effective smashing of the power of the Senate on supply, and of the reserve powers of the Crown.

If I did not act, very great suffering on a nation-wide scale would follow. I was not prepared to gamble with the future of the Constitution, the economy, and the financial security of very great numbers of people, indeed directly and indirectly the whole nation.

I did not believe that I had to wait until this suffering and these illegalities occurred. I conceived it to be within my discretion to take action in time to avoid them. I was not prepared to delay until after the disaster came to pass in order to get a watertight ground for action based upon visible chaos. The price to the community would be too great.

Those who complain that I should have waited until 30 November (by which date money would have run out); or longer, or indefinitely, like no doubt to think that the Senate might have weakened. But as the public demand for and expectation of action by the Governor-General grew, the effect had not been to weaken Opposition firmness. A Governor-General cannot see into the future: I waited until the national purse was almost empty, which was as long as, for the safety of the country, I could; the fact was that the Senate had held to its determination since 16 October with a firmness which was recognised by the Government when it reacted by proposing dubious and makeshift financial arrangements in order to carry on without supply, by-passing the Parliament.

The precise date of 11 November had been widely accepted as the last date permitting an electoral decision in 1975. This was for recognised administrative reasons. They were to some extent tied to national sociological factors, December to late January being the long summer holiday period in Australia, when many things close down and the nation goes away on vacation, much as in July and August in Europe. It has been claimed that such a consideration should not have prevented me from waiting one week — perhaps two weeks — before acting, in the hope that some solution would thus have had time to manifest itself. On what grounds could I have entertained such a hope? Speculation about the possibility of the Senate breaking was fruitless. I could not know whether history would ultimately be able to make a judgment on that point. Such a finding, if it could ever be made, would take a long time. I could not on 11 November make in advance that long term judgment of history.

Professor Sawer, although he put forward this idea, went on to conclude:

> Unless, therefore, palliative measures could be taken fairly promptly and their legality promptly tested, a time must soon have arrived when on the 'maintenance of law' test, the Governor-General could act.

In addition to this test I had the 'Constitution preservation' test upon which to rely.

Sawer continued:

> On this as on other matters, the more precise formulation in the Constitution of matters not previously so plainly stated supported the view of the Governor-General that he could not let matters go too long. Probably Sir John Kerr, as a constitutional lawyer, attached especial significance to the requirement of appropriation of public moneys in ss. 81, 82 and 83 of the Constitution and the associated Audit Act provisions under which he himself had specific responsibilities (ss. 32, 33 and 34). However, even a Governor-General without such special sensitivity would need to be a worthless puppet or a party hack before he could sit back, draw his permanently appropriated pay and allowances and take no action in a situation of increasing chaos with revolutionary possibilities.[4]

Of course all of this weighed heavily upon me. To time my action differently would in my view have been to wait until the country was over the edge of the precipice.

As to the basis of the dismissal, Mr Whitlam and his colleagues should, I thought, be dismissed because they insisted, contrary to the customary procedures of constitutional government, on governing without parliamentary supply, failing to resign or advise an election. These were the two sides of a single coin. From the positive viewpoint, the Government was departing from proper conduct in doing something specific — insisting on governing without supply; from the negative, it was departing from proper conduct in its failure to do something — advise dissolution when supply was denied. Using Forsey's language it was at the same time an occasion for a forced dissolution and an occasion for a dismissal inevitably followed by dissolution. The words of the description do not matter: the same result had to follow, whatever the way of viewing it.

I then turned to the nature of the dismissal — the decision to get from a caretaker Government advice in favour of a double dissolution. I knew that there were some twenty-one Bills, twice presented to but not passed by the Senate, and that these could provide solid objective grounds for a double dissolution. It was obvious that Mr Fraser if he accepted a commission, as I had no doubt he would, would be prepared to advise it. It seemed to me that if I felt compelled to dismiss the Government it would be the fairest outcome if a double dissolution could be produced, rather than a dissolution only of the Lower House.

Some have argued that the decision I made to proclaim a double dissolution was invalid because in my memorandum of 11 November I gave as a reason for the intended double dissolution, not the Parliamentary situation as to the many Bills which would have justified a double dissolution but the deadlock over supply, which taken alone would not have satisfied the requirements of section 57. However, although the deadlock on the twenty-one Bills was not referred to in my memorandum of 11 November, the double dissolution was carried out by a Proclamation of that day based on section 57 and on twenty-one Bills which met the conditions of that section.[5] The satisfaction of section 57 was fully in mind when I obtained Mr Fraser's undertaking. The deadlocks were undoubtedly established and well known when Mr Fraser was commissioned and they provided the solid objective basis upon which the undertaking was obtained and later the double dissolution proclaimed.

Mr Fraser gave, in the event, the necessary advice, and the double dissolution took place unchallenged. Rushed though the timetable of events on 11 November was, the conditions of section 57 were, on examination, seen to be fully satisfied. Mr Fraser's advice was supported by legal opinion as to the twenty-one Bills by the Secretary of the Attorney-General's department, who came with Mr Fraser to Government House early in the afternoon. Professor Sawer says, understandably enough: 'Having regard to the timetable it is unlikely that the kind of advice usually given by an Attorney-General and Solicitor-General as to the conditions required by s. 57 of the Constitution could have been given by the time that the document dissolving both Houses was executed on 11 November.'[6] Proper legal advice was given.[7]

Professor Sawer discusses this question of the double dissolution. He says that even where the requirements of section 57 are met the Governor-General is under no obligation to grant one:

> He 'may', not must do so. Much of the discussion of the role of the Governor-General in the past has been concerned with the implications of this 'may', as well as with the satisfaction of the conditions as to a Bill or Bills. In the 1914 and 1951 cases, both the language of the advice and the observations of the Governors-General when accepting it were consistent with a view that the Prime Minister needed to show political circumstances making a double dissolution *desirable*, or at least raising a *prima facie* case that it was desirable, and with the further view that the Governor-General might be entitled to refuse the double dissolution, even where the conditions of s. 57 were satisfied, on wider political grounds.[8]

Later Professor Sawer said:

> There can be no doubt that s. 57 is in terms making it legally quite within power for the Governor-General to have in his mind, when acting under the section, other considerations than the specific history of a particular Bill or Bills *as well* as that history.[9]

Professor Sawer says that the objective circumstances of the twenty-one Bills were there and adverted to in my Proclamation:

> The deadlock over supply referred to in the memorandum provides further political reasons to justify a double dissolution which are properly to be considered because of the word 'may' in the power to dissolve. This view removes all possibility of legal attack on the double dissolution of 1975.[10]

338

These extracts give a good indication of the considerations I had in mind in coming to my decision.

In thinking out my position over the final weekend — which included a long day of public engagements in Melbourne on Saturday — I took deep account of all these matters. I did not act blindly or pursuant only to a purpose or motive of solving the supply crisis. I looked squarely at the objective situation in relation to the twenty-one Bills and section 57, and had no doubt what legal advice about them I could and would get at the critical moment.

My position as to the action I should take was now clearly formulated in my mind.

On a matter on which a Governor-General comes to feel he has a right and duty to act on his own responsibility under the reserve powers he is entitled to take unofficial advice from anyone whose judgment he trusts. This is quite a different process from that involved in his normal duty to act on the Prime Minister's advice or that of the Executive Council. It is only on those rare but real occasions when he can act constitutionally contrary to the Prime Minister's advice, the extreme example of which is dismissal of a Prime Minister and his Government, that he is entitled to such consultation if he feels the need for it and, in my opinion, on a matter of such great importance he can go where he believes he will get the best help.

As part of his general thesis that I was entitled to no advice at all from anyone but himself, Mr Whitlam several times explicitly said that I was not entitled to the direct advice of the Law Officers of the Crown; that I could ask him, the Prime Minister, for legal advice; that if he saw fit he would ask the Law Officers to advise him; and that, if he wished, he would then advise me on the question involved, sending me a copy of the Law Officers' opinion if that seemed to him to be appropriate.

There is, of course, a very great difference between being entitled to direct advice and getting legal help only as permitted by the Prime Minister. Sir Paul Hasluck had said the Governor-General was entitled to the advice of the Law Officers and to that of the Chief Justice. I asked Mr Whitlam to let me have the advice of the Law Officers on Mr Ellicott's published opinion on the reserve powers, with the non-result that I have described. Time had passed and the problem was now immediate. My mind inevitably turned to the Chief Justice. To obtain constitutional advice from that source was approved by Sir Paul Hasluck and backed by historic precedent.

There are no legal advisers to whom a Governor-General can turn in any institutionalised way — no specially appointed legal adviser or panel of advisers, and no practice in Australia of employing private legal advisers. All such alternatives would *a fortiori* have been objected to by the Prime Minister.

Professor O'Connell in his *Parliamentarian* article said:

> There is, perhaps, a lesson in this. The Governor-General should, perhaps, nominate standing counsel of intellectual and professional repute who stand outside politics and are not members of the judiciary, to whom he can turn for independent advice when the occasion arises. (Not always will the Governor-General be an ex-Chief Justice.) The example of the Palace could be followed, but it would be desirable for a group of counsel to be nominated so that in the event of a repetition of this type of crisis their identity can be known and their opinions made public. In this way the Crown would be best sheltered from the charge of political involvement, and the personality of the Governor-General — now greatly exposed by these events — could be protected.[11]

It would indeed have been less onerous had I had the help of personal constitutional advisers on the merits of the situation. But to have this would mean acting in the teeth of the Prime Minister's objection to my having outside advice, and would therefore — unless I were willing to court dismissal — be possible only in secret, which would greatly increase the prospect of conspiratorial assertions being made. I did not in the highly emotional and explosive conditions of the time, which after the decision would become more pronounced, wish to put at risk of misinformed or malicious reflections on his motivation an adviser to whom I might turn.

That I was considering my powers and authorities — my position generally — was made known to the Prime Minister when I asked for an opinion of the Law Officers about Mr Ellicott's views on the reserve powers. In all of these circumstances I was fortified in my view that I could go to the Chief Justice if the latter were willing to advise me. I knew from earlier talks with the Prime Minister, before the crisis, that he did not believe that a Governor-General could ever consult or take the advice of the Chief Justice; but I did not agree with this. It was a matter for the Chief Justice, if consulted, to decide what he could properly do.

Late on Sunday afternoon 9 November, having arrived conclusively at my decision as to what I must do on the following Tuesday unless, at their meeting that morning, a compromise were reached by the political leaders or one of the two withdrew from the field of battle, I decided, on one aspect only of my decision, to consult the Chief Justice. I would ask him if he were prepared to advise me as to my constitutional authority and power to make a decision of dismissal and force a dissolution, if I were minded to do so. I would seek his constitutional advice, not on what I should do, but in the form of an opinion as to whether I was empowered to take a step which I felt I should probably have to take two days later and which I believed to be within my powers.

My solitude was tempered by conversation with one person only other than the Chief Justice. The conversation did not include advice as to what I should do but sustained me in my own thinking as to the imperatives within which I had to act, and in my conclusions, already reached, as to what I could and should do.

The person with whom I spoke was not and has never been engaged in politics. His name has never been mentioned in any of the speculations about persons I might have consulted. The substance of our conversation is recorded and will some day, when for history's sake the archives are opened, be revealed. I will not disclose it further.

Towards the evening on Sunday I spoke to Sir Garfield Barwick on the telephone and said that I had come to certain conclusions, not at that time stating what they were, about the constitutional crisis, and would like an opportunity of ascertaining from him whether he was prepared to advise me constitutionally as to my powers to do what I had in mind. He said he would call at Admiralty House—I was in Sydney at the time—the following morning before court and we could discuss the matter.

Sir Garfield called early on 10 November. We talked about the supply crisis from the constitutional point of view. I asked him if he would be willing to express an opinion as to whether in any circumstances I had the authority and power to terminate the Government's commission, appoint a caretaker Government under the leader of the Opposition if the latter would accept the commission, and dissolve one or both Houses on the advice of the caretaker Prime Minister. I asked him if he would be prepared to indicate in what circumstances, as a matter of constitutional principle, I could in his view take such a course. I did not, of course, ask the Chief Justice whether existing circumstances would warrant my doing this.

Sir Garfield thought about this. He then said he would be prepared to advise me on this constitutional question because it related to a situation which of its nature was unlikely to come before the High Court, but that he would like to do it in writing to avoid any historical misunderstanding of what had happened and what his advice was. He agreed to have lunch with me at Admiralty House that day and to tell me then what he advised. He came to lunch after his morning in court, bringing with him the text of his letter of advice. The letter was typed, and signed by the Chief Justice, during the afternoon and delivered to me before I left for Canberra. We agreed that the text of his letter would not at that stage be released, future release being left for future decision.

I had not at any time previously discussed with Sir Garfield this question of my authority and power to terminate the Government's commission.

Sir Garfield's letter to me was later published, by mutual agreement, and is well known to all interested.

Dear Sir John,

In response to Your Excellency's invitation I attended this day at Admiralty House. In our conversations I indicated that I considered myself, as Chief Justice of Australia, free, on Your Excellency's request, to offer you legal advice as to Your Excellency's constitutional rights and duties in relation to an existing situation which, of its nature, was unlikely to come before the Court. We both clearly understood that I was not in any way concerned with matters of a purely political kind, or with any political consequences of the advice I might give.

In response to Your Excellency's request for my legal advice as to whether a course on which you had determined was consistent with your constitutional authority and duty, I respectfully offer the following.

The Constitution of Australia is a federal Constitution which embodies the principle of Ministerial responsibility. The Parliament consists of two houses, the House of Representatives and the Senate, each popularly elected, and each with the same legislative power, with the one exception that the Senate may not originate nor amend a money bill.

Two relevant constitutional consequences flow from this structure of the Parliament. First, the Senate has constitutional power to refuse to pass a money bill; it has power to refuse supply to the Government of the day. Secondly, a Prime Minister who cannot ensure supply to the Crown, including funds for carrying on the ordinary services of Government, must either advise a general election (of a kind which the constitutional situation may then allow) or resign. If, being unable to secure supply, he refuses to take either course, Your Excellency has constitutional authority to withdraw his Commission as Prime Minister.

There is no analogy in respect of a Prime Minister's duty between the situation of the Parliament under the federal Constitution of Australia and the relationship between the House of Commons, a popularly elected body, and the House of Lords, a non-elected body, in the unitary form of Government functioning in the United Kingdom. Under that system, a Government having the confidence of the House of Commons can secure supply, despite a recalcitrant House of Lords. But it is otherwise under our federal Constitution. A Government having the confidence of the House of Representatives but not that of the Senate, both elected Houses, cannot secure supply to the Crown.

But there is an analogy between the situation of a Prime Minister who has lost the confidence of the House of Commons and a Prime Minister who does not have the confidence of the Parliament, i.e. of the House of Representatives and of the Senate. The duty and responsibility of the Prime Minister to the Crown in each case is the

343

same: if unable to secure supply to the Crown, to resign or to advise an election.

In the event that, conformably to this advice, the Prime Minister ceases to retain his Commission, Your Excellency's constitutional authority and duty would be to invite the Leader of the Opposition, if he can undertake to secure supply, to form a caretaker government (i.e. one which makes no appointments or initiates any policies) pending a general election, whether of the House of Representatives, or of both Houses of the Parliament, as that Government may advise.

Accordingly, my opinion is that, if Your Excellency is satisfied in the current situation that the present Government is unable to secure supply, the course upon which Your Excellency has determined is consistent with your constitutional authority and duty.

Yours respectfully,
(sgnd Garfield Barwick)

His Excellency the Honourable Sir John Kerr, K.C.M.G.
Governor-General of Australia,
Admiralty House,
SYDNEY
10 November 1975.

On Monday at the usual time in the late afternoon my Official Secretary, on my instructions, distributed in the normal manner to the Press Gallery in Canberra copies of the Vice-Regal News. It stated:

> His Excellency the Governor-General received the Rt Hon. Sir Garfield Barwick, Chief Justice of Australia, at Admiralty House, Sydney, yesterday.
>
> Later, the Governor-General entertained the Chief Justice at luncheon at Admiralty House.

These words were published in the Vice-Regal column of the usual newspapers on the morning of Tuesday 11 November 1975.

Having returned to Government House on Monday I began to draft a statement of my reasons for withdrawing Mr Whitlam's commission, for use if it were to become necessary the following morning, and a letter withdrawing the commission. These were typed early on Tuesday morning.

I must record my state of mind on Monday evening. I believed it was virtually certain that at their meeting the following morning the leaders would make no progress towards a solution. I would be told by Mr Whitlam that his position remained unchanged: that he would continue to govern without parliamentary supply and would not advise a dissolution of the House. I would be told by Mr Fraser that his position was unchanged and that the Senate would continue to deny supply. Moreover I expected Mr Whitlam to ask for a half-Senate election and to seek to have it on 13 December, without supply if supply were still blocked.

I believed on Monday evening that events would take this course but I did not know it for certain. My line of action had to be prepared in case events did develop as I apprehended they would. The most difficult question in my mind was exactly how to handle my conversation with Mr Whitlam if he came to see me next day to seek a half-Senate election. This was a very delicate judgment to make. I believed that as soon as I gave Mr Whitlam any indication at all that his commission might be withdrawn he would instantly, whilst still Prime Minister, seek my recall.

Professor O'Connell showed a very clear insight into my situation when shortly after 11 November he wrote:

> Finally, it has been said that the Prime Minister is entitled to an ultimatum, and that the Governor-General's letter to him of 11 November fell short of that, whatever it reveals of what had gone on beforehand. A Prime Minister is entitled to bluff and to have his bluff called, but the only proper way of calling it is by way of ultimatum. To the contrary case it has been suggested that had the Governor-General on 11 November given Mr Whitlam 24 hours in which to advise a dissolution or to tender his resignation (which it seems clear he had committed himself not to do), Mr Whitlam would immediately have asked the Queen for Sir John Kerr's recall, so dragging the Monarchy into the controversy. This is speculation, but it points to the delicacy of the situation in which the Governor-General found himself. And it overlooks the question of what the Governor-General was to do about the advice that was to be tendered to him on that day concerning a half-Senate election.[12]

I decided upon the following way of handling the situation. I would sign a letter of dismissal and a statement of my reasons. I would have them available for immediate use if required. They would be placed face downwards on my desk. I thought it likely that Mr Whitlam would come to see me on Tuesday to report the result of the morning's meeting and to advise a half-Senate election. If he were not to come of his own accord I should, on the worst view of it, have to send for him. Immediately Mr Whitlam arrived, before he put his proposal to me about a half-Senate election if that were his intention, I would ask him whether any change had occurred as regards the deadlock on supply. If the answer were 'no' I would tell him that I had decided to withdraw his commission. This in itself would not amount to a legally effective withdrawal. That would not occur until I told him I had terminated his commission. Whether I would do this or not was to depend on his reaction. If his reaction, as I expected, were to indicate that he would have me recalled, I would decide to act upon the documents on my desk and tell him he was no longer Prime Minister, handing him the documents.

If, contrary to my expectation, he did not do this but changed his mind, offering to recommend a dissolution so that he could go to the people as Prime Minister, I would get that advice formally from him there and then, ensure that it was made public, and act upon it immediately I had secured supply. Supply would certainly be granted if he were willing to advise dissolution. The people would still be called upon to decide the issue that the two leaders had failed to settle; but the Labor Party would remain in office, with Mr Whitlam as Prime Minister, until elections were held. If Mr Whitlam wanted to he could walk out of my study as Prime Minister to conduct the coming election campaign.

Alan Reid has said in his book *The Whitlam Venture*, on the subject of what Mr Whitlam might have done in my study on 11 November:

> The natural thing, to my mind, would have been to say that he had not realised that Kerr took such a serious view of the Supply question, point out that Fraser had agreed to pass Supply if Whitlam in turn would agree to hold general elections simultaneously with the next half-senate election which need not be held until June, and ask Kerr to hold or withdraw the verbal dismissal and hold back the letter until he had consulted with his Cabinet as to whether they

should in view of the serious view the Governor-General took of the Supply position accept the Fraser compromise offer.[13]

Although I was contemplating, over the weekend, the possibility of changed advice from Mr Whitlam which, if it were offered, could be for an immediate election or an election in terms of the Fraser compromise, I did not think it a likely development. After all my talks with the Prime Minister I believed it to be impossible psychologically for him to climb down from the position he had adopted. I felt it would be totally inappropriate, indeed worthless, after his many public statements for me to volunteer once again the suggestion that he should stay in power and go to the people. It was for him to decide what his final advice was to be; and both publicly and privately he had made sufficiently clear what he was determined to do. He could still change his advice if it were in him to do so. But my belief was that he would try instead to make speed to the Palace and recommend my dismissal. If this were his reaction I must cope with it.

Professor West has commented:

The Governor-General might have presented Mr Whitlam with a choice: advise a double dissolution or be dismissed. The Governor-General must have made an informed judgment upon Mr Whitlam's character to know how likely he was to accept such an ultimatum; he may very well have assumed that Mr Whitlam stood firmly by what he had been saying since the Senate failed to pass Supply. And concluded that on form, so to speak, the choice was a foregone conclusion. If he had offered the Prime Minister such a choice and Mr Whitlam had asked for time to think it over and had then gone to the Queen to remove the Governor-General — which again on form, he might very well have concluded would happen — two things would have followed. Supply would still have been denied to the Government and the constitutional crisis would have deepened. Future Governors-General would have become ciphers of the Prime Minister for the effect would have been to deny the existence, certainly to prohibit the use, of any discretionary or reserve powers in the office of head of state.[14]

The loneliness of the decision I was engaged in making in these final days was one of the most burdensome experiences I have known. Most policy or executive decisions are made with the aid of advisers or colleagues, both as to what can and what should be done. There are others to consult and to offer counsel. But the decision to dismiss the Prime Minister could be made only by me. It was a time of intense mental solitude.

Nothing could have been farther removed from the truth than a story spread abroad after the dismissal that I had engaged in a conspiracy, with fellow-plotters alleged to include the Chief Justice of Australia Sir Garfield Barwick, the present Prime Minister Mr Fraser and the former Solicitor-General, later Attorney-General and Minister, Mr Ellicott. The story was false and ridiculous. Nothing whatever passed between Mr Fraser and myself, directly or indirectly, except what is recorded in this book; nothing whatever passed between myself and Mr Ellicott except that I read his press statement giving his opinion; and my only discussion with Sir Garfield Barwick, on the subject of the exercise of the reserve powers, is fully related here. Other 'conspiracy' stories, all equally fictitious and absurd, surfaced from time to time in the press and elsewhere. Perhaps the most extravagant was the tale that I was conniving to 'call out the Armed Forces' — how, where, and to do what, not being made plain. This was connected in some way with a dinner party we gave at Government House a few days after the dismissal (it had been arranged of course some time beforehand) to farewell on his retirement Admiral Sir Victor Smith, Commander of the Defence Force Staff. To the dinner, as a matter of course, the other service chiefs were invited; and in the reshuffle of posts consequent upon Sir Victor's retirement a number of high-ranking officers had made the customary courtesy calls at Government House at about that time. So much for conspiracy. There was no conspiracy — military, political or other.

My loneliness included isolation from my wife Anne on the question of what I should do. She, of course, knew what was public knowledge as the crisis developed. She knew that I was deeply worried about the seriousness of the evolving situation. She knew something, as a non-lawyer, about the constitutional situation and she knew, as the whole community knew, that events were rapidly moving towards a climax.

On Sunday 9 November I decided to tell my wife what I had made up my mind to do if things remained unchanged on the Tuesday morning. She had to be prepared for the course events would take. She had come to Government House after our marriage the previous April and, as I saw it, there was a real risk of a dramatic change in our lives. In the short six months since our marriage, warmth in our reception by the public had been one element in what had been in personal terms a happy time. My wife was entitled to know what could now happen and why.

I told her that I was convinced the course of action on which I had decided was the only course to take, and that she should be prepared for a very difficult series of reactions beginning immediately after publication of my decision. I knew the decision, though constitutionally unavoidable, would be con-troversial and have some bitter consequences for which I had to prepare her. She had been a source of love and support in the weeks leading up to 11 November and has been at all times since. She did not, as someone has said, advise me not to tell Mr Whitlam of my decision in advance; she did not advise me to resign or not to resign; she did not interfere in any way. A story, told later, that she was exerting some behind-the-scenes influence is an invention. The period leading up to the decision was for me, so far as decision making was concerned, a period of profound intellectual isolation.

It was obvious, of course, that what I was considering doing was something which had never been done in Australia before, just as no Senate had actually denied supply before and no Prime Minister had tried to govern without it. My action would be bitterly resented and profoundly misunderstood in some quar-ters. Among the range of matters to be pondered, one was the question: what would in the future the effect of such action be on the Senate, and on the Governor-Generalship itself as an institution?

Considering first the Senate: there would doubtless be a campaign to condemn the Senate for refusing supply, and argument that the Constitution should be amended to strip the Senate of this power. As to whether the Senate should have failed to grant supply, that was a political question. It had the power to

349

do so. What its decision should have been was not among the matters that called for my judgment. In my opinion no campaign to take from the Senate its power to reject supply was likely in the foreseeable future to succeed, and no constitutional amendment to that effect was likely to be passed. I knew some people believed the Senate should be only a House of review, with no more power over money Bills than the House of Lords; but I also knew others disagreed and I believed the smaller States, or strong sections within them, and many other Australians, saw the provision concerning money Bills as having been put into the Constitution *inter alia* for the protection of the smaller States, and as one which should remain.

If the exercise of that power, followed by the dismissal I was contemplating, were to precipitate a national constitutional debate and a referendum on the Senate's power this, in my mind, would not be an unhealthy development. If it were to happen as a consequence of my decision, or partly so, it would be an orthodox exercise in democracy. I therefore rejected as immaterial the fact that a dismissal might precipitate vigorous constitutional discussion as to the Senate's powers and a possible referendum for amendment of section 53 of the Constitution. My obligation was to apply the Constitution as it stood, accepting it and acting within it.

I also considered the likelihood of constitutional controversy and discussion about the Governor-General's powers, especially the reserve powers of dismissal and forced dissolution. It seemed most likely that there would be a school of thought, especially among those who on this occasion felt themselves to be the losers, that such powers should not exist or if they existed should be exercised by an elected, and not by an appointed, Governor-General or by a republican President.

In order to abolish the reserve powers, or to make the office of the Governor-General an elective one, or to establish a republic, a constitutional amendment would be necessary. If the people of Australia wish to do any of these things they can do them. To denude the Governor-Generalship of the reserve powers would be to change it very significantly but it can be done con-stitutionally by a referendum. I should myself be sorry to see this happen. But the mere fact that the people might later decide to change the Constitution in this way could not as I saw it deter me from doing my duty under the Constitution as it stood. I could not be deterred by the fact that the very act of doing what I judged to be necessary might itself precipitate a constitutional discussion, leading to a referendum on the abolition of the power that I was exercising. It is not a bad thing in a democracy to debate whether a Head of State should have a reserve power to dismiss a Prime Minister in circumstances such as existed in November 1975.

Professor West writes:

> It is hard to see how vice-regal intervention is undemocratic if the result is an election . . . I find the alternative proposition — that the Senate cannot refuse Supply, cannot therefore compel an election, and that the Governor-General has no discretionary power to resolve a deadlock — rather more disturbing. For, without a Senate with that power, a federal constitution might indeed prove unworkable. The dominance of the House of Representatives would in effect create a uni-cameral parliament under the control of one party without the checks and balances necessary to federations. One such party at the centre, with a Prime Minister whose creature the Governor-General was, seems to me to open up the possibility of a Prime Ministerial dominance holding more dangers for democratic government than a Governor-General with limited reserve powers to meet an exceptional situation created not by him but by the political misjudgments of a Prime Minister.[15]

Similar points have been debated in many newly independent countries whose constitutions have been written since 1947. Whether such a referendum should be held or if held would be passed, in Australia, is a political question. Had I been held back by such considerations the vice-regal power would have been destroyed by non-use — that is, by the failure to use it when its use was called for — instead of by the legal process of constitutional amendment. I believed that Mr Fraser feared this and that Mr Whitlam in truth was counting upon it.

Similarly the power of the Senate over supply might be destroyed by failure of the Governor-General to recognise that power and its valid exercise.

351

One possible argument I took into account was that a result of the dismissal might be that some future Prime Minister, in order to get his own way and subvert the Constitution without amending it, would appoint a Governor-General who, in advance, bound himself to act upon the rubber stamp theory. Here again one must assume that normally Prime Ministers would act responsibly within the limits of proper constitutional principle. But even if any risk that they would not were increased by a decision I might make, such a risk must be accepted. I doubt in any case that Australians would tolerate a 'Caligula's horse' Governor-Generalship.

If, as a result of my action, support developed for a change to an elective Governor-Generalship or a presidential system of some kind, I could not be discouraged by this from carrying out my duty under the Constitution. I thought long and seriously about all of these matters. I did not believe any elected Prime Minister of any political party would want an elected President or Governor-General with stated constitutional powers; and I did not think it likely my action would precipitate fundamental changes such as might alter the constitutional basis of the Monarchy, the Governor-Generalship or the Senate in Australia. What mattered was that people should examine and fully understand their institutions, including those ultimate safeguards little remembered because they are rarely needed. Changes if made should be made by the Australian people, in full understanding of what they were changing, and what they were getting in its place. I have great faith in Australian common sense and stability on all questions of constitutional change.

Basic to my position was that I am a convinced constitutional monarchist, as the Monarchy exists under the Constitution in Australia, and I believed in November 1975, as I do today, that the majority of Australians think in the same way. Although I weighed the possibility, I did not believe, nor do I now, that what I had to do would adversely affect the Monarchy or the Governor-Generalship.

My final thought was of the special character of the Australian Constitution which requires, on vital issues, the consent of the governed. Sir Kenneth Wheare comments that a feature distinguishing the Australian Constitution from the British is that 'it recognizes the people (i.e. the electorate) as an essential part of the machinery of government'[16]; and mentions 'the strong . . . confidence of Australia about the part that the people should play in Government'.[17] The consent of the people is constitutionally necessary, under section 57, before any proposed law blocked by the Senate can become law. The consent of the people is similarly necessary, under section 128, for the adoption of an amendment to the Constitution. Sir Kenneth points out that 'the constitution gives the electorate the power to decide these matters, not because the electorate is certain to be right, but because it is right that it should decide'.

I believed strongly in this power of the Australian people.

November the Eleventh

We arrived back at Yarralumla from Admiralty House on Monday afternoon 10 November. That day I drafted my statement of reasons for terminating Mr Whitlam's commission so that it would be ready if the situation remained unchanged the following morning.

I realised from my reading of events, from my assessment of Mr Whitlam's character and strategy and from my study of the subject that an exercise of the reserve powers by dismissal of Mr Whitlam would cause much debate and controversy and much emotional reaction in some sections of the community. Violence or civil commotion was not to be expected, but the lives of my wife and myself would be deeply changed and from the moment of action, should it prove necessary, there would be a real possibility of demonstrations and trouble.

Early on 11 November I put in hand the typing of a number of documents some of which, according to how events fell out, I would need later in the day.

It was the usual busy morning at Government House with official staff and aides coming in and out of my study on a host of official matters. Three young Army captains were arriving that morning to stay with us so that the choice could be made of a successor to the outgoing Army aide. My wife and I were to attend the Remembrance Day ceremony at the Stone of Remembrance and were to be there at 11 a.m. We had to dress for the occasion which was one, according to practice, for full morning dress and decorations for me. Just as I was about to dress I had a telephone call from my daughter Gabrielle to tell me that one of my grandchildren had been taken to hospital with a serious illness. She said she would ring me again presently with more information. Almost at once the Prime Minister rang to say that nothing had changed as a result of the meeting with the Opposition leaders and he would like to see me immediately with a view to advising a half-Senate election on 13 December.

I told the Prime Minister I had to go to the ceremony and would see him after I arrived back. He replied that he would be in the House facing a censure motion and would come out to Yarralumla as soon as he could before lunch. He said supply was still not available and he intended to proceed with his plan to govern without it. This was in response to a question from me. He did not say he could get temporary supply for the half-Senate election.

I next spoke to Mr Fraser who confirmed that the position and the Opposition policy remained the same. I said nothing else to him about the situation. Mr Fraser's statement that things remained the same confirmed that temporary supply would not be available for a half-Senate election, his position being that such an election must be accompanied, when it took place, by a House election, in which event only, supply would be granted.

As a result of these two conversations I knew that when Mr Whitlam came out later in the day for a half-Senate election he would not be able to tell me that he could get even temporary supply to cover the election period. I had either to let him have that election without supply, with consequent financial chaos, or to act, so as to ensure full elections for both Houses with full supply produced at the last realistic moment before supply ran out. Mr Whitlam had left his half-Senate election too late.

During the morning although I did not know it, being probably then at the War Memorial, Mr Whitlam was describing in the House, while replying to Mr Fraser's censure motion, the situation as it existed in Australia on 11 November.

In his speech Mr Whitlam recognised that there was an unprecedented constitutional crisis. He conceded that his banking scheme, even with the best arrangements his Government could make with the banks, would still leave thousands of persons and businesses damaged. He referred to the damage 'done by the action of the Senate — not just the potential damage but the damage already set in train to thousands of our fellow Australians'. He said that the truth was that long-standing government contracts were likely to dry up; that investment decisions were already being postponed; the purchase of major consumer items such as refrigerators, cars and television sets was already being delayed; retail sales were already being affected and purses were being tightened at the crucial Christmas period. By mid-November, he said, the Government would not be able to meet its commitments in respect of certain works and construction. The Darwin Reconstruction Authority would run out of funds before the end of November with dire consequences in Darwin. It might be impossible to relieve the Antarctic expedition due for relief in mid-November. Morale and efficiency of the defence forces could be seriously and adversely affected. Funds would not be available to pay locally recruited staff overseas or payments owed to international organisations.[1]

The two leaders having put their positions in the censure debate were about to come to see me at Government House.

On my return to Yarralumla after the ceremony at the Stone of Remembrance I made an arrangement for the Prime Minister to come at 12.45 p.m. when he expected to be finished in the House, and for Mr Fraser to come a quarter of an hour later. Mr Fraser was not told why I wanted him to come.

The three Army captains from whom we were to choose a new aide-de-camp were, in accordance with practice, to lunch with my household and with my wife and myself. They were all gathered in the private drawing-room. I greeted them but did not join in the pre-lunch drink they were having.

Mr Whitlam was late in arriving and Mr Fraser was early and arrived first. When notified of this I told my Official Secretary to look after Mr Fraser until I had finished my interview with Mr Whitlam, and he stayed with him in an ante-room near the State entrance. I did not see or talk to Mr Fraser until after Mr Whitlam had left.

When Mr Whitlam arrived he entered, as is the practice for the Prime Minister (and no one else except the Governor-General's family) by the private entrance and was ushered in to my study. I had meantime gone to the study and had asked for the doors of the private drawing-room to be shut; they are opposite the study door and I wanted Mr Whitlam and later Mr Fraser to arrive in privacy.

My senior aide of that time, Captain Stephens, told me that he said to Mr Whitlam as he brought him to my study, indicating the private drawing-room, 'My successor is being selected in there.' It was later put about that my aide had said 'Your successor is in there' or words to that effect. This was of course false and indeed nonsensical. There were seven or eight people in the private drawing-room including my wife. They were engaged in filling time sociably until lunch, already delayed. My aide-de-camp, conducting the Prime Minister to the Governor-General, was making a gesture at polite conversation. The notion that one of my young aides could have been privy to my thinking or have any knowledge of the great events of State that were in course is a flight into fantasy land.

It was a morning of various themes — preparation of final policy documents of great national significance, ceremonial at the Stone of Remembrance, illness of my grandson, routine selection of an aide, careful thought about what must actually be said to Mr Whitlam and if necessary to Mr Fraser. A great historic moment was gradually getting closer but meanwhile life went on, as it always does.

During that morning, once I knew that a half-Senate election would positively be asked for by a Prime Minister determined to conduct that election without supply, whereas the Senate had refused supply and was equally determined to adhere to that course, the issue crystallised finally. I had no clairvoyant's glass to enable me to see the future. I had a set of existing facts which were known to me and which were critical for the country.

The time had come when I had to act and act decisively. In matters of ultimate discretion, such as that unfolding, in practical human affairs as opposed to coffee-table or common-room theorising, in real life in short, there comes a time for decision, for action — or for letting the moment pass and accepting forever the consequences of passivity. Such a moment had arrived. I had not wished to be caught in the vice of history; but I was. I acted in the

357

only way open to me. I have no regrets and I have had, despite all the ferment of debate and argument, no second thoughts.

The Senate had denied supply, the Government had sought to govern without it: the people must resolve this great issue, and if Mr Whitlam would not go to the people I should have to send him.

The stage was now set for our vital conversation.

When Mr Whitlam entered my study he put his hand into his inside coat pocket and I said to him, 'Before you say anything, Prime Minister, I want to say something to you. You have told me this morning on the phone that your talks with the leaders on the other side have failed to produce any change and that things therefore remain the same. You intend to govern without parliamentary supply'. He said, 'Yes'. I replied that in my view he had to have parliamentary supply to govern and as he had failed to obtain it and was not prepared to go to the people, I had decided to withdraw his commission.

Things then happened as I had foreseen. Mr Whitlam jumped up, looked urgently around the room, looked at the telephones and said sharply, 'I must get in touch with the Palace at once'. He did not interpret what I had so far said as an actual withdrawal of his commission and indeed it was not. He still had time in which to act; and he made it obvious what his action would be: not to seek to discuss with me any change of attitude, not to seek to go to the people in an election as Prime Minister, but to move at once for my dismissal by so advising the Queen.

The documents, duly signed, were face downwards on my desk. I now knew there would be no changed advice, only the certainty of constitutional disruption if any time were allowed to elapse. I therefore made my final decision to withdraw his commission and hand him the signed documents. He could still say, 'Let us talk about this. If you are determined to have an election, I would rather go to the people myself as Prime Minister'. Had he done so I would have agreed, provided he committed himself by action there and then. I was not prepared to run any further risks.

When he said, 'I must get in touch with the Palace at once', I replied, 'It is too late'. He said, 'Why?' and I told him, 'Because you are no longer Prime Minister. These documents tell you so, and why'. I handed them to him and he took them. He did not read them. There was a short silence after which he said, 'I see', and stood up. He made no gesture towards discussion. He turned to the door and I came around my desk towards him. I said, 'I tried to get a compromise and failed'. I waited but he still said nothing. I said, 'We shall all have to live with this'. Mr Whitlam said, 'You certainly will'.

My parting words were, 'You could win the election. You are doing well in the polls. You have the supply issue and now the dismissal issue. Anyhow, good luck'. I held out my hand to shake his. We shook hands and he left. I understand that soon after leaving he did ring the Palace and spoke to the Queen's Private Secretary, doing so as a private member. At a press conference that afternoon he said: 'The Governor-General prevented me getting in touch with the Queen by just withdrawing the commission immediately.'[2]

There has been a suggestion that Mr Whitlam could have refused to take the documents or could have torn them up and thus in some way avoided the legal consequences of a completed legal termination of his commission. The lawyer in Mr Whitlam would have told him this was impossible. His only option was to seek to negotiate to go to the people as Prime Minister by agreeing to an election. This he could not bring himself to do and he did not do it.

The text of my letter of 11 November to Mr Whitlam and of my attached statement was as follows:

Dear Mr Whitlam,

In accordance with section 64 of the Constitution I hereby determine your appointment as my Chief Adviser and Head of the Government. It follows that I also hereby determine the appointments of all the Ministers in your Government.

You have previously told me that you would never resign or advise an election of the House of Representatives or a double dissolution and that the only way in which such an election could be obtained would be by my dismissal of you and your ministerial colleagues. As it appeared likely that you would today persist in this attitude I decided that, if you did, I would determine your commission and state my reasons for doing so. You have persisted in your attitude and I have accordingly acted as indicated. I attach a statement of my reasons which I intend to publish immediately.

It is with a great deal of regret that I have taken this step both in respect of yourself and your colleagues.

I propose to send for the Leader of the Opposition and to commission him to form a new caretaker government until an election can be held.

Yours sincerely,

(sgnd John R. Kerr)

The Honourable E. G. Whitlam, Q.C., M.P.

11 November 1975

Statement by the Governor-General

I have given careful consideration to the constitutional crisis and have made some decisions which I wish to explain.

Summary

It has been necessary for me to find a democratic and constitutional solution to the current crisis which will permit the people of Australia to decide as soon as possible what should be the outcome of the deadlock which developed over supply between the two Houses of Parliament and between the Government and Opposition parties. The only solution consistent with the Constitution and with my oath of office and my responsibilities, authority and duty as Governor-General is to terminate the commission as Prime Minister of Mr Whitlam and to arrange for a caretaker government able to secure supply and willing to let the issue go to the people.

I shall summarise the elements of the problem and the reasons for my decision which places the matter before the people of Australia for prompt determination.

Because of the federal nature of our Constitution and because of its provisions the Senate undoubtedly has constitutional power to refuse or defer supply to the Government. Because of the principles of responsible government a Prime Minister who cannot obtain supply, including money for carrying on the ordinary services of government, must either advise a general election or resign. If he refuses to do this I have the authority and indeed the duty under the Constitution to withdraw his commission as Prime Minister. The position in Australia is quite different from the position in the United Kingdom. Here the confidence of both Houses on supply is necessary to ensure its provision. In the United Kingdom the confidence of the House of Commons alone is necessary. But both here and in the United Kingdom the duty of the Prime Minister is the same in a most important respect — if he cannot get supply he must resign or advise an election.

If a Prime Minister refuses to resign or to advise an election, and this is the case with Mr Whitlam, my constitutional authority and duty require me to do what I have now done — to withdraw his commission — and to invite the Leader of the Opposition to form a caretaker government — that is one that makes no appointments or dismissals and initiates no policies until a general election is held. It is most desirable that he should guarantee supply. Mr Fraser will be asked to give the necessary undertakings and advise whether he is prepared to recommend a double dissolution. He will also be asked to guarantee supply.

The decisions I have made were made after I was satisfied that Mr Whitlam could not obtain supply. No other decision open to me would enable the Australian people to decide for themselves what should be done.

Once I had made up my mind, for my own part, what I must do if Mr Whitlam persisted in his stated intentions I consulted the Chief Justice of Australia, Sir Garfield Barwick. I have his permission to say that I consulted him in this way.

The result is that there will be an early general election for both Houses and the people can do what, in a democracy such as ours, is their responsibility and duty and theirs alone. It is for the people now to decide the issue which the two leaders have failed to settle.

Detailed Statement of Decisions

On 16 October the Senate deferred consideration of Appropriation Bills (Nos. 1 & 2) 1975–1976. In the time which elapsed since then events made it clear that the Senate was determined to refuse to grant supply to the Government. In that time the Senate on no less than two occasions resolved to proceed no further with fresh Appropriation Bills, in identical terms, which had been passed by the House of Representatives. The determination of the Senate to maintain its refusal to grant supply was confirmed by the public statements made by the Leader of the Opposition, the Opposition having control of the Senate.

By virtue of what has in fact happened there therefore came into existence a deadlock between the House of Representatives and the Senate on the central issue of supply without which all the ordinary services of the government cannot be maintained. I had the benefit of discussions with the Prime Minister and, with his approval, with the Leader of the Opposition and with the Treasurer and the Attorney-General. As a result of those discussions and having regard to the public statements of the Prime Minister and the Leader of the Opposition I have come regretfully to the conclusion that there is no likelihood of a compromise between the House of Representatives and the Senate nor for that matter between the Government and the Opposition.

The deadlock which arose was one which, in the interests of the nation, had to be resolved as promptly as possible and by means which are appropriate in our democratic system. In all the circumstances which have occurred the appropriate means is a dissolution of the Parliament and an election for both Houses. No other course offers a sufficient assurance of resolving the deadlock and resolving it promptly.

Parliamentary control of appropriation and accordingly of expenditure is a fundamental feature of our system of responsible government. In consequence it has been generally accepted that a government which has been denied supply by the Parliament cannot govern. So much at least is clear in cases where a ministry is refused supply by a popularly elected Lower House. In other systems where an Upper House is denied the right to reject a money bill denial of supply can occur only at the instance of the Lower House. When, however, an Upper House possesses the power to reject a money bill including an appropriation bill, and exercises the power by denying supply, the principle that a government which has been denied supply by the Parliament should resign or go to an election must still apply — it is a necessary consequence of Parliamentary control of appropriation and expenditure and of the expectation that the ordinary and necessary services of government will continue to be provided.

The Constitution combines the two elements of responsible

362

government and federalism. The Senate is, like the House, a popularly elected chamber. It was designed to provide representation by States, not by electorates, and was given by Sec. 53, equal powers with the House with respect to proposed laws, except in the respects mentioned in the section. It was denied power to originate or amend appropriation bills but was left with power to reject them or defer consideration of them. The Senate accordingly has the power and has exercised the power to refuse to grant supply to the Government. The Government stands in the position that it has been denied supply by the Parliament with all the consequences which flow from that fact.

There have been public discussions about whether there is a convention deriving from the principles of responsible government that the Senate must never under any circumstances exercise the power to reject an appropriation bill. The Constitution must prevail over any convention because, in determining the question how far the conventions of responsible government have been grafted on to the federal compact, the Constitution itself must in the end control the situation.

Sec. 57 of the Constitution provides a means, perhaps the usual means, of resolving a disagreement between the Houses with respect to a proposed law. But the machinery which it provides necessarily entails a considerable time lag which is quite inappropriate to a speedy resolution of the fundamental problems posed by the refusal of supply. Its presence in the Constitution does not cut down the reserve powers of the Governor-General.

I should be surprised if the Law Officers expressed the view that there is no reserve power in the Governor-General to dismiss a Ministry which has been refused supply by the Parliament and to commission a Ministry, as a caretaker ministry which will secure supply and recommend a dissolution, including where appropriate a double dissolution. This is a matter on which my own mind is quite clear and I am acting in accordance with my own clear view of the principles laid down by the Constitution and of the nature, powers and responsibility of my office.

There is one other point. There has been discussion of the possibility that a half-Senate election might be held under circumstances in which the Government has not obtained supply. If such advice were given to me I should feel constrained to reject it because a half-Senate election held whilst supply continues to be denied does not guarantee a prompt or sufficiently clear prospect of the deadlock being resolved in accordance with proper principles. When I refer to rejection of such advice I mean that, as I would find it necessary in the circumstances I have envisaged to determine Mr Whitlam's commission and, as things have turned out have done so, he would not be Prime Minister and not able to give or persist with such advice.

The announced proposals about financing public servants, suppliers, contractors and others do not amount to a satisfactory alternative to supply.

Government House,
Canberra. 2600

11 November 1975.

I now sent Captain Stephens to bring Mr Fraser to my study. When he came in I told him of the action I had just taken. Mr Fraser's face revealed nothing of the impact this news must surely have had upon him.

I offered to commission him as caretaker Prime Minister upon certain conditions. I said, 'In accordance with constitutional principle you will, if you accept the commission, have also to accept the political responsibility for my decision to dismiss and later to dissolve'. This had to be done without consulting Mr Fraser in advance. There was no doubt he would accept: his whole tactic had been designed to arrive at this result if Mr Whitlam would not go to the people himself.

Mr Fraser replied, 'Your Excellency, I will accept that responsibility'. I asked him whether, if I commissioned him, he could guarantee supply. He said he could. I explained to him that any Government he formed would have to be a caretaker Government and he would have to undertake to initiate no new policies and make no new appointments of importance before an election took place. I added that I would like an undertaking to that effect and also that he would initiate during the caretaker period no enquiries into the policies and activities of the previous Government. Such investigations would be inconsistent with the nature of a caretaker Government. Mr Fraser said he would give these undertakings and through him any caretaker Ministers sworn in would do likewise.

Professor Sawer remarks that one of the minor curiosities of the dismissal of Mr Whitlam and the commissioning of Mr Fraser is that, although in a general sense Mr Fraser 'supported and had indeed advocated in parliament and elsewhere the course which Sir John took in all its parts, nevertheless nothing he wrote officially or said in parliament on or after 11 November 1975 in terms accepted responsibility for the dismissal of Mr Whitlam'.[3] I do not know whether Mr Fraser in any public statement accepted the responsibility for Mr Whitlam's dismissal. He would no doubt think it was understood by the public that he could not in the circumstances become the Prime Minister in a caretaker Government unless he took that responsibility. From what I have narrated of events it will be clear that Mr Fraser accepted full responsibility. Furthermore next day, before I swore in the caretaker Government, all Ministers when they were present together accepted responsibility for the dismissal of Mr Whitlam and the dissolution of the Houses in the same way as Mr Fraser did.

Having dealt with the matter of responsibility I told Mr Fraser that I assumed he would not get the confidence of the House and that he would advise an election. I pointed out that this would involve a dissolution and the question was whether it would be a dissolution of the House only, or a double dissolution. He said he was prepared to advise a double dissolution.

I next made the point that in my understanding the Parliament was deadlocked not only on supply but on twenty-one Bills which the previous Government had passed and his parties had rejected in the Senate. It seemed to me that all deadlocks should be dealt with and should go to the people. The coalition parties had of course opposed all of the twenty-one Bills; however, Mr Fraser agreed that what I proposed was fair. He said he would immediately get legal advice and would, he felt sure, have the proper legal basis for advising a double dissolution both to resolve the twenty-one deadlocks and also to put to the people the issue involved in the dismissal and dissolution, as well as all the other general issues on which in his opinion the people should make their judgment. I asked him to give a formal undertaking to advise a double dissolution.

My fundamental reason for making this a condition was that I believed all outstanding deadlocks should go to the people, and that if Mr Whitlam won the election for the House and had the appropriate majority in both Houses or for a joint sitting thereafter, he should be immediately entitled, after the forced dissolution, to put his Bills through if he wanted to. I could not achieve this without the proper advice from the new caretaker Government, but in the light of Mr Fraser's previous public statements felt confident this would be given. Had he refused, saying he could advise no more than a dissolution of the House, I would have accepted that advice and let him take the political consequences, which as I saw it would be adverse.

A double dissolution, in addition to setting in motion the machinery for resolving the twenty-one deadlocks, would have the effect at which I was aiming, namely sending to the people at the same time as the House the Senate which had denied supply. This seemed to me, though fortuitously possible, eminently fair and desirable.

In different circumstances, in which a double dissolution might not be possible, the result would be that a Senate denying supply could force a House to the people. At first sight it might seem incongruous that an Opposition which had created the twenty-one deadlocks should end up in the position, having become the caretaker Government, of agreeing and advising that the people should have a chance to settle all the deadlocks it had created. In reality it had no political alternative. Mr Fraser had no problems with what I proposed and I was able to achieve all of this without obstacle.

I next said, 'I think it important to swear you in immediately and I will do that now'. I sent for Mr Smith, told him what had happened, and asked him to bring the documents prepared that morning. There was ready for Mr Fraser to sign a letter setting out the terms upon which he accepted a commission to form a caretaker Government. He signed it. Not all the undertakings I obtained from Mr Fraser are set out in this letter, but they are all stated in this chapter. His letter was as follows:

366

Your Excellency,

You have intimated to me that it is Your Excellency's pleasure that I should act as your Chief Adviser and Head of the Government.

In accepting your commission I confirm that I have given you an assurance that I shall immediately seek to secure the passage of the Appropriation Bills which are at present before the Senate, thus ensuring supply for the carrying on of the Public Service in all its branches. I further confirm that, upon the granting of supply, I shall immediately recommend to Your Excellency the dissolution of both Houses of the Parliament.

My government will act as a caretaker government and will make no appointments or dismissals or initiate new policies before a general election is held.

Yours sincerely,

(sgnd J. M. Fraser)

His Excellency the Honourable Sir John Kerr, A.C., K.C.M.G., K.St.J., Q.C.

11 November 1975.

I then proceeded to swear in Mr Fraser as caretaker Prime Minister. Having done so I shook hands with him and wished him good luck as I had done earlier with Mr Whitlam. Normally after such a ceremony there would be a congratulatory glass of champagne and photographs would be taken, but because of the stressful nature of the whole occasion and the caretaker element in the appointment I did not feel this would be appropriate. I said to Mr Fraser, 'I think we ought to dispense with the traditional glass of champagne. I feel sure you would rather get back to your desk—there's a lot to be done'. At this Mr Fraser smiled slightly, and thanked me. As we walked towards the door he told me he believed he could obtain supply during the afternoon but could not recommend that the double dissolution take effect until the Senate granted supply. He hoped to ask to see me later in the day to advise a double dissolution and in the meantime would face the House.

It was certain that there would be a vote of no confidence in him in the House. This would in itself entitle him in the

367

circumstances to ask for a dissolution to enable the whole issue to go to the people. It seemed to me unlikely he would be unable to get supply from the Senate and as it turned out, immediately after lunch, he succeeded. This put him in the position of being able to advise a double dissolution, which he did by telephone as soon as supply was passed.

There has been discussion of various tactics on the part of the Labor Party which might have resulted in the grant of supply being delayed or prevented. I thought such a development unlikely. Had there been problems they would have had to be faced, as they occurred, by the caretaker Government and perhaps by me.[4]

Mr Fraser asked for an appointment to put the formal material before me that would produce a double dissolution; he said he would bring Mr Clarence Harders, the Secretary of the Attorney-General's Department, with him. I gave him an appointment and told him that, subject to the opinion of the lawyers which I had no doubt would support a double dissolution, I would grant such a dissolution.

Later, after the vote of no confidence in the House which took place after the grant of supply by the Senate, Mr Whitlam rang and told me about the vote. He said that as supply had now been granted and the House had expressed its lack of confidence in the caretaker Prime Minister he was entitled to be recommissioned and he wished to call upon me to put his point of view. He said, 'You saw Fraser often enough. I suppose you have no objection to seeing me?' I said, 'I saw Mr Fraser only with your approval and for reasons with which you agreed'. He said he assumed I would have no difficulty in getting 'Fraser's approval'. I said I would speak to Mr Fraser, which I later did. Soon after this I heard that the Speaker wanted to see me to communicate the terms of the House resolution. It was clear the ground was being laid for a proposal that I should recommission Mr Whitlam. This being so I wanted to have the benefit of legal advice as to the effect of the grant of supply and the expression of no confidence in Mr Fraser upon my course of action. I therefore wanted to see Mr Harders before I saw Mr Scholes.

In my order of priorities I decided to get the Parliament

dissolved as soon as possible. Nothing the Speaker could say could affect that. I had dismissed the previous Government, appointed a caretaker Prime Minister and was in the process of producing a dissolution. In order to complete this act I wished to have the opinions of the lawyers on the validity of a double dissolution in these circumstances.

Assuming there was nothing to bar this action I wanted it legally completed as soon as possible. I knew what had happened that afternoon in Parliament. The consequences of my earlier decision and action could not be blocked nor could I be turned from my course by it. On the contrary, what had happened in both Houses made it inevitable that I must carry through to finality the procedure necessary to send the issues to the people. Certainly I had no desire to be discourteous to Mr Scholes. But it was not possible to give priority to receiving him and explaining matters to him when there was pressing need to complete the formalities of the changeover in Government, which had already taken place, and must be formalised without delay so that smooth functioning of government could proceed. Speedy action was advisable, indeed necessary. Furthermore I wished it to be quite clear that the dissolution flowed from the dismissal and, with it, formed a planned exercise of the reserve and other constitutional powers, which I had undertaken on my own initial responsibility but in circumstances in which the new caretaker Prime Minister had now taken over that responsibility. This course of events could not now be changed whether the House had expressed its lack of confidence in Mr Fraser, or not.

My first business was with the Prime Minister and Mr Harders, and I arranged for an appointment to be given to Mr Scholes following my appointment with them. When Mr Fraser and Mr Harders arrived my first act was to give the royal assent to the Appropriation Bills. Supply had been assured by action of the coalition parties pursuant to the undertaking given earlier in the day.

The Proclamation dissolving the two Houses was then presented to me. It listed the twenty-one Bills which I was told satisfied the conditions of section 57. Mr Fraser told me that upon legal advice these Bills did satisfy section 57. Mr Harders repeated this advice to me and also said that in law I could act under section 57 on this oral advice which I had been given by the Prime Minister and by him. I agreed with this. He said that it would be confirmed in writing as soon as possible but I need not wait for the written confirmation. It was on the next day confirmed in writing.

My Official Secretary was present during this conversation and he and I, as well as Mr Fraser, believed that Mr Harders had said that Mr Byers agreed with him not only about the validity of my continuing to carry out, under the reserve power, the 'forced dissolution' procedure, but also as to the availability of the twenty-one Bills to support a double dissolution.

However, both Mr Harders and Mr Byers have since said that it was only on the first point about the continued use of the reserve powers that Mr Harders had Mr Byers' agreement, the latter feeling the need to check the position as to the Bills. He did so and I received the confirmatory advice the next day. The facts were that Mr Harders brought out, when he came with the Prime Minister, a Proclamation for a double dissolution based on the twenty-one Bills and he as Secretary of the Department advised Mr Fraser in my presence that all satisfied the requirements of section 57 of the Constitution. We all thought that Mr Byers concurred at that time as he did the next day. In any case it was immaterial, since Mr Harders had, in his department, been keeping an accurate running check on the Bills which would satisfy section 57 and he had no doubt about the twenty-one Bills.

When, before lunch, I had asked Mr Fraser for an undertaking that he would advise a double dissolution, we had mentioned legal advice. From my own study of the situation I had no doubt that a double dissolution was warranted, but had Mr Harders advised Mr Fraser, as would have been his duty had it been true, that no Bill justified a double dissolution, Mr Fraser would doubtless have been compelled to ask me to release him from his undertaking on that point. On the contrary, Mr Harders advised that each one of the twenty-one Bills warranted a double dissolution. No question accordingly arose as to a release from the undertaking about a double dissolution.

I then referred to my conversation with Mr Whitlam after the no-confidence vote, to the resolution of the House and to Mr Scholes' desire to see me. I asked whether Mr Byers and Mr Harders saw any legal or constitutional problems, arising from the passing of supply in the Senate and the resolution of the House, standing in the way of my carrying out the decision I had made before lunch. Mr Harders said he had spoken to Mr Byers and both of them were of the view that, as I had exercised the reserve power in the morning, I could complete its exercise and could accept the advice of the Prime Minister in favour of a double dissolution. I could in the existing circumstances dissolve both Houses. I was in effect being told that I did have a reserve power to exercise which would justify a dissolution.

If I had had no power to do what I had done in dismissing the previous Government it would have been the duty of Mr Byers and Mr Harders to advise the Prime Minister and me that what I had done before lunch was invalid and in those circumstances, as supply had been granted and Mr Whitlam had the confidence of the House, my duty would have been to undo my invalid act, withdraw Mr Fraser's commission and send for Mr Whitlam. This they did not do.

It was obvious to everyone that what was involved was the exercise of the reserve power to dismiss Mr Whitlam and thus to force a dissolution, under that reserve power, of at least the Lower House. The advice given to me had to be based on the view that it was within the reserve power to carry through the plan to force a dissolution of the Lower House and within section 57 to make the dissolution a double dissolution based upon the concurrent existence of the additional deadlock, beyond supply, on the twenty-one Bills. I do not of course wish to imply that either Mr Byers or Mr Harders was or was not of the view that I should have exercised these reserve powers when I did. I was not asking for their views about what I had done in the exercise of my discretion but merely for their views as to the existence of my power to do what I had done and intended to do. I refer elsewhere to Mr Byers' opinion on the reserve powers.[5]

I then signed the Proclamation dissolving both Houses. Mr Fraser and Mr Harders left Government House.

The Proclamation read:

PROCLAMATION

Australia   By His Excellency the
JOHN R. KERR   Governor-General of
Governor-General   Australia

WHEREAS by section 57 of the Constitution it is provided that if the House of Representatives passes any proposed law, and the Senate rejects or fails to pass it, or passes it with amendments to which the House of Representatives will not agree, and if after an interval of three months the House of Representatives, in the same or the next session, again passes the proposed law with or without any amendments which have been made, suggested, or agreed to by the Senate and the Senate rejects or fails to pass it, or passes it with amendments to which the House of Representatives will not agree, the Governor-General may dissolve the Senate and the House of Representatives simultaneously:

AND WHEREAS the conditions upon which the Governor-General is empowered by that section of the Constitution to dissolve the Senate and the House of Representatives simultaneously have been fulfilled in respect of the several proposed laws intituled —

Health Insurance Levy Act 1974
Health Insurance Levy Assessment Act 1974
Income Tax (International Agreements) Act 1974
Minerals (Submerged Lands) Act 1974
Minerals (Submerged Lands) (Royalty) Act 1974
National Health Act 1974
Conciliation and Arbitration Act 1974
Conciliation and Arbitration Act (No. 2) 1974
National Investment Fund Act 1974
Electoral Laws Amendment Act 1974
Electoral Act 1975
Privy Council Appeals Abolition Act 1975
Superior Court of Australia Act 1974
Electoral Re-distribution (New South Wales) Act 1975
Electoral Re-distribution (Queensland) Act 1975
Electoral Re-distribution (South Australia) Act 1975
Electoral Re-distribution (Tasmania) Act 1975
Electoral Re-distribution (Victoria) Act 1975
Broadcasting and Television Act (No. 2) 1974
Television Stations Licence Fees Act 1974
Broadcasting Stations Licence Fees Act 1974

NOW THEREFORE, I Sir John Robert Kerr, The Governor-General of Australia, do by this my Proclamation dissolve the Senate and the House of Representatives.

(L.S.)   Given under my Hand and the Great Seal of Australia on 11 November 1975.

By His Excellency's Command,

MALCOLM FRASER
Prime Minister

God Save The Queen!

My Official Secretary then made arrangements to read the Proclamation from the steps of Parliament House. What happened there is well known.[6] I did not watch television or listen to the radio at that time although I have seen a replay since, and heard Mr Whitlam urge his listeners: 'Maintain your rage'.

I will make only one comment on the conduct of Mr Whitlam on the steps of Parliament House. Mr Whitlam is well known for his interest in words and their meanings. The Shorter Oxford Dictionary defines *rage* as follows:

RAGE 1. Madness; insanity; a fit or access of mania. Obs. exc. poet.   2. Violent anger, furious passion; a fit or access of such anger; *angry disposition ME.   3. transf. Violent operation or action, 'fury' (of wind, the sea, fire, etc.) ME. b. A flood, high tide, sudden rising of the sea. late ME.   4. A violent feeling, passion, or appetite. Also, violence (of a feeling, etc.). late ME. *b. Violent desire; sexual passion; heat-1697.   5. A vehement passion for, desire of, a thing. Also, const. infin. and absol. 1593.   6. Poetic or prophetic inspiration; musical excitement 1600.   7. Martial or high spirit, ardour, fervour, manly enthusiasm or indignation 1591.   8. Excitement or violence of an action, operation, etc.; also, the acutest point or heat of this 1593.

Denis Warner wrote next day in the London *Daily Telegraph*:

'Well may we say God Save the Queen', Mr Whitlam said on the steps of Parliament House after the proclamation dissolving Parliament had been read, 'because nothing will save the Governor-General'. No responsible political leader has ever made such a remark before. It should not be taken lightly.

373

At the appointed time Mr Scholes arrived. He handed me the following letter:

Your Excellency,
    I have the honour to transmit to you the following Resolution which was agreed to by the House of Representatives this day—

'That this House expresses its want of confidence in the Prime Minister and requests Mr Speaker forthwith to advise His Excellency the Governor-General to call the Hon. Member for Werriwa to form a government.'

Yours sincerely,

(sgnd G. G. D. Scholes, Speaker)

His Excellency the Hon. Sir John Kerr,
    K.C.M.G., K.St.J., Q.C.,
Government House,
CANBERRA.

11 November 1975.

I informed Mr Scholes that I had already dissolved both Houses of Parliament and that there would be an election for both on 13 December. There being nothing else of relevance to say the interview ended.

On 17 November the Queen's Private Secretary addressed to Mr Scholes a letter which was released by the Palace for publication a week later. The text was as follows:

    I am commanded by The Queen to acknowledge your letter of 12th November about the recent political events in Australia. You ask that The Queen should act to restore Mr Whitlam to office as Prime Minister.
    As we understand the situation here, the Australian Constitution firmly places the prerogative powers of the Crown in the hands of the Governor-General as the representative of The Queen of Australia. The only person competent to commission an Australian Prime Minister is the Governor-General, and The Queen has no part in the decisions which the Governor-General must take in accordance with the Constitution. Her Majesty, as Queen of Australia, is watching events in Canberra with close interest and attention, but it would not

374

be proper for her to intervene in person in matters which are so clearly placed within the jurisdiction of the Governor-General by the Constitution Act.

I understand that you have been good enough to send a copy of your letter to the Governor-General so I am writing to His Excellency to say that the text of your letter has been received here in London and has been laid before The Queen.

I am sending a copy of this letter to the Governor-General.

On the subject of the request from the House of Representatives that I should ask Mr Whitlam to form a new Government, Professor O'Connell writes:

The Governor-General has also been criticised for dissolving Parliament when the House of Representatives had demonstrated that only Mr Whitlam enjoyed its confidence. It has been contended that he should have called upon Mr Whitlam to form a new Government. But the Governor-General knew that the vote of no-confidence in the House was a charade. The Senate had passed the Supply Bill in the knowledge that Parliament was to be dissolved. If now Parliament was not to be dissolved and the Labor Party was to be put back in power, the Senate would have been defrauded, and the political crisis would have been exacerbated. Mr Whitlam could not have expected this result because the rules of the democratic game are not designed to promote political stunts.[7]

Such a day was November the eleventh.

23

The Aftermath

Next day Mr Fraser as Prime Minister advised me of the Ministers he recommended for appointment in the caretaker Government. Before swearing them in, in the main drawing-room of Yarralumla, I said to them: 'Gentlemen, the Prime Minister before being commissioned yesterday assumed responsibility for my dismissal of the previous Government and for the double dissolution which followed. He has told me you are all prepared, with him, to assume that responsibility. To emphasise the importance of the matter I will ask each of you to confirm it, before I administer the oath of office.' All confirmed it. I then spelled out the specific undertakings given by Mr Fraser the day before and asked if all understood they were bound by those undertakings. All answered yes and the swearing-in proceeded.

I have said that I knew my decision would be controversial. I was however convinced that the election would proceed in a reasonably normal manner. There would be emotional scenes and perhaps some forceful demonstrations during election meetings but, I hoped, no violence. I did not exclude the possibility of some election violence but trusted the Australian people to have an election no more marred by it than other earlier elections. Even if before 11 November I had feared violence at the elections it could have made no difference to my decision. Violence would be a police matter and one cannot be deterred from one's tasks by fear of lawless violence. I turned out to be not sufficiently optimistic. The election was a non-violent one — Dr David Butler called it 'the flattest of the four Australian campaigns that I had watched'.[1]

Whereas I expected, after such a serious and bitter constitutional crisis, much controversy about what had been done, I did not expect later violence against myself and my wife. Protest and verbal assault, yes; violence, no. I felt my wife had to be prepared for attacks upon me of an offensive verbal kind, sometimes in her presence. Even if I had expected violence against us personally I would still have had to do what I did. On this I was in fact not pessimistic enough as it turned out. I did not foresee the highly organised 'rage' of which I was to be made the object.

In the election, where economic issues were to the forefront, the Labor Party fought its campaign primarily on the denial of supply, the dismissal of the Labor Government and the dissolution of Parliament. There can be no doubt these were basic questions put to the people.

Mr Whitlam, on the steps of Parliament House on 11 November had said, 'It must be made plain, by the secret votes of the Australian people, that they decide who will be the Australian Government—not Governors-General, not Chief Justices, not newspaper proprietors.' In the special circumstances of that day one cannot help adding, 'Not Prime Ministers who cannot get supply, not parliamentarians in deadlock—but the Australian people!'

The very purpose of my action was to produce this result. What was needed was the consent of the people. Would they consent to the return of Mr Whitlam as Prime Minister, or to Mr Fraser's replacing him? To what solution of the nation's problem would they give their consent?

The result of the election was a landslide victory, with a record majority, for the coalition parties. I have already explained that in my understanding of constitutional theory the result of an election in these circumstances is not really relevant to the constitutionality of what was done. Nevertheless, it was heartening to me to see that, with these matters squarely before the people, their vote could not fail to be recognised as an expression of approval of my action. Given a chance to decide, the people had done so politically and in unequivocal terms.

Had the result been the other way round—had Mr Whitlam and his party won the election—I would, having regard to Labor

377

attitudes since the dismissal, most probably have resigned. Between 11 November and 13 December the possibility of this had to be faced by my wife and by me and she had to look for a place to which we could move, if necessary, after the election.

It will be obvious from what I have written that my action on 11 November 1975 was taken neither blindly nor without thought about the future. In view of the predictable controversy I gave some thought to what should be my policy about resignation whatever the outcome of the election, or indeed before the election.

Alternative views I could take were these: on the one hand, that having made a decision certain to provoke argument in the community, I should best serve the common interest by withdrawing from the scene and letting the political issues be determined in my absence, rather than have my presence remain an element in the political dispute; alternatively that I should carry on as a clear expression of confidence in the rightness of my decision, since public reaction to a resignation would almost certainly in many quarters be to attribute it to a sense of error or failure on my part, and this besides being false could only cause confusion and disarray in the public mind.

Soon after swearing-in the caretaker Government I told the Prime Minister that I was considering these alternatives and trying to make up my mind which course was in the best interests of the country. He expressed the very strong opinion that I should in effect apply to myself the *status quo* principles I had imposed on the caretaker Government and await the judgment of the people. He said that although the decision had to be mine he would offer me advice on the subject after the election if he won. I said I would raise it again at that time.

My own view crystallised in the form that resignation during the campaign would cause bewilderment and confusion in the community and widespread misunderstanding of my own view of what I had done. I decided I should not complicate the campaign, already complicated enough, by resigning while it was in progress, but should leave the matter until after the electoral judgment had been given.

My confidence in the rightness of this decision was fortified by a letter which Sir Robert Menzies wrote to me on 19 November 1975. His strongly worded, supportive letter was highly valued by me—as were others received at that time from many exceptional men. Sir Robert, although the letter is described in its terms as a private one, offered me the freedom to publish it at any time if so minded, and I publish it now. Sir Robert Menzies was an elder statesman and lawyer of great repute and his constitutional statements are resorted to frequently in constitutional arguments. The full text runs:

19th November 1975

Your Excellency,

I have refrained from writing to the press because I do not want to encourage any continuation of the 'smoke screen' that has been put up about your decision. But after much thought, I have decided that I ought to write to you personally. I write, of course, as a man with a considerable knowledge of the Constitution, both in its interpretation and in its practice, and I want to tell you, if I may do so without appearing to be impertinent, that your conduct in this matter has been, in my opinion, beyond reproach.

You were right as a matter of constitutional law. You exercised a power which you undoubtedly have and you exercised it at a time when any failure to act to resolve the political crisis would have inflicted great injury on many many thousands of people who look to the Commonwealth for their payments. It is quite clear that the last thing that Whitlam wanted was a Double Dissolution. The last thing he wanted was an election that would clear the air. You had a complete right to do what you did. No competent Constitutional lawyer has offered a view to the contrary. The future Constitutional historian will unquestionably say you did what it was your power and duty to do.

My second comment is that you displayed remarkable moral courage in doing what I believe to have been your duty. Indeed when competent people have assessed these events in a study of our constitutional history, they will say, not only that you were right, but that you did something which has established your term of office as one of the most remarkable in our constitutional history.

I fear that some people when they nominate some distinguished man to be Governor-General of Australia imagine that he is their humble, obedient servant and that he must do as they say. This is, of course, pathetic nonsense. It is not only an insult to the holder of the office, but it converts the Governor-Generalship into a merely automatic post in which the Governor-General must, under all circumstances, do what his advisers tell him to do. If this is what a Governor-General is for, we might just as well not have one; we might as well have an automatic machine — a kind of robot. And if that is what we are to have, then plainly we do not need a Governor-General at all, but merely a recording machine.

I beg of you not to be unduly worried. No man ever ought to be when he has done the right thing.

In this purely private letter, I offer you my congratulations and my profound admiration.

With my warmest personal regards,
Yours sincerely,

(sgnd Robert Menzies).

It is a remarkable circumstance that Sir Robert's career, spanning as it did the period between the great constitutional crisis in New South Wales in 1932 and the national crisis of 1975, made it possible for him to write letters about those crises both to Sir Philip Game and to me. I had a number of detailed conversations with Sir Robert after he wrote his letter to me. We talked mainly about constitutional principles and their application in practical affairs over the years. He had a real feeling for these matters, apart from wide knowledge and experience; it was, in the end, as a great constitutionalist that I came to know him and to appreciate his wisdom. He had lived a controversial life, which fell into perspective as the years passed; and he enjoyed, by the time of his recent death, wide esteem and great reputation. He was, between November 1975 and his death, of great comfort to me personally.

In the early days after the vote of 13 December 1975 I again raised the question of possible resignation with the Prime Minister, as I had said I would do. His firm advice was against resignation. The people, he said, had spoken on the issue and they should be left in no doubt about my own certainty that I had done right in remitting it to their judgment. I had myself come to the same view, believing that it would be foolish to create uncertainty in the minds of the people, since none existed in my own. We canvassed the likely consequences of my staying — the possibility of protests and demonstrations. I pointed out that once I embarked on the course of staying on it would, should there be an attempt to drive me out by breaking my spirit, be out of the question for me to resign under attack.

Shortly after the election my wife and I left for London so that I could personally report to the Queen. During the visit we had the privilege of spending a snowy January weekend as guests of Her Majesty at Sandringham.

Hostile demonstrations began soon after we returned to Australia in February 1976. Since it was now clear the predicted pressure was beginning to mount, I warned the Prime Minister that if he wanted to change his mind and advise resignation it would need to be done at once, since in a very short time resignation would become impossible. He was emphatic that provided my wife and I felt we could stand the heat we should stay on.

In early 1976 my estimate of the position was proved to be only too accurate. I was boycotted by the Labor Party and increasingly wild demonstrations were organised. A tolerably mild demonstration was mounted outside Parliament House on the day when I opened the new Parliament — 17 February 1976 — and the Labor Party boycotted the opening. From that day until the end of my Governor-Generalship the boycott persisted, as regards both my external activities and invitations to Government House, which we continued to issue politely to the leader of the Opposition in accordance with protocol until after the royal visit fifteen months later. (At that time, he having refused an invitation to a State banquet at Yarralumla held to honour the Queen and to celebrate the fact that Her Majesty was in residence with us, the practice of inviting him was allowed to lapse.) The boycott was applied by parliamentarians; occasionally however a few Labor Party members holding positions about the country did not regard themselves as bound by it, and I had congenial conversation with them. The supportive crowds in many places must have included many Labor voters.

On 25 March 1976 the press published the result of a gallup

poll on the following questions: the correctness of my November decision; whether Mr Whitlam had done himself harm or good by his criticisms; and whether the Governor-General's power to dismiss an elected Government should be eliminated. On the first question, 52 per cent said they believed my decision was right and 42 per cent that it was wrong. On the second question 76 per cent said they believed Mr Whitlam had done himself harm by his criticisms and 17 per cent that he had done himself good. On the third question 53 per cent said that the power of dismissal should not be eliminated and 42 per cent that it should.

Wherever my wife and I went throughout 1976, except for organised militant demonstrations, we were received with much enthusiasm and by ovations on all kinds of public occasions. There were also some boos; and a small number booing were news and headlines in the media while hundreds, sometimes thousands, clapping and smiling and cheering were not. Hissing, practised by my more cultivated opponents, was increasingly dealt with by prolonged and determined applause from the host of well-wishers, whose acclaim easily drowned it out and did far more than compensate for the grimaces of the few. It became increasingly difficult for anyone to misrepresent the reception we were receiving; there was even some enlightened teasing in the media about misrepresentation by others of their number. The *Canberra Times* on 26 April 1976 printed the following account:

Three Boo Sir John Kerr

Three people in a crowd of more than 10,000 booed the Governor-General, Sir John Kerr, as he arrived at the Australian War Memorial for the main Anzac service later yesterday morning.

Sir John's arrival and departure were greeted with sustained applause in what the ABC news service was able to describe as 'a mixture of cheers and boos'.

It was notable that during the uglier demonstrations, in one of which a brick smashed through the car window and my aide, Flight Lieutenant Ross Fox, was cut about the face, television floodlights seemed invariably to be directed on to the car and its occupants as targets and rarely on to aggressors in the crowd. Violent demonstrations, being newsworthy, were given dramatic publicity in the media, and people relying on press, radio and television could be excused for believing that massive protests were taking place. They were not. Although disagreeable and sometimes dangerous, the demonstrations were the work of a few and did not reflect the national scene. I have often been told both in Australia and overseas that press and television coverage created an impression of widespread violence. This was not a true picture.

As the months passed we travelled widely north, south, east and west throughout Australia, accepting the broadest possible range of public engagements. I opened many national and international conferences in many parts of Australia, and audiences of every sort — accountants, doctors, engineers, law-yers, real estate agents, war veterans, welfare organisers and many other Australians — showed their loyalty to the Monarchy and their support for the Queen's representative. These were most heart-warming experiences.

In addition many thousands of people wrote to me in very moving terms.

While the media was concentrating on the noises of the extreme oppositional elements, I continued to receive constant evidence of widespread support, and felt sure those who were working to maintain their tedious rage were conducting a counter-productive exercise.

The ugliest of the demonstrations were mounted in Melbourne and Canberra, while the most offensive was probably the desecration of a Sydney church, where we were to attend a service, by the painting of a slogan on its wall. There was plenty of evidence that demonstrations, especially the violent ones, were organised by militant left-wing unionists and students. The numbers participating were to be counted, at the worst, in hundreds, but generally consisted of twenty to sixty persons supported by apparently pre-arranged media coverage. Some faces recurred in widely separated locations, and in each State they included individuals who were well known to police.

Concurrently with the organising of violence had gone, from the very beginning, a campaign of character assassination by innuendo and falsehood.

I have tried to make it clear what is my main purpose in writing this book. It is to demonstrate that what was done on 11 November by me had to be done and was correctly done. In undertaking this task I have thought it proper and necessary to repudiate certain false charges calculated to cast doubt on the good faith and honesty of my approach to my task as Governor-General and its performance.

It would have been wrong indeed for me to do what I did to injure those whose careers suffered in the outcome. It would have been wrong for me to act maliciously and in bad faith, to act in a partisan way with the object of favouring some at the expense of others. From the true account, given in this book, it can be seen that none of these things happened. But it has not been my object and it would have been impossible in such a book to list individually and refute all of the false accusations, suggestions, theories, fictions, inventions and simple abuse which after 11 November were concocted and poured in an ever-ready stream upon me. I have not attempted this. The fact that here and there for one reason or another I have taken the opportunity of denying some particular piece of nastiness is not to be taken as recognition that there is any truth whatever in any of the many others. To the extent that the attacks have attached themselves to my wife, the same comment applies.

I have already denied the charge of having 'deceived' Mr Whitlam and his Ministers.[2] In the very book — *Kerr's King Hit* by Clem Lloyd and Andrew Clark — that Mr Whitlam launched on 22 March 1976 with his speech attacking me on the grounds of my 'deception', a false statement of a very serious kind was made. The false statement referred to myself and to the Chief Justice of New South Wales. In the pre-launching publicity great prominence was given to this statement.

In the *Sydney Morning Herald*, to quote one instance, on 20 March 1976 it was said that the authors of the book, although finding no evidence that Mr Fraser had any early knowledge of my intentions before 11 November ('his actions are not consistent with over-confidence or awareness of a pre-determined course') wrote as follows:

384

There are other puzzling aspects of Kerr's behaviour, however, which tend to reinforce the conspiracy theory. Barwick was not the only distinguished jurist Kerr sought out for advice which would fortify his inclination to dismiss the Whitlam Government.

He approached the Chief Justice of NSW, Mr Justice Street, who had succeeded Kerr at the head of the NSW Bench.

If Kerr was looking for support or a favourable legal opinion from Street, he was badly disappointed. Street rejected the proposal to use the reserve powers out of hand.

The *Sydney Morning Herald* stated that 'according to the book, Sir Laurence advised Sir John in the strongest terms against such a course of action'.

This story is totally untrue.

The Chief Justice of New South Wales rang me up in Adelaide on 20 March to tell me the allegation had been published in the Sydney press that day and that he had written me a letter which he thought could and should be published. I at once directed that it should be, and it was widely published in the press on 22 March.

The text of Sir Laurence's letter was as follows:

Dear Sir John,

In this morning's Press there is reference to a passage in a book entitled 'Kerr's King Hit' by Mr Clem Lloyd and Mr Andrew Clark. It is stated in this passage that you approached me for advice on the resolution of the constitutional crisis last year. It is stated 'If Kerr was looking for support or a favourable legal opinion from Street, he was badly disappointed. Street rejected the proposal to use the reserve powers out of hand'. It is further stated that I advised you in the strongest terms against such a course of action.

As is, of course, well known to both of us, there is not a shadow of justification for these statements. I write, however, to place this on permanent record.

So far from your seeking, or my proffering you, any advice on any aspect of the situation at any time prior to the events of 11 November 1975, there was no discussion or communication whatever, direct or indirect, between us in any way touching on this matter.

In response to requests I have received from the Press I have followed the convention binding holders of judicial office by refraining from commenting on this matter of public controversy. At the same time I am agreeable without reservation to your exercising a free discretion to make known the entirety or any part of this letter or to make reference to it at any time as you may wish.

Yours sincerely
(sgnd) L. W. Street

I know of no attempt by the authors to check their false story either with the Chief Justice or with Government House. It is ironic that Mr Whitlam—launching the book on the very day when the denial by the Chief Justice that there was any truth in the story was widely published in the press—made a speech denouncing me on the ground of my 'deception'. Praising the book, Mr Whitlam said it was good to have the facts brought out by impartial writers.

It was of some comfort to know that I was sometimes in good company as the object of this sort of attack. The distinguished and authoritative constitutionalist Sir Kenneth Wheare draws attention to an example of this in his article 'Australia's Constitutional Crisis'[3], in which he reviews the book *Labor and the Constitution 1972–1975*.[4] Sir Kenneth, referring in his review to a section entitled 'The Blocking of the Budget and Dismissal of the Government' by Colin Howard and Cheryl Saunders, observes:

> There follow some rather critical remarks about the actors in these events and the commentators upon them, in so far as they disagreed with Professor Howard and Miss Saunders: 'The events of 1975, arising as they did out of nothing more dignified than a political brawl of unusual bitterness, were characterized to an exceptional degree by intellectual dishonesty.' And they did add on an even sourer note: 'Most of what passed for interpretation of the constitution by way of justifying the major events which occurred is a travesty of legal reasoning.'

This is a bit hard on some of us.[5]

Labor and the Constitution 1972–1975 is a collection of papers and commentaries originating in the proceedings of a seminar held at the University of Melbourne in August 1976. Dr David Butler's introduction, which appears in the United Kingdom edition of the book, includes the following comment on it: 'Many of the facts and arguments about the crisis are set out in the pages that follow. But the story is told by lawyers, mostly with a strong *parti pris*'.[6] Dr Butler goes on to make clear that the bias is pro-Labor. Sir Kenneth Wheare calls his introduction 'a model of how to behave in these circumstances — understanding, fair-minded, sympathetic but, as one would expect, intelligent and intelligible'.[7]

Mr Whitlam was reported as recently as 11 June 1977[8] to have said the day before in London, 'largely to an audience of Australian reporters' at the launching of the United Kingdom edition of *Labor and the Constitution* (after a further reference to my 'deceitful, dishonourable partisan conduct'):

> Undoubtedly if my Government had not accepted what [the Governor-General] did . . . he would have acted as Commander-in-Chief . . . he would have called out the Army if there had been any administrative or other action which displeased him.

The report commented that Mr Whitlam presented no evidence to support his claim.

It is hardly credible to me that such a statement could be made. It is an allegation that I had it in my power to precipitate something in the nature of a civil war, and would have done so.

In the extraordinarily unlikely event that Mr Whitlam's Government 'had not accepted' their dismissal, the courts would have had to pronounce as to the legality or otherwise of non-acceptance, and injunctions would have had to be sought against any 'administrative or other action' constituting that non-acceptance. Had there been civil commotion so serious as to warrant the use of troops it would have been for the Government to handle it. And surely even a person innocent of much knowledge of what is involved in 'calling out the Army' must know it cannot be done by waving a magic wand. Large numbers of people would have to know about it and be involved in its planning.

No such possibilities entered my mind. Mr Whitlam did not take the issue of the legality of his dismissal for judicial determination, and when the matter went to the people, so far from there being civil commotion and war-like response to it, democracy worked with perfect smoothness in a quiet election. Verbal absurdities abounded during the aftermath period. They included — seen among the disappointingly unwitty slogans of the manifestants — the term *Judas*. Judas, as most people must surely know, was the disciple who betrayed Christ for thirty pieces of silver. Where is the Messiah whose disciple I am supposed to have been? To whom or to what cause can it be claimed I was a traitor? Can anyone seriously claim that I was or should have been Mr Whitlam's disciple?[9]

Another striking misuse of words was in the description of my action as a *coup d'état*. It is such an obvious piece of nonsense to say that referring a great national crisis to the people for their decision in a democratic election is a *coup d'état* that it seems impossible anyone could put it forward with a hope of having it accepted. Yet the expression is still heard from time to time. I am told of one person who uses it when travelling in France, and when in Germany substitutes in a versatile way the word *putsch*.

Mr Whitlam, reading a paper at the Melbourne seminar mentioned above, said, 'The constitutional *coup d'état*, the *putsch*, must never occur again.'[10] In the same speech he remarked on the highly proper manner in which the Labor Party had fought the ensuing election and accepted its result.[11] This comment, which clearly shows the dismissal and dissolution as leading in an orderly manner to the routine unfolding of the democratic process, underlines the incongruity, to my mind, of suggesting there was any element of the *coup* or *putsch* in my recourse on 11 November to the reserve powers of the Crown.

One of the sillier myths circulated during the period was one which attributed to my wife an attempt to affect the course of events, having herself a political axe to grind. Nothing could be wider of the mark. My wife has never made herself a member of any political party or taken part in any political activity. To endeavour to build her into a political force influencing my decisions as Governor-General is ridiculous — or would be, except for the sorry lack of taste in details of the campaign to punish me by an attack on my wife. James McAuley, at whose house the myth was alleged to have found its source, called the 'attempt to explain Kerr's decisions by petticoat government a fabrication for which there is no excuse'.

Behind the two-pronged assault, by violence and by vilification, was a defined strategy, the object of which was to make it impossible for me to stay in office. The intention was either to make me a prisoner in Yarralumla or to break my spirit so that I could not carry on. My counter-strategy was to accept every invitation I could. I would never have resigned in the face of aggression.

To carry out my counter-strategy I had the courageous support of my wife. I often tried to persuade her not to accompany me on risky official engagements but she refused firmly. She was always there—cool, serene, dignified. This helped enormously and as time passed her cool courage was recognised by the people, as correspondence and spoken assurances showed.

Something must be said about the federal and State police forces, including the special security police attached to me under Chief Inspector Barry Brown. I saw police at work at close hand and far from 'over-reacting' their attitude was moderate and careful—never provocative. They suffered violence themselves and gave every sign of devotion to duty. By returning again and again to focal points I was, in effect, imposing burdens upon them which they accepted. A recollection comes of Barry Brown getting us through the first of the wilder demonstrations one night in Melbourne by running for several hundred yards alongside the car, his hand on the door-handle, guiding the driver by instructions through a slit of open window as thrown paint and posters blocked out the windscreen, while police horses reared alongside him alarmed at feeling marbles thrown under their hooves, missiles and fists battered the car and a brick smashed through a window.

As it happened, when I was a federal judge in 1970, I had had to consider legal aspects of demonstrations during the Vietnam War period and, in particular, police handling of them. In relation to one such demonstration outside the American Embassy in Canberra there had been allegations, as there frequently are, that the police had over-reacted. In fact the police had been restrained and had engaged in a well-planned containing action, arresting few though breaches of the law had been many. They had resorted to discretionary selective law enforcement. A planned police attempt to deal with demonstrations which may become violent generally requires and produces selective decisions not to arrest rather than excessive use of the power to arrest, since it is often undesirable in an over-excited crowd situation to arrest all law-breakers who could properly be arrested. But of course, violence breeds violence. My judgment in that case indicates what I then thought, and still think, about the interacting problems involved in such encounters. I quote the following extract:

> Peaceful demonstration is an important part of the democratic process and at the beginning of a demonstration it is not necessarily known whether persons are present who intend to resort to violence in order to provoke retaliatory violence from the police, nor, if such persons are present, whether they are few in numbers. It is important to handle a demonstration to permit peaceful demonstrators to exercise their lawful rights and restrained and prudent selective law-enforcement may in some cases permit this to be done but in the final analysis the discretions are police discretions which they must exercise in the interest of preventing breaches of the peace, violence and illegal activities, and only careful training and wise guidance can ensure that they do so fairly.[12]

First-hand experience six years later confirmed me in the views I expressed in that judgment.

My wife and I witnessed violent attacks on the police and upon our party, not provoked by the police but deliberately calculated, I believe, to produce situations in which it could be alleged police had 'over-reacted'. I am referring here to small numbers of mobilised and organised activists who had no intention whatever of confining their action to peaceful demonstration. The problem of increasing violence deliberately fostered could be a serious one for a community that tolerated its growth. Australians do not like this organised violence and they tend to come together, irrespective of their political views, in objecting to it and rejecting it.

The combination of my strategy and police perseverance gradually got the message across that the tactic of violence was valueless. Most people came to realise the battle of the streets was being won, and rage, much of it artificial, was declining. (One cartoon said: 'I maintained my rage but I couldn't sustain my interest'.[13]) This was apparent many months before the royal visit. There was still bitter disagreement in certain quarters but violent rage was disappearing. The campaign of character assassination had diminished—in public at least—and it seemed my opponents might be concluding there was only electoral disadvantage to be derived from continuing the personal vendetta against me, and gradually accepting that they must somehow succeed in disciplining their tongues.

In about August–September of 1976 the pressure began to abate and it was possible to forecast confidently that the royal visit in the following March would be free of violence and of significant protest. Indeed the visit was to be a triumph for the Queen. My objective had been to take the sting out of the protest movement well in advance of the Jubilee Year, and in this we succeeded.

Some public rallies and debate in support of republicanism were held in 1976. These lessened in vigour and were well on the way to dying down by the time of the royal visit, though some special republican meetings were hospitably arranged to coincide with it. It is evident that more and more people have come to see that republicanism is unlikely to achieve significant support in Australia in the near future. The republican debate has now taken its place as one issue in a wider constitutional discussion.

On 11 November 1976, a date which *les enragés*, and some of the media, had been boosting and brandishing in front of us as a sort of Ides of March when we could expect a mighty commemorative demonstration, presumably at the Remembrance Day ceremony, a large crowd at the Stone of Remembrance received us with a warm and sustained ovation. Even quite well-known demonstrators failed to turn up; the media were relatively balanced and moderate in tone; and we could fairly say from then on that the battle was won.

Dr David Butler, in his introduction to *Labor and the Constitution*

1972–1975, reflected what I felt was a spreading understanding in the community of the realities of the 1975 events as time passed. Examining various of the options that writers had claimed were open to me in November 1975, Dr Butler began by making the following points. First, that I would argue that, granted my duty to uphold the Constitution, I pursued the only sure-fire way to solve the crisis. Indeed I do so argue. Second, that I accepted the view that the Senate had the power to deny supply. I did and do accept this view, which Dr Butler does not dispute. Third, that it was not for me to abandon my constitutional obligations because the parties on all sides were fighting their political battles too roughly. Certainly it is true to say that I had no impulse to abandon my constitutional obligations, in a political situation not of my making. Dr Butler wrote:

In retrospect various alternative courses of action have been prescribed for the Governor-General. The most obvious is that on November 11, he should have done nothing beyond acceding to Mr Whitlam's request for a half-Senate election on December 13. But it was very doubtful whether that election would have by itself solved the crisis, and by December 13 Supply would have run out, if the Senate remained obdurate. Of course, many argue that the Senate would not have remained obdurate—a weakening on the part of only one of the four or five Liberal senators who had indicated reluctance over the blocking of Supply would have ruined the opposition strategy. Yet the Governor-General could hardly gamble on such a weakening. If the Opposition senators stood firm, then Supply would run out by early December.

It has also been suggested that the Governor-General should have waited until the end of November to do what he did on November 11. On November 30 he could perhaps have persuaded Mr Fraser to the course that he invited him to take on November 11 and Mr Fraser could, in return for a dissolution, have got the Senate to provide fresh Supply before the money actually ran out. But an election announced on November 30 (indeed any election announced after midnight on November 11), could not have taken place until well into the New Year and the uncertainties of the whole situation would have been much prolonged at great risk to Australia's internal and external credit. There would also have been confusion if a dissolution, perhaps a double dissolution, had occurred while a half-Senate election was actually under way, with candidates nominated and the poll a fortnight off.

Many have contended that the Governor-General should, after pressing Mr Whitlam harder to call the election himself, have given him time to consult his colleagues about the ultimatum. But that ignores the possibility that Mr Whitlam would instantly have asked the Queen to replace the Governor-General with a more complaisant appointee. Such a request would have put the Queen in an impossible dilemma: acceptance, or refusal, or even delay in answering, would only have heightened the crisis.[14]

These conclusions were of particular interest and weight coming as they did from the pen of an eminent English political scientist who for a decade or so had made the Australian political scene his special field of study.

Sir Kenneth Wheare, reviewing the same book in his article 'Australia's Constitutional Crisis', remarked that the Governor-General's power of dismissal and the power of the Senate to reject Appropriation Bills 'must be regarded as the medicine, not the daily bread of the Constitution'.[15] He wrote:

The letter of the Governor-General dismissing Mr Whitlam and the statement of his reasons which accompanied it are printed in Appendix C of the book. The first paragraph of the statement expresses the position very well: 'It has been necessary for me to find a democratic and constitutional solution to the current crisis which will permit the people of Australia to decide as soon as possible what should be the outcome of the deadlock which developed over Supply between the two Houses of Parliament, and between the government and the opposition parties. The only solution consistent with the constitution . . . is to terminate the commission as Prime Minister of Mr Whitlam and to arrange a caretaker Government, able to secure Supply and willing to let the issue go to the people'.

My opinion, for what it is worth, is that the course of action taken by the Governor-General was one of several options open to him under the constitution, and that it was the appropriate course of action for him to take. To refer the issue to the people, as provided by the constitution in case of a deadlock, is not the action of an autocrat. There was nothing to indicate in advance which party would be returned to power. For the Governor-General it was a case of putting the matter in the hands of the people. In the outcome Mr Fraser's party was returned with a majority in both Senate and House of Representatives. To say that the Governor-General dismissed the Whitlam Government is true so far as it goes. But it fails to mention that the people also dismissed the Whitlam Government. Had they not done so, the argument between the two Houses may or may not have continued but the resources of the constitution would have been exhausted, and no doubt the Governor-General might have been replaced.

Among other options open to the Governor-General which have been or were canvassed are that he ought to have taken no action at all, or that he might have waited and acted later on. It is possible to speculate upon the consequences of these courses, but it is particularly fruitless to do so.

It is easy to understand Mr Whitlam's feelings and even to sympathise with them. He must have been shocked by the Governor-General's action. He thought he had a tame house-dog, appointed on his own nomination, but it proved to have teeth which bit. He was a distinguished lawyer and he knew the constitution. Sir John Kerr was a distinguished lawyer also. It was understandable that Mr Whitlam should raise the historic cry of the Australian football crowd in moments of anguish: 'Shoot the umpire.' That there was much to be said on both sides is the message of this book. Where experts differ, who is to decide? The answer was available in Australia. 'No other decision open to me,' wrote the Governor-General, 'would enable the Australian people to decide for themselves what should be done . . . the people can do what, in a democracy such as ours, is their responsibility and duty and theirs alone. It is for the people to decide on the issue which the two leaders have failed to settle'.[16]

Describing himself as feeling 'a little foolhardy in expressing an opinion so much in opposition to the academic constitutional experts' who had written in *Labor and the Constitution*, Sir Kenneth quotes as strengthening him in his own opinion of the 1975 events the constitutional opinions of former Chief Justice of Australia Sir Owen Dixon and former Solicitor-General of Australia Sir Kenneth Bailey. From Dixon he quotes:

We insist, too, that if a difficulty arises between the executive Government and the Parliament it shall be resolved by an appeal to the people, and we place on the representative of the Sovereign the responsibility of saying whether the case is one for the dissolution of Parliament and a general election;[17]

and from Bailey:

One of the distinctive features of the British constitution is the combination of the democratic principle that all political authority comes from the people, and hence that the will of the people must prevail, with the maintenance of a monarchy armed with legal powers to dismiss Ministers drawn from among the people's elected representatives and even to dissolve the elected legislature itself. In normal times the very existence of those powers can simply be ignored. In times of crisis, however, it immediately becomes of vital importance to know what they are and how they will be exercised . . . It is not too much to say that the whole future of the British constitutional system is likely to depend on the extent to which in the next few years, it is demonstrated that the reserve powers of the Crown are not the antithesis but the corollary of the democratic principle that political authority is derived from the people.[18]

Wheare concludes:

Whether or not Sir Kenneth Bailey would have approved of the action taken on 11 November 1975, I, of course, cannot say, but what he wrote above, strengthens me in my own opinion of those events.[19]

The year 1977 was a far easier and more congenial year for me with the success of the royal tour, the Silver Jubilee celebrations in London and the visit to us in Australia of the Prince of Wales. There was little evidence now of hostility or protest. During the Queen's visit, an attempt was made to assert that the reason I did not accompany Her Majesty around Australia was fear of some public scene. This was nonsense. Protocol has always required the Queen's visits to the States to be occasions for the State Governors to play their role. The Governor-General does not attend Her Majesty in the States, and for this reason, in accordance with long-standing practice, I did not. When I was with the Queen on the appropriate public occasions in Canberra, and in Perth where we farewelled her from Australia after being her guests at luncheon in HMY *Britannia*, no such problems arose.

In Canberra I was sworn in as a member of Her Majesty's Privy Council at a meeting presided over by the Queen at Yarralumla. During an audience on board *Britannia* in Fremantle harbour Her Majesty invested me as a Knight Grand Cross of the Royal Victorian Order. (I had previously, in 1975 when the Queen established the Order of Australia of which she is Sovereign, become the first Chancellor and a Companion of the Order and later, when the rank of knighthood was introduced, the first Knight of the Order of Australia. In 1976 Her Majesty had promoted me to the rank of Knight Grand Cross in the Order of St Michael and St George. Throughout my Governor-Generalship I was Prior in Australia and a Knight of The Order of St John of Jerusalem and in April 1977 was awarded the Grand Cross of Merit of the Sovereign and Military Order of Malta, the Catholic Order which exists in brotherly relationship with The Order of St John.)

My Governor-Generalship, by the time of the Queen's visit in March, had been a stirring one, marked by a great historic clash and the dramas of its sequel. The period since November 1975 could be looked back on now with a satisfying sense of accomplishment. The constitutional debate was proceeding in a relatively calm way, and 1975 was retreating into history, so far as rage and violence were concerned. The nation's politics were, it seemed, on the way to becoming normal. Wounds suffered by some were beginning to heal. I believed the Jubilee Year would leave the Monarchy greatly strengthened in Australia. By the end of it the healing process would I hoped be nearly complete. When I mention the 'healing process' and 'wounds healing' I am not referring to society generally but to hurts in limited political areas. Society as a whole was working smoothly and democratically.

But some aspects of party politics were not yet normal. In particular, the Labor Party was, as I saw it, burdened with its boycott of the Governor-General. I believed that whatever members of the party might themselves think about it their position in the country was being damaged by their general attitude towards me, as expressed for example in the boycott. I regarded it as very important that irrational elements in our politics should disappear as soon as possible. I could not believe that within the ranks of the Parliamentary Labor Party there were not some who took this larger view of what was of true importance to the future of the party.

I therefore began to consider whether, in the interests of making a final contribution towards restoring normal functioning to our national political life, at the same time enabling the Labor Party to have better hope of returning to sound health, I might look afresh at the question of my resignation. It seemed to me, as I reflected early in 1977, that by resigning I might be able to help one area in our national politics to return to normal, or more nearly to normal than had happened so far, though a great deal had been achieved. I believed there were elements in the Labor Party which would welcome the opportunity to avoid perpetuating the divisive attitude to which it had been so regrettably committed since 1975.

To offer resignation would be contrary to all the advice I had so far received. It would in particular go against that wise and experienced adviser Sir Robert Menzies, who emphatically urged that I should stay 'for years' on the clear ground that what I had done was right.

When I had assumed the office at the age of fifty-nine it had been on the understanding that it would be for a substantial term if I wished; and this consideration had weighed with me when I at length decided to give up the Chief Justiceship. In renouncing the Governor-Generalship I would be leaving what may fairly be regarded as one of the most desirable positions in Australia, one that I enjoyed, with whose aims I identified, and through the extreme rigours of which I had now passed. Vice-regal life had resumed the happy aspect of its early days. In all truth it cannot be said that the Labor boycott affected us at Government House in any way.

On the other hand I had a very strong sense of a big task completed. On the personal side, my wife and I had had a pretty brisk time since our marriage in April 1975 — it would, I felt, be permissible for us to look towards a more personal life and constructive new work. Certainly no one could credibly claim that I had gone defeated under attack. The scene would be set for a successor to take over in circumstances as propitious for him as possible. By the time of the Queen's visit I had concluded that I would stay on only until the end of the Jubilee Year.

The people of Australia are entitled, for reasons that will appear later, to know the timing of the resignation talks. It was during the Queen's visit that I engaged, upon my sole initiative, in certain conversations.

I believe it has been said that one reason why I resigned was the possibility of a Labor Government coming into office. Almost certainly had there been any prospect of a Labor victory I would have resigned. But there was no such prospect when early in 1977 I began to set things in train for my resignation. The Fraser Government had been less than fifteen months in office and was governing with a huge majority. I know of no one who would have forecast an early Labor victory at that time.

In March 1977, at the beginning of the Queen's visit and while Her Majesty was in residence at Yarralumla, I asked if I might be received by her in audience. Following that audience I had my first conversation with the Prime Minister, in which I explained to him my thoughts at that time on the question of resignation. The Queen received me again in audience at the end of her visit, in HMY *Britannia* in Fremantle harbour. I cannot of course disclose the content of the discussions I had with Her Majesty, but it must be emphasised that I made my decision solely on my own initiative and that there was at no time any direct or indirect suggestion from the Queen of what course I should take.

In talks soon afterwards I told Mr Fraser what I wished to do and why. He agreed that I should follow the course I had chosen. Questions of timing would be left until we were both in London in June for the Jubilee celebrations. In the meantime, shortly after these talks, the Prime Minister turned his mind to deciding whom he should recommend as my successor. My decision was already being fully acted upon in April.

In London in June I was again received by Her Majesty, and afterwards had further discussions with Mr Fraser. Later Mr Fraser and I agreed that the formalities should be concluded whilst we were overseas. My wife and I were making a stop in Rome where we had the privilege of being received in audience by His Holiness Pope Paul VI. In June, from Rome, I sent a handwritten letter to the Queen by courier. The decision was that an announcement would be made in Australia on our return from London. It was made in July and my departure from office, it was then agreed, would be in early December 1977.

It was not until I had committed myself firmly to resignation that I turned to considering what, after leaving Yarralumla, my life and work might be. What I was preparing to do was indeed a very real sacrifice by me. Having in mid-1974 given up an office which assured me of a good salary and pension and stimulating work to do until I turned seventy, in December 1977 on leaving the Governor-Generalship I would, at sixty-three, be on a pension far less than my former judicial salary and very far less than my emoluments as Governor-General. It did not occur to me for a moment that retirement from the latter office would mean retirement from active life in the service of Australia. I made it clear on many public occasions that what I was doing, as I hoped for the country's sake, did not mean that I was reconciled to giving up forever all public service to Australia or the possibility of worthwhile work simply 'to go fishing', as I metaphorically expressed it several times. No hint of opposition greeted these speeches.

From March 1977 on I thought about what I might be able to do after leaving the Governor-Generalship. Barristers who become judges develop, indeed it is part of what attracts them to judicial life, an attitude of mind which takes for granted real work till the age of seventy. This was always my attitude and I carried it with me when leaving the Bench. It never occurred to me that I should lead an inactive 'retired' life at sixty-three. When entering what I had every reason to believe would be an extended period in office as Governor-General I could not foresee that I should be caught by the disruptive series of historical events that had now unfolded; but since it was so my thoughts ranged actively about the question of some work into which I could get my teeth when I ceased to be Governor-General.

I could myself see no reason in principle why I should not do some public work for Australia after leaving my office. Judges often engage in long enquiries after retirement. Politicians and senior bureaucrats also work for the country after leaving politics or administration. Ministers of the Crown have become ambassadors, Chief Justices, judges, Governors-General. Chief Justices Latham and Dixon stepped across, during a period of leave from their office, to ambassadorial work. Sir Owen also undertook international work on the Kashmir question. Dr Evatt from being a High Court judge became a Minister of the Crown and later a Chief Justice. Such movement to and fro across the board of high national office is regarded as proper and appropriate for men of integrity. Very often, such careers have included periods of great controversy. Is the Governor-Generalship the only office in the country which is to be regarded as automatically excluding its occupant, on retirement, from all further service to Australia?

The British system does not lack precedents for former vice-regal appointees moving across to other public offices after completing their vice-regal period. Sir Philip Game, after retiring as Governor of New South Wales, became the Commissioner of the London Police Force. It would appear to be a strange circumstance if having voluntarily stepped aside from the highest public office in Australia I were unable to accept an appointment which I found interesting and worthwhile, and were to be debarred from accepting any opportunity for further public service.

Moreover my own hope is that Governors-General should in the future not be found exclusively amongst those approaching full retirement. Younger men should be able to accept appointment knowing that they were not thereby closing off all prospect of further public service.

After my resignation was settled, a number of people in the course of conversation raised the subject with me of what I proposed to do next. Three main possibilities were discussed — some kind of work for the country, which meant in effect ambassadorial or other international work; activity in the business world; and writing as a way of life. I am not one of those who think and speak slightingly of the ambassador's role — I know the real importance of its diplomats to the life of any country and especially of a smaller Power, which has to work hard and skilfully to achieve its objects on the international stage and can perhaps afford to make fewer mistakes than a great Power. My thoughts turned back to the choice I had made many years ago when, at the outset of my career, I had with some reluctance turned my back on the possibility of diplomacy in order to return to the Bar. It would have pleased me greatly to see the strands of international activity showing up again in the pattern of my life.

In Paris in 1977 I had looked over our new embassy building, designed to sustain a threefold diplomatic activity — the Australian embassy to France and our two embassies to international organisations having their headquarters in Paris, the OECD and Unesco. I was reminded that our activity with Unesco had been suspended for economy reasons in 1975.

One line in my thinking which developed later as a result of this visit was that if the Unesco embassy were ever reopened it would present a field of activity which would have a strong appeal for me. I have commented on this interest of mine earlier in my life story when outlining my previous international activities.[20]

Among those to whom I mentioned the various possibilities I had in mind was the Prime Minister who, as his public statements show, did not subscribe to the view that a former Governor-General must retire into inactivity. He showed a sympathetic understanding of my wish, in all the circumstances of my retirement, to continue in some active occupation: and I believed when I left Australia that, if and when he could, he would apply his mind positively to the matter of my doing public work in future.

It will be seen from the history of the resignation talks that anyone considering the circumstances of my resignation must start from the following facts: that I saw the Queen first and then the Prime Minister; that I saw the Prime Minister after each audience with the Queen; and that my decision was made in March 1977 and at that time communicated by me both to the Queen and to the Prime Minister.

It is surely inconceivable that on a matter which I had taken up and was pursuing directly with the Queen, it could be alleged that there was some kind of bargaining going on between me and Mr Fraser; or that I was being pressed by Mr Fraser to resign and being offered a reward for doing so. Yet these were among allegations made in February 1978 when after I left Australia I learned that I was still to be the object of bitter attack if I accepted further work for my country—or perhaps, work of any kind. In the same episode it was alleged that, additionally or alternatively, I was being rewarded for the decision I made on 27 October 1977 to accept Mr Fraser's advice for a dissolution of the House of Representatives. In view of this I shall fully discuss the 1977 dissolution, although it was not constitutionally very interesting in itself, in the next chapter. The events of February will have also to be recounted.[21]

But I prefer to leave this present chapter of my life as it in fact ended. There had been, in the normal way, very pleasant official farewells in Canberra and some State capitals. But the Labor-governed States gave us no official farewell; and that meant none in my own home town of Sydney. To this fact I owe one of the most congenial occasions of my long Sydney life—a farewell dinner organised by the citizens of Sydney a week or two before we left stays in our minds as a symbol of the many warm and splendid occasions of the aftermath period. That period, from November 1975 to December 1977, although not a placid time was I believe a time of achievement. My feeling is that those who saw the Monarchy and the Governor-Generalship under attack during that time also saw them proved to be institutions of real significance and durability in our democracy.

24

The 1977 Dissolution
of the House of Representatives

From the timing of my conversations in Canberra and London on the subject of resignation it will be seen that my March initiative was taken before the referendums of 1977 and long before any contemplation of a 1977 election. The results of the referendums came out before the June discussions in London, and the referendum about joint House and Senate elections was lost; but when finality in my resignation talks was reached earlier it was at a time when nothing was known about the result of the referendums or when the next election would occur. Indeed one point specifically mentioned by me when deciding the timing of my resignation was that I should avoid as far as possible having it take place at a time close to an election. It was only as the second half of the year passed, and after my resignation had been finalised and was publicly known, that I came to consider the possibility that I might have to deal with the question of a dissolution before I left the Governor-Generalship.

When setting out to write this book I had in mind to make no more than a passing reference to the dissolution of the House of Representatives granted on 26 October 1977, since the constitutional circumstances of its granting, abundantly supported by well-known and recent precedent, were without complication and therefore in my eyes without particular interest; and because that dissolution appeared to have little relevance to the story this book sets out to tell.

True, there had been some attempts towards the middle of 1977, when speculation about an early election began to attract the interest of the media, to foster a theory that I might feel obliged to refuse an early dissolution if it were advised by the Prime

Minister, on the basis of some comments I had made to the Indian Law Institute in 1975 on a different subject — that is, the grant of dissolution in circumstances involving doubt as to the 'workability' of the Parliament, and therefore such as might lead to a substantive exercise of a vice-regal discretion. The 1977 circumstances raised no question at all about the workability of the Parliament.

No constitutionalist would have entertained such a theory unless he had seriously misunderstood what I said in India. Professor Geoffrey Sawer explained what I was dealing with, in an article in the *Canberra Times* as early as 6 July, shortly after my talk was publicised. There was apparently some misunderstanding of what I said, when the paper was read in Australia, and in retrospect I realise that it would have been better to deal with the subject of dissolution more fully. In order to clarify the observations made in my New Delhi address I shall set out in full the considerations and circumstances surrounding my granting early dissolution of the House of Representatives, which enabled elections to be held simultaneously for that House and for half of the Senate in December 1977.

For some months before the 1977 dissolution became a fact there was speculation about when the next election would take place. The options open were discussed increasingly in the press. Normally an election for the House, if that were to be considered alone, would take place in December 1978 at the latest. A half-Senate election had to be held before the end of May 1978.

A referendum designed to ensure that House elections and half-Senate elections would in future be synchronised was held in the first half of 1977 but, though supported by both parties and by 62% of the voters, it failed to pass because of lack of a majority in three States.

In practical terms, however, both leaders believed that the next elections for both Houses should be simultaneous. Mr Fraser was generally understood not to want separate elections with a half-Senate election preceding a House election. Such an election, it was said in the media, would in the expected economic circumstances of 1978 permit the earlier half-Senate election to be a 'by-election-protest' kind of occasion, without the

Government being directly at risk at the time. The possible outcome, on this theory of things, could be damaging for the Government in a later House election at which the occupancy of the Treasury benches would be at stake. The general opinion appeared to be that though the Labor Party accepted the principle of joint House and Senate elections it preferred them to be in May 1978 because of expected worsening of the economic climate.

The Government's options were regarded as limited to a joint election either in May 1978 or December 1977. Mr Whitlam urged a May election, saying that an election as early as December 1977 would not be proper as being too early in the term of the House. It would be two years instead of three after the previous election, and five months before the deadline if joint elections were to be held.

Mr Fraser kept his choices open until the last minute. On the several occasions when I spoke with him during the few months before 26 October 1977 he discussed options, but never indicated whether he had a preference or intention in favour of one option or the other until I saw him on 26 October. He always said he would keep December 1977 open as a possibility, but until 26 October did not say that he would advise that date. At no stage did Mr Fraser put forward arguments to me that if he did advise a December election it would be my duty to grant it. Although he did not say so, he would have had advice, whilst considering his options, that it was virtually inconceivable that a Governor-General would refuse such a request in the circumstances existing in late 1977.

The dissolution granted in 1955 by the Governor-General Sir William Slim to the Prime Minister Mr Menzies is an outstanding modern precedent of a dissolution similar in nature to that advised by Mr Fraser in 1977 and it is examined in Chapter 10.[1] Mr Whitlam would no doubt have a personal recollection of it as he was in Parliament at the time and stood in the ensuing election.

Mr Menzies' 1955 argument for dissolution was that although the House was only eighteen months old the Prime Minister, being firmly in control of the Parliament and of his coalition parties, was entitled to an early election for reasons of general policy on which he was in a position to advise. It is one of the great advantages of being in control of his party and of the House that a Prime Minister has the opportunity, in advising an election, to do so with considerations of policy in mind at a time regarded by him as being most helpful to his side of politics. There is nothing new about this. As Professor Sawer has said: 'It is established by two centuries of UK precedent that Prime Ministers are entitled to confer some electoral advantages on themselves by the timing of elections.'[2]

Not all those making pronouncements in 1977 on where my duty would lie if I received advice for a December or May election appeared to appreciate the significance of the Slim-Menzies precedent, or even to be familiar with it. A Prime Minister in seeking such a dissolution is seeking nothing illegal or unconstitutional. It is hard to see how his advice could justifiably be rejected or on what ground a Governor-General could intervene in a decision-making or influencing role.

During the speculation period of 1977 there was frequent reference in the press to the talk which I gave to the Indian Law Institute in New Delhi on 28 February 1975. What I said in that address was interpreted by some as making it unlikely I would grant a 'mid-term' election. I gathered several writers were hoping I would feel bound to refuse Mr Fraser a December election. This could be only on a misconceived view of constitutional principle.

It was during a brief State visit made to India and several other countries after attending the ceremonies of the coronation of the King of Nepal, that I was asked, and agreed, to give a talk to the Indian Law Institute. The subject chosen was the Governor-Generalship, and the talk was to be of a general and informal nature and not a learned legal dissertation, since I was of course not travelling with a law library and had little time to prepare. I began the relevant part of my paper by saying:

I cannot in an informal address such as this deliver a learned paper about the modern Governor-Generalship in Australia, but I should like to touch upon a couple of points. People are always interested in whether the Governor-General is a mere figurehead or whether he has any role to play.[3]

I had with me in my briefcase Sir Paul Hasluck's Queale Lecture, to which I referred and upon which I drew extensively in the course of the talk.

The powers of the Crown in relation to dissolution raise complex issues, and the subject has attracted much detailed study by text writers. It will be obvious from, for instance, the fact that Eugene Forsey wrote a substantial book on this single subject that a glancing reference made to it, in the course of my New Delhi talk, could hardly be exhaustive. The following is the full text of my comments on the subject of dissolution in the course of my address on the general subject of 'The Governor-Generalship in Australia':

> There is one other aspect of the Governor-General's role which is important. This has to do with the power to dissolve Parliament. You will all be familiar with the way in which this works under the Westminster system.
>
> One particular point I should like to mention is the Governor-General's role in relation to the dissolution of Parliament in mid-term. Sometimes the situation arises in which a Prime Minister may seek to have Parliament dissolved before its constitutional term has expired. It is of course not sufficient for him to obtain from the Governor-General a dissolution of Parliament simply because he would like to have an election. The basic constitutional issue in such cases is whether or not Parliament has become unworkable. Sometimes this may occur because of the conflict between the two chambers, the Senate and the House of Representatives. This is a special case and raises special issues in Australia which I shall mention later.
>
> Parliament may become unworkable because of the defeat of the government on an important issue in the House or it may be that the Prime Minister is in difficulty with his own supporters. The essential question is whether the Governor-General can be satisfied that Parliament has in fact become unworkable.
>
> He has to consider whether an alternative government can be brought into existence without an election, whether the government parties can find a leader with a majority. Parliament should not be dissolved simply to help a party leader, or a party solve their own

difficulties. The country should not be forced to an election merely to help leaders solve internal party questions but only to deal with a situation which Parliament itself cannot solve. The decision to dissolve Parliament in mid-term is one of the matters which the Constitution leaves to the Governor-General to decide on his own. It is not a power exercised by the Governor-General in council.

In considering, now, what I said in New Delhi I realise that the impression could be gained — particularly when this glancing reference to the subject has been treated in the press as if it were a full statement of my views on dissolution — that I was dealing, however briefly, with mid-term dissolutions as though they could occur only if Parliament were unworkable. Of course, no constitutional lawyer would imagine that another constitutional lawyer was seriously saying this. There is too much evidence in history to the contrary. There are two kinds of occasion on which a dissolution may be sought in mid-term: one in which it is sought by a Prime Minister in full control of his party and of the House; and secondly, when it is sought by a Prime Minister in circumstances where he has not or may not have the confidence of the House and perhaps where the House may be workable under another Prime Minister though not under him.

In the first case the Governor-General has very little cause, if any, to have recourse to his vice-regal discretion. In the second he has a very real call upon it. Because I was seeking an illustration which would show a vice-regal discretion operating, that is, a set of circumstances in which the Governor-General is not a figurehead only, I did not discuss case one but dealt only with case two. The resulting confusion flowed from my failure to make it quite clear I was dealing with one kind of situation only and that was not the only kind that could occur. Professor Sawer recognised this and explained the position clearly in his article; but many people, especially those who were not constitutional lawyers, may have failed to understand. I felt it was difficult for me in the latter half of 1977 to clear up the matter myself.

Part of the confusion no doubt results from my statement: 'It is of course not sufficient for him to obtain from the Governor-General dissolution of Parliament simply because he would like to have an election.' This is true in the kind of situation I was discussing; but in the other kind of situation where the Prime Minister has the full confidence of the House, while he must be able to produce satisfactory reasons for his advice, he is in a very strong position to have that advice accepted.

Evatt, writing in his *Canadian Bar Review* article in 1940 on the two types of situation in which the request by a Prime Minister for a dissolution may occur, remarked:

> It is unnecessary to elaborate the great difference between cases where Ministers remain in full possession of the confidence of the Lower House and cases where they face, or have met with, defeat in that House. In the former case, *ex hypothesi*, no alternative Ministry is possible, and the King's representative, who is thereby precluded from obtaining other advisers, must act upon the advice to dissolve, even if, as is often the case, that advice is affected entirely by party considerations. But, in the latter case, very different considerations arise, particularly where the 'parliamentary situation' embraces three distinct parties and the Ministry has no working majority in the House. In 1923 the complex three party situation in England led Mr Asquith, a highly distinguished authority, to denounce the theory of Professor Keith that, whatever the circumstances, the King is under a duty automatically to grant a dissolution on the advice of the Prime Minister for the time being. Asquith said that the theory was 'subversive of constitutional usage' and 'pernicious to the general and paramount interests of the nation at large'.[4]

Evatt, as leader of the Opposition in 1955, had to live with the dissolution of the House of Representatives in that year. He understood the difference between that type of situation and the type I was discussing in New Delhi. His views on the difference between the two were publicly known. The 1977 dissolution in Australia, like that of 1955, was an example of 'the former case'. What I was discussing in New Delhi was exactly what Evatt refers to as 'the latter case'. Of this he goes on to say:

> So far as Australia is concerned, a long course of practice tends to negative the proposition that the Governor-General of the Commonwealth or the Governor of a State is a mere automaton in the hands of Ministers who have lost, or are about to lose, the support of the Parliament. Prior to 1914, there were three occasions upon which the Governor-General of the Commonwealth had refused a

request by the Prime Minister for a dissolution of the popular House (the House of Representatives). On each occasion the Governor-General believed that an alternative Ministry was possible, and on each occasion subsequent events proved that he was correct in his belief.[5]

It was exactly this point that I was making in India. The 'former case' was not present to my mind, though I think now that I should have referred to it and set it aside. I can only recall, in explanation, the rushed circumstances in which I dictated my paper to a secretary at the Australian embassy, in the midst of the official programme of a State visit — with, of course, the co-operation, knowledge and approval of the ambassador, who saw the paper before I delivered it. My impression is that no lawyer at the New Delhi meeting went home imagining that I had been dealing comprehensively with the vast subject of dissolution. Just as I do not imagine, because Sir Paul in his Queale Lecture concentrated his examination on a limited area of exercise of the power of dissolution, that he disregarded or failed to recognise the important precedent, applicable in quite different circumstances, of the dissolution of 1955, at which time he was himself a Minister in Mr Menzies' Government. When my Indian paper began to be combed through by non-lawyers, who did not know the constitutional context into which my remarks would have to be fitted, I was very pleased to see that Professor Sawer had elucidated what I had said; but no doubt many interested persons did not see what he wrote.

If some of the conceivable complications of the example I used in New Delhi are considered it will readily be understood why I singled it out when talking about vice-regal discretion to an institute of lawyers. Sir Paul Hasluck was directing his attention, as I did, to cases where in 'mid-term' the Prime Minister is in some kind of difficulty with the House or Parliament or his party and is asking for a dissolution to help him solve it. Supposing, upon consideration, that the Governor-General is convinced that the House or Parliament, at present 'unworkable', would be workable under an alternative Prime Minister: he then has to exercise a very active discretion in determining how he will respond to the advice for dissolution.

If Parliament itself cannot solve the difficulties by finding someone to whom to give its confidence, then Parliament has become unworkable and a dissolution will no doubt be granted to the Prime Minister. If someone else has been found and the Prime Minister resigns to enable him to take office, the new Prime Minister may secure the confidence of the House, but if he cannot in fact obtain or retain it the unworkability of Parliament may be thus confirmed. It may be a difficult question whether the new Prime Minister should be granted a dissolution or should in his turn resign, enabling the Governor-General to send for the previous Prime Minister and grant him a dissolution. It will be remembered that this is what happened at State level in Victoria in 1952[6], though in Canada in 1926 the Governor-General granted the dissolution to the new Prime Minister.

The situation may become very complicated if the new or the outgoing Prime Minister refuses to resign to help the constitutional processes to unfold. Conceivably if this happened the dismissal power might ultimately become engaged.

Of course, carried to its extreme, the 'unworkability' criterion could, as Professor Sawer interestingly points out, be applied even in the uncomplicated circumstances where a Prime Minister is in firm control. If he feels that the Governor-General may not want him to have a dissolution which he wants, his position is very strong. Sawer says:

Suppose a Prime Minister like Mr Fraser, with a substantial majority in both Houses, wished to call a general election considerably earlier than the usual $2\frac{1}{2}$ to $2\frac{3}{4}$ years — perhaps to take advantage of the impact of another Petrov case — and was refused a dissolution: he can at once make Parliament 'unworkable' by resigning, leaving the Governor-General incapable of finding an alternative government with majority support or the ability to guarantee supply.

The stronger the parliamentary position of a Prime Minister in Parliament, the greater is his ability to make that Parliament unworkable.

A Governor-General who provoked that response might well soon find himself writing his memoirs.[7]

It would be worthless for a Governor-General to provoke such a situation. The Prime Minister would get his dissolution.

In such an example as the Slim-Menzies dissolution of 1955, in practical terms the vice-regal power is exercised, but discretion though present is barely engaged and the dissolution is therefore far less significant for demonstrating the reality of vice-regal discretion than the example I chose. Evatt's view was that there is no room for exercise of a discretion in such a situation. This may be a semantic question but I believe there is notional room.

When dealing with the Prime Minister's advice that there should be dissolution in late 1977 I had well in mind the facts of 1955. I had studied them carefully before I received Mr Fraser's letter of 26 October since I assumed the 1955 precedent would be referred to and relied upon in any advice for a December election.

No doubt Prime Minister Menzies and Sir William Slim had the usual frank talks about what the Prime Minister was advising. Sir William's approach to that advice would undoubtedly have been that in considering it he should do so not so much from the point of view of whether there were reasons for accepting it, but rather from the point of view of whether there were any reasons for rejecting it. This would be the classic view and in the absence of good reasons for rejection the Governor-General should accept it. In 1955 it is inconceivable that Sir William Slim did not realise that the advice tendered would result in a clear political advantage being gained by the Prime Minister and his parties. But this would be no justification for rejecting the advice and I am sure that Sir William would not have regarded it as a justification. If Mr Menzies were, in choosing his date for an advised dissolution, seeking a political advantage the Governor-General of the time would, I have no doubt, have adopted the view that the Australian electors would be as much aware of this as anyone else, and if they firmly objected they would be able to register this at the polls. In fact they did not. Mr Menzies gained a real victory. My own view was, and is, that Sir William acted in an entirely constitutional manner and if, being conscious of any political advantage likely to be gained by Mr Menzies he ignored this, he acted with absolute constitutional propriety.

My analysis of the 1955 case was in my mind when considering Mr Fraser's 1977 advice. As to any alleged political advantage which Mr Fraser might gain from an early election my impression at the time was that he was having great difficulty in deciding whether he wanted to go to the people in December 1977 or not. The election as we now know produced a landslide result in his favour, but this was certainly not predicted in October 1977 or at any time up to the elections. The press widely canvassed the possibility of Mr Fraser's defeat over the early period of the campaign, and not long before polling day some were still using such expressions as 'Government expected to limp home'.

There had been sporadic revival over the months before 26 October 1977 of the claim that my Indian address was inconsistent with the proper granting of an early dissolution. The point from my text that was quoted in support was:

> The essential question is whether the Governor-General can be satisfied that Parliament has in fact become unworkable.

Professor Sawer amply commented on this in his *Canberra Times* article of 6 July 1977. He made clear, first that I was discussing only one example of circumstances warranting dissolution. He wrote:

> I would have thought that the precedents raise no doubt at all about the ability of a government to call for a general election at any time during the last six months of its normal existence, and probably earlier.
>
> However, assuming that this part of the 'reserve power' does come into existence at any time short of, or almost up to, the three-year period, then Sir John appeared to lay down a very severe general test for granting the dissolution—namely 'whether that Parliament has in fact become unworkable'.
>
> I think, however, that both he and Sir Paul Hasluck in his similar remarks had in mind the sort of parliamentary impasse caused by three-party situations, or close division between major parties with 'floating' independents, or by party splits . . . [Examples followed.]
>
> It is only in such situations that the Governor-General can reasonably reject advice to dissolve, in order to try out the possibility that another leader can obtain a majority to support him: if the

alternative leader fails to do so then the one who first advised a dissolution is entitled to be put back in office and granted a dissolution, as Sir Dallas Brookes did during the McDonald-Hollway saraband in Victoria in 1952.

Professor Sawer went further, and demonstrated that even in the simple and clear-cut cases (of which 1955 and 1977 are examples) where a Prime Minister is *not* in difficulty with his party or the Parliament, such a Prime Minister could easily make Parliament unworkable if he had to.

In the same article he wrote:

> If Mr Fraser did call for a general election next May [the same reasoning applies to December] it would not be in Sir John Kerr's phrase 'simply to help a party leader, or a party to solve their own difficulties': it would be to bring half-Senate elections once again into line with Reps elections. To do this is Fraser Government policy, endorsed by the Labor Party and by 62 per cent of the electorate.

In such a clear-cut constitutional situation as 1977 I should have thought no question as to the propriety of granting dissolution could seriously be raised. Furthermore, I think it very likely that had I refused it, in circumstances where it should so clearly be granted, there would have been an immediate outcry to the effect that some irrational urge further to exercise the vice-regal powers was driving me to absurdly erroneous decisions. A critical outburst would have been justified in relation to the dissolution only if I had refused it.

There had, in the preceding months, occasionally been floated the theory that I might be seduced into refusing the dissolution in the hope that this in some mysterious way would serve as proof of my impartiality as between the political parties. Of course it is never a proof of impartiality to deprive someone of something to which he is entitled. Such seeking after a spurious appearance of impartiality would be guaranteed to produce severe, and legitimate, criticism.

It could be said to be bad luck for me that for the second time a decision that I must make called for action which, in the result, would prove to be to the advantage of the coalition parties. It was only by the merest chance that I and not my successor had to make this decision. It was not until 26 October, on the very eve of my retirement, that I knew — and presumably that Mr Fraser decided — that dissolution would be advised to produce a December election.

Mr Fraser did not discuss with me directly or indirectly his political calculations in relation to the 1977 elections, but my impression at the time was that he believed he was taking a very real political risk rather than gaining a clear political advantage. Hindsight of course shows that the mind of the electors was much firmer than appeared from opinion polls and the press, and the political advantage was considerable as things turned out. If before advising an election Mr Fraser's political decision was, and I do not know whether it was, that it was better to gamble on a perhaps narrow victory and avoid fighting an election in the expected economic climate of 1978, that was a political decision for him to make and was irrelevant to my decision to grant him a dissolution. His entitlement to a dissolution was so clear that when it came to the point I unhesitatingly granted it. This is what undoubtedly would have happened in similar circumstances in Great Britain.

25

Winter in Auvergne;
the Unesco Appointment

When my wife and I left Australia on 10 December 1977 the strongest drive operating in me was to write. We had decided to move, after a period in Europe, to London, sending some of our furniture and other household and personal effects by sea. In London I was to have an office, and the Australian High Commission would seek temporary living accommodation to enable us to look at leisure at the question of the longer term. We kept our home in Australia since we intend in due course to return there.

I left feeling that there had been a strong movement back to normal politics and that I had rounded off, as well as I could, my period in office. I felt no regrets about anything, was sure I had done the right things and was not unhappy to move into an unknown future. Despite the calumny and defamation from which I had suffered I was secure in my own conscience and not bitter. I knew that what I had had to do on 11 November had brought to finality an immediate crisis, induced by hard-fought politics in the Parliament, in such a way that the careers of a number of people had, substantially as a result of their own policies, been most adversely affected. I had never been involved myself in any emotional way and never committed to either of the particular political interests in conflict. I was committed only to my responsibility as Governor-General to uphold the Constitution. It afforded me no personal satisfaction whatsoever that a number of careers had suffered a setback. On the contrary, I could understand and indeed, as I have said, expected the intense initial reaction; but it was clear that what had happened had followed implacably upon party policies pursued and I

416

believed that, privately at least, most people were capable of sufficient objectivity to recognise it.

I heard the results of the 1977 election in Hong Kong late on 10 December and was greatly surprised, as I know many people were, by the sweeping nature of the Government's victory.

It was our intention to travel slowly to London, arriving there after our household gear would have arrived by ship. I planned to have a short holiday followed by a period of undisturbed writing. It was my aim to write a book, mainly about my Governor-Generalship but with autobiographical content, and I carried a collection of documents and books, including such records, notes, tapescripts and other material as I could conveniently put together and carry. Writing started immediately but we reserved time too for relaxation outdoors.

We moved from Hong Kong to Zürich, and after a stay there to a beautiful village high in the Austrian Tyrol, where we spent Christmas and New Year. The mountain snow scenery with its grandeur and silence brought both calm and stimulation, and my writing proceeded daily at a satisfactory pace. We travelled by train through the Bavarian Alps to Munich and during this and other trips continued to be lifted out of the past by the majestic mountains of the Alpine landscape.

From Austria we moved to a charming French village in the Auvergne mountains, to the house of friends who welcomed us there before returning to their home in London. It was a winter of continuous snow in Auvergne. This kept us substantially and warmly at home, with work advancing daily. The village — we are still there as this is written — is very small and a true French mountain village. It is horseshoe-shaped, in a sheltered hollow, with its steepled church built of lava blocks, as are most of the houses. No shops, almost no telephones. Provisions are brought by visiting tradesmen who arrive with meat and fish, bread baked over charcoal in big country ovens, groceries, fruit and vegetables, farm eggs, guinea-fowl and chickens and a rich variety of fresh French cheeses. Each tradesman comes at a known time, and the villagers do their marketing and gossiping at the trucks, to which we are summoned by the sounding horn. These quickly convert to small stores as awnings are flung forward, sheltering customers from the snow. The village is very much as it always was. Some of the older people still speak the ancient French language, the *langue d'oc*. This language is now being studied at a provincial university not far away, and a good friend of ours in the village helped to provide conversation courses in *langue d'oc*, which was the first and childhood language of his parents. On one occasion we heard him conversing in *langue d'oc* with the shepherd, whom we met heading off to the pastures with the village flock. My wife realising they were not talking French asked about the language and was fascinated to learn that the *langue d'oc* of her early philological studies is still spoken as a living language, though few can speak it now.

The shepherd summons the sheep from the cottages by blowing on a horn—an imposing ancient instrument bound in silver—just as has been done in the villages for centuries. It is a musical and haunting sound on the snowy air.

During our stay here we had a week of contrast visiting friends in Morocco. It was a week of friendship and sociability, sightseeing and shopping in the souks, with intervals of leisurely writing in a tropical garden. I bought a warm woollen djellabah to wear in the mountains when writing and was nicknamed *le bourgeois de Fez*.

We made a couple of private visits to Paris from our village. Much of our travel after Zürich was done by rail. We had Eurail tickets and enjoyed the train journeys, as both of us have done since earliest childhood. We also had a short journey to Brussels before our Eurail tickets expired.

There was one somewhat dramatic interruption to our quiet life—a legacy from my period as Governor-General. I refer to the offer to me of appointment as Australian Ambassador to Unesco.

Early in February, with the help of our Paris embassy, Canberra tracked me to our village. In practice this meant that a small girl arrived in the early morning with a telephone message (messages could be received through the village café whose efficient *patronne* contrived to transcribe them although having little English) asking that I should ring a senior official in Canberra.

We muffled ourselves as usual in hunting-coats and other snow-defeating gear belonging to our hosts and made the requested call.

I was asked whether I would accept the post of Australian Ambassador to Unesco. This would mean living in Paris, with duties beginning in March. I was told that the conditions of my appointment including matters of salary and pension would be the same as those that applied to ambassadors who had formerly been Ministers, coming to diplomacy by the political path.

My wife and I gave the question as careful consideration as we could in our isolation — we had deliberately chosen to live where we should be as little disturbed by outside contact as possible. While I had hoped that in due course Australia might have some worthwhile work for me to do, it had not occurred to me that anything would happen so soon or so suddenly. There had been speculation in the press before I left Australia about whether I might be offered an ambassadorship and among several possible futures I was seriously interested in that avenue. Coming to me in the latter stages of our tranquil isolated working holiday the Government's offer confronted us with the unexpected choice of abandoning our flexible London plans and staying in France for three years.

I knew that to take this appointment on a full-time basis would exclude me, no doubt for its duration, from other activities which were important to me. They included in particular the publication of these memoirs, the writing of which was well advanced when I received the Unesco offer. Plans to spend some time in London would have to be abandoned, perhaps permanently.

I knew also that I was being asked to re-establish a full-time embassy to Unesco. I knew there would be some who would claim this was a sinecure. But a glance at my record in community and international activities should reveal that I have been energetic and I hope useful in most things I have undertaken. Mr Whitlam established the Unesco post, Mr Fraser expressed a wish for Australia's activity with Unesco to assume more importance. Unesco is one of the great specialised agencies of the United Nations. Even the short time I soon afterwards spent in Paris, having decided to accept the appointment, in looking at Unesco background material showed me among the wide range of its activities many where Australia's interest could be real and valuable, and my mind was beginning to range constructively about them. In our relations with the third world in particular — an area which had deeply interested me during my involvement in the South Pacific territories, Papua New Guinea and Asia — it seemed to me the Unesco embassy could play a positive role.

I did not believe any job would be a sinecure in my hands, and I supposed my activity would shortly convince critics this was so. Had it turned out, indeed, not to be possible as ambassador to develop full-time worthwhile activity I would not have stayed — at my stage of life the last thing I wanted was the boredom of a sinecure. This book may help people to judge how, over a lifetime, I have tackled an undertaking, and whether it has been in the spirit of avoiding or disliking or being incapable of effective work.

Although to accept would mean giving up plans for London (where our furniture and effects had by now been unshipped) the notion of living in Paris was very attractive both to my wife and to me. The new Australian embassy building where we would be living is well sited by the Seine close to the heart of Paris. My life had offered me a wide variety of international experience: the international character of the environment I would be entering had strong appeal for me.

Being asked to give my answer promptly, I decided I would accept the appointment, abandoning the visit to London and early publication of my writings.

In the mountains we were largely cut off from news. When radio conditions were good we listened to the BBC and Radio Geneva or Paris, and to Radio Auvergne for local news and the state of the snow; Radio Australia news summary came to us by mail, and that was all. So it was not until I reached Paris at the end of February that I learned in detail of criticisms of my appointment by the Australian media, and in particular heard with stunned disbelief of the allegations made in Parliament by members of the Australian Labor Party.

I had not yet taken up office, though I was within a few hours of doing so, when I learned of that attack.

When I had been called upon after 11 November 1975 to endure vilification I had done so because I was then engaged in a fight which had to be won and only I could fight it. It had to be proved that a Governor-General who had properly exercised the reserve power could not be driven from office by such methods.

But was I willing to engage in another war against this petty malice merely for the sake of the personal satisfaction which would come to me from the work of the ambassadorship? Once again my wife would be involved, and my family and friends. Work could be impeded by continued attempts at persecution; and once again I should be obliged by my official position to put up with it in silence.

A deciding factor in my instant reaction to the situation was the knowledge that as ambassador I should again be unable to answer my critics and dispose of their errors and falsifications. I had been under much pressure to write this book. It was nearing completion. I felt at once a very powerful impulse to free myself from any obligation to withhold publication. Those who cannot live with the truth will not read it. But those who want to can find out the truth by reading this work through and learning why as Governor-General I was bound to act as I did, and what sort of man I am.

I have always led an independent life. The motto in my coat of arms is Independence Under Law. By this I have lived. When I realised on emerging from my isolation how uninformed or how malevolent were certain reactions in Australia I realised that this appointment was not one which in the circumstances I wanted. It was an act of independence to reject the embassy. Early on 1 March, in Paris, I wrote in the following terms to the Prime Minister:

My dear Prime Minister,
    I have become aware since arriving in Paris of the attacks that have been made upon me and upon the government as a result of my appointment as Australian Ambassador to UNESCO. These attacks have been made in the Parliament, under parliamentary privilege,

by members of the opposition parties; and they have also been made in various branches of the media.

I am bound to say that the virulence of these attacks and their unfairness has shocked me. I have to contemplate serving in this appointment in the face of them, and possibly—perhaps likely—their continuation. There is no doubt that in these circumstances my ability successfully to undertake the work of Ambassador to UNESCO would be severely impaired. For most of the time I should be absent from Australia and, holding an ambassadorial appointment, be unable to reply in the way I would wish, and to overcome them as I believe I did during my term as Governor-General.

Beyond this, I have had to consider whether the purpose that led me to leave the Governor-Generalship earlier than the normal term will be defeated if controversy over this new appointment continues. As you know, I felt that by leaving the office of Governor-General when I did there would be an opportunity for remaining wounds to heal and controversy to die down. The importance of the Governor-Generalship and its protection stand high in my objectives. My consideration of these matters has led me to the conclusion that I should ask to be relieved from taking the post of Australian Ambassador to UNESCO, in which I would have begun duty today. I believe there is too much at risk, greatly as the position would have attracted me personally and much as I feel I would have been able to contribute to Australia's interests with UNESCO.

There is a further reason which concerns me in the decision I now make. That is the feelings of my wife and family, who with me have had to withstand vilification and attack for part of my term as Governor-General, and now in prospect through a term as Ambassador to UNESCO. They, with many others, have stood by me without question through all that has happened. I am not prepared to demand more of them. I am not prepared to subject them to this further trial by innuendo and falsehood, even though my personal instinct is to stand firm and make certain once again that this tactic of persecution fails.

Prime Minister, I trust that you will understand the considerations that have led me to this decision. I appreciate the support I have had from the government and your desire to allow me to continue to serve Australia in public office. My decision however is made. It is with sadness and regret that I inform you of it.

Yours sincerely,
(John Kerr)

The Prime Minister in informing the House on 2 March made the following comments:

On 14th July, 1977, Sir John Kerr announced his intention to relinquish the office of Governor-General. He made his decision because he believed that the events of 1975 and the position into which he had been forced while serving as Governor-General of Australia had left some scars on the Australian body politic, which would be more quickly healed if he stepped down. Sir John protected the Australian people and Parliament according to the law, according to the Constitution and according to his duty as Governor-General.

The attempt of the Labor Government to stay in power in defiance of Parliament compelled his proper and inevitable dismissal of that Government. An Executive governing without the sanction of the Parliament is the hallmark, not of a democracy, but of a dictatorship. His difficult decision gave the people the opportunity to vote and upheld the parliamentary system. The people of Australia passed their clear judgment on these events and Sir John's actions in the election of 1975. History will judge them just as clearly. It will support the actions Sir John Kerr was compelled to take in the extraordinary circumstances in which the Government of the day so reprehensibly placed him.

Australia, as a nation of free people, owes as much to the courage of Sir John Kerr as to any man in our history. If he had not acted as he did, had he not prevented the unconstitutional designs of the last Government being consummated the shape of Australian democracy would have been twisted and distorted. Sir John's action was opposed by a hostile and bitter minority. Division was caused by the statements of the then Leader of the Opposition, by Senator James McClelland and other members of the Labor Party who sought to make the Governor-General a scapegoat for their own actions. Because of this unjustified bitterness, the office of the Governor-General became a matter of national controversy. Sir John recognised this—we all did.

He believed he could best serve Australia by standing aside, by allowing another to serve as Governor-General. This he did. His action was applauded. I believe his action was right, that it contributed to our nation's healing process—to a return to normalcy.

In this Parliament two days ago, I drew attention to Sir John's

423

long and notable career of public service, and to the fact that both as Chief Justice of the Supreme Court of New South Wales and as Governor-General, he would have been able to devote more of his life to serving Australia had not most unusual events intervened.

At the time of Sir John's resignation, he said he looked towards new fields of constructive activity. It was clear that he still wished to serve this country in some other capacity where he could serve energetically but out of the public gaze. Recognizing Sir John's desire to continue serving Australia, I after consultation with my senior colleagues, offered him on behalf of the Government the opportunity to do so. This became possible after the Minister for Foreign Affairs wrote to me on 1 February, advising that in his judgment the Australian diplomatic posts at Los Angeles, Bombay and Unesco should be re-opened. As a result of that advice from the Minister for Foreign Affairs and after consultation with my colleagues, the Government decided to offer Sir John Kerr the post of Ambassador to Unesco.

The Government took this step in the firm belief that Sir John Kerr would fill the post with honour and as ably as any man available from within or without the public service. The Government believed that having served this nation honourably, Sir John should not be cast aside, relegated to the shadows, simply because he was forced by the Government of the day to make a difficult decision. The Government believed that he had earned the right to serve the nation quietly, at peace with himself, at peace with the nation—at peace with his family.

There were people in this community who were determined that this should not be so. Since his appointment as Ambassador to Unesco, the attacks on him in the Parliament and attacks outside it have been renewed. Sir John Kerr, once having discharged his duty to the nation under the most difficult circumstances, has no wish to continue as the centre of public dispute, making it impossible for him and his family to live the normal life to which we are all entitled.

An Ambassador at Unesco trying to carry out his functions under these conditions would find it impossible to discharge the responsibilities of his office.

Mr Speaker, I inform the House that I have today received a message from His Excellency Sir John Kerr who was today to have commenced duty as Australian Ambassador to Unesco. Sir John has informed me that with great regret he feels he cannot take up this post.

(Mr Fraser then read the text of my letter of 1 March.)

I can only deplore the actions that led to this decision. The bitterness of the attack, especially in another Chamber, since Sir John left the protection of the office of Governor-General, has shown that the Labor Party still blame him, when in logic and in justice, they should be blaming themselves.

They are still seeking to find a scapegoat for their own misdeeds. The A.L.P.'s refusal to allow Sir John to serve his country in peace has been despicable: their actions and statements on this matter have served only to discredit themselves.

There have been some who have sought to confuse the high purpose of this man with the remuneration he would have received in his new post. If this is to be a point of principle, then it should equally have been applied to appointments such as that of Senator Murphy to the High Court, Mr Barnard to an Ambassadorship.

The principle of taking a full salary while retaining their pension was established by the previous Labor Government. It is plain that this itself is not the major matter of dispute.

If there are others who believe Sir John's actions in 1975 to have been proper and necessary, but who now want to pass him by, who want to forget he ever existed and deny him the possibility of service: I only ask them to ask themselves how much justice, how much fairness there is in that view.

By his decision, Sir John Kerr leaves public life. A long and distinguished public career is thus ended. I respect his decision. I cannot argue with it.

To be an Ambassador, constantly pilloried, constantly in the public glare, who had his family placed under intolerable stress, was something he did not want: he deserved better.

I feel shame for those events which led to this decision. I expected less meanness, more generosity and more understanding of a person who only wanted to serve his nation. I can only hope that all Australians will now show Sir John the decency and respect in his retirement that his great integrity and courage in public office have earned him.

Sir John Kerr can hold his head high as he leaves the public arena he has served so faithfully and well.

My wife and I did not return at once to our village after my decision to reject the appointment, not wishing its peace to be put at risk by possible intrusions on our privacy. Instead we turned towards a medieval city of southern France, the great historic events of whose past presently made my own burdens seem more trivial. We walked among its soaring architecture and watched the apricot light of the south fall across the austerity of its stone. It was a period of great beauty in spite of some fatigue of spirit.

Back in the mountains, I set out to reply to the attacks made on account of the Unesco appointment, dealing first with lesser criticisms and passing on to accusations of a very serious kind.

There was criticism, as I had foreseen, on the ground that the office of ambassador to Unesco (indeed of any ambassador, according to some writers) is a sinecure. Earlier I have discounted the idea that any office I undertook would be a sinecure in my hands. Here I add that there is, I think, a certain mentality which readily views any desirable post occupied by someone else as a sinecure. The office of Governor-General was described by some as a sinecure when I entered upon it. The word *sinecure* means 'without care'. Some sinecure.

I should add that the Unesco post has now been filled by a distinguished microbiologist who presumably, on the basis of his knowledge and experience, does not believe it to be a sinecure. Unesco deals with scientific matters in which he is an expert. I am an experienced lawyer with a wide range of social interests. Unesco also deals with important legal and social questions. No one can by direct training be an expert in the whole range of scientific, educational and cultural matters with which Unesco deals. The professional diplomat, too, cannot be a universal expert. Some criticised my appointment upon the ground that I did not have the qualifications to perform the duties of the office. This would appear to assume at least that the office was not a sinecure. It can hardly be immodest if I say that I believe I could have done what the position requires, as assuredly the distinguished professor of science who will be in the post will be able to do.

There was criticism also on the ground that a Governor-General should not, after retirement, engage in further work for the Government — 'on the apparent view', as a young friend wrote to me, 'that viceroys should so time their tenure as to have

426

entered dotage when that tenure expires'. Heavy criticism centred also on the fact that I would receive my pension earned as Governor-General in addition to my income as ambassador. Here I point out further that the very Labor Party now attacking me, in 1974 introduced legislation which assumed it was proper that a Governor-General should keep his pension if he undertook work for Australia, or any other work, after retirement from his office, as was the position with retired Ministers.

The law governed the conditions offered me. The same conditions applied to several other ambassadors. Why should it be for me, alone of all those benefiting by them, to question or reject those conditions?

Some people have said that it would have been better for me to offer to suspend my pension or take the appointment without salary. Although this would seem an unfair discrimination between me and others in a similar position I would, I think, have been ready to consider one or the other had the matter come up for discussion. But because of the accepted practice this does not seem to have occurred to anyone before the great outburst. It did not occur to me. Looking back on it now I realise that my reaction was so much one of repugnance that I did not consider alternatives to simple rejection; and I am glad, now, that I have had the freedom to write.

Fantastically blown-up accounts were given of the conditions I would enjoy, and astronomic figures quoted as to my future income. In fact, the conditions offered were routinely those applying to Australian diplomatic posts around the world. There were the representational and post allowances which operate in a principled way for all such posts in order to enable a diplomatic job to be done. The total of pension and salary I would receive amounted to much less than a capable Queen's Counsel could earn and very far less than the effective remuneration of a Governor-General. Had it been money that interested me I had merely to remain at Yarralumla. There I should have enjoyed too the continued protection given the Governor-General by the Standing Orders of both Houses against calumny and defamation in the Parliament. I had apparently overestimated the Labor Party in imagining that, my action in dismissing their

Government from office having twice been politically ratified by the Australian people, they would at last accept that verdict and cease their petty and unfair attacks.

I will refer now to the most serious of the allegations made against me by the Labor Party—the infamous allegation of venality.

A number of Labor members were involved in this. It was surprising and shocking to me to see the new leader of the Labor Party Mr Hayden, instead of maintaining what he said had previously been his policy of not making personal accusations against the Governor-General, join in the attack, and do so in the extreme way illustrated by his words to Parliament:

> The appointment of Sir John Kerr as Ambassador to the United Nations Educational Scientific and Cultural Organisation in Paris is not just an indecent exercise of the rankest cynicism. It is, in every respect, an affront to this country. More than that, it is a further demonstration of the degree by which the high office of Governor-General has been abused by the former incumbent for personal gain and manipulated by the Prime Minister (Mr Malcolm Fraser) for political advantage.
>
> The matter of Sir John Kerr's actions in November 1975 has been an issue of the most divisive political debate in the Australian community. More recently, his acquiescence to the Prime Minister's demand for an unnecessary election a full year before it was due similarly created widespread controversy. This latest appointment can do nothing but confirm the views of those who believe Sir John acted with gross impropriety in each case. The dimension that is added to the debate is that he did so—certainly in the most recent instance—for his 30 pieces of silver.[1]

A third reason for my being 'rewarded' was alleged by others to have been my resignation from the Governor-Generalship.

It is incomprehensible to me that Mr Hayden, the new leader, could speak as he did.

To those who adduced these 'reasons' for 'rewarding' me I say this.

(1) As to the dismissal of Mr Whitlam: this whole book bears witness to the necessity and good faith of my action. To suggest

428

that I would have assumed such a burden if it could have been avoided is grotesque.

(2) As to the grant of dissolution in 1977: the constitutional principles governing that grant and all the circumstances surrounding it are set out in Chapter 24. They are set out in detail to show how indefensible would be the claim that I was doing even something erroneous. I have said in that chapter that I have no doubt dissolution would have been granted in similar circumstances in Great Britain. In Australia, the operation of our Constitution and the precedents of our history led inevitably to its granting. I know of no statement by any constitutional authority that has challenged its correctness.

(3) As to my resignation as Governor-General: the true account of all the circumstances of that resignation is given in Chapter 23. History will confirm its truth when the time comes for the related documents to be published. And what sense does it make to say that the Unesco appointment would *reward* me for leaving the Governor-Generalship?

It is a truly disgraceful thing that the former Governor-General of Australia, a member of Her Majesty's Privy Council, formerly Chief Justice of his State, for years a federal judge, should be accused of having venally bargained with a political leader to dismiss a Government, place him in power, later resign from the Governor-Generalship, and before actually leaving — presumably as some sort of final encore — grant him improperly a dissolution of the House of Representatives.

And all for the sake of being 'rewarded' with a minor diplomatic posting. Taking the great sweep of politics I would have to be the most incompetent seeker after corrupt rewards in history.

It is astounding to me that any responsible person should associate himself with an allegation at once so base and so far-fetched. It is also deeply disturbing that any Australian should accept or wonder about or entertain the idea that the Governor-General would negotiate for or expect or take a reward for doing his duty, or that the Prime Minister would conspire with him or offer him a reward for doing that duty.

I repudiate the allegation as being entirely inconsistent with

429

my character, my long public career in Australia, my whole life and philosophy of life. There is no spark of truth in it.

A person who makes such an allegation defames himself. It is he who has to live with what he has said, not I.

Moreover some who in no way believe I committed any dishonest act apparently think that I should be debarred from putting such talents as I have at the service of my country, simply because there are others who falsely allege that I did.

It would surely seem unfair and indeed absurd that I alone of all the participants in the 1975 crisis should be excluded from further work for Australia simply on the ground that to allow this might lead to an unjustified suspicion that I am being 'rewarded'.

There is a far bigger issue which should be of serious concern to all Australians. I believe that it is grossly irresponsible of the Labor Party to say to the world that the Governor-General of Australia in a great constitutional crisis such as we had in 1975, and later in relation to the 1977 dissolution, acted corruptly or in conspiracy. It is a terrible thing to do to the country to say to the world that it is capable of producing and permitting such a situation.

I have been selected for high office in many national institutions and for high public office by both sides in politics. And now it has been said that the person selected as Chief Justice of New South Wales and Lieutenant-Governor of that State by the Liberal-Country Party coalition, and for the office of Governor-General by Mr Whitlam as leader of the Labor Party, is guilty of corruption and of high constitutional conspiracy. What an appalling state of affairs it depicts as the Australian condition.

How false and distorted a picture it paints, of me and of the country I have served.

26

Reflections

One evening in November 1976 I was in the Chief Petty Officers' mess on board the aircraft-carrier HMAS *Melbourne*. My wife and I were spending a couple of days at sea, watching air and sea exercises and celebrating the ship's twenty-first birthday. It was a magnificent short voyage. We arrived on board by helicopter in heavy grey mist and rain, and woke to brilliant blue skies and windswept decks. The drink in the mess with the Chiefs was an informal affair, and one of them asked me a question. He said, 'Sir, you may not be willing to answer this one but I shall ask it, if you don't mind, in case you are. Looking back on it all, do you think that if you had known what was going to happen you would still have given up being Chief Justice and taken on being Governor-General?'

I said, 'I shall answer it as well as I can. May I put it this way. If I had known in advance that there would be a great constitutional crisis during my term, that would not have deterred me from accepting the commission. Of course, I did not know . . .'

Had I not accepted the office my life since 1974 would have been very different. Yet looking at everything that has happened I must say that I would do it all again. I have no regrets about being where I was in a great constitutional crisis of essential importance to my country. I am glad and indeed proud that I was where I was in 1975 and that I had the knowledge, experience and will to do in my lonely office what needed to be done.

Earlier I have said something of my general philosophy of life.[1] It has never been my way to seek a routine, repetitive life with

431

each day following the last in a predictable fashion. Certainty about the future has never been attainable by or attractive to me. The sweep of a lifetime with its depressions, wars and recoveries, its economic and political crises, its opportunities and its buffeting brings great chances and great choices. My Governor-Generalship was a climax for which life, with its pattern of experiences, had been preparing me, though I never could have anticipated that I would come to such a point. Perhaps I can say that at the critical time I felt able to call upon reserves which were the product of my life up to that time, and which both guided me towards what had to be done and fortified me in the doing of it. These reserves fortify me still.

That I accepted responsibility for my decision of November 1975 does not mean, however, that any responsibility rests on me for the crisis itself—for the tough unyielding political confrontation of 1975. It seems to me woolly-minded to the point of unreason to assert that it does. The decision to deny supply was a political decision, made not by me but by the Senate and the then Opposition. The decision to govern without supply was a political decision made not by me but by the then Prime Minister and Government. The resulting constitutional crisis was dealt with by me by getting the issue to the people, who resolved it. I am still surprised occasionally to find people of some mental stature saying that the Governor-General 'put Mr Fraser where he is' or some such phrase.[2] The Australian people put Mr Fraser and the coalition in office in 1975; and in 1977, long after the agitation and stress of that crisis had subsided, just as firmly put them back again.

But the Labor Party, rather than face up to its share of responsibility, sought a scapegoat. The lot fell to me. It would have been political suicide for Labor members in active politics to boycott their conservative opponents: they had to debate and meet from day to day with the political group with which they had been locked in conflict. The boycott, the resort to a scapegoat, were phenomena directed against me without regard to fairness or logic.

Professor Francis West on 9 April 1976, concluded his Notes on the News by saying:

What is disturbing about the present situation is not that government will as a result become unstable — for that has not, nor is likely to happen, no more than it did when the Victorian Upper House rejected supply in 1947. Indeed Victorian government became notably stable, as may, for the next nine years at least, be federal government. The disturbing thing is the repetition, by senior Labor party members, of statements they know or could easily ascertain to be untrue as a weapon of politics. It is very hard to avoid the conclusion, on the public and available evidence, that the Governor-General is being made a scapegoat for Mr Whitlam's political misjudgments.

But this does not reflect upon the health of the nation. The Australian people as a whole have no need for such an escape from reality.

It is well known that in the west today many people are worried about the brittle quality of the basic consensus on which society rests. Laws are defied by persons who organise themselves for the purpose and who are not prepared to accept legal punishment as a consequence of their illegal acts. This defiance of the law is aimed at making it difficult to administer its punitive processes. To what extent has such a breakdown of consensus occurred in Australia? Does it threaten? What indications are there that as a result of the events of 1975–7 Australia has suffered or is about to suffer a consensual breakdown or serious weakening or instability?

Professor R. S. Parker, Professor of Political Science at the Australian National University, in his 'Thoughts on the Constitutional Crisis'[3], wrote:

I am not outraged. I do not think the future of parliamentary government in this country is at stake. I do not believe the Governor-General has 'defamed the very basis of the Constitution'. I do not think that either the Labor Party or the Liberal and Country Parties have been trying to subvert democracy with dastardly plots. I find it particularly hard to see that calling a general election for both houses of parliament is an attack on democracy . . .

The constitutional text-books are studded with similar cases of governments and oppositions jockeying for power by manipulating parliamentary procedures and conventions — or ignoring them —

and of Governors and Governors-General using their reserve powers in ways that were bitterly criticised by one or other of the contesting parties and superciliously questioned later by scholars and pundits. But seen in a perspective these crises have left scarcely a ripple on the stream of our history and scarcely a mark on the main institutions of our government. Is this crisis any different? I am not sure.

Of course, the question must be asked: was the 1975 crisis any different from those mentioned by the professors? Will it be found, as time passes, to have left damaging marks on the main institutions of our government? Will it be seen to have been a factor of significance in inducing or increasing instability or fragility in the consensus on which those institutions rest?

In a sense our institutions, not being embalmed unchanging in history, are being marked all the time by the unfolding of events. This is an evolutionary process which far from indicating fragility may well show their resilience. The real question is: have those institutions, and the acceptance by Australians of the rules upon which they depend, been weakened, undermined, made more brittle and readier for collapse by the events of October–November 1975? Has the Australian people, or significant groups within the people, as a result of 1975 ceased to accept the customary social rules? Have we begun so to question or discard them as to weaken the political system?

In expressing opinions on these big questions one can be confounded by events. If one looks for answers in terms of Australian common sense, self-discipline, social conservatism, reluctance to accept fundamental constitutional change; if one finds it hard to see signs of Australians in general ceasing to believe in the customary concepts of Australian democracy; if in taking the long view one has a belief that rage dies and institutions outlive temporary emotional phenomena, one could be proved wrong if our Australian house were in fact to fall down around our ears or were seen to have become a wobbly structure likely to fall under pressure.

In truth I have faith in Australian social stability. Whatever may be the state of affairs elsewhere, I see heartening signs that testing circumstances have served to reveal not the weakness of our national consensus but its strength. There are groups in any society who do not embrace the principles on which its political system rests. We have had protests on a number of issues in Australia, especially in recent years, and protest has sometimes been accompanied by confrontation with the forces of law and order. If this went too far we should have a dangerous anarchic element in society, and if society's basic rules were widely and violently challenged the result could be to weaken the consensus which underpins the constitutional apparatus. In my view this tendency, taken in its broad national context, has not gone to any threatening lengths in Australia.

There are undoubtedly groups in our society having a militant revolutionary ideology which seek to weaken the nation and its economy and which engage in protests and demonstrations on many policy issues having nothing to do with constitutional matters. I have no doubt they also protested and demonstrated on recent constitutional issues. One has to be wary about such groups and they have a not insignificant nuisance value; we need to bear in mind the situation in many western countries and to be vigilant and not indifferent to them and their doings. Legitimate protest groups whose aims are peaceful can find themselves penetrated by, and unwittingly giving a cloak of legitimacy to those whose private aims are violent and subversive of social stability. But I see no signs that the Australian people are allowing them to bring our structure down around us.

Ordinary political and constitutional debate, even when it is ill-informed or poorly reasoned — or irrational or abusive, as it sometimes regrettably is — does not in itself undermine or threaten the structure and supports of society. Rather it expresses its democratic robustness. I do not regard argument about actions and decisions of mine, even irrational and uninformed argument on false premises, as undermining our national consensus, but rather the reverse, when taken against the background of the successive electoral judgments.

The constitutional debate, in so far as it consists of argument in good faith engaged in on an intellectual and not a hysterical emotional level and using words not as emotive jargon but as the valuable means of achieving clear thought, helps to strengthen

435

our consensus, our willingness to abide by broadly accepted rules. Peaceful protest as I have said can be useful; but violence is the negation of rational debate and of progress in one's thinking. Rage is a destructive emotion which had it spread widely might well have eaten into the foundations of our national structure. The Australian people did not allow this to happen. *Les enragés* are, I think, a temporary phenomenon.

Until now I had not participated in the debate. But I no longer feel that silence of mine on all these matters can achieve any calming purpose, and I accordingly publish this book. If it is argued that its publication will keep old issues alive, I say simply that those who wish to keep them alive will, on my recent experience, work at stirring the pot whatever I do. The country has nothing further to gain from my silence. On the contrary I regard it as necessary in the public interest to speak out now.[4]

People will continue to write and argue. There has already been an outpouring of books and articles and other comment on the events of 1975–7. Some learned studies have appeared. Many writings have shown little constitutional knowledge, little attempt to check fact. Others are based on greater knowledge but marred by ideological bias. Dr Butler, when commenting in his introduction to *Labor and the Constitution 1972–1975* on the strong bias of most lawyers who took part in that seminar[5], referred to the 'still more political perspective' to be reached from the 'instant history-writing which the affair produced in paperback'. Nonetheless, far from the discussion damaging our institutional stability there has, I detect, been evidence of a growing desire in the population to understand what happened constitutionally. The vitality of debate is an excellent thing.

One element in the argument has centred on the role of the Governor-General in Australia. Some have said my decision and action will be treated as a precedent, ratified by the Australian people at the elections and putting the Governor-General in a more active and responsible position than he had been thought to occupy. Does argument about this threaten the stability of our institutions? We must surely be able to discuss what sort of powers the Governor-General should have without imperilling the firmness of our foundations — provided, of course, that any change argued for is to be achieved democratically and that the argument does not itself incite revolutionary violence.

At a critical point in our history our written Constitution with our constitutional usages, which are at the heart of our national consensus, operated; our electoral processes, ratifying politically what had been done constitutionally, operated: our democratic processes operated. Our consensus is a federalist consensus — a factor which tends to be obscured by use of the phrase 'national consensus' — and our federal processes operated. All of this was repeated in 1977. Lord Home in his address at the thanks-giving service for Sir Robert Menzies in Westminster Abbey spoke of Sir Robert's belief in 'the self-disciplined society accepting the responsibility for preserving the basic individual freedoms'. Anyone surveying our national scene must be impressed by the quiet self-discipline of the millions of Australians who were not distracted from normal consensual politics by attempts to create deep splits in their society that would prevent it from working according to its accepted principles.

One comment still heard quite often is that the events of 1975 have made us an excessively polarised community, split seriously on political lines; and that the office of Governor-General has been brought to the forefront in this highly polarised political strife. The bitterness of the political division at the time of the confrontation, and its association, on a superficial view of events, with the vice-regal office were real and serious. But the causes must be sought in the tough politics of the second half of 1975 as played by the political parties. That the result has been some kind of sick weakness in the body politic I do not believe. If it has, two doses of ordinary electoral medicine seem to have done a lot to mitigate the trouble.

I do not regard Australian society as abnormally divided in any socially dangerous way. Of course we have political divisions — we should be a very strange democracy if we did not. My feeling is that most Australians on both sides of politics were profoundly uneasy as the 1975 confrontation, with its 're-volutionary possibilities',[6] built up, and heaved a deep sigh of relief that its dangers had been avoided. Remaining divisions do not cut deep into vital social tissue. Most people can now see that

437

Australians, whatever their politics, for the most part want what has been the normal political system to go on working; they positively want stability and not a threatening cleavage in society.

A significant point about 1975 is that we were confronted by the prospect of a disaster which did not occur. The very real dangers that threatened were avoided at the last moment. In the result it is now difficult to remember how truly threatening that crisis was. We can remember terrible tragedies, depressions and wars which actually happened but it is harder to remember crises which would have been disastrous *had they happened*. The blade may pass within a millimetre, but we will not remember it, because it did not strike. It now requires a positive act of imagination as well as of memory to appreciate how frightening the crisis would have been had things gone really wrong in 1975. The ultimate reason why our stability *was not* undermined is that the disaster *was not allowed to happen*.

The time since I left office has been one of great spiritual refreshment. The revelation, at the time of my appointment to Unesco, of enmity persisting was distressing at the time but has receded from my mind. Reflecting on the more sombre side of the events of my Governor-Generalship I am reminded of what I wrote earlier of my perception of life:

> Even the most stressful circumstances, the most agonising and lonely moments, the most difficult decisions have had their creative aspects in their effect upon my life. Certainly I have experienced evil and suffering and destructive forces at work over the years but at the same time and in relation to the same circumstances I have also generally experienced love and support. Even when lonely in one or other aspect of life I have never felt that I was alone.[7]

I have spoken here and there in this book of the warmth that has always come to me from contacts with the Australian people and from my strong sense of identity *as an Australian*. I have been a very lucky Australian. Life has enabled me to see a great deal of the wide, variegated country that is mine and that I love. It is the variety of Australia that underwrites its federalism and gives promise for its future. If we look forward over the great sweep of future years, imagining an Australian population of fifty million, our rich resources developed and great States prospering in the north and west as well as in the south and south-east, it cannot be supposed that the whole vast country, spread out over such distances, would accept to be dominated and run from one central point. Such States will have emerged within the freedom of federalism and will want to keep that structure.

It has been argued that the crisis of 1975 provided a victory for federalism over responsible government, as if these two concepts were incompatible. This I do not believe. We in Australia have found a means to enable the principles of responsible government to express themselves both within the States, and at national level within a federal structure. They flourish today, as always since responsible government was introduced in our country. Sir Kenneth Wheare remarked: 'An important difference between the Australian and the British constitutions is . . . that the former establishes a federal system and not only a federal system but also a federal system *combined* with responsible cabinet government.'[8]

One has only to watch the flow of politics over the decades in Australia to see Governments being formed and exercising their powers according to the pattern of responsible government but within a system of checks and balances which is our federalism. Lord Hailsham wrote recently:

> Alienation begins to appear in all large conglomerates of human beings which are run from the centre. Some form of devolution, federalism, call it what you will, seems to be necessary in all branches of human activity. There is depersonalization in all large-scale human activities for which a heavy price in terms of human relationships has to be paid.

We are lucky in Australia that we have our constitutional matrix within which over the years the political philosophy of diversity within unity can grow.

Epilogue

To be asked to write an epilogue to Sir John Kerr's book was an honour I could not refuse. For the book gives us not only a thorough, detailed account of what actually took place in the Australian crisis of 1975, but is also a masterly and definitive statement, amply supported by authorities, of the principles which governed Sir John's action, and which should govern the actions of the representatives of the Crown in other countries of the Commonwealth.

Because of my own experience of a Canadian constitutional crisis involving a very dissimilar reserve power of the Crown (refusal of dissolution), and because of the immense importance for all the Queen's realms of the issue at stake in Australia, I followed intently, from the first, the course of events which culminated in the dismissal of Mr Whitlam and the double dissolution of the Australian Parliament. Canadian newspaper accounts were, of course, necessarily very incomplete. But I had the advantage of further information from the Canadian Department of External Affairs and from the Australian High Commission in Ottawa; and I was exceptionally fortunate in having at my elbow Mr Graham Eglington, LL.M., an able Australian-born and Australian-trained constitutional lawyer. Almost from the beginning, therefore, I was able to rely on a massive collection of documents and a clear explanation of certain special features of the Australian Constitution which might otherwise have been obscure to me.

Never for a moment did I doubt the correctness of the action Sir John took. For the life of me, I could not see, and still cannot see, what else he could have done in the circumstances. The constitutional right of the Senate to refuse, or defer, supply, seems to me incontestable. Perhaps it should never have been given that right. But it was; and the result of its exercise of that right, and of Mr Whitlam's response to that exercise, was that, but for Sir John's action, the Government of Australia would have been left for some months with no funds to meet some 40 per cent of its expenses, except by the use of measures of very doubtful legal validity and even more doubtful effectiveness.

The duty of a Prime Minister denied supply by an Upper House is either to resign, or to advise a dissolution of the Lower House. Mr Whitlam declined to do either.

He could have resigned; whereupon the Governor-General would have had to call on Mr Fraser to form a Government, which, being manifestly unable to secure a majority in the House of Representatives, would have had to put the supply Bill through the Senate and then ask for a dissolution of the House, which could not have been refused.

Or he could have asked for a dissolution of the Lower House, as Asquith did when faced with a similar situation in Britain in 1910; and, again, the request could not have been refused.

Thanks to the peculiar provisions of the Australian Constitution, Mr Whitlam had a third choice open to him, a choice which would not be available to a Canadian Prime Minister, nor to a British in the days before the Parliament Act deprived the House of Lords of its power to veto money Bills. He could have asked for a double dissolution, for which the necessary legal conditions precedent already existed in ample measure. Had he done so, the Senate would undoubtedly have passed the supply Bill, and the electors would have decided whether Mr Whitlam should remain in office, with a clear mandate to carry out his policies, or whether he should give place to Mr Fraser.

If he had followed any one of these three courses, and had won the election, the Senate would not have dared hold up a fresh supply Bill; and if it had persistently obstructed his other legislation, the obstruction could have been overcome by using the devices provided by the Constitution for overcoming a deadlock. No question of the Crown's reserve powers would have arisen. The Governor-General would have had no reason not to follow the advice of his Ministers in the normal way, and the electorate would have settled the question in the normal way.

Mr Whitlam's refusal either to resign, or to advise a dissolution (single or double), was a flagrant breach of the principles of responsible government. It would, on his own and his Ministers' showing, have led to 'utter financial chaos', 'a major economic collapse', and severe hardship for 'the suppliers of goods and services to the Government and the suppliers of goods and services to people who serve the needs of government, community agencies, States and overseas governments', no pay for the armed services. The only way to prevent this was a dissolution, preferably a double dissolution. Only the people could settle the question. Mr Whitlam was refusing to let them do so. It then became the plain, indeed the inescapable, duty of the Governor-General to give them the opportunity which Mr Whitlam would have denied them.

There, it seems to me, are the bare bones of the matter. The Governor-General alone could preserve the rights of the people of Australia; and he did his duty.

I do not think it can be denied that the Crown and its representatives have, in strict law, the power to dismiss a Government. I do not think it can be successfully argued that, by November 1975, this prerogative had been so long unused that, like the power to create life peers (as decided in the Wensleydale case) or to give borough seats in the House of Commons, it had lapsed. Like the power to refuse a dissolution of Parliament, it remains, as one of the 'reserve' powers which, in very exceptional circumstances, the Crown and its representatives can exercise without, or against, the advice of the Ministers in office; provided always, of course, that they can find other Ministers prepared to accept responsibility for their action. In this Australian case, Sir John Kerr had to find a Ministry prepared to advise the double dissolution which was plainly the best way of enabling the people to deal effectively with the situation. This he had no difficulty in doing.

Some question has arisen as to whether Sir John's action did or did not involve a 'forced' dissolution; and Mr M. H. Byers, Q.C.,

442

has quoted me (with a slight typographical error) to support the argument that the 'rarity' of forced dissolutions 'and the long years since their exercise cast the gravest doubt upon the present existence of that prerogative'. I had, at one point, defined a 'true' forced dissolution as one following a dismissal of Ministers because they had refused to advise a dissolution desired by the Crown or its representative in order to put to the test a Government policy with which the Crown or Governor disagreed, had noted that there appeared to have been only one, anywhere in the Empire or Commonwealth, since 1855, and that the power to force a dissolution would now 'never be used as a means of bringing about some positive end desired by the King himself or his representative'. I had contrasted with the 'true' forced dissolution the fairly numerous cases, ranging from 1807 to 1932, where Governments were dismissed 'for quite other reasons' than their refusal to advise a dissolution, and 'dissolutions were granted to their successors because they could not hope to carry on government with the existing Lower House'. Rather confusingly, I had then called these latter also 'forced dissolutions', and had stated plainly that they would nowadays 'take place only if the Crown considers them necessary to protect the Constitution or to ensure that major changes in the economic structure of society shall take place only by the deliberate will of the people' (this last was in the heyday of British socialism). 'In other words', I had added, 'the power . . . is now likely to be used only negatively, preventively', and had gone on to give hypothetical examples.

Sir John makes it perfectly clear that his action in dismissing Mr Whitlam's Government had nothing whatever to do with its general policies, or any desire on his part to force Mr Whitlam to submit them to the people. The dissolution he granted was certainly not a 'forced' dissolution in the sense of being one where he insisted on an election with the aim or in the hope of getting the electors to turn down Government policies with which he disagreed, and dismissed the Government for that purpose. It certainly was, however, a 'forced' dissolution in the sense that a Government which insisted on governing without supply had to be dismissed, with the inevitable consequence of a dissolution granted to its successor; and I can only repeat my conviction that it was constitutionally correct, necessary and inescapable.

Sir John himself has dealt so thoroughly with this matter that my comments are perhaps otiose. None the less, because Mr Byers had directly quoted me, I feel it necessary to make it perfectly clear that his interpretation of my views was incorrect and irrelevant.

I have only to add my earnest hope that Sir John's book will be 'read, marked, learned and inwardly digested' by public men and constitutional scholars not only in Australia but throughout the Commonwealth, wherever genuine parliamentary government prevails, and will serve to dissipate whatever vestiges remain of the dangerous and subversive rubber stamp theory of the powers of the Crown and its representatives.

Eugene Forsey

Appendix

Papers and Articles by John Kerr include the following publications:

1958   'Re-opening the Orr case' (with J. H. Wootten) in *The Free Spirit*, v. 4, no. 10, August 1958: 3–15.

         'A rejoinder' (with J. H. Wootten) in *The Free Spirit*, v. 4, no. 11, September–October 1958: 13–23.

         'The political future' in *New Guinea and Australia*, Sydney, Angus and Robertson, 1958.

1960   'The struggle against Communism in the trade unions — the legal aspect' in *Quadrant*, September 1960: 27–41.

1961   'An Australian view — an elite and target dates' in *New Guinea* . . . a series of lectures given in September 1961 to the N.S.W. Branch of the Australian Institute of International Affairs. Sydney, Anglican Press, 1962.

         'Trade unions and industrial relations in Australian New Guinea' in *Journal of Industrial Relations*, vol. 3, no. 1, April 1961: 17–31.

         'A new labour policy for New Guinea' in *Journal of Industrial Relations*, vol. 3, no. 2, October 1961, p. 148–150.

         'Procedures in general wage cases in the Commonwealth Arbitration Commission' in *Journal of Industrial Relations*, vol. 3, no. 2, October 1961: 81–91.

1963   'Centralising tendencies in industrial arbitration' in *Federal Public Service Journal*, (Melbourne), new series, v. 43, November 1963: 16–21.

1964   'Higher education in New Guinea' in *Australian Outlook*, v. 18, December 1963: 266–277.

'Human rights in Asia and the Far East' in *Hemisphere*, vol. 8, December 1964: 8–12.

'Industrial relations, 1963–1964' in *Journal of Industrial Relations*, v. 7, July 1965: 112–130.

'Modern approach to legal aid' in *Australian Lawyer*, v. 5, November 1964: 172–174.

'Work value' in *Journal of Industrial Relations*, v. 6, March 1964: 1–19.

1965   'Uniformity in the Law—Trends and Techniques'. The Robert Garran Memorial Oration delivered to the Australian Regional Groups, Royal Institute of Public Administration at Canberra, 11 November 1964. Canberra 1975.

'Changing White Australia: controlled immigration?' in *New Guinea and Australia, the Pacific and South East Asia*, v. 1, June–July 1965: 31–36.

'Industrial relations 1964–1965' in *Journal of Industrial Relations*, v. 7, July 1965: 112–130.

'The Future Pattern (of the legal profession)' in *Commonwealth and Empire Law Conference Record Sydney* 1965: 693–703.

'Reflections on the third Commonwealth and Empire Law Conference' in *Law Council Newsletter*, v. 1, October 1965: 1–3.

'The rule of law and the role of the lawyer' in *University of Western Australia Law Review*, v. 7, June 1965: 71–87.

1966   'The Australian commitment in New Guinea' by Harold F. Bell. (Includes discussion by J. R. Kerr) in *Economic Papers*, no. 21, March 1966: 31–53.

1967   Report of the Inaugural Conference of the Law Association for Asia and the Western Pacific. Law Book Co. 1967: VII–XVI.

1968   'Australia's role in New Guinea's development'. Paper presented at H.R.H. The Duke of Edinburgh's Third Commonwealth Study Conference, Melbourne 1968.

'Law in Papua and New Guinea' (19th Roy Milne Memorial Lecture) Australian Institute of International Affairs, 1968.

1969   'Wanted a constitution: before it is too late' in *New Guinea and Australia, the Pacific and Southeast Asia*, v. 4, September/October 1969: 19–30.

1971   'A constitutional suggestion'. Paper presented at the Council
        on New Guinea Affairs Seminar at the University of Papua
        and New Guinea, Port Moresby 30–31 May 1970 in *New
        Guinea and Australia, the Pacific and South East Asia*, January
        1971.

        Australia. Administrative Review Committee. *Report*
        Canberra Government Printer 1971.

        Australia. Committee of Inquiry into Financial Terms and
        Conditions of service for Male and Female Members of the
        Regular Armed Forces. *Report*. Canberra. Government
        Printer 1971.

        Australia. Inquiry into the Salaries and Allowances of
        Members of the Commonwealth Parliament. *Report*.
        Canberra, Australian Government Publishing Service 1971.

        'A constitutional suggestion: mixing the systems' in *New
        Guinea and Australia, the Pacific and South East Asia*, v. 5,
        December 1970—January 1971: 51–61.

1972   '757th anniversary of Magna Carta' in *Justice* no. 5,
        September 1972: 53–57.

        'Bureaucracy and Society' in *Who Runs Australia?*,
        (Proceedings of 38th summer school of Australian Institute of
        Political Science), Sydney 1972.

1973   'Legal studies and the university' in *University News*
        (Macquarie University), no. 60, June 1973: 8–11.

        'New approach by our courts' in *The Sydney Morning Herald*,
        23 October 1973: 7.

        'The role of science in industrial conflict and dispute
        settlement: industrial harmony or conflict' in *Australian
        Journal of Forensic Sciences*, v. 5, March–June 1973: 115–119.

1974   'Modern problems of judicial administration: address' in
        Australian Law Journal, v. 48, March 1974: 116–117.

        'The modern task of judicial administration in New South
        Wales' in *Journal of the Australian Regional Groups of the Royal
        Institute of Public Administration*, September 1974.

        'Renewing the law' in *The Sydney Law Review*, vol. 7, no. 2,
        September 1974: 157–165.

        'The ethics of public office'. Robert Garran Memorial
        Oration delivered to the Australian Regional Groups, Royal

447

Institute of Public Administration at Canberra, 11 November 1974. Canberra 1974.

1975 'The Governor-Generalship in Australia' in *Journal of the Indian Law Institute*, v. 17, no. 1, January–March 1975: 1–7.

1976 Oration delivered at the Inaugural Dinner of the Australian Association of the Sovereign and Military Order of Malta, Sydney, November 1976.

Notes and Sources

2—Appointment as Governor-General
1. John Burney, Sydney *Daily Telegraph*, 3 March 1978.
2. H. V. Evatt, *The King and his Dominion Governors*, Frank Cass and Company, 1936, p. xxxv.
3. For a fuller discussion of the reserve powers see in particular Chapters 4, 5, 6 and 14.
4. I feel free to outline the circumstances of my appointment because they have been publicly discussed, often on the basis of inaccurate data. An example is Graham Freudenberg's *A Certain Grandeur*, Macmillan, 1977, pp. 366 *et seq*. Mr Freudenberg was special adviser to Mr Whitlam throughout his Prime Ministership.
5. See J. R. Kerr, *The Ethics of Public Office*, Garran Oration 1975.
6. For an examination of this problem in the United States see the article 'The Role of the Chief Judge in a Modern System of Justice' in the *Record* of the Association of the Bar of the City of New York, vol. 28, no. 5, April 1973, pp. 291 *et seq*.
7. For those interested in the nature of problems of judicial administration and its reform in New South Wales during my tenure of office reference may be made to my writings of the period, published then or early in my Governor-Generalship. See for example: J. R. Kerr, 'Modern Problems of Judicial Administration', in *Australian Law Journal*, vol. 48, Mar. 1974, pp. 116–7. J. R. Kerr, 'The Modern Task of Judicial Administration in New South Wales', in *Journal of the Australian Regional Groups* of the Royal Institute of Public Administration, Sept. 1974. J. R. Kerr, 'Renewing the Law', in *The Sydney Law Review*, vol. 7, p. 157.
8. Further reference to my Chief Justiceship is to be found in Chapter 13.
9. Freudenberg, p. 367.
10. Similarly when I left office in 1977 the salary was adjusted for the benefit of my successor.
11. Mr Freudenberg, in what is to me a particularly objectionable

intrusion into matters of which he could have no knowledge, alleges (p. 368) that I told Mr Whitlam one of the reasons for both my hesitation and my final acceptance was the critical health of my wife. He states that she was terminally ill and that I told Mr Whitlam at that time that she was desperately ill. Both are untrue. When I accepted the office she was well, and fully occupied with her professional work and in family and social life. She became seriously ill at Easter 1974, after my appointment had been announced.

12. I had long known, and my reading in late 1973 reminded me, that the vice-regal office not only was one held at pleasure but could be a warmish seat in times of constitutional crisis.

13. Graham Freudenberg (p. 369) says that Mr Whitlam 'was negligent—with hindsight culpably so—in never having opened up with Kerr in any profound way Kerr's view of the constitutional role of the Governor-General'. It is true at all events that he did not.

14. Mr Freudenberg (p. 370) says that the initiative in this matter came from me after I accepted office and that Mr Whitlam encouraged this approach, 'with qualifications'. This is quite erroneous. The facts are as I have said. I did, after entering upon the new role, take up the Prime Minister's idea of 'showing the flag', which appealed to me, as it was no doubt intended to do.

15. See Chapter 15.
16. *Parliamentary Debates*, vol. H. of R. 88, p. 1048.
17. *Parliamentary Debates*, vol. H. of R. 88, p. 1054.
18. *Parliamentary Debates*, vol. H. of R. 88, pp. 1110–11.

3—Childhood and Youth—School, University and Early Post-graduate Life
1. Somerset Maugham, *Of Human Bondage*, Penguin Books, p. 523.

4—Evatt and the Reserve Powers
1. H. V. Evatt, *The King and his Dominion Governors*, p. xxxv. This passage from Sir Kenneth Bailey was quoted by the learned and authoritative constitutional theorist Sir Kenneth Wheare when commenting in January 1978 on the events of 1975: see Chapter 23.
2. Evatt, p. xxxv.
3. Evatt, p. xxxvii.
4. Evatt, p. xxxviii.
5. See Chapter 5.
6. See p. 62.
7. Evatt, p. xv.
8. Evatt, pp. xv–xvi.

9. See Chapter 11 and my article 'Wanted a Constitution—before it is too late' in the journal *New Guinea* of Sept–Oct 1969.
10. Evatt, p. 286.
11. Evatt, pp. 115–6.
12. Evatt, p. 286.
13. Evatt, p. 72.
14. Evatt, p. 72.
15. Evatt, p. 78.
16. See Chapter 17.
17. Evatt, p. 80.
18. Evatt, p. 83.
19. Evatt, p. 89.
20. Evatt, pp. 288–9.
21. Evatt, p. 200.
22. Evatt, p. 199.
23. Evatt, p. 200.
24. I faced the dilemma in 1975. My reasons for dismissing Mr Whitlam before he had an opportunity to have me dismissed appear in Chapters 20–22.
25. Evatt, p. 299.
26. Evatt, p. 300.
27. Evatt, pp. 304–5.
28. Evatt, p. 268.
29. *Journal of Comparative Legislation*, November 1934, p. 292, quoted by Evatt, p. 305.
30. Evatt, p. 305.
31. The opinions of the last three Chief Justices of Australia as to the powers of the Crown, i.e. the Governor-General, are relied upon by me in this book. Sir Owen Dixon is quoted on p. 394 and Sir Garfield Barwick on pp. 341 *et seq.* The combined period in office of these three Chief Justices is from the thirties until the present time.
32. J. G. Latham, *Australia and the British Commonwealth*, pp. 65–6, in Evatt, p. 306.
33. Evatt, p. 311.
34. See Chapter 22, p. 374.
35. Evatt, p. 306.
36. Geoffrey Sawer, *Federation Under Strain*, Melbourne University Press, 1977, p. 154.
37. Sawer, pp. 154–5. The 1952 Victorian case is discussed in Chapter 9.

5—The Game-Lang Crisis
1. John Manning Ward, 'The Dismissal' in *Jack Lang*, ed. Radi and Spearritt, Hale and Iremonger Pty Ltd, Sydney, 1977, p. 164.

2. H. V. Evatt, *The King and his Dominion Governors*, p. 163.
3. Evatt, p. 164.
4. Evatt, p. 164.
5. Evatt, p. 168.
6. Evatt, p. 173.
7. Evatt, p. 174.
8. Evatt, p. 171.
9. John Manning Ward, in *Jack Lang*, ed. Radi and Spearritt, p. 160.
10. See Chapter 14, p. 213.
11. Mr Menzies' letter is quoted on pp. 81–2.
12. Geoffrey Sawer, *Federation Under Strain*, p. 164.
13. Ward, p. 174.
14. Ward, p. 161.
15. Bethia Foott, *Dismissal of a Premier*, Morgan Publishers, Sydney, 1968.
16. See Chapters 4 and 14.
17. Evatt, p. 151.
18. Evatt, p. 104.
19. Evatt, p. 165.
20. Evatt, p. 166.
21. Evatt, p. 172.
22. *Parliamentary Debates*, vol. H. of R. 97, p. 2108.
23. Mr Whitlam's reply, *Parliamentary Debates*, vol. H. of R. 97, p. 2108 *et seq.*

6—Evatt and Outside Advice
1. *Canadian Bar Review*, vol. xviii, no. 1.
2. John Manning Ward, in *Jack Lang*, ed. Radi and Spearritt, p. 168.
3. H. V. Evatt, *The King and his Dominion Governors*, p. 43.
4. Evatt, p. 44.
5. Evatt, p. 49.
6. *Canadian Bar Review*, vol. xviii, pp. 4–5.
7. *Canadian Bar Review*, p. 5.
8. *Canadian Bar Review*, p. 5.
9. *Canadian Bar Review*, p. 6.
10. *Canadian Bar Review*, p. 7.
11. See Chapter 9.
12. *Canadian Bar Review*, p. 7.
13. *Canadian Bar Review*, p. 9.

9—Post-war Supply Crises; Double Dissolution 1951; Labor Endorsement for Lowe

1. Parliament of Tasmania, *Votes and Proceedings of the House of Assembly*, 1948, no. 36.
2. For an examination of the Senate's power to deny supply see Chapter 19.
3. Parliament of Tasmania, *Votes and Proceedings of the House of Assembly*, 1948, no. 22.
4. Parliament of the Commonwealth of Australia, 1957, no. 6: Documents relating to the 1951 Dissolution.
5. See Chapter 6.
6. H. V. Evatt, *The King and his Dominion Governors*, p. xxv.
7. Evatt, p. xxv.
8. *Parliamentary Debates*, vol. H. of R. 10, p. 2451.

10—The Great Labor Split of 1954–5; the 1955 Dissolution
1. *Sydney Morning Herald*, 4 and 9 November 1950.
2. A *cause célèbre* in Australian academic circles: see Chapter 12, pp. 175–6.
3. For a further discussion of this question see Chapter 24.

11—Return to New Guinea Interests
1. See Appendix.
2. See Appendix.
3. *New Guinea*, Sept.–Oct, 1969, pp. 24–5.

12—Crowded Years
1. *Quadrant*, January 1976.
2. See pp. 183 *et seq.*

13—Judicial Life
1. The Administrative Review Council was established under my committee's recommendations.
2. *Australian Law Journal*, vol. 51, no. 12, December 1977, p. 804.
3. *Australian Law Journal*, p. 811.
4. *Sydney Morning Herald*, 1 April 1972.
5. *National Times*, 3–8 April 1972.
6. J. M. Bennett, *Portraits of the Chief Justices*, John Ferguson, Sydney, 1977, p. 61. The original portraits hang in the Supreme Court.

14—Forsey—the Power of Dismissal and Forced Dissolution; the Rubber Stamp Theory
1. Oxford University Press.
2. Introduction to Evatt, pp. xviii-xix.
3. McClelland and Stewart Limited, Toronto, 1974.
4. See Chapter 25.

5. *Australian Law Journal*, vol. 50, 24 November 1975, pp. 273–90. See also Chapter 19.
6. *Globe and Mail*, 24 November 1975.
7. See Chapter 18, pp. 301 *et seq.*
8. E. Forsey, *Freedom and Order*, p. 1.
9. *Freedom and Order*, p. 2.
10. *Freedom and Order*, pp. 16–18.
11. *Freedom and Order*, p. viii.
12. E. Forsey, *The Royal Power of Dissolution of Parliament*, foreword by J. A. R. Marriott, pp. ix–xi.
13. Forsey, p. 270.
14. Forsey, p. 46.
15. Forsey, p. 46.
16. Forsey, p. 71.
17. Forsey, p. 3.
18. Forsey, p. 7.
19. See Chapter 21, pp. 337 *et seq.*
20. Forsey, p. 104.
21. Forsey, p. 122.
22. *Freedom and Order*, p. 34.
23. *Freedom and Order*, p. 35.
24. *Freedom and Order*, pp. 37–8.
25. *Freedom and Order*, p. 48.
26. *Freedom and Order*, pp. 48–9.
27. *Freedom and Order*, pp. 87–8.
28. *Freedom and Order*, pp. 89–90.
29. *Freedom and Order*, p. 30.
30. See Chapter 9, p. 137 *et seq.*

15—The Loan Affair and Justiciable Issues
1. G. Sawer, *Federation Under Strain*, p. 98.
2. Sawer, p. 98.
3. Sawer, p. 102.
4. Sawer, p. 102.
5. Sawer, pp. 102–3.
6. Sawer, p. 103.
7. *Parliamentary Debates*, Senate Weekly Hansard, no. 12, 1975, p. 2620.
8. Sawer, p. 74.
9. Sawer, p. 75.
10. Sawer, p. 164.
11. See Chapter 17, p. 260.

16—July to October 1975
1. A fifth edition of Mr Odger's work appeared as Parliamentary

Paper No. 1, 1976, Commonwealth Government Printer, Canberra, 1977.

2. Alan Reid in his book *The Whitlam Venture* (Hill of Content, Melbourne 1976, pp. 268–70) refers to this incident, saying that it 'pointed to Whitlam having in mind even at that early stage that the confrontation between the Senate and the House of Representatives could reach a point at which the question of his sacking would have to come under gubernatorial consideration'. Reid says; 'Subsequent to Whitlam's dismissal, the rationalisation was that it never entered Whitlam's mind that the Governor-General might withdraw his commission as Prime Minister in the event of Australia being threatened with economic chaos by the Senate's rejection of Supply. If that was so, Whitlam's tongue was shaping words for which his mind took no responsibility.'

Whitlam was later reported, says Reid, as telling associates that it was meant as humor. But 'on the reports which Tun Abdul Razak gave later to his staff and diplomatic associates, Tun Abdul Razak was mildly astonished'. The Malaysian Prime Minister, Reid comments, had never before heard a conversation like this between a prime minister and the person occupying an office similar to that of the Governor-General. Reid goes on: 'If the reports which circulated through Canberra's diplomatic community at the time were correct, Tun Abdul Razak's intuition was not astray. The reports gave Tun Abdul Razak as observing that though Whitlam's contribution to the conversation might on the surface be intended as humour there was an undertone of real threat and that Tun Abdul Razak would not be surprised if in certain circumstances the humour vanished and was replaced by seriousness.'

David Butler also mentions that 'there were well-publicised stories of his speaking jokingly to visitors about how in a crunch it would be a race to the telephone between the Governor-General and himself to see which could dismiss the other first'. (*Current Affairs Bulletin*, 1 March 1976, '20 questions left by Remembrance Day'.)

17—The Deferral of Supply

1. *Parliamentary Debates*, vol. S. 66, pp. 1221 and 1241.
2. *Parliamentary Debates*, vol. H. of R. 97, p. 2199.
3. *Parliamentary Debates*, vol. H. of R. 97, p. 2103.
4. *Parliamentary Debates*, vol. H. of R. 97, p. 2104.
5. *Parliamentary Debates*, vol. H. of R. 97, p. 2104.
6. *Parliamentary Debates*, vol. H. of R. 97, p. 2105.
7. See Chapter 5, pp. 74 *et seq.*
8. See Chapter 16, p. 254.

9. See pp. 288–9.
10. Quoted by Evatt, *The King and his Dominion Governors*, p. 78.
11. See pp. 270–1.
12. See Chapter 18, p. 302 *et seq.*
13. See Chapter 19, p. 313.
14. Published in leading newspapers throughout Australia on 22 October 1975.
15. *Parliamentary Debates*, vol. H. of R. 97, p. 2200.
16. *Parliamentary Debates*, vol. H. of R. 97, p. 2201.
17. *Parliamentary Debates*, vol. H. of R. 97, p. 2203.
18. *Parliamentary Debates*, vol. H. of R. 97, pp. 2205–6.
19. *Parliamentary Debates*, vol. H. of R. 97, pp. 2295–6.
20. *Parliamentary Debates*, vol. H. of R. 97, p. 2299.
21. *Parliamentary Debates*, vol. H. of R. 97, p. 2307.
22. *Parliamentary Debates*, vol. H. of R. 97, p. 2308.
23. *Parliamentary Debates*, vol. H. of R. 97, p. 2309.
24. *Parliamentary Debates*, vol. H. of R. 97, p. 2310.
25. *Parliamentary Debates*, vol. H. of R. 97, p. 2311.
26. *Parliamentary Debates*, vol. H. of R. 97, p. 2316.
27. Alan Reid, *The Whitlam Venture*, p. 374.
28. *Parliamentary Debates*, p. 2325.
29. *Parliamentary Debates*, p. 2414.
30. *Parliamentary Debates*, p. 2419.
31. *Parliamentary Debates*, pp. 2522–3.
32. *Parliamentary Debates*, p. 2524.
33. *Parliamentary Debates*, p. 2527.
34. Julius Stone, 'Why Not a Moratorium?' *Sydney Morning Herald*, 21 October 1975.
35. See Chapter 5, p. 76 *et seq.*
36. See Chapter 18, p. 291.

18—The Week Before
1. *Parliamentary Debates*, vol. H. of R. 97, p. 2723.
2. *Parliamentary Debates*, pp. 2720 *et seq.*
3. *Parliamentary Debates*, p. 2725.
4. *Parliamentary Debates*, p. 2726.
5. *Parliamentary Debates*, p. 2833.
6. *Parliamentary Debates*, pp. 2833–4.
7. *Parliamentary Debates*, p. 2835.
8. *Parliamentary Debates*, p. 2835.
9. *Parliamentary Debates*, pp. 2835–6.
10. *Parliamentary Debates*, p. 2837.
11. See Chapter 16, p. 252.
12. See Chapter 22, p. 364.
13. Regional Employment Development Scheme.

14. *Parliamentary Debates*, vol. H. of R., 2 March 1978, p. 350.
15. See pp. 324 *et seq.* for further discussion of the banking scheme.
16. Mr Byers no doubt meant to write: New Brunswick in 1856.
17. See pp. 213 *et seq.*
18. See Chapter 19, pp. 312–21.
19. See Chapters 4 and 14.
20. See Chapter 16, pp. 246–7.
21. See Chapter 16, p. 258.
22. See Chapter 17, p. 263.
23. See p. 292.
24. The results which would have flowed from dismissal of the Governor-General in the circumstance of the crisis are discussed in Chapter 20, pp. 329 *et seq.*
25. See also Chapter 23, p. 384.
26. The programme, 'Face the Press'; reproduced in Australia on 'This Day Tonight', 20 July 1976.

19—Supply—Power to Deny, Responsibility to Obtain
1. See Chapter 4, pp. 54 *et seq.*
2. *Australian Law Journal*, vol. 50, no. 6, June 1976, pp. 273–90.
3. *The Parliamentarian*, January 1976, p. 4.
4. G. Sawer, *Federation Under Strain*, p. 117.
5. Sawer, p. 127.
6. Sawer, p. 128.
7. (1975) 134 CLR 81.
8. 134 CLR 81, p. 121.
9. 134 CLR 81, p. 143.
10. 134 CLR 81, p. 168.
11. 134 CLR 81, p. 185.
12. *Parliamentary Debates*, vol. H. of R. 97, p. 2701.
13. *Australian Law Journal*, vol. 50, no. 6, June 1976, pp. 273–90.
14. See Chapter 16, p. 246.
15. See Chapter 16, p. 252.
16. *Parliamentary Debates*, vol. H. of R. 68, pp. 3495–6.
17. *Parliamentary Debates*, vol. H. of R. 69, p. 463.
18. *Parliamentary Debates*, vol. S. 44, p. 2647.
19. On the point that the Government is not a committee of the Parliament but the Queen's Government see Chapter 14, p. 221.
20. Section 61 of the Constitution.
21. Section 64 of the Constitution.
22. Sawer, pp. 215–6.
23. Sawer, pp. 213–4.
24. Sawer, p. 217.
25. Sawer, p. 212.
26. *The Economist*, 15 November 1975.

20—The Queen and November the Eleventh
1. See Chapter 22, pp. 374–5.
2. See Chapter 4.
3. Appendix to *The King and his Dominion* Governors, p. 311.
4. Evatt, p. xxxviii.
5. G. Sawer, *Federation Under Strain*, p. 147.

21—Final Thoughts
1. Professor West is Dean of Social Science and Professor of History and Government at Deakin University, Geelong.
2. *The Australian Quarterly*, vol. 48, no. 2, June 1976, pp. 53–5.
3. For comments on my alleged 'deceiving' of Mr Whitlam and his Ministers see Chapter 18, pp. 308–9.
4. G. Sawer, *Federation Under Strain*, pp. 163–4.
5. See Chapter 22, pp. 369 *et seq.*
6. Sawer, p. 143.
7. See Chapter 22, pp. 369 *et seq.*
8. Sawer, pp. 59–60.
9. Sawer, p. 60.
10. Sawer, p. 61.
11. *The Parliamentarian*, January 1976, p. 10.
12. *The Parliamentarian*, p. 11.
13. A. Reid, *The Whitlam Venture*, p. 413.
14. *The Australian Quarterly*, vol. 48, no. 2, June 1976, p. 57.
15. *The Australian Quarterly*, p. 58.
16. *The Parliamentarian*, January 1978, p. 67.
17. *The Parliamentarian*, p. 68.

22—November the Eleventh
1. *Parliamentary Debates*, vol. H. of R. 97, pp. 2917–21.
2. Quoted by David Butler, '20 Questions left by Remembrance Day', *Current Affairs Bulletin*, 1 March 1976.
3. G. Sawer, *Federation Under Strain*, p. 142.
4. For a discussion of some moves which might perhaps have been made by the Labor Party in the Senate and the House see J. R. Odgers, *Australian Senate Practice*, Fifth Edition 1976, pp. 69–70.
5. See Chapter 18, pp. 302 *et seq.*
6. See Chapter 1, p. 4.
7. *The Parliamentarian*, January 1976, p. 11.

23—The Aftermath
1. *Current Affairs Bulletin*, 1 March 1976, '20 Questions left by Remembrance Day'.
2. See Chapter 18, pp. 308–9.
3. *The Parliamentarian*, January 1978, pp. 66–70.

4. Gareth Evans ed. *Labor and the Constitution 1972–1975*, Heinemann Educational Books Ltd, 1977. Mr Evans is now a Labor senator.
5. *The Parliamentarian*, p. 70.
6. *Labor and the Constitution 1972–1975*, U.K. edition, p. xix.
7. *The Parliamentarian*, p. 66.
8. *Sydney Morning Herald*, report from Mr Peter Bowers in London.
9. My repudiation and opinion on the suggestion of venality implied in the term can be found in Chapter 25, pp. 428–30.
10. *Labor and the Constitution 1972–1975*, p. 327.
11. *Labor and the Constitution 1972–1975*, p. 321.
12. See Wright v McQualter, 1970, 17 Federal Law Reports, p. 320.
13. *National Times*, 8–13 November 1976.
14. *Labor and the Constitution 1972–1975*, introduction by Dr David Butler, pp. xviii–xix.
15. *The Parliamentarian*, p. 69.
16. *The Parliamentarian*, p. 354.
17. Sir Owen Dixon, 'Government under the American Constitution', (1944) in *Jesting Pilate*, Melbourne, 1965, p. 107.
18. See also Chapter 4, pp. 54–5.
19. *The Parliamentarian*, p. 70.
20. See Chapters 11 and 12.
21. See Chapter 25.

24—The 1977 Dissolution of the House of Representatives
1. See pp. 154 *et seq.*
2. *Canberra Times*, 6 July 1976.
3. *Journal of the Indian Law Institute*, vol. 17, January–March 1975, no. 1, p. 1.
4. H. V. Evatt, 'The Discretionary Authority of the Dominion Governors', *Canadian Bar Review*, vol. XVIII, p. 1.
5. Evatt, p. 2.
6. See Chapter 9, pp. 130 *et seq.*

25—Winter in Auvergne; the Unesco Appointment
1. *Parliamentary Debates*, H. of R., 28 February 1978, p. 207. For my comment on the 'Judas' reference see Chapter 23, p. 386.

26—Reflections
1. Chapter 3, pp. 46 *et seq.*
2. Sir Kenneth Wheare has commented pithily on this point: see pp. 393–5.
3. A paper prepared after 11 November 1975 for a seminar held at the Australian National University on 14 November; published in the *Newsletter* of the Royal Institute of Public Administration (A.C.T. Group), vol. 111, no. 2, pp. 14–15.

4. See Preface.
5. See Chapter 23, p. 386.
6. G. Sawer, *Federation Under Strain*; see Chapter 21, p. 336.
7. Chapter 3, p. 48.
8. *The Parliamentarian*, January 1978, p. 67.
9. Lord Hailsham, *The Dilemma of Democracy*, William Collins (Publisher), London, 1978, in the Chapter 'Small is Beautiful', pp. 70–1.

Index

464